DATE DUE

DEMCO, INC. 38-2931

DEVELOPMENTAL ENTREPRENEURSHIP: ADVERSITY, RISK, AND ISOLATION

INTERNATIONAL RESEARCH IN THE BUSINESS DISCIPLINES

Senior Series Editor: Mike H. Ryan

Recent Volumes:

INTERNATIONAL RESEARCH IN THE BUSINESS DISCIPLINES
VOLUME 5

DEVELOPMENTAL ENTREPRENEURSHIP: ADVERSITY, RISK, AND ISOLATION

EDITED BY

CRAIG S. GALBRAITH

University of North Carolina, Wilmington, NC, USA

CURT H. STILES

University of North Carolina, Wilmington, NC, USA

ELSEVIER
JAI

Amsterdam – Boston – Heidelberg – London – New York – Oxford
Paris – San Diego – San Francisco – Singapore – Sydney – Tokyo
JAI Press is an imprint of Elsevier

JAI Press is an imprint of Elsevier
The Boulevard, Langford Lane, Kidlington, Oxford OX5 1GB, UK
Radarweg 29, PO Box 211, 1000 AE Amsterdam, The Netherlands
525 B Street, Suite 1900, San Diego, CA 92101-4495, USA

First edition 2006

British Library Cataloguing in Publication Data
A catalogue record for this book is available from the British Library

ISBN-13:   978-0-7623-1358-7
ISBN-10:   0-7623-1358-7
ISSN: 1074-7877 (Series)

Transferred to digital printing 2007

CONTENTS

PART III: ENTREPRENEURSHIP AND CRISES

LIST OF CONTRIBUTORS

Ricardo D. Alvarez	Centro de Enseñanza Técnica y Superior, CETYS Universidad, Tijuana, Mexico
Robert B. Anderson	Faculty of Administration, University of Regina, Regina, SK, Canada
José Renato de Campos Araújo	Escola de Artes, Ciências e Humanidades, Universidade de São Paulo-USP Leste, São Paulo, Brazil
Charlotte Benson	Independent Researcher, Kuala Lumpur, Malaysia
Dallas Brozik	Lewis College of Business, Marshall University, Huntington, WV, USA
Edward J. Clay	Overseas Development Institute (ODI), London, UK
Leo Paul Dana	Department of Management, University of Canterbury, Christchurch, New Zealand
Alex F. DeNoble	College of Business Administration, San Diego State University, San Diego, CA, USA
J. Michael Finger	Policy Research Department, World Bank Group, Washington, DC, USA
Christian Friedrich	Department of Management, University of the Western Cape, Bellville, South Africa
Craig S. Galbraith	Cameron School of Business, University of North Carolina, Wilmington, NC, USA
Michelle Howard-Vital	General Administration, University of North Carolina, Chapel Hill, NC, USA
Richard J. Hunter, Jr.	Stillman School of Business, Seton Hall University, South Orange, NJ, USA

Eslyn Isaacs   Department of Management, University of
                         the Western Cape, Bellville, South Africa

Örn D. Jónsson   Department of Business and Economics,
                         University of Iceland, Reykjavik, Iceland

Don Jung   College of Business Administration, San
                         Diego State University, San Diego, CA, USA

Porlákur Karlsson   School of Business, Reykjavik University,
                         Reykjavik, Iceland

Friedrich Kaufmann   GTZ Ministry of Industry and Trade,
                         Maputo, Mozambique and Universidade
                         Católica de Moçambique, Beira,
                         Mozambique

Nichola Lowe   Department of City and Regional Planning,
                         University of North Carolina, Chapel Hill,
                         NC, USA

Michael R. Luthy   Rubel School of Business, Bellarmine
                         University, Louisville, KY, USA

Katrín Ólafsdóttir   School of Business, Reykjavik University,
                         Reykjavik, Iceland

Odair da Cruz Paiva   Faculdade de Filosofia e Ciências de Marília,
                         Universidade Estadual Paulista Júlio de
                         Mesquita Filho, Marília, Brazil

Wilhelm Parlmeyer   Prilep Region Enterprise Development
                         Agency (PREDA), Prelip, Macedonia

Ana María Peredo   Faculty of Business, University of Victoria,
                         Victoria, BC, Canada

Howard S. Rasheed   Cameron School of Business, University of
                         North Carolina, Wilmington, NC, USA

Pat Roberson-Saunders School of Business, Howard University,
                         Washington, DC, USA

Carlos L. Rodriguez   Cameron School of Business, University of
                         North Carolina Wilmington, Wilmington,
                         NC, USA

Leo V. Ryan	Kellstadt Graduate School of Business, DePaul University, Chicago, IL, USA
Rögnvaldur J. Saemundsson	School of Business, Reykjavik University, Reykjavik, Iceland
Erich J. Schwarz	Department of Innovation Management and Entrepreneurship, University of Klagenfurt, Klagenfurt, Austria
David Smallbone	Small Business Research Centre, Kingston University, Kingston-upon-Thames, UK
Raymond D. Smith	School of Business, Howard University, Washington, DC, USA
Hernando de Soto	Founder and President, Institute for Liberty and Democracy (ILD), Lima, Peru
Curt H. Stiles	Cameron School of Business, University of North Carolina, Wilmington, NC, USA
Kobus Visser	Department of Management, University of the Western Cape, Bellville, South Africa
Malgorzata A. Wdowiak	Department of Innovation Management and Entrepreneurship, University of Klagenfurt, Klagenfurt, Austria
Friederike Welter	School of Economic Disciplines, University of Siegen, Siegen, Germany and Jonkoping International Business School, Jonkoping, Sweden
Alina M. Zapalska	Department of Management, United States Coast Guard Academy, New London, CT, USA

PREFACE

Developmental Entrepreneurship: Adversity, Risk, and Isolation is the fifth volume in the series *International Research in the Business Disciplines*. It is the second volume in our series that has followed a thematic format. Professors Galbraith and Stiles, the editors of the volume, have once again done a superb job of identifying an important area for study and providing an array of interesting viewpoints for readers to consider. Over time, I believe this volume will be viewed as another critical contribution to the overall study of entrepreneurship and business.

Volume 5 of this series is an indicator of both the quality and relevance of the research that this series provides an outlet for. In the future, additional volumes will continue to focus on what we believe to be are equally interesting topics. The next volume (Volume 6) in the series is tentatively titled *Space-Based Entrepreneurism: Stepping Off the Edge of the Earth*. Although the space business arena has long been a passion of mine, it has remained somewhat on the periphery of most business research. My hope is that the next volume will help bridge that gap. Regardless, I anticipate a significant number of very unique articles from a variety of perspectives.

As with the previous volume, I believe it is useful to reiterate and/or restate a few of the more salient editorial and review policies for the series. Each volume, under the direction and complete control of its editor or editors, is a stand-alone work intended to provide a better understanding of its focal topic. The thematic approach now in place for the series requires some slight adjustment of our editorial processes. Although each editor will continue to actively seek submissions from any one having an interest in the topic of a specific volume, he or she will also be interested in having as complete and balanced a volume as possible. To that end, we expect to solicit articles from some authors whose expertise and viewpoints we believe to be critical to an understanding of the topic at hand. Every article either submitted or solicited for each volume will continue to go through a rigorous process of peer review. In addition, to help ensure thematic consistency, each article, as needed, will undergo an editorial review process as well. This dual review process ensures both the overall quality of each volume and our commitment to commonly accepted review practices. Articles, whether solicited or submitted, that do not meet the necessary standards of quality deemed essential for a volume will not be accepted for publication. All of the editors of this series are committed to proving a research outlet that is not only timely and interesting but also of the highest possible caliber. As always, please feel free to address any questions or comments to either myself or any of the volume editors. I would hope that those of you that have an interest in any of the current volumes or their future counterparts would contact either me or Professors Galbraith or Stiles.

Mike H. Ryan
Senior Series Editor

INTRODUCTION

In this fifth volume in the series *International Research in the Business Dis ciplines* we build upon a theme that emerged in our previous volume titled *Ethnic Entrepreneurship: Structure and Process.* In this earlier volume, several of the contributors investigated entrepreneurship under difficult circumstances, such as within poor communities or isolated indigenous economies. This inspired the present effort, a volume dedicated to examining the issue of entrepreneurship specifically under conditions of adversity, isolation, or risk. The importance lies not only in the difficulties entrepreneurship faces under these conditions but also in the ability of entrepreneurs to significantly participate in the development of their community's economic and social structure.

We often forget that much of the world struggles under severe conditions. Within the last decade alone, the world has seen a myriad of both natural and human created disasters. The most publicized of the natural disasters include the tsunami disaster of December 2004 that destroyed broad populated areas around the Indian Ocean, killing an estimated 310,000 individuals, the 2005 Kashmir earthquake in Pakistan, and the series of hurricanes striking the Gulf States of the U.S. in 2005 killing over 1,000 people and causing extensive damage with estimates as high as $ 200 billion. Many other disasters do not receive the same press coverage but are equally destructive to their communities.

Disasters are not just natural events, nor are they all sudden in occurrence. Much of the world suffers from chronic violence, chaotic governments, crushing poverty, population displacements, and mass starvation. Other regions are undergoing difficult transitions from communist economies to those based on more free market principles. A large percentage of the world's population are members of indigenous communities, often isolated from the surrounding economy, while others struggle in the inner city ghettos of even the most developed countries. Disease, particularly the HIV/AIDS pandemic, is crushing the lives, social fabric, and fragile economies of much of sub-Saharan Africa.

Given these differences, there still emerges a common theme from these struggles. People everywhere, regardless of their particular situation, all try to better their lot in life, and many attempt this by participating in the entrepreneurial, small business sector of their economy. More often than not, entrepreneurial activity anchors economic development within impoverished regions, it stimulates recovery after natural disasters, and it elevates the self-esteem of the disadvantaged. This hard struggle, the failures and the success stories combined, is what inspired the theme for this volume – *Developmental Entrepreneurship: Adversity, Risk, and Isolation.*

Yet, in spite of the billions of dollars of foreign aid, the humanitarian efforts of countless international and domestic agencies, and the proliferation of small business assistance and micro-loan programs, we actually know very little about the real dynamics of entrepreneurs under stress, adversity and risk, or how to best assist in the illusive goal of stimulating economic growth. More than any other business sector, entrepreneurs struggle under ill-defined institutional frameworks and poorly enforced intellectual property right laws, often competing unnoticed in the shadow economies of the world.

This volume attempts to examine many, but certainly not all, of the themes that are slowly emerging in our eclectic approach to developmental entrepreneurship under adversity. We have organized the chapters into seven different groups.

PART I: ENTREPRENEURSHIP AND INSTITUTIONS

The first paper by Hernando de Soto is titled, "Trust, Institutions and Entrepreneurship." Hernando de Soto certainly needs no introduction. As the author of two best-selling books, *The Other Path* and *The Mystery of Capital*, and the founder of the Institute for Liberty and Democracy in Peru, Hernando de Soto has made his mark on examining critical issues related to economic development among poor people. In 1999, *Time* magazine chose Hernando de Soto as one of the five leading Latin American innovators of the century. *Forbes* magazine highlighted him as one of 15 innovators "who will re-invent your future." *The Economist* magazine identified his Institute for Liberty and Democracy as one of the top two think tanks in the world. The essay in this volume, based upon a speech given at the University of North Carolina on October 26, 2004, examines the important relationships between institutions, trust, property rights, and the ability of entrepreneurs to participate in economic growth and development. This stimulating essay sets a foundation for much of what is discussed in this volume.

In the next chapter titled, "Poor Peoples' Knowledge: Helping Poor People to Earn from their Own Intellectual Property," J. Michael Finger, recently retired from the World Bank, explores several case studies of how indigenous and poor people throughout the world are starting to capture the commercial value of their intellectual property. The examples in this chapter tend to illustrate a simple principle; the normal commercial and legal instruments that work well in richer societies can work for poorer people. However, within the poorer or indigenous environments, it is important that these normal legal regimes be properly understood, managed, and enforced. And concurrently the property to be commercialized must be properly articulated and described.

PART II: ENTREPRENEURSHIP IN TRANSITIONAL ECONOMICS

A theme becoming increasingly more popular with entrepreneurship researchers is how entrepreneurial firms participate in the transition of economies, particularly economies that are transitioning from previous communist or Marxist rule to a more open economy. The first chapter in this section, "Institutional Development and Entrepreneurship in a Transition Context," by David Smallbone and Friederike Welter, suggests that it is time to reflect on some of the emerging policy issues affecting small business development in these countries. An appropriate and effective institutionalization is still one of the main preconditions that need to be fulfilled in countries such as the Ukraine, Belarus, and the Russian Federation before sound and sustained private sector development can become embedded. The authors use Estonia as an example in this paper, arguing that Estonia has shown considerable progress with respect to institutionalizing small business policies. Here, the anticipation of EU accession on the policy approaches and priorities has both positive and negative aspects. The authors argue that while EU accession appears to have given a boost to the development of institutions and policies to encourage and support small business development, there are also some hidden dangers.

In the second chapter, "Entrepreneurial Environment and the Life-Cycle Growth and Development Approach to Analyzing Family Businesses in the Transitional Polish Economy," authors Alina M. Zapalska and Dallas Brozik analyze common characteristics among successful family-owned and -operated businesses in the tourism and hospitality industry in the transitional Polish economy. The results of the study indicate that tourism and hospitality industry growth in the southern region of Poland is hindered mostly by high taxation and the unavailability of low-cost, long-term financing to small business. Other perceived difficulties include unfavorable credit terms, the attitude of banks toward small business, the lack of tax incentives and preferences, and the lack of venture capital and project financing. To promote more family business development in Poland, the authors suggest that it is important that local authorities pursue a joint economic policy to improve the general infrastructure and promote the creation of the necessary economic conditions to support the growth of existing firms and encourage the development of new entrepreneurial activities.

In the third paper, "Transition in the Polish Economy," Richard J. Hunter Jr. and Leo V. Ryan take a critical look at the process of economic change in Poland since 1989 in the transition from rigid central planning to a market economy. The paper describes the conditions that existed under the command-rationing mechanism (CRM) and the elements of the Balcerowicz Plan for dismantling the CRM and transitioning to decentralized markets. Along with the difficult economic conditions, the transition had to cope with the privatizing of huge and inefficient state-owned industrial enterprises and to restrain during the privatization process the temptation of the former communist nomenklatura to play political entrepreneur and use state-owned assets to become business entrepreneurs. The article takes a detailed look at growth, international trade, privatization, foreign direct investment, transition costs, technology and infrastructure lapses, and ination. It concludes with a look at Poland's future as a full member of the EU and the promises it might hold for development.

In the final chapter, Erich J. Schwarz and Malgorzata A. Wdowiak develop a model of entrepreneurial performance in transitional economies. The chapter, "New Venture Performance in the Transition Economies: A Conceptual Model," explores the idea that the survival and growth of new ventures are dependent on the country's stage of economic development and cultural features. A crucial issue of the paper is the entrepreneur who creates its venture under condition of high uncertainty, weak institutional framework, and with scarce resources. By examining the relevance of the founder's cultural and social capital for new venture performance in transition economies, the chapter contributes conceptually to prior models of new venture performance.

PART III: ENTREPRENEURSHIP AND CRISES

The third collection of papers examines a little discussed aspect of entrepreneurship, that of entrepreneurship in natural and human created disasters. In the first paper, "Disasters, Vulnerability and the Global Economy: Implications for Less-Developed Countries and Poor Populations," Charlotte Benson and Edward J. Clay, authors who have written prolifically on the dynamics of less-developed countries and natural disasters, explore the relationship between integration in the global economy and sensitivity to natural hazards – that is, to events caused by geophysical, hydrological, and atmospheric forces. It takes a macroeconomic perspective and draws on both the published literature and on evidence accumulated by the authors in a series of studies of the economic impacts of natural disasters. The paper also presents one of these case studies, the country of Malawi in Southern Africa.

The second paper, "Disasters and Entrepreneurship: A Short Review," by Craig S. Galbraith and Curt H. Stiles takes a more micro-approach. They recognize that not only is a disaster felt within the painful context of human tragedy, loss of life, and physical suffering, but disasters can also destroy the immediate socio-economic fabric of the affected population as well as the ability of a region to sustain itself during the slow process of recovery and reconstruction. Yet in spite of the tremendous effort placed by the world governments on post-disaster recovery, the authors argue that from an empirical point of view, the actual impact, and proper focus of post-disaster recovery strategies remains somewhat unascertained. While there are certainly many dimensions that need to be considered in understanding the relationship between disasters, economic recovery, and the broader socio-political context, this paper focuses on only a narrow slice of the "disaster" literature – that related to small business and the relationship between post-disaster recovery strategies and entrepreneurial efforts. Within this context, several streams of research are reviewed.

The final paper in this section by Eslyn Isaacs and Christian Friedrich explores a critically important subject that has only recently started to gather some attention, the impact of disease and crime on entrepreneurial activity. The chapter entitled "HIV/AIDS, Crime, and Small Business in South Africa" raises several questions about this important topic and reviews some of the relevant research. The results of an empirical study of service providers in South Africa are then presented.

PART IV: POVERTY TRAPS, ENTREPRENEURSHIP
AND DEVELOPMENT: THE CASE OF MOZAMBIQUE

Parts 4 and 5 of the volume present papers representing two very different countries. Part 4 addresses the case of Mozambique, one of the poorest countries in the world, while Part 5 examines Iceland, currently one of the wealthiest nations in the world, but a country that only a century ago was isolated, technologically backwards, and economically impoverished. In Part 4, the first paper, "Poverty, Developing Entrepreneurship and Aid Economics in Mozambique: A Review of Empirical Research," by Leo Dana and Craig S. Galbraith, reviews the small body of empirical literature that examines the small business and entrepreneurial process in Mozambique. The topics covered in the chapter include issues related to the importance of micro-enterprises and the shadow economy, the policies and functions of micro-loan institutions, the role of Mozambican labor unions, the successes of international efforts to support micro-enterprise development, and micro-enterprise cross-border exchanges. The authors argue that one reason for the failures of aid programs in Mozambique, and other sub-Saharan African countries, is the lack of real empirical data at the micro-entrepreneurial level of the economy.

The second paper about Mozambique is by Friedrich Kaufmann and Wilhelm Parlmeyer. In "The Dilemma of Small Business in Mozambique: A Research Note," the authors discuss a empirical study of Mozambican micro-enterprises that were part of a ten year assistance program, the Projecto de Apoio às Pequenas Industrias Rurais (PAPIR). The authors found that there was high attrition in spite of the assistance and training. They also argue that different aid assistance programs should be designed differently, depending on whether the target firms operate in the shadow, extra-legal economy or the formal, legal sector.

PART V: ISOLATION AND WEALTH
DEVELOPMENT: THE CASE OF ICELAND

The essay by Örn D. Jónsson and Rögnvaldur J. Saemundsson, "Isolation as a Source of Entrepreneurial Opportunities: Overcoming the Limitation of Isolated Micro-States," traces the unique history of entrepreneurship within Iceland. The authors suggest that the remarkable success of Iceland can be traced to three underlying factors. First, World War II opened up the economy in a radical manner, in spite of the isolationistic interests of the farming sector. Second, Iceland's imitation of the Nordic "welfare state" only became possible due to the window of opportunity created by the combination of the micro-size character of the society and its location. In addition, a strategy of education abroad developed global networks that could be utilized later by the emerging cohort of alert entrepreneurs. And third, the latest phase of Icelandic economic development is characterized by a changing entrepreneurial relationship between the financial and technological components of the economy.

The second paper, "Portrait of an Entrepreneurial Trade Mission: Iceland Goes to China," by Þorlákur Karlsson, Michael Luthy, and Katrín Ólafsdóttir, examines a trade mission to China, and the attitudes of participants of the trade mission. This presents an interesting overview of the problem of isolation, and the need to reach out to other economies.

PART VI: ENTREPRENEURSHIP AND HISTORICAL DISADVANTAGES

Many population groups around the world struggle from disadvantages that have long historical roots. The first paper in this section, "Indigenous Entrepreneurship Research: Themes and Variations," by Ana Maria Peredo and Robert W. Anderson presents an overview of the current study of indigenous entrepreneurship. The paper covers several critical issues, including the application of the term "indigenous," and a discussion of the pursuit of multiple goals, including social objectives; the notion of collective organization, ownership and outcomes; and a population's association with the land, leading to a higher degree of environmental sensitivity.

The next chapter titled, "Gender Differences in Minority Small Business Hiring Practices and Customer Patronage: An Exploratory Study," by Pat Roberson-Saunders and Raymond D. Smith sampled four major racial/ethnic subgroups of minority entrepreneurs (Black, Hispanic, Asian/Pacific Islander, and Native American/Alaska Native) with respect to hiring practices and customer profiles. Significant differences were found in the co-racial/ethnic customer profiles of firms owned by Black men and women and in the tendency of Native American men and women entrepreneurs to hire co-racials/ethnics. By comparison, no such differences were found in the co-racial/ethnic hiring practices and customer patronage of Asians and Hispanics. Across race/ethnicity, however, there were significant differences among women entrepreneurs with respect to the tendency to hire persons of their own race/ethnicity.

In the chapter, "Immigration and Entrepreneurs in São Paulo, Brazil: Economic Development of the Brazilian 'Melting Pot'", authors José Renato de Campos Araújo, Odair da Cruz Paiva, and Carlos L. Rodriguez describe the trajectories of four major ethnic groups that migrated to São Paulo, Brazil, during the period 1850–1965: Syrian/Lebanese, Armenians, Koreans, and Spaniards. These groups were an important element in the spurt of development that transformed that area, from the center of production and trade in Brazil's best-known commodity – coffee – into South America's largest metropolis and the country's main engine of industrial development. Basic characteristics of these groups in terms of patterns of employment, entrepreneurship, religiosity, networking, social capital development, and integration into the new society are briefly described and compared in an attempt to connect their developmental paths with the foundations of the business-creation initiatives of their most entrepreneurial members.

PART VII: ENTREPRENEURSHIP AND BUILDING HUMAN CAPITAL

In the final section of the paper, four papers are presented that examine the issue of building human capital among economically disadvantaged people through entrepreneurship education and skill acquisition. The first essay, by Nichola Lowe titled, "Acquiring the Skills and Legitimacy to Better Manage Local Economic Development and Adjustment: The Case of Jalisco, Mexico," approaches the question from the perspective of regional planning and development theory, and takes a broader, more foundational look at economic development. She explores three basic questions, how do state governments acquire the skills and legitimacy needed to better manage the economic and industrial adjustment and growth of their region? What historical legacies and relationships can local authorities build on and further develop in order to help them hone these skills and design more "inclusive" development strategies? And what events and actions trigger policy innovation and reform in the area of economic development? These questions emerge from an extended case study of economic development planning in Jalisco, Mexico.

The last three papers focus directly on the effect entrepreneurship education has upon historically disadvantaged students. In the paper, "Building

Human Capital in Difficult Environments: An Empirical Study of Entrepreneurship Education, Self-Esteem, and Achievement in South Africa," Christian Friedrich and Kobus Visser describe an entrepreneurship program directed toward previously disadvantaged individuals in South Africa. The program included students from a broad spectrum of South Africa, including Colored, Xhosa, Tswana, Sotho, Asian, and Zulu students. The authors discuss the impact and outcome of the module on students' perceptions of entrepreneurship training as a viable work-related alternative, and then examine if entrepreneurship training is successful. Several instruments were used in the study, and the authors found that in comparison to the control group, the students taking the entrepreneurship-training module significantly improved in innovation, self-esteem, and achievement orientation.

The third paper, "Educational Curricula and Self-Efficacy: Entrepreneurial Orientation and New Venture Intentions among the University Students in Mexico," researchers Ricardo D. Alvarez, Alex F. DeNoble, and Don Jung recognize that a key environmental force that enables entrepreneurs to pursue their venturing goals is education. Education provides a way for nascent entrepreneurs to gain the necessary business skills and to nurture their self-efficacy to the point of initiating actions toward starting a new venture. The paper describes an empirical study that examined the impact of entrepreneurship education on students' perceived self-efficacy and orientation toward new venture intentions in three different Mexican universities. They found that the level of students' exposure to entrepreneurial events had a positive correlation with their level of entrepreneurial intentions and orientation, and that such relationships appeared to be different among the three schools.

The final paper, "Entrepreneurship Education: A Cautious Ray of Hope in Instructional Reform for Disadvantaged Youth," by Howard S. Rasheed and Michelle Howard-Vital reviews empirical findings from an entrepreneurial, intervention project implemented in nine public schools in Newark, New Jersey to improve student achievement. This article proposes that specific instructional strategies, in a curriculum that interests students, have the potential to increase academic performance and engage students in a life of learning. These specific instructional strategies are learner centered and include personalized, small learning communities that reflect students' interests, learning projects related to solving real-life problems, cooperative group learning, an environment of respect and support, and hands-on activities. The authors then conclude that their findings regarding classroom environment, instructional strategies, and teacher–student interactions are particularly relevant to ethnic minorities who often become disengaged in traditional classrooms.

CONCLUDING REMARKS

The series, *International Research in the Business Disciplines*, is a scholarly blind peer-reviewed series, and is listed in *Cabell's Directory of Publishing Opportunities in Management* (2005, pp. 1166–1168). For this volume, two separate calls for papers were issued, one in late 2005, the other in early 2006. The calls for papers were generally directed toward those scholars that had published or presented in the areas of developmental entrepreneurship, aid and developmental management, ethnic entrepreneurship, and indigenous entrepreneurship. The editors reviewed 41 papers. Of these, 18 were accepted for the volume. All of the papers were reviewed by both editors (non-blind) and by two other external reviewers as a "blind-review" process (including those that were co-authored by the editors). For most of the accepted papers, the review process resulted in a request for revision. The external reviewers were all on the staff of the University of North Carolina, Wilmington. In this respect, the editors would like to thank Jessica Magnus, Devon Galbraith, and Robert Keating of the Department of Management; Tom Baker of the Department of Marketing; Steve Robinson of the Department of Economics; Jacqueline-Benitez of the Department of Foreign Languages; Pam Evers of the Department of Business Law and Accounting; Leslie Hossfeld of the Department of Sociology; and two other anonymous reviewers, for their kind assistance in reviewing papers. Two papers in this volume were invited chapters, those by Hernando de Soto and J. Michael Finger.

Craig S. Galbraith
Curt H. Stiles
Editors

PART I:
ENTREPRENEURSHIP AND INSTITUTIONS

TRUST, INSTITUTIONS AND ENTREPRENEURSHIP ☆

Hernando de Soto

Consider the developed countries; one sees so much wealth, so much beauty, highways that are landscaped, and so many extraordinary developments. This is something people see everywhere in developed economics.

However, this is something not seen in most other places. There are about six billion people in the world. One billion people come from developed countries like North America, Western Europe, Japan, and perhaps four other Asian "tigers." But the majority of people are not in that situation. The other five billion come from what is typically called the developing world, or the Third World, and the former Soviet Union countries.

Until a few years ago, most of these countries were really following other systems rather than the capitalist system. That has all changed since the fall of the Berlin Wall. Even Deng Xiaoping in 1978 started marching in a different direction in China when he said, "It doesn't matter what color a cat is, as long as it catches mice."

In the developing world, we've all begun to change, we've all been trying to get our macroeconomic systems in place, we've all been making sure that we have fiscal balance, and we've all been making sure that we don't issue too much currency. We are all trying to get our account balances in order, especially since the fall of the Berlin Wall.

☆ Based upon a speech given at the University of North Carolina, Chapel Hill.

Developmental Entrepreneurship: Adversity, Risk, and Isolation
International Research in the Business Disciplines, Volume 5, 3–19
Copyright © 2006 by Elsevier Ltd.
All rights of reproduction in any form reserved
ISSN: 1074-7877/doi:10.1016/S1074-7877(06)05001-X

The general expectation at that time, according to Francis Fukuyama, was that this was "the end of history." Now there's only one game in town it was thought – capitalism, and we're all going to thrive. It will take some time, but we're all basically going to get there. And if you take away North Korea, and perhaps a couple of other countries, then every other country in the world has been following that road.

But if we look at the newspapers in these countries and study the level of actual progress, we discover that we're not all being that successful. We've made some progress – I think the numbers are there. But at the same time, expectations have risen incredibly. And there are a lot of unsatisfied people in these countries, something often manifested by the anti-globalization movement. Some economists have argued that anti-globalization is anti-capitalism, anti-free trade, anti-systems of the kind that has brought about the manicured lawns, the landscaped roads, the beautiful buildings, and the high standards of living and quality of life of the developed world.

But that is not the case in Afghanistan. It's not the case in Iraq. It's not the case in Saudi Arabia. For these countries, the news doesn't appear very good. In Pakistan things are not really working out; there's more violence than ever before. In less developed countries one can see the poverty; it screams out at you. One can see especially the exclusion, how some people are excluded from being able to do the right kind of things. One can see that even in Latin America, which everybody thought had been won over in the 1990s to the "good cause of the West."

And now you have governments that aggressively talk against the West. That's the case of Venezuela and its reliance on its Cuban alliance. One can see the problems in Sudan. Russia can't quite get on its feet, even though it has made progress recently. A Bolivian President just got thrown out. There are guerrillas in Columbia. It has not been an easy road.

Today the conclusion is quite different. It's not that capitalism has won. It's that communism has failed. Capitalism has yet to win.

Part of this, among other things, is because "capitalism" is a word that is never said in sympathy. It's not a nice word. I travel around the world and have never seen anybody get up in the middle of the town square and say, "Long Live Capitalism!" That just doesn't happen. It probably doesn't even happen in the United States where capitalism has brought so much success. Capitalism is a nasty word, guys with long-tailed coats and striped pants.

And when somebody brings up the idea of capitalism, one usually discusses all sorts of other things. When discussing the problems of capitalism, one talks about structural adjustment or about retooling. But nobody says the real words, which are that when somebody fails, they've got to try again and again to succeed.

There are many explanations about why capitalism has been more successful in some places. One of the most commonly heard is the "cultural" explanation. This explanation is the easiest one to assimilate and makes developed nations feel good, especially if we come from the North Atlantic. This explanation suggests that culturally, some people are just more prepared for capitalistic systems than others. This was an argument of the great master, Max Weber. And, of course today, some eminent scholars, like Samuel Huntington, say there's something to it. It is, after all, the Anglo-Saxon culture, which has caught on and spread to all the other cultures that have become part of the melting pot of the United States.

All of these are based upon a series of qualities, which most of China and most of Latin America just don't have. It is true that some Latins dress like Westerners, talk like Westerners, and even imitate Western accents and phrases. Some Asians also act like this. But the majority of Chinese, the majority of Latin America, and the majority of Iranians are really outside this framework. For these people, they've got their own cultural reasons for identifying themselves separately. This, in fact, at least on the surface, seems to give credibility to the cultural thesis, the one proposed by scholars such as Huntington.

1. TRUST

Recently a study on expectations was published. The researchers went to about 80 different countries and asked, "Do you trust other people?" When they asked this question in Norway, it turned out that about 65% of a region responded, "Yes, I do trust." So the cultural theorists might come back and say, "Ah, see, trust."

Trust, in fact, is very important, because in the end, what is a market economy? A market economy is essentially an exchange economy where everybody specializes in something. Somebody makes glasses, somebody purifies water, and somebody cuts the wood. We have to be able to exchange so that we can specialize, and specialization is the basis of wealth. So how can one specialize in something with the expectations that it will be exchanged for something else if one doesn't basically trust people?

What about trust in other countries. The survey suggests that about 60% of Swedes trust other Swedes. Most Europeans, they're at about 50%. In the United States, trust is just under the 50% line. But in Latin American, the level of trust is really horrific. Only 4% of Brazilians trust each other, and only about 7% of Peruvians trust each other.

So when I get invited to speak at places like American universities, I am really very happy, because finally I am going to a place where somebody really trusts me. And it's been a long time, because back home in Peru, some people like me, some people dislike me, but I can see in their eyes that most people don't really trust me.

When I travel, I often come into the United States through Washington DC, and I really feel the exhilaration. Just recently, I walked through immigrations in DC and went up to this uniformed officer of Homeland Security with a big badge on his arm.

He asked me to identify myself, and I said, "With pleasure. My name is Hernando de Soto. I am a native of Peru. My family's been there for about 380 years since they migrated from Spain. Some actually came from Italy. The first place they went to was Moquegua. That was actually on my mother's side of the family. On my father's side of the family, they went to Arequipa. Then when my mother and my father ...."

And this nice gentleman said, "Will you do me a favor? Please just show me your passport."

So I took out my passport, and the moment I took out my passport, I saw this "Gringo," with his blue eyes, trusting me. He looked at it, ran it through a machine, then came back and said, "Yes, you are Mr. de Soto."

He stamped it, and then I was in free inside your country. So I told myself, "That's very interesting. I read about that."

1.1. Knowledge by Acquaintance and Description

The philosopher Bertrand Russell wrote that there are really two ways that humans manage knowledge. One is knowledge by acquaintance. When I give speeches, I meet a lot of people. That's knowledge by acquaintance. I've shaken their hands, touched their shoulders, talked to them, smiled with a few, and had great conversations. Russell says that the *basis* of all knowledge is acquaintance.

But there's another type of knowledge, which is knowledge by description. Most of the knowledge that we *have* is by description. Most everybody knows, for example, that Kazakhstan exists, but people know it by description. Most people haven't actually been there. Everybody knows that my country Peru exists, but most people haven't been there. That's description.

Bertrand Russell points out that most of the truth is actually known through knowledge by description. Often people actually find out if someone is right or wrong when somebody is taken to court. In court, somebody comes up with documents and says, "Your Honor, this is the truth." Most of the time attorneys don't come in and show the court somebody actually stabbing somebody. Instead, the attorneys show a series of documents that prove that he did stab or did not stab somebody, so description actually tries to capture the truth. So I wasn't surprized that the immigrations officer in Washington, DC was able to begin trusting me, because I had come in by description.

In Washington I always stay at a small hotel. I've been going to this hotel for 15 years. They have a very small lobby, and I now know all the people who work there by name. There's Jack, there's Herb, and there's Dionne. I know them all. One night Herb was working, and I walked up to the registration desk.

As I came in, Herb said, "Mr. de Soto, good to see you. You haven't been here for some time."

I said, "Yes, I've been busy elsewhere."

Then Herb did the usual check-in and said, "Mr. de Soto, how do you intend to pay?"

That surprised me. I said, "Promptly as usual. What you mean?"

And he said, "I mean Mr. de Soto, where's your credit card?"

So I took out my credit card and realized that after all these years, Herb, that North American, never really trusted me. He trusted my credit card, which of course is knowledge by description. In other words, this piece of plastic told Herb, whether he knows me or not, that I actually have some resources in Peru, and it allows these resources to become liquid and travel through the communication and banking system, get into his computer at that small hotel, and then pay for my lodging.

So I told myself, "This is really interesting, because it means that there are *things* that bring you information about something else, something beyond themselves."

In other words, as the American philosopher Daniel C. Dennett would argue, there are two types of things in the world: there is "us," and there are things "about" us. And those things that are about us are those that describe.

It's a different world now. It's a world of descriptions. It's a world of connections that qualifies me such that you can now trust me. It's what makes the hotel worker, Herb, trust me, because I did get my room at the hotel. And I did get into the United States.

Descriptions are what really establish who I am, my identity. My identity is not born in my body, but rather my identity actually travels in this passport. And my creditworthiness is definitely not established by the fact that I can smile at you or that I do not twitch or tremble. Rather it is established by a plastic card.

Both of these documents are really a visible part of a larger iceberg of laws and regulations that underlies the whole system.

And our wealth depends on it. Consider the example of my apple that I hold in my hand. I actually bought this apple. I have a couple of witnesses at the hotel that actually saw me purchasing this apple. If you look at this apple, in spite of the fact that it is clearly my apple, there is nothing in this apple that says this is Hernando's apple. There's nothing in this apple that says that I got it at the inn. As a matter of fact, there's nothing different between an absolutely legitimate apple and a stolen apple. They are exactly the same, but they can be very different in some purposes. There's nothing in this apple that says I can sell it, I can buy it, I can lease it, or I can give it as collateral. There's nothing in this apple that says I can transfer it, or use it as a point of reference to have a dialogue with somebody to get credit, to get electricity, to get clean water, to have the sewage system work. What gives this apple a whole range of different functions, other than simply eating it, happens to be a legal environment.

In other words, humans seem to have created a meta-world. This world now goes beyond the physical world of apples to a world of ideas. We have created a world that has gone from beliefs to becoming enforceable statements. It now allows you to take a whole package of resources that are not visible out of physical objects, or out of human relationships, and give significance to these things. Thus, this apple, by itself, has little economic significance. What gives it economic significance is that it can be property. What gives it economic significance is the institution that sold it to me, or my organization, who bought it.

1.2. The Real Value of Property

Some years ago in Peru, students at my Institute for Liberty and Democracy were invited by the government to examine the privatization of the Peruvian Telephone Company, CPT. At the time, supposedly, the company belonged to all the people who used phones. If you bought a telephone, you got a share in the company. But it was run by the government for all practical purposes. You could sell your shares on the market, and according to this, the company had a total value of shares of $53 million.

When Peru wanted to privatize the telephone company, we had to sell it to someone, but nobody wanted to buy it. The reason nobody wanted to buy it was because the title wasn't clear, the law wasn't well defined. So it took us three years to redefine the law. We had to copy the laws of the United States to make them compatible with our laws. Finally, the law was defined, and we called for bids.

The company was finally sold to a consortium headed by Telefónica de España of Spain, which is one of the largest multinationals today in information technology and telecommunications. They bought it for $2 billion – 37 times its original value. And we didn't even touch the telephone building, we didn't repair any broken windows, the doors still don't open very well, nobody mowed the lawn, and nobody touched the wires. All we did was give it a "passport." And all of a sudden, the Peruvian Telephone Company was not just real estate and a lot of wires, but rather was something that in a representative manner, through its representation like my credit card, like my passport, could travel to different places, raise money, and issue bonds. Now one could divide the property up into little pieces of property and call them shares and raise investment. All of a sudden one had functions defined, and they were so well defined that future inventions would be incorporated. Everybody who bought the company knew exactly what they had, not only on the basis of what they had today, but also on the basis of abstract future definitions, such as advanced telecommunications.

Thus, we are back to the two worlds: the world of facts and the world of beliefs. All the people in developing countries have beliefs. Whenever you go to a developing country, whether for tourism or education, you will always see the things that make us different from you and even different among each other. We have different beliefs. But in the United States, you have beliefs too, but your beliefs are enforceable on a broad scale, and therefore you can be trusted on a broad scale.

Developed legal systems are able to capture nonmaterial values. They allow people to not only organize themselves, but also identify the values of things in such a way that creates wealth.

For example, consider credit. For many years, we all thought that credit was all about how much money you have. And now we know that it's not true. Latin Americans have issued more money than the United States, but we're still not any richer for it. So obviously issuing more money doesn't give one more credit.

Instead, think of the property that is behind credit. In the United States, 80% of employment comes from small and medium enterprises, and 85% of all the credit these enterprises acquire is based on collateral. Collateral is the basis of credit and why not? Credit comes from Latin "credo," which means "I believe you." But I believe you because you've got something to lose.

I remember having had the privilege of meeting the chairman of the U.S. Federal Reserve, Alan Greenspan. I was very much honored by this. I asked him two very simple questions. They were, in fact, trick questions. I asked, "Mr. Chairman, I have a question. When you go out and you put more money into the market, what are the criteria?" He knew that I was preparing a talk and would be indiscreet enough to tell the story. So Mr. Greenspan played along and said, "All right, what tells me how much money is how many transactions there are in the market."

I said, "You must have a very powerful intelligence survey. You've got agents out there watching in front of the shops to see how much merchandise goes out, how many cars are being sold?"

And he looked at me with a certain impatience and said, "No, of course not. What happens is that I look at what the markets say."

I said, "The markets? What markets? Like when John Wayne takes ten thousand head of cattle and goes to the Chicago mercantile exchange?"

"No." He said, "What I actually see – and I know where you're going – is people exchanging property titles. They exchange property titles over companies, they exchange property titles over money, they exchange property titles over real estate, and, of course, these are all recorded. I can figure out how much they're exchanging, and I know how much liquidity to put into the market."

I said, "Very interesting. This is really good stuff, because it substantiates my thesis. Now I have a second question. When you actually give credit, how does it work?"

"Well, somebody securitizes it one way or another, or they've got enough evidence, like the passports, like the credit card, that I've got the flow of funds necessary."

"And then what does the Central Reserve Bank do?" I asked.

"Well, then once a credit is done, we rediscount it."

So again, it's property. It is property that allows one to give or receive credit; it is what allows people to accumulate capital. If anybody ever sees capital that's not on a piece of paper, please let me know. It is essentially the property system that allows the United States to be the biggest capitalist nation in the world.

The "symptom" of the system is that there are a lot of capitalistic types of people in suits. But behind it essentially is a legal system that is able to capture values. And it is a legal system that has been built over time. It is a system that captures values whether a person knows it or not, and it is a system that allows people to understand things in a way that developing nations can't quite understand yet.

It is a system that allows the Federal Reserve to know, for example, how much liquidity to put into the market or how much credit it should allow the banks to give. It is a system that allows one to not have runaway inflation and to put resources in the right hands. Just like one cannot do carpentry with bare hands, one cannot have a market economy with just bare brains.

Developing countries need the foundations of a good legal system. All these economists who have been coming to Latin America, and even our own economists, keep saying, "you've got to get your 'macros' right, you got to get your 'measurements' right." But if we don't come in with a legal institutional system that is created by an informed and aware state, there will never be all these other good things a good economy can offer, such as proper credit and better investments. The legal system is what gives you trust.

2. THE ECONOMICS OF ORGANIZATION

We may all be brothers and sisters in this world, but obviously there's no way any American will really know the other 280 million Americans. There is no way I can know the overwhelming majority of 27 million Peruvians. I only know an immediate circle of acquaintances. In fact, I know the majority of the people by description, thanks to the legal system that provides the security, which allows us to cooperate in a wider and expanding network.

This legal system, however, is not in place for 5/6ths of the world's population. And unless something is done – and it's a very complex task – it's going to remain the same. Or maybe every decade or so, one or two more developing countries will slowly become developed, but it'll take hundreds of years for the world to completely develop. The answer is not around the corner, because it requires the creation of law.

Then there is division of labor. Adam Smith said it, and Marx agreed. Adam Smith talked about what causes wealth. He talked about the little pin factory and saw a couple working, and they were producing 14 pins a day between both of them. Sometime later Adam Smith went to the outskirts of Edinburgh, and he saw 10 workers making 48,000 pins per day. And this led into his famous discussion of division of labor.

But what was not seen at the time was what it takes to bring 10, mostly unrelated, people together to work. I have traveled in different parts of the world, and my conclusion is that what people often call "micro-enterprise" or "small-enterprise" is really not. It's just families, families where people get together to seek out a living. They, in fact, do not have the tools necessary to bring 10 people together, and as families they tend not to be very productive.

In most of the developing world, or in about 70% of the former Soviet Union, when you deal with a productive group, you really don't know who actually runs it. Ask the children in a small enterprise who runs the operation, and they tell you Dad does. The father then looks at you, smiles and looks at the mother. Now you think that she runs the place, but you don't really know.

But when one talks to an American firm or to a Swiss firm, you know exactly who runs it. It's in the statutes, in the corporate charter. At least you know who's going to jail if something's not right. People know who's the CFO, who's the CEO, who's in charge of what.

In addition, there's little asset partitioning in developing countries. In other words, if you ask a small firm in the United States if they have the assets to back up a contract, they might say, yes, our house. In the United States, one can find out not only whether the house is theirs or not, but also whether they can use it as collateral and for how much. The statutes also tell you that.

Asset partitioning, limited liability, and corporate statutes, which really came into being for most Americans only about 150 years ago, is something most developing nations don't have. And until somebody has this system, it is impossible to make 48,000 pins. Instead, you stay at 14, no matter how righteously and hard these people work.

In many developing countries there are only weakly enforceable property rights. So one can't take a company and divide it up into a 100 pieces, a 1000 pieces, or 10,000 pieces, then put them into the market to get investments. In many developing countries there are no standard accounting books or even standard measurements. For example, at the time of the French Revolution, there were about 280 ways of measuring things, weights, or sizes. We had to bring it down to the metric system before we could all understand each other.

But we can't do this right now in the developing world. The number of micro-enterprises in these countries shows that people everywhere are entrepreneurial. But until the rule of law comes in, we can't be orderly in our transactions or economic relationships. Without the rule of law there's no way of organizing oneself internally to be credible. There's no way of passing from Adam Smith's 14 pins to Adam Smith's 48,000 pins.

In fact, how many people in developing countries have the benefit of just these two things: property rights and the ability to divide labor?

3. CALCULATING VALUE

We've learned how to calculate value going from country to country. The figures presented below have been published and announced by the governments of these two countries: Mexico and Egypt.

3.1. Mexico

In the case of Mexico, roughly 50% of the population is in the "extralegal sector." The Russians call it the "shadow economy," in Kazakhstan they call it the "black market," and many people refer to the "gray economy" or the "informal economy." In Mexico that is approximately 50% of the population working full time. Other people work in the extralegal sector part of the time and the legal sector part of the time, so about 80% of the Mexican population works at least part of the time in the extralegal sector. Thus, only 20% of the Mexican working population is fully legal. So if somebody asks whether the flow of Mexicans or Peruvians to the United States will go down in the near future, the answer is "no." Why? It will keep going up because this is the only place nearby where you can make 48,000 pins with 10 people.

How important is this to Mexico, how valuable? There are 11 million buildings in Mexico – we've calculated them – which are not on the official records. There are about six million enterprises or families that are producing things that are outside the legal system. The total value of their assets, the slums, the little houses, and other things, is about $315 billion. How much is $315 billion to Mexico? It is roughly seven times the value of Mexico's total oil reserves.

In other words, the real capital, the real potential for Mexico is not its oil or natural resources, it is located in this "dead" capital.

Consider the Saudis. For the Saudis, the majority of the population is not participating in the division of labor, and they don't have enough property rights. That is one reason why their GNP per capita is continually decreasing regardless of how much oil the Saudi's have. On the other hand, some of the wealthiest countries in the world don't have many natural resources. Switzerland doesn't grow its own cocoa and doesn't produce most of its own

milk for its chocolates. Nor does it make the steel from which its watches
and turbines are made. The same is true for the Japanese. Rather, their
success is built upon their institutional system and good laws to enforce
property rights.

3.2. Egypt

In the case of Egypt, when we were called by President Mubarak, we organized a team of 120 people. We began by looking at their extralegal
economy and its associated assets. We presented the Egyptian government
with maps of all the buildings, and it turned out that 92% of all the real
estate is outside the law. Ninety-two percent of all the buildings, and about
88% of Egyptian enterprises were outside the legal sector. In other words,
only about 10% of Egypt was fully legal. What is the value of these assets
for people outside of the law – about $248 billion, according to our cal-
culations.

When the Egyptian government didn't believe us, we took them to their
own public housing system. They asked, "What is it about our public
housing system that isn't legal? After all, we built it."

Here we are in El-Nasser (Nasser City), with probably the largest and
most generous public housing system for poor people in the world, and we
look at it and say, "It's absolutely true that you built it, but have you seen
this photograph of the 1960s when it was inaugurated?"

They take the early photograph and say, "Yes, I can see the buildings – all
two stories of them."

Then we ask, "Then why do these buildings have seven stories. Who built
the other five?"

And then all of a sudden people started to realize what has been happening over the last 40 years. It is what has happened throughout the developing world and is now happening in the former Soviet Union,
particularly when people have begun to migrate toward the cities.

3.3. The New Industrial Revolution

Oliver Twist has come to town. It's the Industrial Revolution. For example,
Algerian cities have grown 15 times in the last 35 years. The cities and towns
of Haiti have grown 17 times in the last 35 years. Likewise, the cities and
towns of Ecuador have grown 17 times. It's the beginning of the industrial
revolution in these countries. It's not when industry comes, but rather when

people start getting together in sufficient masses to begin the division of labor. When it comes, all of a sudden, everybody will find how to become productive. But until then, people will keep flooding the cities. What is missing, however, is the legal system. And until these countries get their legal system into place so that people can cooperate, no longer at the village level or the family level but at the expanded level of dozens, or hundreds, or even millions of people, people will continue to come but not participate in this new industrial revolution. We need to trust each other by description, through passports, credit cards, and the whole legal and property rights system.

The same thing happened in the United States. For example, consider the California gold rush. Americans invaded California in search of gold, three million big Americans with their big guns. They immediately created mining claim associations, about 800 associations throughout California. Each association had a different legal system, just like the shantytowns in developing countries, just like guys who move onto the land in Colombia or Sudan. Until you pull it all together so that you have the same standards, the same "Uniform Commercial Code," there will be problems. The Rule of Law means no anarchy, no different legal systems.

Until you were able to create a uniform legal system in the West, you didn't have the growth in the United States, no manicured lawns, and no landscaping of highways. It was a very, very violent place up until 1870, west of the Mississippi. There was no Standard Time, the sheriffs gave the time. So it could be 2:00 PM in Twin Rivers with Hopalong Cassidy and another time two miles south. It took effort and time to bring these standards together. A couple of hundred years ago, there were 700 currencies – the yellow back, the brown back – now there is one.

The same thing happened in Germany. Before the Napoleonic Wars, there were about a hundred different property systems across the numerous German principalities. Then Napoleon defeated the King of Prussia, and the King subsequently tried to raise more armies among the German princes and the free cities to fight this wave of revolutionary fervor coming from France. But he couldn't recruit. The farmers now wanted to participate in the new system. So they started with the Stein–Hardenberg reforms and proceeded through a later second phase in the 1870s with Bismarck until they had created one system, one Rule of Law, and a nation that guaranteed access to property. Then they got organized.

The same happened in Switzerland. Up until about 1908, Switzerland was one of the poorest countries in Western Europe. Today it's one of the most prosperous in the world. What happened? They got organized in such a way that they were able to give the country one property law, one company law, and they brought it all together in a complete system. And today the property is so secure that not one Latin American dictator puts his savings anyplace but Switzerland.

3.4. The Common Link

So the history of the West is the history that we in developing countries are living today. In the 1930s and early 1940s, lots of poor Japanese started migrating toward Latin America. There were two countries that were absolutely open to Asian migration. These countries had always welcomed immigrants and were multiracial. One is Brazil, and the other is my own country Peru. As a result, about one million Japanese families came to live in Peru and Brazil. The Fujimori family came to Peru, for example, and the Yoshiyama family went to Brazil. The Fujimoris later had a son called Alberto who became president of Peru. An interesting question, the real issue, is why did the Fujimoris and Yoshiyamas come to Peru and Brazil? Why didn't the Toledos and the Lulas go to Japan, the other way around?

The reply to that is very simple. In the 1940s, the gross national income per capita in Peru and Brazil was twice as high as Japan's. Japan may have had a huge army in the 1930s and 1940s, but it's like Saddam Hussein. One can have a powerful army and still be a poor country. Japan during this time, was, in fact, a poor country. But why did it change? One reason was that certain Japanese officials wanted it to change from its feudal past. In the 1940s, Japan was really a feudal country, with feudal lords like in Afghanistan today. In fact, much of the world is still being run by feudal lords.

3.5. U.S. Policy

While preparing to invade Japan, General MacArthur put together a team to study the problem. They concluded that the solution was to get rid of the feudal class. Get a property system into place. This was even more urgent after Japan surrendered, because Mao was starting to march down from Manchuria to the south and eventually beat Chiang. Mao's army swelled, because he started a property revolution. He started titling people as he marched south. He did it simply by giving them collective title. It's not private property, but it gets you closer to your assets when you previously had nothing. And all people, just like the immigrants flowing into Rio de Janeiro or other places today, want to hold onto something.

And MacArthur did this in Japan. By providing the possibility for private property and private corporations, he basically created a huge constituency for the market economy and fueled economic growth.

I never understood why Americans always talk about the Marshall plan. It was peanuts compared to what the United States did in Japan. In the Marshall plan you already had Germany, a prosperous country at one time and one that was rebuilding. But Japan was not prosperous. In fact, they were all migrating to my country, which is still poor. Ultimately, the region got so organized and so prosperous that by 1978, Deng Xiaoping couldn't resist it anymore and had to start the march toward a market economy.

It was a brilliant strategy. It *is* a brilliant strategy even if most people don't realize it. You've taken one of the most powerful Communist countries in the world and turned it to a market system. They started the march, and they've now got the same problems that Western Europe and the United States had in the 19th century; that is, about 150 million Chinese now have property title and enterprise. At the same time, China is struggling to reach the other 1.1 billion. The distance between the most powerful Chinese, the richest, and the poorest is wider in China than anywhere else. All the same, there is no way they can stop the march, and that was brilliant U.S. policy.

But that policy was forgotten in Vietnam, and it was forgotten in Iraq. So it's important for us to imitate the United States, but mostly the American great-grandfathers and what they did in the 19th century. It's also important for the United States to remember its own history, because people have a tendency to forget, and that's very dangerous. It's very dangerous, because it is easy to forget what the genesis of one's own system is. This history should not just be an academic subject; it should also be a policy that is applied in the modern world.

3.6. Why Do People Forget?

Nobody knows why people forget these things. But I like what Karl Popper, an Austrian philosopher who became British due to persecution by the Nazis, used to say when it came to forgetting. He tells about his experience with a celebrated violinist, Karl (Adolf) Busch. Once when Popper was going to go see him at the theater, a friend of Popper's said, "Oh, if you're going to see Karl Busch, please take me along. I'm an incredible fan. He's a maestro."

So they went together and they listened to him. I forget if the violinist was interpreting Bach or Vivaldi, but when he went from the third to the fourth movement, it was absolutely the finest spectacle you've ever seen or heard. And Karl Popper's friend was moved to tears. Afterward they went behind the stage to talk to the maestro. Karl Popper introduced his friend, and the friend asked the maestro how he did that transition. And Karl Busch said, "As you know I'm an old man so I don't mind giving away trade secrets. It's rather simple; let me tell you how it's done." So he put his violin to his neck, took out his fiddlestick, and showed the trick. And he was never able to play the transition of the third to the fourth movement again.

Here is another example. The spider has got eight legs, and it's got trouble managing the eight legs, and so it goes to the centipede and says, "I've got real trouble managing these eight legs. How do you manage a hundred legs?" The centipede says, "It's actually quite simple. You take the front 20 legs and move them like this," and he's never been able to move those 20 legs again.

In other words, once we solve a problem, like when we learn to walk as children, we pass the knowledge on to our motor system. And we have to make an intellectual effort to remember what it is we did that actually got us where we are today.

This is what we are trying to do. The system in the United States is an example to all of us all over the world, and we're trying to imitate it. Look at the impact of American culture, the inventions, and products.

In a way, it is what Darwin would have called adaptation. He refers to adaptation as to those things that one does but not necessarily consciously. I believe that when one builds property systems and a system of ownership, one actually builds a much bigger edifice, and that is something that people are not very aware of. It's not really in your foreign aid, and it's not really being exported right now. Why not? Because the United States has forgotten the "consciousness of MacArthur." But the United States got it right in the past, and it's very important to remember it.

It's much easier for me to embody the 18th- and 19th-century history of the United States in my approach to economic development, and I don't even know that history that well. I just find little spots in places that put the whole picture together for me, because that is when the United States really became great. The United States built a great nation, and it is in a position to help the world immensely, but unfortunately that is not always being picked up in theory.

We have come to the conclusion that the power of man goes way beyond manpower. It's not only how people work, but also how people get organized. It's how people get into the market, and that is simply not a pure economic theory.

That's the reason we like to study other countries; that's the reason we bear ourselves in a certain way to reflect our heritage. But those are really the leaves of the tree that we are all a part of. The basic trunk of the tree is our human capacity to absorb knowledge in pretty much the same ways. So I believe that though there are differences, what we have in common is much greater than what separates us.

Why should we care what Americans think? For a very simple reason – because the United States has most of the money in the world. So, when the United States decides that it is going to do a road development program instead of helping build a legal system, all the economists in our country study road building rather than legal and economic institutions. The modern U.S. sets the trends, the music, the dance, and the fashion.

But what about the historical system of laws and property rights? If the developing countries learn only about how the United States lives today and not its fundamental history of economic success, then more and more poor people in my country will do two things. Some will dislike you immensely, and others will come to the United States to visit and work.

POOR PEOPLES' KNOWLEDGE: HELPING POOR PEOPLE TO EARN FROM THEIR OWN INTELLECTUAL PROPERTY

J. Michael Finger

1. INTRODUCTION

How can we help poor people to earn more from their knowledge – rather than from their sweat and their muscle? This chapter is about promoting the innovation, knowledge, and creative skills of poor people in poor countries – and particularly about improving the earnings of poor people from such knowledge and skills. My principal message is that a lot is being done in this regard. On the whole, this useful work is a matter of straightforward application of familiar legal and commercial instruments and skills such as copyrights, trademarks, and patents. This does not mean that it is easy, however.

Rather than presenting a learned discourse, I will tell a few stories about people who have made the market for intellectual property work for poor people. I will also try to pull together a few lessons or generalizations.[1] A complementary point that I also take up is that perhaps too much has been made of the need for legal novelty; special legal regimes to deal with "traditional knowledge" or "indigenous knowledge" that exists only among poor people. Their knowledge, my experience suggests, is of the same sort as

Developmental Entrepreneurship: Adversity, Risk, and Isolation
International Research in the Business Disciplines, Volume 5, 21–34
Copyright © 2006 by Elsevier Ltd.
All rights of reproduction in any form reserved
ISSN: 1074-7877/doi:10.1016/S1074-7877(06)05002-1

that of richer people. What helps in the "modern" economy also helps in the "traditional."

2. SUCCESSES

There are many examples of poor people capturing the commercial value of their intellectual property. The examples tend to illustrate a simple principle; the normal commercial and legal instruments that work well in richer societies can work for poorer people.

2.1. Property Rights for Indigenous People

Nelly Arvalo-Jiménez (2004) is a Venezuelan woman, with a Ph.D. in anthropology from the University of California. For most of her professional life she has worked with the Yekuana people who live in the tropical forests of the Amazon and the Orinoco Basins.

It is hard to find a way to describe Yekuana society in a way that does not sound supercilious. "Natives" they would have been called in the days of Tarzan movies, "traditional groups" as we have tried to become more culturally sensitive.

Though the Yekuana people live in an area we would describe as remote, they have experienced major incursions of modern society, some associated with attempts to exploit natural resources through large-scale mining and rubber plantations. As the Yekuana people attempted to avoid being impressed as plantation or mining labor, their settlements became widely dispersed. As they became more dispersed, takeover of their land was an increasing threat.

The Venezuelan constitution recognizes traditional property rights, but those who would claim them must put together the necessary information and apply for the property ownership documents that we in the "modern world" take for granted. In 1993, with technical support recruited by the Asociación OTRO FUTURO, the Yekuana started a program to identify and mark the land that was by tradition theirs, so that they could apply for formal deeds of ownership.

The program was informally named Esperando a Kuyujani. Kuyujani is the Yekuana's cultural hero, who at the beginning of time identified – by walking across them – the lands he left in trust to the Yekuana people. Once the land was so marked and Kuyujani's teachings were assimilated, he went away, leaving with his people a promise to return.

From their oral history, the Yekuana were able to reconstruct all of Kuyujani's original treks. From this knowledge they marked their borders with stakes and stones. By 2001 they had completed a map that not only identified their borders but also included cultural data, topographic features, historical and sacred monuments, and natural resources. A parallel effort put together an archive of Yekuana visual images, crafts, medical knowledge, and so forth. These archives are a necessary base for claiming copyrights, trademarks, and patents on the Yekuana's knowledge. The Yekuana have organized themselves into a corporate unit, a legal "person" in whom ownership can be vested. This property identified and recorded, the Yekuana have entered into a contract with a U.S. company to explore and develop the commercial value of some of their knowledge, particularly their medical knowledge.

The initial motivation behind the project was as much social as economic – to preserve Yekuana folkways and culture. The written and photographic record of Yekuana cultural heritage has become an important pedagogic tool in the Aramare school, which the Yekuana established. The school emphasizes the teaching of religion, ceremonies, dances and sacred music, playing of musical instruments, and oral history. The teachers there are wise old specialists in oral history, religion, and the ancient ways. Their role in the school is helping to restore the status that elders and wise men once had in Yekuana society.

It would be a mistake to presume that the traditional schools are backward-looking. They also offer workshops in modern matters such as tourism and the legal mechanics of registering and merchandising property rights.

The main lesson from this experience: creating a record of the Yekuana's property that will serve them in their dealings with the modern world was done in a way that strengthened rather than weakened indigenous culture. Culture and commerce complement rather than conflict. A complementary lesson is the need for an active program to maintain and build on indigenous culture. The momentum of the interface between the traditional world and the modern is toward the latter, but Yekuana experience demonstrates that, creatively managed, the dynamic of the indigenous culture can be maintained.

2.2. Indian Crafts

Maureen Liebl grew up in the United States and now lives in India. Her passion is Indian art and handicrafts: weaving, jewelry, embroidery, furniture, dolls, and such.

Handicrafts in India provide a modest livelihood to large numbers of poor people, particularly to the rural poor. Currently, about 10 million people earn some U.S.$4 billion a year from such work – until recently more than India earned from computer software.

Handicrafts have value beyond their capacity to generate income. Numbers of connoisseurs avidly collect examples of specific craft genre, numerous scholarly treatises and expensive coffee-table books have been written on various craft forms. Ms. Liebl's expertise is to find ways to maintain such art and to improve the economic situation of its artists. Her particular expertise is in adapting the skills and products of Indian artisans to new market conditions.

In applying this expertise, Ms. Liebl is a realist. Commercial realities do not paint an optimistic picture for all artisans. Take, for example, weavers of everyday garments. In the past, wrapped, unstitched cloth was the basic mode of dress throughout the country (the woman's *sari* and the man's *dhoti*). The local weaver was thus an important member of the community and his economic well-being was assured. Many women today prefer the brilliant chemical colors, novel synthetic texture, and low price of machine-made *saris*, and many are shifting to tailored clothing. Throughout India, women still prefer *saris* for formal and ritual occasions, and there will always be a market for the exclusive (and often expensive) high-end woven *saris*. But the livelihood of the multitude of local weavers has disappeared.

The consumer has spoken. Except in a museum setting, Ms. Liebl concludes, no traditional craft skill can survive unless it has a viable market.

Upscale markets offer more optimistic examples. One is the designer Ritu Kumar. In the 1970s, Ms. Kumar revived a traditional form of embroidery done with silver and gold wire to create fine evening and bridal outfits. In time she expanded into other traditional crafts, such as other forms of embroidery, mirror work, and hand-blocked prints. At first she incorporated these into traditional Indian outfits, but has since moved into fusion and Western clothing, as well as into accessories and home decoratives. Today, Ritu Kumar has boutiques throughout India as well as in London, and is an international presence.

Ritu Kumar has been the inspiration and model for a new generation of designers who see traditional craft skills as the foundation for a contemporary Indian design aesthetic. One group is working with traditional palm-leaf manuscript painters from the eastern state of Orissa, teaching them carpentry and opening their eyes to the ways in which their paintings can be incorporated into fine furniture. In the southern Indian state of Kerala, sensitive development of "backwaters tourism" has saved the *kettuvallom* and its makers. The *kettuvallom* is a type of boat that was originally used for cargo transport and is now used as private floating hotels. They have become fashionable with high-end international tourists.

People in the crafts business are pessimistic about obtaining design and process protection through enforcement of patent and copyright laws by the Indian government. Ms. Liebl and economist Tirthankar Roy (2004), interviewed many dealers, manufacturers, and exporters on the matter, and not one expressed optimism. The most positive answer they received, she told me, was a polite laugh. The entire system of property rights enforcement in India has problems, and these problems are unlikely to be overcome for the sole purpose of protecting crafts producers.

The study illustrates that many people engaged in commercial activities to help developing country artisans are motivated by their love for the art, their concern for the artists, as well as by the opportunity to profit from their work. The effective ones are market accepting; they realize that except in a museum setting, no traditional craft skill can be sustained unless it has a viable market.

A second lesson is that the lack of enforcement of Intellectual Property Rights (IPRs) in the domestic economy orients activity toward foreign markets where such protection is available, or toward the high end of the home market. Here the artist is protected from unauthorized copying by the uniqueness of his or her skill and the appreciation of his or her customers for the objects that skill can render.

2.3. African Music

African music has significant business potential. It currently makes up about half of the fast-growing "world music" segment of recorded music, and music industry experts suggest that African music today may be at the jumping-off-point where country music and rock and roll were in the United States in the 1950s.

Frank J. Penna's distinguished work has ranged from the international marketing of railroad equipment to community organizing in the northeastern United States. He has recently led an effort to help African musicians to boost their earnings. His team (of which I had the pleasure to be a part) began with a series of meetings in Dakar, Senegal, with local musicians.

"What are your problems," we asked, "and what do you see as solutions with which we might help?"

The musicians came forward with a long list of complaints. The following are only a few of those listed in a longer report by Penna, Thormann, and Finger (2004).

- Most Senegalese musicians make their living from the local market. Of some 30,000 musicians, perhaps a dozen derive income from foreign sales.
- Piracy of local music is rampant. Cassettes sold locally are quickly counterfeited, and radio stations play the music without paying royalties. Most musicians are unaware that there are laws to combat such piracy, they do not know how to use the laws, and they do not have the resources to engage lawyers to represent them.
- Pirates have more resources at their disposal and better connections with influential politicians than do the people responsible for enforcing intellectual property laws.
- Musicians who enjoy success in the international market produce and record their music in foreign studios; their success provides neither pressure for copyright enforcement in Senegal nor jobs for local sound technicians and engineers.

"Big fish eat little fish" is how Africans describe the economic structure of their music industry.

Finding a place to start in such a situation is difficult. When we investigated the problem of pirated cassettes being sold on the street, we learned that the pirates were not little guys who bought a cassette, then went to make copies on a little machine. The owner of the recording studio, where the band went to record its song and have 250 cassettes made, usually kept a master tape. If the song turned out to be popular, he made copies for himself, and had his salespeople go out on the street to hawk them.

When we inquired of the radio stations why they did not pay royalties they complained that the government did not transmit to them the money from the license fees that each owner of a radio in Senegal was obligated to pay. The government agency responsible told us that they did not have the resources to collect the license fees.

We were lucky to find in the local Senegal Musicians' Association a President who was both dynamic and honest, Mr. Aziz Dieng. The Association already had on its drawing board a sensible plan to attack these problems. We signed on to help.

The government, aware of a 30,000-member organization now active on the local scene, became supportive; after all, which politician could be opposed to music? Spurred by the government's interest and by the activities of the Musicians' Association, the copyright enforcement organization has become more dynamic. It has taken legal action to force radio stations to pay royalties; it has also initiated a system to combat local piracy by providing difficult-to-counterfeit stickers to attach to cassettes and disks on which royalties have been paid. The sticker system will help to identify counterfeit products; its success of course depends on the rigor of the police and the courts to enforce the law. No small amount of credit here should go to Ms. Sibyl Schlatter, an intellectual property lawyer. She helped the Musicians Association to put the fear of the law to the agency.

From this start, the government of Senegal has inserted into its tourism development plan the provision of additional business infrastructure (studios, performance halls, etc.). The Ford Foundation has picked up on the need to educate local musicians as to their rights under Senegalese copyright law, to provide legal and business education for local musicians, to provide them with templates for performance contracts, etc.

The most forward-looking element in the overall Africa music plan is for an Internet-based distribution system for African music. An African musician plays a song in an African studio. Computerized equipment records the song, creates the records for the copyright, and mounts the song into an encrypted dot.com facility that listeners around the world can address. As a listener downloads or plays the song, his or her bank or credit card account is automatically debited, and the musicians' account automatically credited. Such a system, experts insist, is within the bounds of present technology.

An important lesson here is that empowerment of the poor musicians – getting the government to recognize them as a political force – is an important part of the remedy. Because the local people saw how their interests could be advanced, a dynamic program of reform and development has been initiated for a minimal amount of money.

An important dimension of the music project is the positive impact on African morale that further success in music will bring – building a sense of "can do" that Africans might carry over into other endeavors.

Another lesson is that the World Trade Organization's agreement on the trade-related aspects of intellectual property (TRIPS) has missed the development boat entirely (see Finger, 2002, 2004; Finger & Schuler, 2004 for more detailed discussion).

2.4. Local Designs, Local Identity

Ron Layton (2004) began his career in the New Zealand foreign service. He later ran a successful film production company in California. From that business experience he mastered the commercial mechanics of identifying, defending, and marketing intellectual property. Through his current venture, Light Years IP, he helps developing country producers to capitalize on the value of their designs and their geographic and ethnic identities.

When I first met Ron he was helping a group of Congolese artisans. Ten Thousand Villages, one of the leading fair trade importers of handicrafts in the U.S., was marketing one of the Congolese artisans' products, a toy automobile inspired by the Volkswagen "Bug" but made entirely from strands of wire. These artisans are from a group of people with a long tradition of making adornments from wire, e.g., tall, spiraling women's necklaces. The product attracted the attention of Volkswagen who raised issues of design ownership. Volkswagen has certain rights to the design of a model "Bug" as it is derived from their design of the actual car. Ron knew however that just as Volkswagen owned the design, the interpretation of the design in a particular medium was likewise intellectual property, and could be identified and commercialized. Light Years IP assisted Ten Thousand Villages secure an extended license from Volkswagen to resume marketing the product. Copies of the interpretation in wire cannot be sold in the U.S. without license from the owner of the interpretation.

As a cup of coffee has shifted from an indistinguishable commodity into a boutique item, the identity of the coffee has taken on a value of its own. Light Years IP is currently working with Ethiopian coffee producers to trademark and otherwise identify their coffee by the province in which it is grown.[2] The project involves international registrations of names and also training in intellectual property management for Ethiopian producers.

The idea is simple – if "Harar" or "Lekempti" (regions of Ethiopia) is an identity that consumers value, then the producers in those regions should be able to capture that value. The execution, however, requires skill and patience. The business model Light Years IP is helping suppliers to adopt focuses on earning royalties for products branded as coming from a particular region or tribe. Controlling the rights to supply their product to distributors is a key element in improving poor producers' livelihoods.

2.5. Traditional Knowledge, Modern Knowledge, and Poor People's Knowledge

The term "traditional knowledge" includes traditional and tradition-based cultural expressions in forms such as stories, music, dance, artworks, crafts, etc., including symbols, marks, and other recurring expressions of traditional concepts. It also covers traditional agricultural, medical, and technical knowledge. "Indigenous knowledge" and "traditional knowledge" are more or less synonyms (Visser, 2004).

One characteristic is that such knowledge is handed down from generation to generation, usually as part of an oral tradition. Another is that its use is interwoven in a net of customary obligations and rights of the individuals and the community. Within "indigenous communities," the practical and the spiritual/ceremonial dimensions of life overlap perhaps more than they do in "modern communities." In addition, "traditional knowledge" suggests a sense of common or community ownership.

At the extreme, one might imagine a simple analytical model in which people in modern society and in a traditional community each view the origin and ownership of knowledge in a manner parallel with how they view the origin and ownership of tangible property. Consider a stereotypical community of hunter-gatherers. Persons in such a community are aware that many unseen plants and animals are alive in the wild. Provisioning oneself is a matter of acquiring these rather than of creating them. Knowledge they conceptualize in a similar way. What persons in "modern society" perceive as innovation or creativity they perceive as access to and drawing from a hidden stock of knowledge – to use perhaps an overly sophisticated phrase, drawing from a divinely inspired subconscious.

Modern intellectual property law recognizes "common knowledge" as the property of all – the "public domain." No one can obtain a patent or copyright for it. However, individuals can own *new* knowledge. The conception here is that knowledge, like cars or carrots, is *produced* through the efforts of people rather than taken from a stock that nature provides. The basic elements needed to claim a copyright or a patent are a creative step, an identified creator and a basis to demonstrate that the claimant *is* the creator. In short, to gain ownership of knowledge, it has to be novel, and it has to be yours.

From society's perspective, the rationale for allowing temporary individual ownership of new knowledge is that in time all members of society will gain. Intellectual property protection provides an incentive for creative acts, for progress. It adds "the fuel of interest to the fire of genius," said Abraham Lincoln.

"Traditional knowledge" can be a useful analytical concept, but knowledgeable persons warn against over-drawing the distinction between it and "modern knowledge" (Visser, 2004; Wüger, 2004). An obvious part of this warning is a straightforward point: no one's life is entirely "traditional," no one's life is entirely "modern." Traditional versus modern is better thought of as opposite ends of a scale rather than as a clean sorting. Each community fits somewhere along the scale, having some combination of modern and traditional. Along this scale, many persons who are members of more traditional communities are relatively poor; but many poor people live in the "modern" world. Traditional knowledge is only a part of poor peoples' knowledge, one should not slip into thinking that developing countries' commercial interests lie only in collecting on traditional knowledge.

2.6. Respecting Collective and Individual Ownership

Respecting the collective ownership that some indigenous communities value is a complicated matter. The problem is not, however, that modern conceptions of intellectual property cannot handle collective ownership. Any collectivity that law recognizes as a legal entity can own intellectual property: a corporation, a non-profit organization, etc. Many countries with significant populations of indigenous groups have provisions in their legal systems for recognizing such groups as legal entities.

Organizing such groups, however, brings forward familiar collective action problems. Nelly Arvalo-Jiménez (2004) found the indigenous political systems of the Yekuana to be decentralized and resistant to the surrender of diffused authority to a central agency. The Tropical Botanical Garden Research Institute in India did establish a trust fund among the Kani people to administer royalties from patents taken on their ethno-botanical knowledge, but Wüger (2004) points out that there were significant differences among the Kani as to the wisdom of the venture, and disputes over distribution of the royalties among the members.

Recognition of collective ownership raises questions about where to draw the line between the "traditional knowledge" that belongs to everyone and the innovations produced by individual members of the community. Moving the line too far toward protecting traditional knowledge can have negative consequences for the culture or art of poor people as well as for the earnings they enjoy from its commercial use. In the mid-1970s Accra, Ghana, was a lively center of Africa for popular music: recording studios, record pressing plants, scores of nightclubs, twenty top highlife dance bands, dozens of Afro-rock fusion bands, seventy or so highlife guitar bands and "concert parties" – concert parties being a local form of comic highlife opera.

In 1991, the Ghana government created the National Folklore Board of Trustees, ostensibly to make a register of Ghanaian folklore and to monitor its use outside the Third World. The Folklore Board, and folkloric tax, actually originated from a recommendation of the World Intellectual Property Association (WIPO). The WIPO recommendation was to apply the tax only to use of third world traditional knowledge outside of the third world. The Folklore Board, however, interpreted its charter to give it the authority to regulate commercial use by Ghanaians as well, and it interpreted "folklore" to include the entirety of Ghanaian popular music. The Board regulated and taxed the music business out of existence. Today there is no music in Ghana except techno-pop; techno-pop being computer-generated music that uses no musicians or musical instruments (Collins, 2000).

Daniel Wüger (2004) describes a similar outcome in Ethiopia. The government of Ethiopia authorized the Ethiopian Musicians Association as the agent to license and charge fees for the use of folkloric music. The Association interpreted its authority as extending into popular music that had roots in folkloric music. Wüger warns that if artists are not able to claim ownership of their works they will not be able to make a living from their profession – there will be no music in Ethiopia.

In both cases arrangements intended to protect folklore backfired. Rather than collecting revenues *for* a traditional community an organization with authority over the community's musical or artistic tradition found it easier to collect *from* the community.

Liebl and Roy (2004) report a similar concern about Indian crafts. Dr. Jyotindra Jain, Dean of the Faculty of Arts and Aesthetics at Jawaharlal Nehru University, initially supported creation of a regulatory agency. From his experience with it he has since concluded that any regulatory machinery imposed on the crafts community will ultimately end up hurting, rather than helping, those who need protection most.

Country music in the United States provides a positive example. In the United States, the country music business developed in the first half of the twentieth century from a rich tradition of indigenous music in the southeastern states. This music had evolved in significant part from the music that the people who settled in Appalachia brought with them from Scotland and England. The story of this development is warmly told in a book by Mark Zwonitzer and Charles Hirshberg (2002) that relates the experiences of the Carter family of western Virginia.[3] From the beginning, the entrepreneurs who sought out Appalachian artists looked for music in the Appalachian tradition that was sufficiently novel that it could be copyrighted. Ralph Peer was one of the early entrepreneurs in country music. From time to time he would set up a temporary recording studio in Bristol, on the Virginia–Tennessee border, and word would circulate that he was in town paying for music.

Most of the acts racing toward Bristol would go back home to obscurity, with nothing. Many of the mountain acts Peer saw repeated the same songs: hymns, centuries-old ballads, or popular standards that had been recorded already. Peer needed material he could copyright and cash in on, so he needed musicians who could write their own songs, or at least restitch the traditional songs enough that he could 'put them over as new.' (Zwonitzer & Hirshberg, pp. 94–95)

Within a static conception of knowledge/culture, this might sound like parsing out the common domain – all traditional music would pass into private ownership and the community tradition of music would disappear.

In fact, the opposite happened. Many commercially successful artists enjoy playing and recording more traditional forms. With the income they earn from their more commercial products they can afford to do more traditional things simply for the pleasure of it. Furthermore, commercially successful music tends to "liven" the cultural tradition rather than stifle it. Baaba Maal's and other successful Senegalese artists' music is now part of the Senegalese musical tradition. Carter Family music has become part of the Appalachian tradition. It is celebrated at festivals from Australia to the upper reaches of Canada, in Europe and in Asia, from Newport, Rhode Island, to Alaska. Moreover, as music evolves away from its roots there are commercial opportunities to turn back. Baaba Maal's 2002 album is traditional music performed on African acoustic instruments. In the U.S. country music, Willie Nelson and the "outlaws" who split away from the Nashville version are another example of going back to the roots without sacrificing commercial potential.

The lesson here is that maintaining the liveliness of the culture as well as taking advantage of economic opportunity lies in expanding the dynamics of poor peoples' knowledge much more than in defending a static stock of knowledge from outside exploitation. Culture in a bottle soon becomes an empty bottle.

3. CONCLUSIONS

I will limit myself to four conclusions.

1. *Except in a museum setting, no traditional skill can be sustained unless it has a viable market.*
2. *Good intentions play an important role.*

   Many of the success stories in the chapter are about people motivated in large part by their love for a particular art or for a particular people. Nevertheless, those among them who have been successful are *market accepting.* They use their commercial skills to achieve what they want to achieve, they know that finding an artisan a way to make a living is a reliable way to keep that artisan at his trade. They know that culture and commerce complement each other more than they conflict.

The regulation that throttled viable musical cultures in Ghana and Ethiopia was not, however, market accepting. It compromised, rather than enhanced, the possibility that creative people could make a living from their creativity. They erred in viewing culture as a stock, rather than a constantly renewing flow. They chose to lock up the stock rather than to encourage the flow; from them we learned that culture in a bottle becomes soon an empty bottle.

3. *The development dimension of intellectual property is much broader than the legal dimension.*

Success in defending poor people's knowledge – in helping poor people to increase the return on their knowledge – requires a functioning legal system for intellectual property. It also requires the commercial skill to function in the resulting markets. Indeed, it is more appropriate to think of the legal system as facilitating owners in their defense of their property rights rather than as providing an environment in which capable people advance such interests. The dynamics of the system must come from intellectual property producers; it will not come from the legal system.

4. *Familiar legal and commercial instruments have much to offer.*

Specialized legal systems for poor peoples' knowledge are an intellectual challenge for legal scholars. Economic development however turns on skillful application in poorer countries of the legal and commercial concepts that have proven useful in richer countries.

NOTES

1. The stories, I realize, are what is interesting, not the lessons – though that is hard advice for university professors and other preachers to follow.

2. Coffee grew wild on the Harar plateau before the existence of man, and even for Ethiopia that is a long time ago.

3. The authors are cultural historians, not economists.

REFERENCES

Arvalo-Jiménez, N. (2004). Kuyujani Originario: The Yekuana road to the overall protection of their rights as people. In: J. Finger & P. Schuler (Eds), *Poor people's knowledge: Promoting intellectual property in developing countries* (pp. 37–52). Washington, DC: World Bank/Oxford University Press.

Collins, J. (2000). *The Ghanaian experience.* Presentation at the World Bank – Policy Sciences Center, Inc., available at < http://www.worldbank.org/research/trade/africa_music2.htm >.

Finger, J. (2002). *The Doha agenda and development: A view from the Uruguay Round.* Manila, Philippines: Asian Development Bank.

Finger, J. (2004). Introduction and overview. In: J. Finger & P. Schuler (Eds), *Poor people's knowledge: Promoting intellectual property in developing countries* (pp. 1–36). Washington, DC: World Bank/Oxford University Press.

Finger, J., & Schuler, P. (Eds) (2004). *Poor people's knowledge: Promoting intellectual property in developing countries.* Washington, DC: World Bank/Oxford University Press.

Layton, R. (2004). Enhancing intellectual property exports through fair trade. In: J. Finger & P. Schuler (Eds), *Poor people's knowledge: Promoting intellectual property in developing countries* (pp. 53–74). Washington, DC: World Bank/Oxford University Press.

Liebl, M., & Roy, T. (2004). Handmade in India: Traditional craft skills in a changing world. In: J. Finger & P. Schuler (Eds), *Poor people's knowledge: Promoting intellectual property in developing countries* (pp. 53–74). Washington, DC: World Bank/Oxford University Press.

Penna, F., Thormann, M., & Finger, J. (2004). The Africa music project. In: J. Finger & P. Schuler (Eds), *Poor people's knowledge: Promoting intellectual property in developing countries* (pp. 95–112). Washington, DC: World Bank/Oxford University Press.

Visser, C. (2004). Making intellectual property laws work for traditional knowledge. In: J. Finger & P. Schuler (Eds), *Poor people's knowledge: Promoting intellectual property in developing countries* (pp. 207–240). Washington, DC: World Bank/Oxford University Press.

Wüger, D. (2004). Prevention of misappropriation of intangible cultural heritage through intellectual property laws. In: J. Finger & P. Schuler (Eds), *Poor people's knowledge: Promoting intellectual property in developing countries* (pp. 183–206). Washington, DC: World Bank/Oxford University Press.

Zwonitzer, M., & Hirshberg, C. (2002). *Will you miss me when I'm gone? A history of the Carter family and their legacy in American life.* New York: Simon and Schuster.

PART II:
ENTREPRENEURSHIP IN
TRANSITIONAL ECONOMICS

INSTITUTIONAL DEVELOPMENT AND ENTREPRENEURSHIP IN A TRANSITION CONTEXT

David Smallbone and Friederike Welter

1. INTRODUCTION

The start of the second decade after the transformation process began is an appropriate time to reflect on some of the emerging policy issues affecting small business development. While emphasising that setting up, operating and developing businesses results from the creativity, drive and commitment of individuals, rather than as a result of government actions, the conditions that enable and/or constrain entrepreneurship are affected by the wider social, economic and institutional context, over which the state has a major influence. In this regard, a key point to stress is the variety of ways in which government can affect the nature, extent and pace of small business development in an economy, rather than narrowly focusing on direct support measures. As a result, when considering the question of policies to support small business development, it is necessary to consider the implications of a range of government policies, institutions and actions for the environment in which small businesses can develop, instead of just focusing on direct interventions that are specifically targeted at small businesses. This is because any benefits accruing from the latter may be more than outweighed by the negative effects of other government policies and actions and those of

Developmental Entrepreneurship: Adversity, Risk, and Isolation
International Research in the Business Disciplines, Volume 5, 37–53
Copyright © 2006 by Elsevier Ltd.
All rights of reproduction in any form reserved
ISSN: 1074-7877/doi:10.1016/S1074-7877(06)05003-3

state institutions. This applies in mature market-based economies as well as in those at various stages of transition, although the transition context typically adds further dimensions.

The following types of policy fostering entrepreneurship and small business development have previously been identified (Smallbone & Welter, 2001a; Verheul, Wennekers, Audretsch, & Thurik, 2002): firstly, *macroeconomic policy*, since the macroeconomic environment affects the willingness and ability of entrepreneurs (and potential entrepreneurs) to invest, particularly in projects that may take some time to produce a return; secondly, the *costs of legislative compliance*, which can fall disproportionately heavily on smaller enterprises (Bannock & Peacock, 1989; Fletcher, 2001); thirdly, *tax policies,* including both the total tax burden, but also the cost of compliance that can be affected by the frequency with which changes are made to the tax regime and the methods used for collection; fourthly, the *influence of government on the development of market institutions*, such as banks and other financial intermediaries, business support and training organisations; fifthly, the *influence of the government on the value placed on enterprise and entrepreneurship in society,* which in the long-term is affected by the curriculum and methods of teaching in the education system (at all levels), but also by the stance of government towards business and property ownership and the behaviour of politicians and government officials in their dealings with private firms; and lastly, *direct intervention*, designed to assist small businesses to overcome size-related disadvantages. In a liberal market view, such intervention is justified in order to address areas of demonstrated market failure, such as the effects of a collateral-based approach to lending by commercial banks on the supply of finance for new and small firms. However, in a transition context where a market (e.g., for finance or advice/consultancy) may be underdeveloped, or still emerging, such intervention may have a pump-priming role in helping to build capacity in the market.

While each of these policy areas are applicable in a mature market as well as in transition economies, the key underlying factor in a transition context is the extent of the commitment of government to market reforms (Welter, 1997). This is demonstrated through governmental actions with respect to the shift from public to private sector ownership; the extent to which there is price liberalisation; and the role of government with respect to the creation and effective operation of market institutions. Here, differences in the extent of market reforms, combined with other economic, social and historical differences limit the scope for generalisation across the variety of countries that comprise Central and Eastern Europe and the former Soviet Union. This can be illustrated with reference to economic indicators produced by the European Bank for Reconstruction and Development (EBRD), which show wide variation between countries on a number of dimensions. For example, in terms of the state of small-scale privatisation, which involved retail shops and small service outlets, Croatia, the Czech Republic, Hungary, the three Baltic States, Poland, the Slovak Republic and Slovenia are to be found at one extreme (high), while Belarus and Turkmenistan are at the other (low) (EBRD, 2001). In terms of price liberalisation, the indicators vary from Hungary, Poland, Slovenia, Romania and Moldova at one extreme (high) to Belarus, Turkmenistan and Uzbekistan at the other (low). In this context, the aim in the rest of the paper is not to attempt to summarise progress or policy approaches across all transition economies, but rather to focus on issues of institutional development in countries that are at different stages of market reform (using Belarus and Estonia as examples) in order to develop general policy recommendations, since market-oriented institutions are prerequisites for the sustained development of productive entrepreneurship.

2. TRANSITIONAL ENVIRONMENTS WITH MAJOR INSTITUTIONAL DEFICIENCIES

2.1. An Institutional Approach to Entrepreneurship in Early Stage Transition Economies

Evidence from several empirical surveys in former Soviet republics, such as Russia, Belarus and Ukraine and others such as the Baltic states, suggest that many enterprises are set up, survive and sometimes even grow *despite* government, because of the entrepreneurship of individuals in mobilising resources and their flexibility in adapting to hostile external environments (e.g., Aidis, 2003; Chepurenko, 1994, 1999; Chepurenko & Malieva, 2005; Manolova & Yan, 2002; McIntyre & Dallago, 2003; Smallbone & Welter, 2001b; Smallbone, Welter, Isakova, & Slonimski, 2001; Yan & Manolova, 1998). The problem is that in these situations the number of firms remains small and their contribution to economic development in terms of jobs, innovation and external income generation is rather limited. Thus, in situations where market reforms have been slow or only partially installed, the institutional context becomes a critical factor, since government still has to create the framework conditions for sustainable private sector development.

In such conditions, it has been suggested that the types of entrepreneurship that can be identified and the enterprise strategies adopted are heavily influenced by the external environment in general (e.g., Hoskisson, Eden, Lau, & Wright, 2000; Oliver, 1991; Peng & Heath, 1996; Peng, 2000, 2003; Radaev, 2001; Wright, Filatotchev, Hoskisson, & Peng, 2005) and the institutional context in particular (e.g., Manolova & Yan, 2002; Aidis, 2003; Welter & Smallbone, 2003). In this regard, institutionalist theory offers a suitable interpretative frame of reference, since it emphasises the role of external political, economic and societal influences on individual behaviour (cf. North, 1981, 1990, 1995, 1998, 2004; Williamson, 2000; Voigt & Engerer, 2002). Douglass North understands 'institutions' as the rules of the game within a society, which structure individual behaviour, thereby reducing uncertainty, risk and transaction costs connected with each individual action. He distinguishes between formal institutions, which include political and economy-related rules and organisations, and informal institutions, such as the codes of conduct, norms and values of society (North, 1990). An institutional framework to foster entrepreneurship consists of the fundamental political, social and legal rules, which set the basis for economic actions (Davis & North, 1971). In this regard, examples of formal institutions include the legal framework and the financial system. Informal rules refer to codes of conduct and interpretations of laws and regulations, which further regulate economic actions. Both formal and informal institutions are a major influence on the nature and extent of any entrepreneurial activity, since they determine the scope for the actions and behaviour of (potential) entrepreneurs in practice.

In those transition economies, where progress with transformation towards a market economy is limited, effective formal institutions appropriate to emerging market conditions, are lacking. 'Old' (i.e., unchanged) informal rules predominate, resulting in an incompatible institutional framework, which further slows down the transformation process (Mummert, 1999). In such situations, entrepreneurs solve the 'normative dilemma' of postcommunism (Los, 1992) by resorting to learned behaviour, although this contradicts the new institutional framework. Such behaviour represents a form of path dependency, which plays a major role in explaining certain characteristics of entrepreneurship and enterprise behaviour in transition economies (Welter & Smallbone, 2003).

In addition, an inadequate and often hostile institutional environment in countries where market reforms have been slow, or only partially installed, further constrains the development of small businesses and entrepreneurship (Smallbone & Welter, 2001a, b; Aidis, 2003). In Belarus for example, the very slow pace of privatisation, combined with an increase in the regulation of small enterprise activity after 1996, forced many small firms into liquidation and others into operating abroad in countries, such as Poland, Russia, the Czech Republic, Latvia and the Ukraine (Smallbone et al., 2001). Methods used to restrict entrepreneurship included additional requirements for enterprises to obtain licences, and a more rigorous approach to the implementation of regulations by state officials (e.g., tax officials) towards private firms than towards state enterprises. By 1997, the effect of an increasingly hostile regulatory stance on the part of government towards the private sector resulted in 54% of all registered enterprises becoming illegal, or driven out of business, because of new registration rules, linked to higher minimum capital requirements (Zhuk & Cherevach, 2000).

2.2. The Environment for Entrepreneurship in Early Stage Transition Countries

In many transition countries, where the pace of reform has been slow, the *legal framework* is still the main barrier for the development of small business and entrepreneurship. Creating an adequate legal framework involves laws relating to property, bankruptcy, contracts, commercial activities and taxes, but it also involves developing an institutional framework with the capacity to implement these laws, which has major implications for staffing. In practice, and referring again to the Belarussian context, this requires the establishment of specialised economic courts; a private legal profession and effective enforcement mechanisms, which are still lacking for the most part, which goes hand in hand with a typical lack of adequate personnel in government administration. The reasons include low public sector salaries, combined with a lack of education and training opportunities. All this prevents the proper implementation of new laws and regulations, with negative implications for the business environment and organizations. In addition, frequent changes in tax regulations and other commercial laws, which are characteristics of the early years of transition, require a constant adjustment of knowledge by small business managers as well as by those in government administration. Other problems include a rather uncertain attitude, or even arbitrariness, on the part of public officials regarding law enforcement, which is not helped by a typical lack of specificity in the drafting of laws.

Fundamentally, these institutional deficiencies reflect a lack of political commitment to facilitate private enterprise development. Belarus, under President Lukashenko, may be one of the worst examples, but the issues exist to varying degrees in most of the other former Soviet republics. Political considerations with respect to the enforcement of laws can aggravate the situation, resulting in the fostering of 'old' networks between former state-owned firms and government, as also happened in the early stages of transition in those former transition countries, which joined the EU in 2004 (for Hungary cf. Voszka, 1991, 1994). In some transition countries these networks seem to be one of the major problems (cf. Kuznetsov, 1997), which impede the establishment of independent juridical institutions and the impartial enforcement of a legal framework required for market economies.

Another major barrier to small business development in transition countries, where market reform has remained slow is the *financial infrastructure* (Welter, 1997; Zecchini, 1997). While stock exchanges developed quickly in the more advanced transition countries, in most former Soviet republics, national risk capital markets are virtually non-existent and the banking system is still highly inadequate (Zecchini, 1997; Frydman, Murphy, & Rapaczynski, 1998). Banks under central planning were mere accounting agencies without an active role in the financial transactions of households or enterprises. In less advanced transition economies, the majority of banks still experience difficulties in mastering the task of guiding savings towards capital investment in private enterprises, especially small businesses. The extension of credits to small businesses has also been hampered by the fact that newly created or privatised banks often face liquidity constraints, resulting from insufficient equity capital provision, inherited liabilities from the central planning era and/or from massive repayment delays. In addition, banks have typically followed a conservative strategy with respect to the financing of private enterprises. As a consequence, most banks in less advanced transition countries, such as Ukraine and Belarus, lack the willingness to finance small businesses, reinforced by a lack of expertise and know-how with this new clientele, as well as a shortage of collateral on the side of the enterprises. In these circumstances, informal institutions and practices may compensate for some of the deficiencies in formal market institutions, although not without implications for the types of strategies adopted by entrepreneurs to set up and develop businesses (Peng, 2000, 2003).

2.3. Entrepreneurial Behaviour in an Early Stage Transition Environment

All these factors can contribute to a *negative attitude on the part of small businesses towards government and regulations*, which was a common phenomenon in the early years of transition particularly, and across all transition countries. It typically results in the widespread use of types of enterprise strategy which represent an adaptation by entrepreneurs to a specific set of environmental and institutional conditions (Oliver, 1991). Frequent changes in the legal system, combined with a prohibitive tax level, an unpredictable behaviour of state officials in applying legal and tax regulations, and inadequate access to external capital, encourage entrepreneurs to use evasion strategies (Feige, 1997; Leitzel, 1997). These 'evasion' strategies allow private entrepreneurship to exist and survive in an environment where government typically considers private businesses to be mainly a source of tax revenue and where inadequate public law enforcement leads to arbitrariness and corruption.

'Typical' evasion strategies included combining legal and informal production; setting up a 'fictitious' enterprise; and making cash payments to employees. For example, evidence drawn from a study of employment behaviour in Russian small businesses, indicates a predominance of unofficial payment strategies to workers in order to reduce social security contributions (Welter & Smallbone, 2003). As the owner of a publishing house in Russia put it, "In a trading business the wage actually paid is several times greater than the officially calculated pay" (Welter & Smallbone, 2003). Survey data from the same project in Russia also indicated widespread violation of the labour law, thus providing further examples of evasion strategies being used as part of 'normal' enterprise behaviour, although entrepreneurs were naturally cautious about admitting this openly. Examples included the use of verbal labour contracts, or the socialist practice of 'enrollment on order' (i.e., the enterprise management issues an order to employ a particular employee), thereby violating the labour law. In addition, only-one third included the legally required provisions for labour protection in the conditions of employment. Consequently, in two-thirds of the surveyed Russian enterprises, the labour contracts were not valid legally (Welter & Smallbone, 2003).

Moreover, evidence from various studies across different transition countries confirm these results (e.g., Frye & Shleifer, 1997; Gustafson, 1999; Hendley, Murrel, & Ryterman, 2000; Peng, 2000; Radaev, 2001; Manolova & Yan, 2002). Weakly specified regulations, combined with inadequate law enforcement, encourage corruption, not only when an entrepreneur is first registering a company, but also in everyday economic transactions. As a result, an inadequate legal framework contributes to forms of enterprise behaviour, which although rational from an individual entrepreneur's point of view, is non-productive from the economy's standpoint, falling into the category of unproductive entrepreneurship (Baumol, 1990). This behaviour is considered unproductive because it diverts resources that could otherwise be put to productive use, into dealing with some of the unnecessary costs associated with an institutional context in which the framework conditions for sustainable entrepreneurship have still to be established. Institutional deficiencies lead to mistrust on behalf of the entrepreneur, towards state officials and society more generally (e.g., Raiser, 1999; Rose-Ackerman, 2001; Tonoyan, 2005). This can lead to a potentially vicious circle of mistrust fostering further evasion behaviour of entrepreneurs, which in turn fosters further mistrust and corruption practices (for country-specific examples, see Raiser, Haerpfer, Nowotny, & Wallace, 2001; Service, 2002; Satter, 2003; Welter, Kautonen, Chepurenko, Malieva, & Venesaar, 2004; Chepurenko & Malieva, 2005; Radaev, 2005).

As a consequence, in conditions that pertain in countries such as Belarus and Ukraine, policy needs to focus on the overall institutional framework for entrepreneurial activities, in order to facilitate the development of productive entrepreneurship and minimise unproductive forms of entrepreneurial behaviour. In this context, it is important to recognise that the cost of compliance with regulations and other statutory requirements includes opportunity costs for businesses with respect to the resources devoted to compliance, as well direct money payments in some cases. Improving the quality of laws and regulations are key elements in establishing the framework conditions that are necessary for economic and democratic development. Regulations that are overly burdensome, complex or impractical may reduce business competitiveness by contributing to higher administrative and compliance costs, as well as to a diminution of the rule of law when non-compliance becomes rife. Greater recognition also needs to be given to the fact that policy recommendations for small business support are often connected to specific political and cultural contexts, while conditions and legacies can vary considerably between countries.

3. INSTITUTIONAL DEVELOPMENT IN NEW EU MEMBER STATES AND CANDIDATE COUNTRIES

3.1. The Environment for Entrepreneurship in New Member States

In the new member states of the EU that joined in May 2004, the process of accession contributed to the overall process of institutional development and administrative reform. This can be illustrated with reference to Estonia, which represents a country where rapid and considerable progress has been made in terms of institutional development and regulatory reform with respect to enterprise development, in contrast to some of the countries referred to earlier in the chapter. Although a very small country, Estonia is an interesting example for the purpose of this paper, not least because unlike Poland, Hungary and Slovenia, for example, it was formerly part of the Soviet Union, with a comparable formal institutional context at the start of the reform process to countries featuring in the first part of the paper.

Following independence in 1991, government policy in Estonia has been underpinned by a free market philosophy and a commitment to the institutionalisation of private ownership and market reforms. Rapid privatisation meant that by the end of 1996, most large enterprises had been sold, with attention turning to the utilities, such as energy, telecommunications, railways and ports. However, progress with the privatisation of land was hampered by a complicated restitution procedure. Since 1991, Estonia has also had a liberal trade policy in which trade barriers and tariffs have been largely abolished, leading to a growth in exports on the one hand and an inflow of duty-free imports on the other. The openness of the Estonian economy has also contributed to the country's success in attracting foreign investment, which has been an important enabling factor contributing to the success of its economic reforms and the structural transformation of the economy. As a result, on most indicators of market reform, Estonia scores high in comparison with other Central and East European countries and former Soviet republics. For example, based on EBRD assessment, 75% of Estonia's GDP in 2001 was contributed by the private sector.

During the initial phase of transition in Estonia, government was responsible for administrative and legal reforms, which made it possible for privately owned enterprises to develop, although for a time the continuous nature of these changes contributed to an unstable and uncertain business environment. It also took some time to completely revise the tax system, which meant that the development of small private enterprises was initially constrained by the remains of a tax regime inherited from the Soviet period. At the same time, until recently, direct support measures to support small business development in Estonia have been absent, with the role of government best characterised as one of limited intervention (European Commission, 1999). The first step towards the harmonisation of regulations and business environment with EU requirements in Estonia was the introduction of a new Commercial Code in 1995. This resulted in the introduction of legal forms of entrepreneurship similar to mature market economies; an increase in the minimum capital requirements for public and limited liability companies; and the creation of a new, central Business Register. The influence of Estonia's candidature for EU entry can also be seen in relation to the definition of small business, as the EU definition of small businesses became accepted in Estonia.

As expressed in the Pre-Accession Economic Programme (Republic of Estonia, 2001), the main goals of Estonian economic policy are to achieve sustainable, socially and regionally balanced economic growth. The basis of small business policy was embedded in the National Program for the Adoption of the 'Aqcuis Communitaire' 2002–2003 (NPAA, 2001), which included a number of specific activities, demonstrating how policy development has been affected by the EU accession agenda. Examples include the use of pre-structural funds and other foreign assistance instruments to assist in the implementation of the Action Plan; offering state support services to start-up businesses; offering guarantees for small loans; developing an infrastructure for entrepreneurship, which was supported through Phare projects; and strengthening the capacity of relevant institutions in preparation for receiving assistance through EU Structural Funds.

3.2. Developing the Institutional Framework for Entrepreneurship in Estonia

The development of an appropriate institutional framework is an important part of the market reform process. In general, the institutionalisation of business support includes the development of institutions on three levels: macro- meso- and micro-level (Welter, 1997). In Estonia, during the 1990s, two ministries (the Ministry of Economic Affairs and the Ministry of Internal Affairs) were responsible for implementing the main tasks connected with the support programmes for small businesses at the *macro level*. However, three other Ministries (for Finance, Agriculture and Social Affairs) were also involved through their responsibility for administering various foundations concerned with supporting regional and enterprise development. Since 2000, the responsibility for enterprise support was centralised under the Ministry of Economic Affairs, with the aim of making more effective use of the resources available for enterprise support, on a regional as well as on a sectoral basis (Estonian Ministry of Economic Affairs, 2002).

Considerable progress has also been made in developing the institutional framework for enterprise development at the *meso level*. This includes the banking system which, now largely under foreign ownership, is increasingly developing a range of financial products similar to those available to enterprises in a market economy. It also includes a number of unions, associations and chambers, established by special interests groups, mainly on the basis of voluntary membership. Some of these, such as the Chamber of Trade and Commerce and specialised sector-based organisations, have been the main source of support for businesses in the process of exploiting foreign markets. In 2000, the public business support infrastructure in Estonia was restructured in an attempt to make it more efficient, transparent and accessible. Seven foundations together with the Tourist Board, under the administration of five different ministries, were integrated into two new organisations, namely Kredex (the Credit and Export Guarantee Fund) and Enterprise Estonia, which has responsibility for implementing public business support measures, and through the Regional Development Agency, the responsibility for supporting the local business development centres.

At the *micro-level*, institutional development has focused on the development of a network of business development centres that originated with foreign donor funding in the 1990s. Previous evaluation has identified a number of weaknesses in the donor-financed network, including poor relationships with local authorities and other relevant institutions (such as banks) in many cases, and their impact within local business networks appears to have been weak. Other problems included the ongoing dependence of these centres on subsidies, the poor advertising of their services, and the fact that hitherto their activities have been mainly limited to dealing with start-ups (Bateman, 2000; European Commmission, 1999). As a result, the business support network has recently been the subject of reform, both to improve the quality and effectiveness of services delivered to small businesses, but also to improve the administration, management and cost-effectiveness of the support institutions.

Although the small size of the Estonian economy, combined with the opportunity to exploit historic ties with Nordic neighbours has presented Estonia with potential advantages over many other former Soviet republics, the pace of change has been impressive and considerable progress has been achieved with respect to the institutionalisation of small business policy. The publication of a national policy document for small business development represented a significant step forward in strategic thinking, with related measures and responsibilities for implementation (OECD, 2002). Moreover, linking strategic policy objectives to specific action plans, which are tied into the budgetary process, was a positive step towards overcoming the implementation gap that is a common feature of small business policy in a transition context. The rationalisation of the various agencies into Enterprise Estonia and Kredex also appears to have been a positive step from an enterprise development standpoint. Another positive feature of the current policy environment in Estonia is the opportunities that exist for representative organisations of small businesses (such as the Chamber of Commerce) to express their views on draft regulations and legislation, although it is difficult to establish to what extent their comments have influenced final decision making.

4. CONCLUSIONS AND POLICY AGENDA

Although the specific policy priorities for small business development vary between individual transition economies, a key underlying theme in *early stage transition countries* is the importance of institutional development and capacity building, over which governments exert a key influence. An appropriate and effective institutionalisation of small business policy is still one of the main preconditions that need to be fulfilled in countries such as the Ukraine, Belarus, and the Russian Federation, before productive entrepreneurship and sustained private sector development can become embedded. This also refers to the potential role of regional and local authorities, both in promoting entrepreneurship and in facilitating its development, in view of the fact that it is at the local level that policy and institutions touch entrepreneurs most directly. This can be illustrated with reference to the Russian Federation, where there is a need to clarify the respective aims and responsibilities of federal and regional authorities, improve the coordination of federal and regional support programmes; take steps to reduce bureaucracy at the local level; and establish conditions to facilitate dialogue between public authorities and entrepreneurs (OECD, 2001).

At the same time, developing effective institutional arrangements for the governance and support of small businesses in the economy is a challenge shared by all transition countries. The state has an important role to play in fostering entrepreneurship by developing a strategy for removing obstacles to enterprise creation; establishing a facilitating environment for private sector development; and contributing to the development of appropriate market institutions, which are an important part of the business environment in a market economy. In this context, the appropriateness, effectiveness and overall quality of the *legislative and regulatory framework* is likely to have a greater impact on the development of the small business sector in the long run than direct support measures that are specifically aimed at helping small businesses. Alternatively, the negative effects of an inadequate and poorly implemented legal and regulatory framework can impair the development of legitimate private sector activity at the expense of a burgeoning informal economy. In addition, strengthening the legislative environment can be a highly cost-effective strategy for stimulating and promoting entrepreneurship, particularly when government resources are limited.

Policy priorities are different in *candidate countries for the next accession round and in the EU's new member states*. In this regard, one of the immediate policy priorities is to improve the level of detailed knowledge concerning the likely changes in the operating environment resulting from EU accession that face SMEs in specific sectors, combined with an effective dissemination programme. Priority must also be given to the development of effective business support networks, since the competitiveness of SMEs depends on them being able to extend and supplement their base of internal management resources and knowledge, by drawing on appropriate external inputs when they need them.

Active promotion of entrepreneurship at the regional and local levels is also required, as part of an enterprise-focused regional policy (OECD, 2000). Although the pace of development of the small business sector in core regions in many candidate countries has been impressive, there is typically a need to take steps to stimulate entrepreneurship more widely. However, to be effective, this will need to address one of the current deficiencies of current regional policy, which, in a country such as Estonia, is an institutional one (De Vets, Boot, & Hollanders, 2000). This refers to the need to reform the county and local government structures, neither of which have the capacity or resources to effectively engage in regional policy. There are currently 250 different local authorities in Estonia, ranging in size from Tallinn (with 400,000 inhabitants) to small islands, with a handful of people. Local government reform can help to provide a basis for the development of effective central–local and public–private partnerships that is necessary if candidate countries are to maximise the opportunities for accessing EU structural funds in the future. In addition to reforming the structure of local/regional government structure, priority must also be given to the development of institutional capacity to enable these countries to effectively access appropriate EU funding sources to facilitate the required development.

Other policy priorities with implications for institutional development include the development of effective, market-oriented innovation systems. The development of an institutional infrastructure to support technology transfer and facilitate innovation in SMEs (e.g., innovation centres, technology parks, science parks) has been a feature of economic development in most EU member states during the last 25 years, although in new member states, such initiatives have a much shorter tradition. However, as the experience in western Europe demonstrates, while supply side initiatives (such as innovation centres or science parks) may be a necessary condition for nurturing new technology-based enterprises, they are not a sufficient condition for the development of such enterprises. Hence, another policy priority is to increase the level of involvement of higher education institutions in developing links with the business sector in order to increase the supply of technical entrepreneurs.

Finally, when considering policies to encourage and support enterprise and small business development in transition and emerging market economies, it is important to keep in mind that an ongoing critical debate exists within most mature market economies about policy approaches and priorities and the effectiveness of government intervention with respect to small businesses (e.g., Curran, 2000; Gibb, 2000). In this regard, some of the current policy debates in mature market economies are applicable in economies at earlier stages of market development and vice versa. For example, is a policy for entrepreneurship more appropriate than a policy for small businesses and what are the implications of such an emphasis? What is the role of the state in relation to market forces and market institutions in supporting SME development? How can higher education institutions contribute more to the development of entrepreneurship? How much do policy makers really know about the support needs of the enterprises and entrepreneurs that their policies purport to address? Such questions are currently being debated in EU countries, including the UK, yet they are basic questions, which indicate the limited extent to which policy practice is based on real knowledge and robust evidence of the needs of entrepreneurs, rather than on the assumptions of policy makers and the political agendas of their masters. These remain priority issues for policy, to varying degrees, in most countries.

REFERENCES

Aidis, R. (2003). *By law and by custom: Factors affecting small- and medium-sized enterprises during the transition in Lithuania*. Tinbergen Institute Research Series, 316. Thesis Amsterdam: Thela.

Bannock, G., & Peacock, A. (1989). *Governments and small business*. London: Paul Chapman.

Bateman, M. (2000). Neo-liberalism, SME development and the role of business support centres in the transition economies of central and Eastern Europe. *Small Business Economics, 14*, 275–298.

Baumol, W. (1990). Entrepreneurship: Productive, unproductive and destructive. *Journal of Political Economy, 98*(5), 893–921.

Chepurenko, A. (1994). Das neue russland: Die kleinunternehmen und die große politik. *Internationales Gewerbearchiv, 42*, 260–265.

Chepurenko, A. (1999). Die neuen russischen Unternehmer: Wer sie sind, wie sie sind. In: H.-H. Höhmann (Ed.), *Eine unterschätzte Dimension? Zur Rolle wirtschaftskultureller*

Faktoren in der osteuropäischen Transformation, Analysen zur Kultur und Gesellschaft im östlichen Europa (Vol. 9, pp. 139–152). Bremen: Edition Temmen.

Chepurenko, A., & Malieva, E. (2005). Trust-milieus of Russian SMEs: Cross-regional performance. In: H.-H. Höhmann & F. Welter (Eds), *Trust and entrepreneurship: A West–East perspective* (pp. 136–155). Cheltenham: Edward Elgar.

Curran, J. (2000). What is small business policy in the UK for? Evaluating and assessing small business support policies. *International Small Business Journal, 18*(3), 36–50.

Davis, L., & North, D. C. (1971). *Institutional change and American economic growth.* Cambridge, NY: Cambridge University Press.

De Vets, Boot & Hollanders (2000). *Regional policy in Estonia, Latvia and Lithuania: Main report.* NEI Regional and Urban Development on behalf of the European Commission, DG Regional Policy, March.

EBRD (2001). *Transition report 2001: Energy in transition.* European Bank for Reconstruction and Development, London.

European Commission. (1999). An evaluation of Phare SME programmes. Estonia. In: J.-J. Kudela & U. Venesaar (Eds), *Draft report.* Brussels.

Feige, E. (1997). Underground activity and institutional change: Productive, protective, and predatory behaviour in transition economies. In: J. M. Nelson, C. Tilly & L. Walker (Eds), *Transforming post-communist political economies* (pp. 21–34). Washington, DC: National Academy Press.

Fletcher, D. (2001). A small business perspective on regulation in the UK. *Economic Affairs, 21*(2), 17–22.

Frydman, R., Murphy, K., & Rapaczynski, A. (1998). *Capitalism with a comrade's face.* Budapest: Central European University Press.

Frye, T., & Shleifer, A. (1997). The invisible hand and the grabbing hand. *American Economic Review, 87*(2), 354–358.

Gibb, A. (2000). Small and medium enterprise development: Borrowing from elsewhere? A research and development agenda. *Journal of Small Business and Enterprise Development, 7*(3), 199–211.

Gustafson, T. (1999). *Capitalism Russian-style.* Cambridge: Cambridge University Press.

Hendley, K., Murrel, P., & Ryterman, R. (2000). Law, relationships and private enforcement: Transactional strategies of Russian enterprises. *Europe-Asia Studies, 52,* 627–656.

Hoskisson, R., Eden, L., Lau, C., & Wright, M. (2000). Strategy in emerging economies. *Academy of Management Journal, 43*(3), 249–267.

Kuznetsov, Ye. (1997). Learning in networks: Enterprise behavior in the former Soviet Union and contemporary Russia. In: J. M. Nelson, C. Tilly & L. Walker (Eds), *Transforming post-communist political economies* (pp. 156–176). Washington, DC: National Academy Press.

Leitzel, J. (1997). Rule evasion in transitional Russia. In: J. M. Nelson & C. Tilly & L. Walker (Eds), *Transforming post-communist political economies* (pp. 118–130). Washington, DC: National Academy Press.

Los, M. (1992). From underground to legitimacy: The normative dilemmas of post-communist marketization. In: B. Dallago, G. Ajani & B. Grancelli (Eds), *Privatization and entrepreneurship in post-socialist countries: Economy, law and society* (pp. 112–142). New York: St. Martin's Press.

Manolova, T., & Yan, A. (2002). Institutional constraints and entrepreneurial responses in a transforming economy. *International Small Business Journal, 20,* 163–184.

McIntyre, R., & Dallago, B. (Eds) (2003). *Small and medium enterprises in transitional econo-mies*. Hampshire, UK: Palgrave.

Ministry of Economic Affairs (2002). *Enterprising Estonia: National policy for the development of small and medium-sized enterprises in Estonia, 2001–2006*. Ministry of Economic Affairs, Tallinn.

Mummert, U. (1999). *Informal institutions and institutional policy – shedding light on the myth of institutional conflict*. Diskussionsbeitrag, 02–99, Jena: Max-Planck Institute for Research into Economic Systems.

North, D. (1981). *Structure and change in economic history*. New York and London: Norton.

North, D. (1990). *Institutions, institutional change and economic performance*. Cambridge: University Press.

North, D. (1995). Structural changes of institutions and the process of transformation. *Prague Economic Papers, 4*(3), 229–234.

North, D. (1998). Where have we been and where are we going? In: A. Ben-Ner & L. Putterman (Eds), *Economics, values, and organization* (pp. 491–508). Cambridge: Cambridge University Press.

North, D. (2004). Local knowledge and institutional reform. In: CIPE (Ed.), *1983–2003* (pp. 10–13). Washington, DC: CIPE.

NPAA (2001). *National programme for the adoption of the acquis 2001*. Tallinn.

OECD (2000). *Entrepreneurship and enterprise development in the Baltic region: Policy guidelines and recommendations*. Baltic Regional Programme, Centre for Co-operation with Non-Members, Organisation for Economic Co-operation and Development, Paris.

OECD (2001). *Entrepreneurship and enterprise development in the Russian federation*. Centre for Co-operation with Non-Members, Organisation for Economic Co-operation and Development, Paris.

OECD (2002). *Estonia: a country assessment*. Centre for Co-operation with Non-Members, Organisation for Economic Co-operation and Development, Paris.

Oliver, C. (1991). Strategic responses to institutional processes. *Academy of Management Review, 16*(1), 145–179.

Peng, M. (2000). *Business strategies in transition economies*. Thousand Oaks: Sage.

Peng, M. (2003). Institutional transitions and strategic choices. *Academy of Management Review, 28*(2), 275–286.

Peng, M., & Heath, P. S. (1996). The growth of the firm in planned economies in transition: Institutions, organizations, and strategic choice. *Academy of Management Review, 21*(2), 492–528.

Radaev, V. (2001). Entrepreneurial strategies and the structure of transaction costs in Russian business. In: V. Bonnell & T. Gold (Eds), *The new entrepreneurs of Europe and Asia: Patterns of business development in Russia, Eastern Europe and China* (pp. 191–213). Armonk, NY: M.E. Sharpe.

Radaev, V. (2005). Establishing trust in a distrustful society: The case of Russian business. In: H.-H. Höhmann & F. Welter (Eds), *Trust and entrepeneurship: A West–East perspective* (pp. 114–135). Cheltenham: Edward Elgar.

Raiser, M. (1999). *Trust in transition*. EBRD Working Paper, 39, EBRD, London.

Raiser, M., Haerpfer, C., Nowotny, Th., & Wallace, C. (2001). *Social capital in transition: A first look at the evidence*. EBRD Working Paper, 61, EBRD, London.

Republic of Estonia (2001). Pre-accession economic programme. Tallinn, April.

Rose-Ackerman, S. (2001). Trust and honesty in post-socialist societies. *Kyklos, 54*(2/3), 415–444.

Satter, D. (2003). *Darkness at dawn: The rise of the Russian criminal state.* New Haven and London: Yale University Press.

Service, R. (2002). *Russia: Experiment with a people.* London, Basingstoke & Oxford: Macmillan.

Smallbone, D., & Welter, F. (2001a). The role of government in small business development in transition countries. *International Small Business Journal, 19*(4), 63–77.

Smallbone, D., & Welter, F. (2001b). The distinctiveness of entrepreneurship in transition economies. *Small Business Economics, 16*(4), 249–262.

Smallbone, D., Welter, F., Isakova, N., & Slonimski, A. (2001). The contribution of small and medium enterprises to economic development in Ukraine and Belarus: Some policy perspectives. *MOCT MOST: Economic Policy in Transitional Economies, 11,* 252–273.

Tonoyan, V. (2005). The dark side of trust: Corruption and entrepreneurship – a cross-national comparison between emerging and mature market economies. In: H.-H. Höhmann & F. Welter (Eds), *Trust and entrepeneurship: A West–East perspective* (pp. 39–58). Cheltenham: Edward Elgar.

Verheul, I., Wennekers, S., Audretsch, D., & Thurik, R. (2002). An eclectic theory of entrepreneurship: Policies, institutions and culture. In: D. Audretsch, R. Thurik, I. Verheul & S. Wennekers (Eds), *Entrepreneurship: Determinants and policy in a European-U.S. comparison* (pp. 11–81). Dordrecht: Kluwer.

Voigt, S., & Engerer, H. (2002). Institutions and transition – possible policy implications of the new institutional economics. In: K. Zimmermann (Ed.), *Frontiers in economics* (pp. 127–184). Heidelberg: Physica.

Voszka, E. (1991). From twilight into twilight: Transformation of the ownership structure in the big industries. *Acta Oeconomica, 43*(3–4), 281–296.

Voszka, E. (1994). The revival of redistribution in Hungary. *Acta Oeconomica, 46*(1–2), 63–78.

Welter, F. (1997). *Small and medium enterprises in Central and Eastern Europe: Trends, barriers and solutions.* RWI-Papier, 51. RWI, Essen.

Welter, F., Kautonen, T., Chepurenko, A., Malieva, E., & Venesaar, U. (2004). Trust environments and entrepreneurial behavior exploratory evidence from Estonia, Germany and Russia. *Journal of Enterprising Culture, 12*(4), 327–349.

Welter, F., & Smallbone, D. (2003). Entrepreneurship and enterprise strategies in transition economies: An institutional perspective. In: D. Kirby & A. Watson (Eds), *Small firms and economic development in developed and transition economies: A reader* (pp. 95–114). Aldershot: Ashgate.

Williamson, O. E. (2000). The new institutional economics: Taking stock, looking ahead. *Journal of Economic Literature, 38*(3), 595–613.

Wright, M., Filatotchev, I., Hoskisson, R., & Peng, M. (2005). Guest editors introduction: Strategy research in emerging economies: Challenging the conventional wisdom. *Journal of Management Studies, 42*(1), 1–33.

Yan, A., & Manolova, T. (1998). New and small players on shaky ground: A multicase study of emerging entrepreneurial firms in a transforming economy. *Journal of Applied Management Studies, 7*(1), 139–143.

Zecchini, S. (1997). Transition approaches in retrospect. In: S. Zecchini (Ed.), *Lessons from the economic transition: Central and Eastern Europe in the 1990s* (pp. 1–34). Dordrecht: Kluwer Academic Publishers.

Zhuk, V., & Cherevach, P. (2000). Problems of the current re-registration. *Small and Medium Business in Belarus: Analytical Bulletin, 2000*(1), 26–28.

ENTREPRENEURIAL ENVIRONMENT AND THE LIFE-CYCLE GROWTH AND DEVELOPMENT APPROACH TO ANALYZING FAMILY BUSINESSES IN THE TRANSITIONAL POLISH ECONOMY

Alina M. Zapalska and Dallas Brozik

1. INTRODUCTION

The economies of the former Soviet Union satellite countries have had to evolve during the past decade. Recent changes in the business environment of a transforming Polish economy have made entrepreneurial behaviors acceptable and thus have promoted the founding of new ventures. The private sector in Poland has proven to be one of the key mechanisms in achieving success in the transition of the economy. This study presents interviews conducted with entrepreneurs involved in tourism and hospitality. The major characteristics of the Polish tourism and hospitality industry are examined, and the difficulties that confront these small businesses are identified.

Developmental Entrepreneurship: Adversity, Risk, and Isolation
International Research in the Business Disciplines, Volume 5, 55–70
Copyright © 2006 by Elsevier Ltd.
All rights of reproduction in any form reserved
ISSN: 1074-7877/doi:10.1016/S1074-7877(06)05004-5

The study analyzes common characteristics among successful family owned and operated businesses in the tourism and hospitality industry to identify those characteristics that affect the success of entrepreneurs. Environmental conditions are examined to determine how they influence the development and growth of entrepreneurial activities. The relative frequencies of types of problems during the start-up and later stages are measured to indicate the differences in dominant problems at different stages of entrepreneurial business formation.

Differences in competencies of small business owners may affect the relationship between entry timing and new venture performance, and small business owners can face difficulties in identifying and making use of these competencies. Changes in the patterns of competencies as businesses move from start-up to a later stage could identify factors perceived to contribute to both the success and problems of entrepreneurial ventures.

2. BACKGROUND ON THE TRANSITION AND DEVELOPMENT OF SMALL POLISH BUSINESSES

Under state socialism, domestic tourism was very limited because workers and their families were unable to afford or gain access to domestic recreation. They were also denied access to foreign vacations for a variety of reasons including the lack of hard currency and the lack of bureaucratic status and connections. Several years before the collapse of state socialism, substantial adaptation of a few economic mechanisms had taken place. In the accommodation sector, the government permitted private citizens to operate small hotels and inns. Joint venture investments in high-quality accommodation had also been allowed to take place; however, it was not until 1989 that international tourist arrivals gained real momentum. This was when the changes in the tourism business of the post-communist era became apparent.

The growth in receipts was dramatic in the first half of the 1990s as Polish tourist businesses began to achieve some success in marketing higher-value niche products. The need for staff training in hotel management, catering, and travel agency and in related areas such as computing, telecommunications, and foreign languages was recognized. Multilateral aid from Western institutions had provided an important source of support for infrastructure projects and the encouragement of inward investment. Since the 1990s, small entrepreneurial firms within the tourism and hospitality industry have developed in all parts of the Polish economy. The marketing and image projections were repositioned to encourage higher-spending, season-extending tourists rather than increased numbers. This sector started as a simple, relatively low-skilled segment of the market by offering accommodation and related services to travelers.

The increasing economic prosperity in the Central and Eastern Europe (CEE) economies has created a relatively larger amount of leisure time and discretionary income so that more people can enjoy the benefits and pleasure of domestic and international tourism. Greater mobility has drawn the attention of potential customers to previously unknown destinations within the CEE. Tourism and hospitality is one of the fastest growing industries in Poland today.

Poland has devoted a great deal of effort to reforming its economic system so that it better serves the country's developmental objectives. One objective has been to establish the predominance of the private sector such as individually owned businesses, joint ventures, or wholly foreign-owned enterprises that operate on the profit-motivated basis. Control of state enterprises has been transferred to enterprise managers who are responding increasingly to market pressures rather than official directives. Foreign investors have taken an interest in certain state-run enterprises, and performance records show a significant improvement after privatization of these enterprises.

The current situation of the private sector in Poland is fairly clear, but the transition from a centrally planned economy to a market economy represents an enormous challenge. It has proved to be a difficult and lengthy process for most entrepreneurial ventures. It must be mentioned, however, that the success of Polish reform efforts is attributable to the impressive growth of entrepreneurial firms and the small family businesses during the past decade. The non-state sector has contributed to the reform process through its strong performance and has absorbed surplus labor and provided competition to the state-run enterprises. Much of the growth of the small business sector has been in light manufacturing, service, and the hospitality and tourism industries. These industries were severely neglected in Poland by the communist industrialization strategy that focused primarily on the development of heavy industry. Thus, one explanation for the rapid rise of private enterprises and family businesses is their ability to exploit gaps in Poland's industrial structure and respond to substantial unsatisfied demand in sectors previously repressed.

Entrepreneurs that operate small family businesses face many problems that inhibit the growth and development of their family firms. Access to bank loans is limited because banks are reluctant to lend to untried, private clients with no track record. The positive side of limited bank finance is that the process of private equity creation is underway as profits get reinvested. There is some evidence that as entrepreneurs establish their reputations, access to bank loans becomes easier. The greatest challenges faced by Polish businesses over the last decade have created and strengthened the basic institutions that underpin market systems such as

(1) developing new forms of economic motivation for individuals and organizations to be innovative and productive,
(2) protecting private property rights,
(3) guaranteeing freedom of entrepreneurial ventures,
(4) encouraging decision-making based on market signals,
(5) developing a competitive business environment, and
(6) implementing regulations and laws guiding and restricting private sector activities.

An increased awareness of the perceived problems of entrepreneurial ventures and a better assessment of factors and conditions that either promote or hold back private-sector development in Poland may result in a better understanding of the challenges and difficulties that those firms have to face in an integrated global economy. An evaluation of government policies may have a substantial effect on the development and further growth of the private sector in all countries of the region.

3. THE STUDY

Several models have been advanced that attempt to label and explain the various stages of development of small business firms (Galbraith, 1982; Smith, Mitchell, & Summer, 1985; Cowan, 1990). Models of organizational life-cycles and stages of development provide information on the types of problems encountered by firms over time and suggest that each stage of development is associated with a unique set of problems (Ackoff, 1963; Kazanjian, 1988; Kuratko & Hodgetts, 1989; Zapalska, 1997; Zapalska & Fogel, 1998). Kazanjian (1988) identifies four specific stages that the entrepreneurial firm passes through (Table 1).

This four-stage life-cycle approach permits the examination of the growth and development of the Polish small family businesses in the context of a transitional economy reforming from a centralized to a more decentralized

Table 1. Stages of Growth and Development of an Entrepreneurial Firm.

Conception and development stage	Stage I
Commercialization stage	Stage II
Growth stage	Stage III
Stability stage	Stage IV

means of resource allocation. The model identifies the problems confronted by these businesses at their different levels of growth and development.

Competence plays an important role in strategic management and is particularly important for a new venture and its growth and development. A firm's competence is understood in terms of how it matches the basic requirements for success by the industrial environment and in terms of skills and capabilities relative to firm's competitors. Competence represents entrepreneurial skills that can be applied toward strategic performance. These include financial, managerial, functional, and organizational skills and are influenced by an entrepreneurial firm's reputation and history (Andrews, 1987). Distinctive competencies arise from the strengths and weaknesses of the individuals in the firm, the degree to which an individual's capability is effectively applied to a common task, and coordination of a group task. In order to provide a wider definition of competence, Kay (1995) refers to four types of general competence that a firm may possess: architecture; reputation; innovation; and control of strategic assets (Table 2).

A firm's limited competence indicates that the entrepreneurial firm lacks important contacts, credibility with buyers, and other industry-specific information that may lead to a greater possibility of being a new firm with a greater risk of failure (Bruderl & Schussler, 1990). This implies that industry-specific information is a significant determinant of venture survival (Bruderl, Preisendorfer, & Ziegler (1992). New venture performance, whether seen in terms of survival or the probability of survival, appears to be enhanced by a management team with high levels of industry-related competence. Success is more likely to be achieved by those entering an industry in which they have prior experience (Vesper, 1990; Chandler & Hanks, 1991). Ventures need to be well managed by individuals with solid entrepreneurial and business skills. These individuals need to have entrepreneurial and marketing skills that involve not only knowledge of whom to market to but also how to market.

There have been changes in the entrepreneurial environment, business culture, and management in the post-communist economies, but there have

Table 2.   Types of General Competencies a Firm May Possess.

Type and Characteristics

Architecture

The venture must have the ability to create knowledge, respond to changing circumstances, foster easy and open exchanges of information within the firm and other groups of firms, know where critical interactions occur, and collect information about such interactions in a timely and cost-effective manner.

Reputation

The positioning of the venture and its managers in external status hierarchies communicates information to customers and shareholders on quality, efficiency, dependability, and related performance attributes. Possession of a positive reputation serves to lower the search costs for customers, buyers, and suppliers and thus aids them in their decisions regarding doing business with the venture.

Innovation

Innovations are resources which when skillfully developed and marketed can lead to strong advantages. The capabilities involved in bringing new innovations to market include limiting bureaucratic pressures during product development, providing a place within a firm where new products can mature without being stifled by standardized control systems, and creating channels through which innovations can be matched to customer needs.

Control of strategic assets

Skills at exploiting market situations that limit the extent of price competition, restrict entry or imitation, or raise the price of switching to substitute products can provide long-term advantages to the firms that possess them. Competence in controlling strategic assets enhances a firm's profitability.

been no studies examining family businesses and entrepreneurial firms that operate in tourism and hospitality industries. There is a need for a comprehensive analysis of entrepreneurship in family businesses, and it is necessary to identify and describe the environmental factors that have an impact on the development of family businesses in a transitional economy. The Polish experience may not be the same as other transitional economies, but it can provide an example for the analysis of the role that environment can play in entrepreneurial development. Analysis of the social cognitive variables that may mediate the impact of the environmental forces on entrepreneurial development may suggest new directions for future research and practice.

The data for the analysis were generated by telephone interviews in March and April of 2003. A random sample of 50 small family businesses was selected. The sample is composed of small family businesses that operate within the tourism and hospitality industry in the southern region of Poland.

These businesses are typically small with the number of employees ranging from 1 to 50 with low sales volume and low profit margins. These family businesses engage in such business activities as bed and breakfasts, hotels, coffee shops, restaurants and catering, and tourist bureaus and offices.

The questionnaire elicited information on the size and nature of the operation, business objectives, level of employment, financial assistance received and desired, non-financial support, business training needs, socioeconomic conditions, policies on taxation, preferences, credit financing, and reporting requirements for small businesses. Respondents could give more than one answer to each question.

4. BUSINESS CHARACTERISTICS

Entrepreneurial firms within the tourism industry have developed in all parts of the Polish economy since the 1990s, and the southern region of Poland has experienced the greatest number of new businesses operating within the tourism industry. Tourism activities cover a wide spectrum of services such as bed and breakfasts, hotels, restaurants, transportation services, and tourism and travel agency services. The most common tourist activities provided by these businesses are: pilgrims/visiting pilgrimage places, national parks/nature experience and other outdoor activities, arts festivals/cultural events, visiting art galleries and museums, and visiting historical places.

The businesses are relatively young; the average length of activity is about 10 years. More than 25 percent of the respondents had already set up their ventures before the 1990s when the restrictions on private activity were lifted, however, the skills acquired before 1991 have not always been useful in the new economic and political environment. The sizes of businesses were relatively small. Thirty percent of the businesses employed fewer than 10 employees, and 70 percent of the businesses employed from 10 to 30 employees.

Successful small tourism and hospitality businesses are typically those that developed a strong competitive advantage by focusing on a particular product or niche market rather than by diversifying services. Offering higher quality services and products has been the key to their survival and growth. The new tourism in post-communist Poland is perceived to be oriented toward more tourists who are better educated, more culturally aware, better attuned to the natural environment, and more active. These social trends have generated new demand patterns for travel and tourism and changing product needs.

The decision to set up a business was based on a variety of reasons such as: a better way of life (72 percent), a recognized market opportunity (70 percent), the desire for independence (68 percent), to supplement family income (65 percent) and, unemployment or company layoff (50 percent). Related studies of small and family-based businesses operating within tourism and hospitality have highlighted similar results stressing that strong motivational elements associated with lifestyle and family-related goals contributed to the firm's success (Getz & Carlsen, 2000).

Approximately 71 percent of the small businesses surveyed produce for local market, 15 percent for the national market, 4 percent for both national and local, 6 percent for national and foreign markets, and 4 percent for foreign markets. The overall education level of the entrepreneurs was above the national average. Thirty-four percent of respondents had some college education, 30 percent had graduated from high school, and the rest of respondents had at least some high school education.

The reasons given for going into business were diverse. The most common reason was "to let an entrepreneur do the kind of work he/she wanted to do" (60 percent) and "to continue the family business" (45 percent). More than 16 percent of the entrepreneurs expressed that they wanted to become wealthy, but 98 percent respondents expressed that they wanted to have steady employment. More than 85 percent of the respondents had some previous business experience in the business in which they were engaged while 10 percent had some business experience but unrelated to their present business interests. Eighty-six percent of the firms started with funds provided solely by their owners, 10 percent from bank funds, and 5 percent from Small Business Investment Companies. Forty-eight percent of entrepreneurs operated at the Commercial stage, 46 percent at the Growth stage, and the remaining 6 percent at the Stability stage. The family businesses operating at the second stage had been in business for about nine years.

Respondents were asked to identify important economic concerns regarding running their family businesses at various stages of their growth and development. Several possible factors for concern were suggested and are presented in Table 3. The respondents were asked to comment on the stages they had reached, but answers were not expected on stages that they had not attained. Table 3 presents the relative frequencies of occurrence of each type of problems encountered at the four different stages of family business development.

From the respondents' rankings, the following factors were important economic concerns: domestic competition, high interest rates, unavailability of long-term capital and lack of financial assistance, growth of the economy,

Table 3.   Important Concerns while Running the Family Business According to the Stage of Firm's Development.

Name of Concern	Percentage of Occurrences by Stage			
	I	II	III	IV
High interest rates	77	76	72	75
Unavailability of financial assistance	93	99	87	81
Domestic competition	87	76	56	27
Energy costs	87	84	87	90
Growth of economy	98	87	88	77
Availability of short-term capital	45	67	80	100
Regulatory environment	67	57	45	46
Weak collateral position	75	56	74	6
Lack of quality control	78	74	41	35
Ability to pass on price increases	73	79	8	–
State or local taxes	15	20	46	56
Low demand	36	46	14	4
Lack of commercial Advertising	68	28	4	–
Foreign competition	23	12	7	13

Stage I, conception and development; Stage II, commercialization; Stage III, growth; Stage IV, stability.

state or local taxes, labor costs and labor quality, energy costs, and low demand. The respondents indicate that competition is increasing from other parts of the country and from foreign competitors.

The survey results show dramatic changes from the first three stages of development to the stability stage in some areas. Despite the fact that the majority of problems constraining entrepreneurs occurred during the first three stages, a majority of firms managed not only to survive but also to increase their family business activities. Their businesses identified as major problems those that related to the investment environment such as inadequate energy supply, red tape, non-convertible currency during first years of operation, and the lack of exposure to international concepts of accounting. They also repeatedly expressed that the greatest hurdle to economic growth of the non-state sector is infrastructure bottlenecks. The poor infrastructure represents an enormous strain on the growth of the economy, and its limitations act as a deterrent to foreign investment in many areas. Respondents stated that what is required for business growth and success is to meet international standards, promote the highest quality service, improve management and efficiency, and have the technology appropriate to their needs.

Table 4. Occurrence of Competencies Expressed as Necessary for Success by Development.

	Type of Competency (in Percentages)		
Architecture	Reputation	Innovation	Controlling Strategic Assets
Stage I: Conception and development			
99	26	79	70
Stage II: Commercialization			
82	78	90	89
Stage III: Growth			
96	89	94	69
Stage IV: Stability			
75	94	97	55

The success of these businesses in the presence of an inadequate infrastructure indicates that there must be some competencies working in the background. Table 4 summarizes the competencies reported by the respondents.

Innovation is one of the key elements of competency at all stages of growth and development of the family businesses. New and family businesses that are *innovative* or oriented toward innovative strategies are typically resource poor, that is, low in key resources, such as financial, human, and social capital. Although the resources that a start-up family business has at its disposal may be sufficient to pioneer the market, growth creates a considerable and dangerous strain on these resources. *Architecture* plays an important role as a competency. It involves the skills of knowing where critical interactions occur for a business and collecting information about such interactions in the most timely and cost-effective manner. These competencies play a very important role in the earlier stages of a firm's growth and development.

Reputation plays an important role in the later stages of a firm's growth and development. Possession of a positive reputation serves to lower the search costs of customers, buyers, and suppliers and thus aids them in their decisions regarding doing business with the family business. Because it takes a long time to develop and is difficult to imitate, the reputation of family firms can be a source of sustainable competitive advantage in the very difficult environment of the reforming economy.

Competence in *controlling strategic assets* enhances firm profitability. It will generate competitive pressures from new entrants or industry competitors that eventually lead to the dissipation of excess profits and a return to competitive conditions. Polish family businesses have been operating in increasingly competitive conditions since the economic and political reforms were implemented. Controlling strategic assets has been mentioned as more important at the earlier stages of growth and development. Skills developed in exploiting market situations that limit the extent of price competition, restrict entry, or raise the price of switching to substitute products provide long-term advantages to the family firms that possess them.

The specific sets of competencies that are necessary for success vary widely across Polish family businesses and are difficult to know prior to entry due to the nature of the tourism and hospitality industry. A new family business can be successful with largely industry-specific competencies at the time of initial entry, but it will require organizational and marketing capabilities to grow and prosper.

5. BUSINESS ENVIRONMENT

Information about the elements of the business environment represented as "received" and "desired" are presented in Table 5. In all categories of both the non-financial and financial environment, the level of support "received" was much lower than what was "desired."

The majority of respondents indicated that management training seminars and workshops are desirable but few received them. A large percentage of respondents reported that networks and trade fairs, technical assistance, and management training are needed for their business growth and development. Information technology and communication networks were desired by 90 percent of the respondents, but only 8 percent received them. Only 10 percent of the respondents were able to take advantage of incubator centers or industrial parks.

The majority of respondents, 88 percent, would like to have greater access to tax allowances. Other types of financial assistance required include low-cost and long-term loans (98 percent), project financing (34 percent), and increased opportunities for venture capital (22 percent). The pattern of receiving actual assistance indicated a reliance on personal sources such as borrowing from friends and family. Many of the respondents used reinvesting or short-term credit financing as a source of financial support.

Table 5.   Environmental Evaluation.

	Received (%)	Desired (%)
Non-financial environment		
Information technology/communication networks	8	90
Small business management training	5	87
Technical and financial assistance	14	83
Incubator centers/industrial parks	10	80
Social and entrepreneurial networks	12	76
Trade fairs and industry shows	7	72
Presence of a mentor	2	68
Information technology/communication networks	10	56
Support from friends and family	25	56
Presence of role models	20	34
Educational background	25	32
Financial environment		
Borrowing from friends/family	25	30
Short-term credit	24	40
Foreign investor/venture capital	8	22
Project financing	2	34
Tax allowance and credits	4	88
Preferential loans to small businesses	–	98
Low-cost, long-term loan	–	67

The gradual installation of new telecommunications resources and the advent of increased competition between domestic and foreign banks have resulted in services becoming increasingly more user-friendly and efficient. But according to our respondents, the banks have still been inefficient in their transfer of money into and out of Poland. Regulation of the banking system has also been unsatisfactory. The government's credit policy has not been able to help the private sector. Faced with an inflation rate that remained relatively high, the government maintained high nominal interest rates. The high level of nominal interest rates combined with instability in the real interest rate discouraged private borrowing.

Restructuring the tourist and hospitality industry itself took place during the first years of the economic reforms. At that time, a concentration in the sector and the emergence of international hotel chains came under control of a few tourist operators who previously had controlled a significant part of the international market. These operators still continue to dominate the hotel accommodation market as well as the tourist transport market. By a combination of various opportunities and by using the modern information and communication technology, they have been in a position to control large parts of the travel agency market and the transport market for international tourists. As a consequence, small tourist carriers, hotel owners, and other tourist and hospitality service providers tend to become increasingly dependent on a group of large operators. This situation raises the question of how small businesses in tourism and hospitality can exploit the opportunities of the modern information and communication sector in such an environment.

Respondents were asked to rate their satisfaction with the items identified as policies and procedures for success of their entrepreneurial activities. Table 6 presents data on the respondents' perceptions of environmental conditions for their tourism and hospitality activities. The highest positive ratings were observed on licensing and registration requirements ($M = 3.03$) and business training programs ($M = 2.48$). The lowest levels of satisfaction were reported on credit terms and finance, taxation incentives and exemptions, and competition among businesses within their industry.

During the early years of the operations, macroeconomic problems, particularly high inflation, held back business development. Those who survived realized that the product quality and the strategy of the firm were of paramount importance. Today, these businesses offer high quality, unique products, such as educational, horseback riding, eco-tourism, or pilgrimage tours. The businesses also concentrate on providing products and services with cost advantages. The reduction in costs is achieved by taking advantage of economies of scale that are derived from the integrated operating methods of businesses in the industry. The product or service is no longer considered as a set of individual services but rather as a system with vertical integration among the productive activities that play a role in the final consumption of services and a system with horizontal integration among tourist operators in the region. Those firms that are unable to deal with these processes through

Table 6. Evaluation of Environmental Factors.

Small Business Conditions	Satisfaction Ratings (1–4)*				Mean
	(1) (%)	(2) (%)	(3) (%)	(4) (%)	
Licensing/registration requirements	–	35	27	38	3.03
Business training programs	15	22	63	–	2.48
Laws and regulations	20	24	56	–	2.36
Small network/information availability	25	45	30	–	2.05
Competition within industry	35	45	20	–	1.85
Taxation/incentives/exemptions	33	42	25	–	1.92
Credit terms/finance	75	20	5	–	1.30

*Rating scale: 1 = must be improved; 2 = fair, 3 = average, and 4 = good.

vertical integration strategies must adopt a strategy involving product quality and relational links among the other small businesses of the region. Successful businesses became market oriented, were willing to seek out customers, were concerned with delivering a high-quality product, and were always looking for opportunities to improve their performance.

6. POLICY IMPLICATIONS

In order to promote an active tourist and hospitality industry in the Polish economy, the government needs to create the conditions that will reassure private investors and encourage them to consider tourism development as an attractive investment opportunity. Policy decisions have to consider economic, psychological, and environmental factors. One psychological factor that is important in predicting entrepreneurial success is encouraging or teaching business owners how to be innovative with regard to products and processes. To be innovative requires a clear vision or idea of what one wants to achieve, a safe group climate that allows one to propose ideas, and policies that support innovation.

The importance of economic factors has not diminished. These results indicate that entrepreneurial development and small business growth is still hindered by high taxation and the lack of low-cost, long-term financing to small business. Other perceived difficulties include unfavorable credit terms, the attitude of banks toward small business, the lack of tax incentives and preferences, and the lack of venture capital and project financing. The government needs to assure that the proper financial incentives are available for entrepreneurial firms. It is necessary to reduce political barriers to the development of small businesses and stimulate small-scale entrepreneurs economically. Environmental factors that will assist small business expansion include providing technical support, improving access to technology, increasing opportunities for entrepreneurial and business training, promoting small business success and small business networks, creating societal awareness of entrepreneurship, and reducing reporting requirements for small businesses. Government policies should be enacted to improve these conditions.

7. CONCLUSIONS

The private sector in Poland has proven to be the key mechanism for affecting economic transition. Economic reform unleashed the private sector in a direction that was consistent with industrial and macroeconomic stability. However, after a decade of systemic transformation, entrepreneurial ventures are still facing difficulties. Environmental pressures have altered the basic nature of entrepreneurial businesses creating an increase in the quality of their services and products. Successful entrepreneurs are typically those who have focused on a particular product or niche market and developed a strong competitive advantage there, rather than by diversifying. Offering higher quality and better services and products has been the key to rapid growth, but there are still many barriers to development and growth.

The chances of small family business firms' survival and growth at different stages of development reflect the number and types of barriers to operation. Despite the many problems and obstacles encountered, the family businesses were able to grow. They had to operate under hard budget constraints, uncertain and poor economic conditions, poor banking conditions and preferences, a low level of capitalization, poor infrastructure, and growing competition from domestic and foreign firms, but hard work and a desire to succeed helped overcome these problems. Given all the difficulties, Polish family businesses have displayed intensive activity and a high level of entrepreneurial propensity. The ability to think, be innovative, strategic, opportunistic, and be able to make efficient and rational decisions enabled most of the respondents to succeed, grow and move up to the next stage of development.

Certain policy measures are needed to promote more family business development in Poland. It is important that local authorities pursue a joint economic policy to improve the general infrastructure and promote the creation of the necessary economic conditions to support the growth of existing firms and encourage a development of new entrepreneurial activities within hospitality and tourism industries.

In order to identify the competencies necessary for entrepreneurial success, a new venture can refer to the development of an existing industry and adopt a flexible posture so it can more quickly learn what competencies are necessary for success and then acquire them. The ability to adapt to the environment is often difficult due to a new firm's inertia, however, *architecture, reputation, innovation,* and *control of strategic assets* are examples of how a new entrepreneurial family business can assess the environment and take the risk of entry. As entrepreneurial firms in transition economies face various problems and uncertainties from the continuing instability of fundamental rules of the market economy paradigm, the profile of the environment remains important. Future research should explore the problems these firms face and examine the importance of small business on regional economic growth and development.

REFERENCES

Ackoff, R. (1963). *A manager's guide to operations research.* New York: Wiley.

Andrews, K. (1987). *The concept of corporate strategy.* Homewood, IL: Irwin.

Bruderl, J., Preisendorfer, P., & Ziegler, R. (1992). Survival chances of newly founded business organizations. *American Sociological Review, 57,* 227–242.

Bruderl, J., & Schussler, R. (1990). Organizational mortality: The liability of newness and adolescence. *Administrative Science Quarterly, 35,* 530–547.

Chandler, G., & Hanks S. (1991). How important is experience in a highly similar field? *Proceeding: Research Conference* (pp. 1–10). Babson College.

Cowan, D. (1990). Developing a classification structure of organizational problems: An empirical examination. *Academy of Management Journal, 33*(2), 366–390.

Galbraith, J. (1982). Stages of growth. *Journal of Business Strategy, 3*(1), 70–79.

Getz, D., & Carlsen, J. (2000). Characteristics and goals of family and owner-operated businesses in the rural tourism and hospitality sector. *Tourism Management, 21,* 546–560.

Kay, J. (1995). *Foundation of corporate success.* New York: Oxford University Press.

Kazanjian, R. (1988). Relation of dominant problems to stages of growth in technology-based new ventures. *Academy of Management Journal, 31*(2), 257–279.

Kuratko, D., & Hodgetts, R. (1989). *Entrepreneurship: A contemporary approach.* Chicago: Dryden Press.

Smith, K., Mitchell, T., & Summer, C. (1985). Top-level management priorities in different stages of the organizational life-cycle. *Academy of Management Journal, 28,* 799–820.

Vesper, K. (1990). *New venture strategies.* Englewood Cliffs, NJ: Prentice-Hall.

Zapalska, A. (1997). Profiles of Polish entrepreneurship. *Journal of Small Business Management, 35*(2), 111–117.

Zapalska, A., & Fogel, G. (1998). Characteristics of Polish and Hungarian entrepreneurs. *Journal of Private Enterprise, 13*(2), 132–144.

TRANSITION IN THE POLISH ECONOMY[☆]

Richard J. Hunter, Jr. and Leo V. Ryan

1. TRANSITION IN THE CONTEXT OF A CENTRALLY PLANNED ECONOMY

It has been slightly more than 15 years since Poland embarked on its ambitious program of political and economic transformation. A synthetic review and analysis of this process seems to be in order.

A centrally planned economy is an organizational and economic system in which the factors of production are owned or are tightly controlled by the state. As such, the state makes all or nearly all economic decisions. Central planning agencies of Poland and their counterparts in the political and economic bureaucracy (known as the nomenklatura) set detailed production goals for all segments of the economy, determined inputs, and administratively fixed prices for all, or the great majority, of goods and services. Theoretically, at least, the system of central planning was designed to achieve a wide range of core political, economic, and social objectives – the most important of which was full employment – of course, always as determined by central authorities (Kornai, 1992; Berry & Jaruga, 1983). In reality, it was often said of pre-transition Poland that "They (meaning the bureaucracy) pretend they pay us; so we pretend we work."

☆ This chapter is based upon a earlier paper published in *Global Economy Journal*, 5(2), 2005.

Developmental Entrepreneurship: Adversity, Risk, and Isolation
International Research in the Business Disciplines, Volume 5, 71–87
Copyright © 2006 by Elsevier Ltd.
All rights of reproduction in any form reserved
ISSN: 1074-7877/doi:10.1016/S1074-7877(06)05005-7

By the time of the collapse of the Soviet-inspired system of central planning in "democratic and socialist" Poland in the period 1988–1989 (a system which Stalin had reportedly remarked would "fit Poland like a saddle fits a cow") the nomenklatura system had developed into a highly centralized administrative structure – not only for national economic and political organs but also for small- and medium-sized organizations and enterprises – which operated only as a part of a huge centrally organized and bloated bureaucracy. The other key players in this tripartite structure were the official state or government apparatus and the Polish United Workers' or Communist Party. By the late 1980s, the system of central planning had virtually elapsed into a "lunatic collage of incompetence, privilege, pandering and outright corruption," based on a "principle of underqualification" and a "perverted practice of negative selection" (Weschler, 1982). Although the system of central planning has been systematically dismantled, remnants and quite visible reminders of the nomenklatura system are still present. Not surprisingly, the role of the nomenklatura is still hotly debated in the Polish society.

After 1989, as the prospects for advancing their bureaucratic careers in the new system initially appeared more limited, the members of the nomenklatura in Poland almost immediately became active in privatized businesses and banks in a variant of privatization that has sometimes derisively been referred to as "spontaneous privatization." Others brand it simply "institutional theft" by the nomenklatura of state assets, apartments, property, and profitable state-owned enterprises. Members of the nomenklatura have also benefited politically and economically from popular discontent that is practically unavoidable during economic reforms started under very difficult economic conditions and circumstances. As a result, members of the nomenklatura have been judged to be major "winners" in the transformation process (Hunter, Ryan, & Hrechak, 1994). Ironically, the Democratic Left Alliance or SLD, the successor to the Polish United Workers' or Communist Party and an outgrowth, the newly formed Polish Social Democracy, are populated by many former members of the nomenklatura and are today the mainstay of capitalism in Poland and the champion of the emerging and burgeoning capitalist business class.

The system of central planning is also referred to as the monocentric system or the command-rationing mechanism (CRM). As it operated throughout the region of Central and Eastern Europe, but most especially in Poland, the CRM was characterized by certain derivative traits that were inimical to and destructive of the three cornerstones of potential economic and political transformation. These cornerstones were the privatization process, the development of Poland's export sector, and the attraction of significant amounts of foreign direct investment (FDI) into the Polish economy (Hunter, Shapiro, & Ryan, 2003; Hunter & Ryan, 2001, 2003, 2004). The decidedly negative traits of the CRM included administrative price-fixing by central authorities of all nature of goods and services "officially produced" in the Polish economy, isolation of domestic producers from foreign markets, enterprises' "soft budget constraints" where the "national budget" was literally a "national joke," and extreme monopolization in the hands of the state of everything in society that had any real economic value.

It is no surprise, then, that by 1989 and the historic "round table" that led to the overwhelming victory of Solidarity in the "semi-free" elections in the spring of that same year, the system of central planning literally imploded in Poland, and eventually in the entire region of Central and Eastern Europe. Despite the persistent "propaganda of success" put forth by the Polish government and the blathering of the Polish Communist Party, the central planning system imploded, because of a combination of four interrelated factors. First, the CRM failed to create economic value and to improve the standard of living for the average Pole. For example, it often took 20 years for an individual to secure a private apartment or a private telephone. Second, the Polish economy failed to "measure up" to comparative economics, not only those capitalist economies in the West like the United States, France, Italy, or West Germany, but also several "fraternal" socialist economies in Central and Eastern Europe, especially, Hungary, Slovenia, and Czechoslovakia, later the Czech Republic. Third, the Polish economy failed to satisfy basic consumer needs, essentially creating a dollarization of the Polish economy through the existence of a large, open, "semi-official," and surprisingly efficient black market and long lines or queues for all consumer goods. By the summer of 1988, Polish stores literally had nothing to sell on their shelves. "Special shops," called PEWEX, had shelves stocked with all nature of goods, but sold only for dollars. Fourth, and probably most important, the CRM failed to provide adequate individual and organizational incentives.

1.1. The Attempt at Reform of the CRM

Given the dual economic and political aspects of the CRM and the enormity of its negative legacy of more than 45 years, reform of the central planning system has posed a considerable challenge from the outset and has involved a delicate blending of both political and economic considerations in the adoption of the following macro strategies first advanced by the Mazowiecki government in the fall of 1989:

1. Attaining political stability and pluralism, which would be accomplished through holding free and multiparty elections as soon as possible after the collapse of the prior closed political system (this proved to be the easy part of transition).
2. Implementing a program of "real" economic reform with the evolution to a full private market economy, involving an emphasis on the development of a substantial private sector and a reduction of the state sector through a multi-track program of privatization.
3. Creating the basic institutions of capitalism, including a private banking system, credit institutions, customs and clearing houses, currency exchanges, a private insurance system, the reintroduction of the Polish stock market, and the creation of investment vehicles like stocks, bonds, and mutual funds – all of which are taken very much for granted in the West.

From the outset, three important questions dominated conversations concerning the transformation process: How would it be possible to create capitalism in a nation where there was neither capital nor capitalists? What should be the role of the nomenklatura and ex-communists in the political and economic life of Polish society? And, what would the system do about workers and others most negatively affected by the transition (Hunter & Ryan, 2000)?

The attempt to move Poland from a system dominated by central planning to "some other system" – and no one was exactly sure what the new system would be – was based upon the following core assumptions (Balcerowicz, 1995):

1. The authoritarian nature of the society must gradually change into one based on administrative and bureaucratic competence, so as to weaken the decisive role of central authorities and to strengthen the role of market mechanisms in resource allocations.
2. Accepting that the system of central planning actually hampers economic analysis and hence does not provide sufficiently accurate information for effective decision-making, the top–down "command-and-control" economy and administrative system must gradually change into a system based upon information sharing and verification, consultation, and cooperation among all segments of Polish society (Nikolaenko, 2002).
3. The state-run society must gradually change into a full civil society (Hunter & Ryan, 1998), marked by community self-governance, trade

and economic discipline, honest career building, and "independent individuals characterized by self-esteem, self-reliance, and self-empowerment" (Fulin, 2002).

1.2. A Brief Focus on Polish Privatization

The multi-track approach to privatization adopted in Poland has involved a myriad of concurrent, sometimes seemingly inconsistent, strategies including re-privatization to former owners, the "small" privatization process, eventual privatization by liquidation, "mass" privatization, and the sectoral approach involving the creation of the National Investment Funds. In this context, four main options or variants for privatization were adopted: commercial (traditional) privatization through the capital market; privatization through employee ownership (termed the ESOP option); privatization through some form of "citizenship ownership"; and privatization through institutional investors (Blasczyk & Dabrowski, 1993). In the first half of 1990, more than 100 state-owned-enterprises indicated their interest in participating in the privatization process. On September 27, 1990, the Ministry of Privatization undertook its first major step. De la Rosa, Crawford and Franz (2004) report that the "'Magnificent Seven,' a name given to the first seven enterprises privatized according to the 1990 Law on Privatization, were established as wholly owned companies of the Polish state treasury." This group included Exbud (construction), Fampa (industrial paper production machinery), Inowroclaw (meat packing), Kable (industrial electro-engineering), Krosno (commercial and consumer glass products), Norblin (metal industrial products), and Prochnik (clothing). When the public subscription began on November 30, 1990, shares of Exbud, Kable, Krosno, and Prochnik, as well as a new firm, Tonsil (electro-acoustic equipment), were offered to the public.

Listings on the Warsaw Stock Exchange for 1997 included 15 National Investment Funds, which were initially created to implement the "mass privatization" program and to provide the necessary framework in order to restructure and privatize more than 500 state-owned enterprises. The history of the National Investment Funds is quite interesting. In December of 1994, the Ministry of the Treasury established 15 funds as joint-stock, limited liability companies, wholly owned by the Treasury. During the next two-year period, the Ministry transferred 60 percent of the shares of the selected state-owned enterprises to the National Investment Funds, retaining 25 percent in the Treasury and reserving 15 percent for employees. Share certificates were then distributed to Polish citizens – with more than

27 million Poles eligible to purchase one certificate each for 20 zlotys (approximately U.S.$7.00). One original certificate purchased on the so-called primary market could be redeemed for one share in each of the 15 National Investment Funds. The funds began trading on the Warsaw Stock Exchange on July 15, 1997 (Hunter, Ryan, & Shapiro, 2004). A capital market thus rose literally from the ashes of the CRM.

2. THE FOUNDATIONS OF ECONOMIC TRANSFORMATION IN POLAND

The process of economic transformation in Poland is quite instructive and has provided a more general model for other Central and Eastern European transition economies. Conceived by the then Minister of Finance and Deputy Prime Minister Leszek Balcerowicz, the program was based on five philosophical pillars of economic transformation: (1) rapid transformation of the monocentric system of state central planning into a functioning private market economy; (2) liberalization of economic functions, especially in relation to foreign trade and FDI; (3) privatization of state-owned enterprises; (4) construction of an effective social safety net by reforming the pension, education, health care, and social security systems; and (5) mobilization of international financial assistance to support the process.

In the process of economic transformation, Minister Balcerowicz was aided by a well-prepared transition team consisting of Polish nationals and émigré specialists. Many of the foreign advisers were of Polish origin – so-called Polonia academics and Polonia economists. The leading foreign expert was Harvard Economist Jeffrey Sachs (1993) (Lipton & Sachs, 1990), who currently heads the Earth Institute at Columbia in New York City. Sachs also serves as a Special Advisor to United Nations Secretary Kofi Annan on a group of poverty reduction initiatives called the Millennium Development Goals. Both Balcerowicz, who currently serves as President of the National Bank of Poland, and Sachs remain enigmatic and quite controversial figures even today in Poland.

2.1. Enter the Balcerowicz Team

The "Balcerowicz Team" consisted of numerous foreign advisors, in addition to Sachs, and numerous Polish ones. Along with Balcerowicz himself, on the team were his deputies and advisors in the Ministry of Finance and the top members of the Polish National Bank. Virtually, all of the Poles were graduates of the Faculty of Foreign Trade of the Central School of Planning and Statistics in Warsaw, Poland's premier school for state planning and policy experts and later to become the Warsaw School of Economics. Minister Balcerowicz himself was a graduate of the school and subsequently a Professor of Economics. Between September 1972 and January 1974, Balcerowicz had studied business administration at St. John's University in New York City. In 1978, Balcerowicz presciently had established a "think tank" composed of 10 young economists who met regularly to discuss and debate potential programs for economic reform. These informal meetings shaped the program of transformation adopted by the Mazowiecki government and subsequent Solidarity governments and greatly influenced all post-1989 Polish governments, whether post-communist or post-Solidarity (Hunter & Ryan, 1998).

Mirroring the Balcerowicz–Sachs model, Poland has undertaken the following concrete actions as the main components of its process of economic reform:

- Liberalizing prices from state control, opening up of the foreign trade regime, and formalizing and simplifying the requirements for new market entry.
- Stabilizing inflation, public finance, and foreign debt.
- Effecting changes in the economy leading to privatization of state property and to an increase in the nature and volume of international trade.
- Creating new market institutions, a commercial code, a revised tax code, private property rights, and a financial and capital market sector (perhaps, most importantly, the creation of a viable stock market).
- Remodeling and upgrading the important social-safety net, most especially, the pension, education, social insurance, and unemployment systems.
- Assuring full convertibility of the Polish zloty.
- Gaining extensive external assistance of the International Monetary Fund, and the "London" (private commercial creditors) and "Paris" Clubs (public creditors).
- Gaining full membership in the OECD, NATO, and, most recently, the European Union (Hunter & Ryan, 1998).

2.2. Securing International Financial Cooperation

Because of the sheer mountain of Polish external debt, Minister Balcerowicz decided immediately to tackle this problem. The Paris Club comprised nations that had financed Poland's public debt, and the London Club comprised private lenders, banks, and brokerage houses that had financed Poland's private debt. The Paris Club includes 19 permanent members and other official creditors who have participated in some official government-to-government lending. At the start of the transformation process in the fall of 1989, Poland's official Paris Club creditors included Germany ($5.94 billion), France ($3.63 billion), Austria ($3.60 billion), the United States ($3.46 billion), Canada ($2.64 billion), the UK ($1.65 billion), Italy ($1.32 billion), and Japan ($0.66 billion). Brazil, not a permanent member of the Paris Club, provided $3.0 billion. Poland's Paris Club debt was reduced by a minimum of 50 percent. France and the United Stated agreed to a 70 percent reduction.

Poland's private or commercial London Club debt amounted to an additional $13.2 billion in 1989. It was reduced by 45.2 percent, including a 37 percent reduction in interest and a 52 percent decrease in principal. Poland's largest London Club creditors included Salomon Brothers Inc., BFG Bank, Commerz Bank, Swiss Bank Corp., Lloyd's Bank, BNP, Standard Chartered PLC, Westdeutsche Landesbank, Societe Generale, Bank of America, and Dresdner Bank. Bossak and Kalicki (1994) regard the agreement with the London Club as "the crowning achievement of not only long and sophisticated negotiations, but also the effect of consistent implementation of economic reforms in Poland and their high evaluation by the G-7, the Paris Club, the IMF, and the World Bank."

3. THE STATE OF POLAND'S POST-TRANSITION ECONOMY: A SELECTED MICRO LOOK

What is the current state of the Polish economy? As a context, according to leading experts from the World Bank (2004), Poland may need as much as 30 years to catch up with the rest of Europe. However, on the positive side, *Standard & Poor's* in 2005 changed Poland's rating prospect from "stable" to "positive," reflecting an improvement in the medium-term fiscal prospects of Poland in comparison to its earlier expectations. The rating was changed back in 2006 (AFX International, April 24, 2006; Warsaw Voice, April 3, 2005). As we celebrate the 15th year of the transition from a centrally planned to a market economy, the question may thus be answered in both positive and negative terms, depending on whether the observer sees the Polish glass to be "half full" or "half empty."

3.1. Positive Indicators

Possibly the most important aspect of the transformation of the Polish economy has been the tremendous growth of smaller- and medium-sized businesses. This marks the rise of a business class that is truly entrepreneurial and is not just activity on the part of the remnants of the former nomenklatura. Today, there are more than 3.5 million companies registered in Poland, and 98.8 percent are classified as small- and medium-size businesses, operating with a varied capital mix (Polish Confederation of Private Employers, 2005). Franchises continue to blossom with international brands, including, for example, McDonald's, KFC, Wendy's, Pizza Hut, Dunkin' Donuts, T.G.I. Friday, Blimpie, Sbarro, Midas, Budget Rent-a-Car, and Domino's Pizza. In all, there are about 170 franchise systems operating in Poland that currently employ more than a half-million Poles. There are also host of local Polish companies fighting to develop powerful brands, including: "Pozegnanie z Afryka" ("Out of Africa"), a new specialty coffee shop franchise operating since 1992; A. Blikle, luxury cake shops; A.D. Dragowski, real estate offices; Drogerie Natura, drugstores; U szewczyka, footwear retail chain; and Zielona Budka, ice-cream shops (U.S. Department of Commerce, 2005; Warsaw Voice, April 7, 2004). All of these new businesses are rushing to exploit domestic growth opportunities.

The general economy has continued to grow at an average rate of nearly 6 percent in the previous decade, surpassing most economic predictions and the growth rates of most nations around the world. The private sector now accounts for more than 75 percent of national income, as opposed to 5–10 percent in 1989 arising from the limited private agricultural sector. Real GDP per capita experienced an increase of 3.8 percent in 2003. In 2004, the rate of increase was reported by both the Center for Social and Economic Research (CASE) and the European Commission to be 5.4 percent. For 2005, although private financial firms forecasted 4.5–5.5 growth, CASE and the European Commission were not quite as optimistic and predicted GDP growth in the range of 4.0–4.4 percent (Ratajczyk, 2004b).

The unit of Polish currency, the zloty, continues to remain steady against the dollar. In fact, the *zloty* has consistently appreciated since Poland's accession to the EU. Since the beginning of 2004, the zloty has gained 17.3 percent against the dollar and 11.1 percent against the euro. For Poland's entrepreneurs, however, the high price for the *zloty* may mean more competition from imports and less revenue for Polish exporters who have been a major force behind Poland's economic growth, because an "excessively strong zloty might reduce demand for Polish goods" (Ratajczyk, 2004a).

Real wages and salaries for Polish workers increased by 4 percent in 2003, rising to an average of $618 per month. Poland's Gross National Product stood at $5,483 per capita and was expected to rise to $7,300 per capita by the end of 2005. Labor productivity in the industrial sector has increased by an average of nearly 20 percent during the past four years, led by Polish trucking companies, who increased their productivity in the range of 20–50 percent. Industrial production grew at a 13 percent rate during 2004 as opposed to 8.4 percent in 2003. In the first half of 2004, the production of steel, once considered to be Poland's dead industry, rose by 25.3 percent. Other sectors which saw substantial growth included automobiles, 76.1 percent (Fiat is the largest producer, followed by Opel and VW.); building materials, 58.6 percent; metal production, 43 percent; shipbuilding, 37 percent; and electronics, 24 percent (Ratajczyk, 2004b). In addition, the Central Statistical Office indicated that 14,811 reporting Polish companies reached zl.13.4 billion in profit during the first quarter of 2004, more than four times the 2003 figure for the same period. On a yearly basis, Polish companies in 2004 earned nearly zl.61 billion in net profits, almost 3.5 times more than in 2003. The sharp increase was attributed to a "much lower increase in operating costs than revenue and a reduction (January 1, 2004) in the income tax rate from 26 percent to 19 percent" (Ratajczyk, 2004a).

In terms of international trade, Poland continues to expand its growing export sector, especially to fellow European Union nations – further distancing the Polish economy from its "heavy industry" orientation toward the former Soviet Union and its Eastern European satellites. Polish exports to the European Union have literally soared since May 1, 2004. Surprisingly, considering the dire predictions of the "Polish right," food exports in the period immediately following the accession were 43 percent higher than for the same period in 2003. Sectors that saw the greatest gains were meat and milk, especially dairies close to the German border. Overall, receipts from exports expressed in the euro increased by 10.2 percent, and exporters reported that their sales increased on a year-to-year basis by an impressive 39.7 percent, with three-quarters of Polish exporters reporting net profits. Exports to the European Union now account for more than 80 percent of total Polish exports. Imports increased by 33.4 percent, with 61.2 percent of Polish imports originating from the European Union. Major export partners included (in statistical order): Germany (31 percent), Italy (6.2 percent), France (6.2 percent), as well as Great Britain, the Netherlands, the Czech Republic, Sweden, Belgium, Russia, and Spain. Interestingly, an increase of more than 53 percent in sales to the Russian market occurred in 2004. Major import partners (in statistical order) include: Germany, Italy,

France, Russia, China, the Czech Republic, the Netherlands, Great Britain, Sweden, and Spain. Recently, the importation of Polish meat products was authorized by the United States Department of Agriculture, adding hope of increased Polish agricultural exports to the United States (Central Statistical Office, 2005).

Poland continues to be an attractive destination for worldwide FDI inflows, although at a slower pace than during the peak years of 1998–2000. UNCTAD reports that Poland is in the same category as India and China. In 2003, Poland attracted $6.42 billion in FDI, and the aggregate amount that has flowed into Poland since 1989 stands at more than $72 billion. The recently revamped and reconstituted, Polish Information and Foreign Investment Agency reported that the structure of foreign investment has changed. In 2003, the so-called greenfield projects, involving the construction of new plants from scratch, accounted for half of the FDI, while in 2002, the figure was 37 percent. In previous years, privatization projects attracted a major part of foreign investment.

The manufacturing sector continues to attract much needed capital, with investors showing a continued preference for automobiles, electronics, and pharmaceuticals. Services accounted for 55–60 percent of FDI in Poland. Foreign investors from France, (20 percent – 93 companies), the United States (14 percent – 126 companies), Germany (13 percent – 128 companies), the Netherlands (9 percent – 91 companies), and Italy (6 percent – 62 companies) continue to dominate the scene (Hunter et al., 2003).

3.2. Persistent Negatives

For those who may view the situation in more negative terms, several problems continue to persist, most seriously a pervasive sense of corruption and political instability. Transparency International, an organization that tracks official corruption around the world, reports that Poland stands in 67th place out of 146 countries among the economies of the worlds with 3.5 points. The rating employs a scale from 10 points, no corruption to zero, highest corruption. Out of the 146 countries listed in the rankings in 2004, 60 countries had less than 3 points, meaning that corruption in those countries is of "endemic character." Poland's score of 3.5 stands as the *worst* among all European Union member countries (Agence France-Presse, October 20, 2004; Warsaw Voice, October 31, 2004).

Some investors fear that the continuing political instability may impact negatively on FDI. Following the recent resignation of the Prime Minister, political turmoil and investor fears seem to have ebbed just a bit with the final elevation of the new Prime Minister. However, it was not seen as helpful that there was endemic instability in the important position of Minister of Finance or that the new government survives only as a coalition of disparate left-wing political parties and the opposition generally represents the "right side" of the political spectrum. Frequent calls for parliamentary elections add yet another uncertainty to both the economic and political equations (Shepherd, 2004).

Another area of concern includes the poor condition of Poland's infrastructure, especially roads and highways. Poland has only 483 km of highways and another 216 km of divided expressways. As noted by Jan Cienski (2004, p. 4), "The rest of Poland's 370,000 kilometers of roads includes dirt tracks, picturesque tree-lined lanes, and rutted byways – nothing able to handle the traffic of a modern European nation." Membership in the European Union is expected to provide a cash infusion to speed road construction, amounting to euro 2.3 billion from 2004–2006, and an additional euro 900 million for rail improvements. Other areas of infrastructure problems include the costs of telephone and internet services, and inadequate expenditures for research and development. In addition, continuing lags in patent applications and the number of computers owned by schools, the sometimes confusing requirements for licenses and permits as well as a myriad of tariff and non-tariff barriers that exist for companies that wish to penetrate the Polish market continue to be problematic (Ratajczyk, 2004b).

Inflation had remained under control in 2002–2003 but rose to 3.5–3.6 percent in 2004, spurred by increases in fuel prices, higher oil and food prices, and factors dealing with Poland's accession to the European Union – although the National Bank of Poland estimates that the total effect of price changes related to European Union accession will not cause annual inflation to grow more than 0.9 percentage points. It is well to remember that inflation had reached 585 percent in 1990, 70.3 percent in 1991, finally slowing to 43 percent in 1992. CASE and European Commission experts predict that inflation will rise by a manageable 2.1–2.5 percent in 2005 and beyond (Jelonkiewicz, 2004).

The pension and health care systems are still in serious jeopardy and much anticipated and needed reforms have again been delayed, often for political reasons or for the lack of either Presidential or Parliamentary leadership. Much of Poland's eastern regions are still under the grip of high unemployment. Pockets of unemployment may also be found in regions populated by former "state-owned farms," bankrupted by 1992, and in regions that were previously dependent on a "single industry" that was geared toward the Soviet Union; the figure approaches an alarming 40 percent in some regions. As of April–May 2005, aggregate unemployment hovers between 18 and 19 percent, with as much as an additional 10–15 percent of the population permanently discouraged and no longer seeking employment (Central Auditing Office, 2004).

4. FUTURE PROSPECTS

What are the future prospects for economic growth and development in Poland? Much may depend on settling the seemingly interminable political infighting that destroyed Prime Minister Leszek Miller who left office in 2004 with an approval rating of around 8 percent. A second factor involves the disequilibrium associated with the vetting process that has ripped through Polish society in a sea of recriminations and uncertainty. Poland was hit by a fresh scandal when Josef Oleksy, a former Prime Minister, Sejm Speaker, and the chairman of the SLD, was found guilty of lying about his past as a Communist security agent between 1970 and 1978. Lying about this matter means a 10-year ban on holding public office (Agence France-Presse, 2004).

A third factor revolves around the ability of the government to reinvigorate the privatization process – an important lynch-pin (along with foreign trade and FDI) in the process of economic transformation. Over 5,500 state-owned enterprises have already been subjected to commercialization and privatization over the past 15 years. However, the process stalled in 2003 and the early part of 2004. In response, the government announced plans to speed up the privatization process by replacing many "key people" in Treasury-owned companies, especially in the so-called "strategic companies" in industries such as copper mining, energy firms, and power plants (Jerziorski, 2004). Other privatizations may be scheduled in the pharmaceutical and medical sectors and in the Polish liquor industry (Ratajczyk, 2004b). The government also announced a plan to privatize a part of the heavily subsidized coal-mining sector, by offerings on the Warsaw Stock Exchange, by sales of private investors, and by linking with the privatization of a power plant. Once the staple of Poland's command economy, coal mining employed more than 400,000 miners and was the source of much of Poland's hard currency. Today, the mining sector makes up only about 2 percent of Poland's GDP and parallels the fate of the coal industry in the United States. Poland's coal mines employ about 120,000 coal miners, and 30 mines have been permanently closed. However, with

recent privatizations in the mining sector, it may be asserted that the
government's privatization strategy is beginning to work and that the coal-
mining sector may yet survive.

In the second half of 2004, the largest Polish bank, PKO BP, was privatized by sale on the Warsaw Stock Exchange. The transaction was complicated by the intention of the Treasury to keep a 51 percent "golden
share" for itself, a strategy that has been seen as problematic in the past and
has dampened investor interest, as a golden share may be either a perpetual
50 percent plus ownership by the state or it may be a share with special
voting rights that enables its holder (the Polish State Treasury) to veto
certain changes in the charter of a company. The golden share is under
sustained attack in European Union courts, as well as before the World
Trade Organization (WTO), of which Poland was a founding member. Despite this complication, however, the privatization of PKO was a tremendous success, the largest in the history of the Polish capital market, and
attracted not only individual investors but also more than 250 institutional
investors – including 99 from Poland and more than 150 from abroad (The
Polish Voice, 2004, p. 9).

The Ministry of the Treasury has selected a "privatization adviser" (the
consortium McKinsey and Company Poland Sp.z o.o) for the privatization
of the Warsaw Stock Exchange itself, although the process will not be finally
resolved until 2006. The Government Center for Strategic Studies (RCSS)
reports that while total investment fell by more than 22 percent in 2001–
2003, it increased by 8.7 percent in the first half of 2004, with the increase
reported primarily by medium-sized and large business entities (Warsaw
Voice, May 4, 2004).

5. A TRANSITIONAL CONCLUSION

Poland's entry into the European Union on May 1, 2004 provides a fitting
context for a tentative conclusion. The dream of Poland's full participation
in a united Europe, first exemplified by Poland's membership in NATO and
in Poland's desire to become a member of the European Union, has become
a reality. The formal process began early in Poland's transition, in May
1990, when the government of former Prime Minister Tadeusz Mazowiecki
submitted its official application for the opening of accession negotiations
in Brussels. In order to join the European Union, Poland was required to
fulfil stringent economic and political conditions known as the Copenhagen
Criteria that were established in 1993. These conditions required that a

prospective member must be a stable democracy, must respect the rule of law, human rights, and the protection of minorities, must have a functioning market economy, and must adopt the common rules, standards, and policies (the *acquis communitaire*) that make up the body of European Union law.

A major step was accomplished on February 1, 1994, when Poland and the European Union signed the European Treaty assuring Poland's "associated country status." After a round of intense diplomatic and political summitry, accession negotiations were completed on December 13, 2002 in Copenhagen. It now appears that Poland was able to negotiate final terms that were favorable both to Poland's domestic and international positions. Poland and nine additional "candidate countries" formally joined the European Union on May 1, 2004. It is also expected that Poland will be eligible to join the "euro zone," meeting the so-called Maastricht criteria, and adopting the euro as its medium of exchange, perhaps as early as 2007, but more realistically by 2009 (Taras, 2003; Hunter & Ryan, 2001).

Poland is now a member of the European Union, but four out of five Polish voters stayed at home on the election day. Official results of the National Elections revealed that the turnout was a disappointing 20.87 percent, spread primarily over nine political parties, none of which received more than 24.1 percent of the votes cast (Mierzejewski, 2004). Polls reveal that one-half of the Polish population believe Poland will benefit from membership in the European Union, more than 40 percent of Poles feel that the situation in Poland has "deteriorated," and only one-third of Poles evidence trust in the European Union to solve their major problems, identified as unemployment and a lack of prospects for an improved economic situation, problems that especially effect Polish youth who may once again experience a strong desire to emigrate in the face of economic and political insecurity.

Admittedly, the benefits of economic transformation have not been spread evenly over Polish society, and there is a widespread view that materialism, consumerism, and secularism have corrupted traditional Polish society and provided nothing in return. Yet, as indicated by almost all accounts and an objective review of statistical data, progress has been steady, if not pronounced. In the midst of both political and economic uncertainty, as well as persistent negatives and positives, one thing is certain. Possibly no one, other than perhaps Leszek Balcerowicz, the undeniable "father" of most of the fundamental economic changes that have occurred over the past 15 years, would have envisioned the dramatic progress that has taken place in Poland.

REFERENCES

Balcerowicz, L. (1995). *Socialism, capitalism, transformation*. New York: Central European Press.

Berry, M., & Jaruga, A. (1983). Industrial accounting in Poland's reorganized economy. *International Journal of Accounting, 20*(2), 45–63.

Blasczyk, B., & Dabrowski, M. (1993). Privatization process. In: Y. Akyuz, D. Kotte, A. Koves & L. Szamuely (Eds), *Privatization in the transition process: Recent experiences in Eastern Europe* (p. 64). Geneva: United Nations Conference on Trade and Development.

Bossak, J., & Kalicki, K. (1994). Poland's agreement with the London Club. In: J. Bossak (Ed.), *Poland: International economic report* (p. 203). Warsaw: The World Economy Research Institute.

Central Auditing Office (NIK) (2004). *Warsaw Voice*, July 18, 32.

Central Statistical Office (GUS). *Available at* http://www.gus.pl (last visited April 21, 2005).

Cienski, J. (2004). Road building needs boost. *Financial Times (Poland: Special Report)*, October 26, p. 4.

De la Rosa D., Crawford, D., & Franz, D. (2004). Trading on the Warsaw stock exchange – from reopening in 1991 through 2000. *The Journal of International Accounting, Auditing, and Taxation, 13*(2), 121–134. (forthcoming) (citing Grzegorz Cydejko, "Privatization: Magnificent Seven," *Warsaw Voice*, October 7, 1990, p. 4).

Franchising in Poland. *Warsaw Voice*, April 7 (2004). Available at http://www.warsawvoice. pl/view/5229 (last visited April 29, 2006).

Fulin, C. (2002). Overcoming institutional barriers and sociocultural conflicts in China. *Transition, 13*(Oct–Nov–Dec), 1–2.

Hunter, R., & Ryan, L. (1998). *From autarchy to market: Polish economics and politics 1945–1995* (p. 162). Westport, CT: Greenwood Press.

Hunter, R., & Ryan, L. (2000). The challenge of political and economic change in Poland and Central and Eastern Europe. *International Journal of Value Based Management, 13*, 97–107.

Hunter, R., & Ryan, L. (2001). Economic transformation through foreign direct investment in Poland. *Journal of Emerging Markets, 6*, 18–36.

Hunter, R., & Ryan, L. (2003). Trade and economic transformation in Poland. *Global Economy Quarterly, III*(3), 303–316.

Hunter, R., & Ryan, L. (2004). Privatization and transformation in Poland: An update. *The Polish Review, 49*(3), 919–943.

Hunter, R., Ryan, L., & Hrechak, A. (1994). Out of communism to what? The Polish economy and solidarity in perspective. *The Polish Review, 39*(3), 328–329, 334–335.

Hunter, R., Ryan, L., & Shapiro, R. (2004). *Poland: A transitional analysis* (Appendix 2, pp. 167–173). New York: PIASA Books.

Hunter, R., Shapiro, R., & Ryan, L. (2003). C.S.V., "Foreign direct investment in Poland – 2003. *The Polish Review, 48*(3), 303–316.

Jelonkiewicz, W. (2004). The price of accession, *Warsaw Voice (Business)*, July 18, p. 31.

Jeziorski, M. (2004). Share and share (not) alike, *Warsaw Voice (Business)*, September 12, p. 32.

Kornai, J. (1992). *The socialist system: The political economy of communism*. Princeton, NJ: Princeton University Press.

Lipton, D., & Sachs, J. (1990). Privatization in Eastern Europe: The case of Poland. *Brookings Economic Papers, 2*, 293–339.

Mierzejewski, M. (2004). Who won. *The Polish Voice*, *49*, 17–19.

Nikolaenko, S. (2002). Problems with economic statistics in Russia. *Transition*, *13*(Oct–Nov), 47–48.

Poland can take hope from low corruption ranking: Official (2004). *Agence France-Presse*, October 20, 2004.

Polish Confederation of Private Employers (2005). At www.prywatni.pl (last visited April 25, 2006).

Ratajczyk, A. (2004a). Privatization: Under supervision, *Warsaw Voice (Business)*, September 26, p. 29.

Ratajczyk, A. (2004b). Poland: A growth leader. *Warsaw Voice (Business)*, November 7–14, p. 32.

Sachs, J. (1993). *Poland's march to the market economy* (pp. 45–46). Cambridge, MA: MIT Press.

Shepherd, R. (2004). Belka wins Polish premiership, for now. *United Press International*, June 24.

Slower Growth. *Warsaw Voice*, May 4 (2004). Available at http://www.warsawvoice.pl/view/ 8357 (last visited April 29, 2006).

Taras, R. (2003). Poland's accession into the European Union: Parties, policies, and paradoxes. *The Polish Review*, *48*(1), 3–19.

Weschler, L. (1982). *Solidarity: Poland in the season of its passion* (p. 46). New York: Simon and Schuster.

World Bank. (2004). *Poland: Convergence to Europe. The challenge of productivity growth.* Washington, DC: The World Bank.

NEW VENTURE PERFORMANCE IN THE TRANSITION ECONOMIES: A CONCEPTUAL MODEL

Erich J. Schwarz and Malgorzata A. Wdowiak

1. INTRODUCTION

Entrepreneurial activity is a critical issue in the transition of economies attempting to reduce, or abolish state-owned monopoly enterprises. In many Central and Eastern European countries, privatization, restructuring, and failure of state-owned enterprises as consequences of the reforms typically led to a reduction of the size of the workplace. For example, in Poland, about 3.5 million employees lost their jobs in the period 1991–1996 (PEAD, 2003). After the collapse of communism in Europe, post-communist countries have undertaken reforms to liberalize their economies. These reforms stimulated the development in the private sector of small and medium-sized enterprises. New ventures provide a counterbalance to the loss of jobs at state-owned companies. In the period 1991–1996, new enterprises in the private sector in Poland created more than 1.8 million jobs. By the end of 2002, they provided work for 68% of the total employed persons (PEAD, 2003). Further, new ventures can play a critical role in stimulating economic growth. As a result of market reforms, the contribution of the private sector to Gross Domestic Product, e.g., in Hungary, went from 7% in 1988 to 85% in 1999 (World Bank, 2000). However, many new ventures do not survive

Developmental Entrepreneurship: Adversity, Risk, and Isolation
International Research in the Business Disciplines, Volume 5, 89–111
ISSN: 1074-7877/doi:10.1016/S1074-7877(06)05006-9

the first year of operation. For example, in Poland, about 40–45% enterprises established in the period 1995–2000 failed after the first year of their existence (PEAD, 2003).

The essential intention of the transition process is to replace dysfunctional institutions with new ones that are appropriate for the market economy. The extensive changes regarding long-standing social, political, and economic institutions create considerable uncertainty about the future (Danis, 2003). In addition, the transition from a centrally planned economy to a market economy has been accompanied by external economic shocks (i.e., the stock market crisis in Asia as well as the economic crisis in Russia in the late 1990s) and subsequent sharp drops in GDP growth (EBRD, 1999). In such an unstable environment, surviving the first year of operation is a significant challenge to new ventures. Therefore, a central question is what factors contribute to survival and growth of new ventures in transition economies.

The existing models of new venture performance generally neglect the different situations of entrepreneurs who create ventures in economies in transition with still scarce resources (e.g., Bosma, Van Praag, Thurik, & De Wit, 2004; De Clercq & Arenius, 2003; Cooper, Gimeno-Gascon, & Woo, 1994; Brüderl, Preisendörfer, & Ziegler, 1998). They relate to established market economies with a longer tradition of entrepreneurial activity. Therefore, the results of the empirical studies are particularly valid for new enterprises in relatively stable economies with abundant resources and entrepreneurial role models (Smallbone & Welter, 2003). But the emerging market economies in post-communist countries "do not have the same levels of resource slack, the same founding mechanism or the same flows of capital that exist in the relatively resource rich Western economies" (Muzyka, 1992, p. 33). A question that arises is whether models of firm survival and growth for established market economies are applicable to economies in transition, or whether they should be extended along economic and cultural dimensions.

Research on entrepreneurship and new venture performance in emerging market economies is relatively scarce (Lyles, Saxton, & Watson, 2004). The existing studies that address new ventures in transition economies have primarily a one-dimensional character (Hisrich & Drnovsek, 2002), that is, they analyze only a selected aspect of entrepreneurship and new venture success, such as entrepreneur's locus of control (Kaufmann et al., 1995), founder's managerial competences (Wasilczuk, 2000), or competitive strategies on new enterprises (Ferligoj, Prasnikar, & Jordan, 1997). Further, the investigations are mostly based on small and not representative samples, thus, making the generalization of received findings impossible. Additionally, the studies are primarily limited to descriptive statistics. In general, there is a lack of theoretically grounded and methodologically rigorous studies that analyze factors essential to new venture performance in transition economies in a widespread and systematic way.

In this paper, we propose a model of new venture performance in transition economies. We assume that the survival and growth of new ventures are dependent on the country's stage of economic development, its cultural features, and societal democratization (Wasilczuk, 2000; Köllermeier, 1992). Therefore, we focus on a transition context of entrepreneurial activity that has to be integrated into the model. A crucial issue of the paper is the entrepreneur who creates a new venture under conditions of high uncertainty, weak institutional framework, and scarce resources. We demonstrate the relevance of the founder's cultural and social capital for new venture performance in transition economies. By including within the transition context both cultural and social capital of the founder, we contribute conceptually to prior models of new venture performance.

The paper consists of three main parts and a conclusion. The next part considers the theoretical background and results of previous empirical studies relating to cultural and social capital of the entrepreneur. This section is followed by the discussion of features of the transition process in Central and Eastern European countries and its implications for new venture creation and performance in the transition economies. The next part is specifically concerned with the development of a model of new venture performance extended to a transition context. In particular, the transition context of cultural and social capital of the founder is analyzed. Finally, conclusions and implications for future research are presented.

2. CULTURAL AND SOCIAL CAPITAL OF THE ENTREPRENEUR

Cultural capital is defined to include both an individual's "institutionalized" capital such as occupational certificates, education diplomas, and academic degrees, and an individual's "incorporated" capital such as competences and skills gained through experience and habits consisting of behavior, work norms and values, and personality of a person (Bourdieu, 1986, pp. 243–248). Bourdieu criticizes the traditional representations of human capital theories (e.g., Becker, 1993) that take into consideration only "monetary investments and profits, or those [investments] directly convertible into money, such as the costs of schooling and the cash equivalent of time devoted to study"

(Bourdieu, 1986, p. 243). He argues that they do not take into account the transmission of cultural capital previously invested by the family (Bourdieu, 1986, p. 243). He emphasizes that the incorporated cultural capital always remains marked by its earliest condition of acquisition (Bourdieu, 1986, p. 245). The impact of the communist legacy as it relates to norms, values, and behaviors of individuals in the post-communist societies on the cultural capital of entrepreneurs in transition economies must be considered.

According to the human capital theory, the higher the individual's investments in education, competences, and skills, the greater the individual's productivity and, thus, the higher the expected returns on these investments for the individual (Becker, 1993, p. 17). In a new venture context, entrepreneurs with higher human capital are expected to have wide and valuable knowledge about technologies and markets, the competences to use special work tools, strongly developed analytical intelligence, and the ability to focus on essential problems and make decisions efficiently (Becker, 1993; Chrisman, Bauerschmidt, & Hofer, 1999; Moog, 2004). Therefore, higher investments of entrepreneurs in knowledge, competences, and skills are expected to have a positive impact on new venture creation and performance.

Likewise, the signaling theory provides arguments for an influence of an individual's cultural capital, particularly institutionalized capital, on entrepreneurship and small business development. This approach views the acquired education and work certificates as a signal about an individual's talent and productivity (Weiss, 1995). Entrepreneurs with a high investment in these types of capital appear to be more talented and trustworthy to clients, suppliers, and investors or lenders and therefore have easier access to relevant resources to create and develop a new venture (Bosma et al., 2004). Furthermore, the survival and success of a new venture is affected by behaviors of the founder. The behaviors and decisions of the entrepreneur determine the type of new venture, strategies chosen to enter a market and compete within it, and the process of identification and mobilization of resources (Chrisman et al., 1999).

The importance of cultural capital to the successful performance of new ventures is well recognized in entrepreneurship research. Previous studies that address influence factors on new venture performance concentrate particularly on the level of education, field of education, management experience, start-up experience, industry experience, and entrepreneurial training (Schwarz et al., 2005; Davidsson & Honig, 2003; Brüderl et al., 1998; Cooper et al., 1994; Robinson & Sexton, 1994). However, empirical findings to support the direction and significance of these relationships are inconclusive. For example, Cooper et al. (1994) confirmed a positive impact of education level on new venture performance. In contrast to the above study, Stuart and Abetti (1990) found a negative correlation between formal education and new venture performance. Dunkelberg, Cooper, Woo, and Dennis (1987) reported a non-significant influence of entrepreneurs' investment in education on new venture growth. The inconclusive findings of empirical research can be partly explained by the use of imprecise measures of independent variables as well as different measures of dependent ones (Kennedy & Drennan, 2001).

The common idea of the concept of social capital is the premise that individuals may increase their scope of potential activities by embeddedness in their social environment (Coleman, 1991). Social capital refers to the components of social structures in the society as well as the resources placed in social networks. Bourdieu defines social capital as the "aggregate of the actual or potential resources which are linked to possession of a durable network of more or less institutionalized relationships of mutual acquaintance and recognition" (Bourdieu, 1986, p. 248).

According to the "network approach to entrepreneurship," the entrepreneur is embedded in a social network that plays a critical role in the entrepreneurial process (Aldrich & Zimmer, 1986, p. 4). The relevance of social networks for new venture performance results from two basic premises. First, the entrepreneurial process includes the acquisition of necessary resources from the environment such as financial capital, human resources, and information about customers. Second, resources are mostly gained through the entrepreneur's social network (Ostgaard & Birley, 1996). There are particularly three features of entrepreneur's networks that have a positive impact on new venture performance: network size, network diversity, and composition of strong and weak ties (Hoang & Antoncic, 2003). For example, a large network of contacts can facilitate an access to potential stakeholders of a new venture, such as customers and investors. As network size refers to the amount of resources the entrepreneur can access, the diversity of a network determines the scope of opportunities open to the founder (Dubini & Aldrich, 1991). The contribution of social contacts to the entrepreneurial process is also dependent upon the type of relations within networks. Granovetter (1973) distinguishes between strong and weak ties. He emphasizes the role of weak ties for actors' action because they can gain an access to new information and ideas that lie outside of individuals' cluster of contacts (Granovetter, 1973). Alternatively, strong ties can provide information channels otherwise unavailable (Dubini & Aldrich, 1991) as well as emotional support and trust (Brüderl & Preisendörfer, 1998).

The relevance of networks for the start-up phase of new ventures and their subsequent performance has been confirmed in empirical research (Bosma et al., 2004; Hoang & Antoncic, 2003; Renzulli, Aldrich, & Moody, 2000; Brüderl et al., 1998; Ostgaard & Birley, 1996). However, empirical studies linking entrepreneurs' networks and new venture performance also provide inconsistent results. For example, Batjargal (2000) found a non-significant relationship between strong ties and new venture performance. By contrast, Brüderl et al. (1998) found strong ties to be more critical for new venture performance than weak ties. The inconclusive evidence results primarily from a wide variation in research context, the measurement of networks and performance, and in sample frames (Ostgaard & Birley, 1996).

3. TRANSITION AND ITS IMPLICATIONS FOR NEW VENTURES IN THE POST-COMMUNIST COUNTRIES

Central and Eastern Europe in the 1990s is characterized by deep political, social, and economic changes following the collapse of the communist system that had lasted for over four decades (Davies, 2003). To get a better understanding of the transition process from centrally planned to market economies in Central and Eastern European countries, it is necessary to define the major characteristics of communism. This socio-economic system can be described by the following features (Konrad & Szelenyi, 1991, p. 339):

1. The state had an ownership of the most relevant means of production and a monopoly in the field of production of key goods. Some private activities were also accepted in centrally planned economies but to a very limited extent, e.g., in Hungary, Poland, or former Yugoslavia (Szelenyi, 1988; Piasecki & Rogut, 1993; Mulej, Zenko, Rebernik, Potocan, & Bucar, 2003).
2. One party that followed the ideology of Marxism-Leninism had a political monopoly. In addition, executives of state-owned enterprises were primarily party members.
3. The social structure of the communist societies appeared as a single hierarchy that operated as a single bureaucratic rank-order. Ascent and descent of an individual in the social hierarchy were regulated by only two criteria: political loyalty and educational level. Therefore, persons who had neither "political" nor cultural capital were located on the lowest level of the social pyramid.

After the collapse of communism, transition in economies and societies of Central and Eastern Europe began. The transition processes comprise privatization of state-owned enterprises and development of small and medium-sized enterprises (i.e., transition from public to private-sector ownership), as well as liberalization of trade and capital markets (i.e., transition from central administration of prices to market mechanisms). A further ingredient in the transition process is creation of market institutions that are an integral part of the external environmental conditions for new venture creation and development in established market economies, e.g., financial and business support infrastructure (Smallbone & Welter, 2003). Although legal conditions needed for privatization and liberalization mostly already exist, they are not yet final (World Bank, 2000; Dallago, 2003). An institutional framework for supporting entrepreneurship and small and medium-sized enterprises has not been completely developed yet (Dallago, 2003). Furthermore, establishing a new venture in transition economies is hindered by the existence of considerable bureaucratic barriers (Smallbone & Welter, 2003).

The transition of the economic system runs parallel with social changes. In communism, the professional life of individuals was controlled and organized by the state. Therefore, people in post-communist countries have to learn to be proactive and act independently. Taking responsibility for their own life, however, still seems to be a longer lasting process than implementation of market economy instruments. Expansion of business enterprises coming from established market economies into the former eastern-block countries facilitated knowledge transfer about the principles of the market economy to the resident managers and co-workers (Peterson, 2003). Likewise, the development of business education programs on the basis of Western European or the United States programs enabled the scholars to get knowledge about the principles of business management in the market economy. Despite the changes in the economy and in the educational system, not all individuals have yet acquired competences and skills necessary to act in the emerging market economies. Thus, the transition processes are still not final both on the economic and social levels, even if joining the European Union (EU) by the majority of the post-communist countries in 2004 legitimized their progress in the development of an effective and efficient economy and a democratic society.

The entry to the European domestic market means, for the market participants, new sales and procurement markets, less problematic expansion possibilities, and also more chances of business co-operations. On the other hand, the extended internal market is connected with intensified competition and entrepreneurs' fears of failure of their ventures, in particular, small and new ones in the emerging market economies. They have to compete with the Western European enterprises, which have used instruments of the market economy for decades and, thus, are better prepared for the extension of the domestic market.

We can assume that under conditions of high uncertainty and intensified competition new ventures are exposed to a higher risk of failure. For new ventures, their initial resources are crucial for their survival and early performance in view of the liabilities of newness and liabilities of smallness (Lyles et al., 2004; Cooper et al., 1994). In addition, the resource base of a new venture determines a strategy formulated and realized to obtain competitive advantages in the market (Barney, 1991). Resources can be defined as "bundles of tangible and intangible assets, including a firm's management skills, its organizational processes and routines, and the information and knowledge it controls" (Barney & Wright, 2001, p. 625). Barney distinguishes three categories of resources: physical resources, human capital resources, and organizational capital resources (Barney, 1991, p. 101). In a new ventures context, the entrepreneur (human capital resources) is particularly relevant for performance of new enterprise (Cooper et al., 1994). In her theory of the early growth of the firm, Garnsey (1998, p. 530) emphasizes the importance of the founder for the success of a new venture as follows: "In new firms, the entrepreneurs' experience, personality, perceptions and resources are formative. The founder or founding group not only shape initial conditions, but also provide the venture with its essential assets and impetus. Their ambitions determine whether there will be an early drive for growth or modest aspirations for the firm."

Initial resources of the new ventures in the Central and Eastern European countries are affected primarily by the historic economic legacy of communism, by the experiences of the founders in the market economy, and by the structural change of the economic system. The former socio-economic system shaped the way of thinking of individuals and their behavior, e.g., they were influenced by a strong collectivist ideology (Suutari & Riusala, 2001). Social networks were of great importance under communism both to individuals and enterprises because they had an inadequate and highly uncertain access to resources (e.g., scarcity of financial capital and means of production, insufficient infrastructure, and outdated technology on the organizational level; shortage of food or clothing on the individual level). In her study of the "economy of favors," Ledeneva points out that the systematic use of connections to procure favors was a response to the absence of a market (Ledeneva, 1998). Thus, the financial lack of private households, for example, still determines the initial capital level of the new ventures in transition economies. Likewise, business education in the central planned economy still has an impact on the founders' knowledge of the principles of the market economy. Further, an extended integration of individuals into family and community, and strong reciprocal relationships based on mutual favors still affect behavior and values of the founders (Danis, 2003; Field, 2003). For example, entrepreneurs in transition economies share on average stronger collectivist values than their Western counterparts (Danis, 2003). Therefore, it is to be assumed that the legacy derived from the centrally planned economy and related to the resource scarcity, education system, individuals' behavior, and way of thinking have an influence on the present level of initial resources of new ventures.

4. TRANSITION CONTEXT OF NEW VENTURE PERFORMANCE: AN EXTENDED MODEL

4.1. Transition Context of Cultural Capital

Cultural capital of entrepreneurs in transition economies is affected by the individuals' investments in education, competences and skills, and their habits developed both under communism and in the emerging market economies.

The educational system under communism provided knowledge and developed skills that were required in the state-owned enterprises. Education in economic sciences that provided the principles about the centrally planned economy was of high relevance. Because of the domination of manufacturing enterprises, technical skills were also important competences of the company managers. Technical professionals were paid better than employees in health, education, and culture, although communism assumed an egalitarian wage distribution (Orazem & Vodopivec, 1997). However, managers of state-owned enterprises were rewarded particularly for their political loyalty and for taking control of the state assets. In the selection process of high-level management, party membership played a more important role than a university diploma (Suutari & Riusala, 2001). A survey of citizens of the former Soviet Union who immigrated to the United States in the 1970s and 1980s concluded that "party membership or connections" were decisive influences on a management career under communism (Gerber, 2000). There were also hired managers not possessing the party card, but who were chosen on the basis of their professional competences, i.e., technical ones (Suutari & Riusala, 2001).

Occupational experience of individuals in the centrally planned economy comprises primarily work in state-owned enterprises. These enterprises were characterized by hierarchical structures (Soulsby & Clark, 1996). Information about production, product mix, and cost targets were delegated from the ministers to the top managers (Suutari & Riusala, 2001). In this way, hierarchical structures of planning inhibited the development of business management practices accustomed for the market economy such as marketing and strategic management. In addition, the state supported its enterprises with subsidies, e.g., with financial and material resources, to enable them to perform better (Shipley, Hooley, Cox, & Fonfara, 1998). However, the performance of state-owned enterprises was hindered by the necessity to accomplish a number of inefficient administrative tasks in response to "socialist competition" between executives. Managers tried to be more successful in organizing frequent work meetings, preparing reports, and realizing various types of ideological work (Gerber, 2000). Because of a permanent scarcity of resources in the former socio-economic system, managers had to develop their social networks (Suutari & Riusala, 2001). Therefore, social competences were one of the essential skills of executives (Smallbone & Welter, 2003). In addition, corrupt behavior was a widespread practice under communism, in particular, by seeking scarce resources or promoting someone's position in the organizational hierarchy (Wasilczuk, 2000; Suutari & Riusala, 2001).

As market mechanisms grow in importance following economic reforms and state socialist collapse, the return to education should rise and the return to political position should decline (Nee, 1989). Since the educational system under communism was not oriented toward producing entrepreneurial skills and did not provide knowledge about business management, universities in the Central and Eastern European countries have developed educational programs in business sciences on the basis of Western European and American programs since the collapse of communism. Thus, the younger generations of students have acquired knowledge about business management in the market economy. There are also diverse training courses on small business management offered for potential founders. Further, employees of enterprises coming from established market economies have an opportunity to understand the principles of the market economy easier, i.e., on-the-job (Peterson, 2003). However, working in the state-owned enterprises, which are often inefficient, is likely to be a hindrance in a new venture context; the practices of employees and the management style of executives are still similar to those in the central planned economy.

Knowledge and qualification necessary to manage state-owned enterprises in the centrally planned economy are mostly not applicable to the market economy and not supportive in an entrepreneurial context. However, individuals' social competences, their ability to handle resource scarcity, and the experience of "muddling through" during communism may be valuable skills for entrepreneurship in the transition economies, i.e., under conditions of uncertainty and still weak institutional frameworks (Kusnezova, 1999). Further, entrepreneurs who gained work experience in Western Europe and North America under the former system got to know the principles of the market economy before the collapse of communism. Aidis and Van Praag (2004) found out that work experience of the Latvian entrepreneurs gained abroad under communism is positively related to objective business performance measures such as business turnover. Founders' work experience gained abroad after the collapse of communism may also have a positive impact on new venture performance.

Maybe the most difficult challenge of the transition in the post-communist countries is to change the mentality of individuals (Kenny & Trick, 1995). Entrepreneurs in the developed and emerging market economies are likely to have different values and practices reflecting their historically contrasting environments (Danis, 2003). For example, the realization of production targets was a crucial issue in the state-owned enterprises under communism. Profits were less relevant (Danis, 2003). Therefore, a lasting legacy of the centrally planned economy may be the production-first mentality of entrepreneurs that can be not supportive for new venture performance in the market economy, where profit orientation is predominantly required (Suutari & Riusala, 2001).

In view of the above, the following hypotheses related to the transition context can be proposed:

Hypothesis 1. There will be a negative correlation between the entrepreneur's investments in business education done under communism and new venture performance.

Hypothesis 2. There will be a negative correlation between the state-owned enterprise experience of the entrepreneur and new venture performance.

Hypothesis 3. There will be a positive correlation between prior work experience of the founder gained abroad and new venture performance.

Hypothesis 4. There will be a positive correlation between work experience in Western enterprises acting on markets in transition countries and new venture performance.

Hypothesis 5. There will be a negative correlation between entrepreneur's habits developed under communism and new venture performance.

4.2. Transition Context of Social Capital

Similar to the cultural capital, it is necessary to explain the function of social contacts in the former socio-economic system to better understand the role of social capital in the post-communist societies and economies.

Social networks were essential for the everyday life of individuals and enterprises under communism. Primarily, they reflected a defensive attitude of individuals toward the former regime and bureaucratic administration (Kolankiewicz, 1996). Executives of state-owned enterprises were rewarded principally for their political loyalty and for taking control of the state assets. In addition, they controlled the private life of employees to screen their political views. In order to take a tangible advantage or to get a better position in the organization, many work colleagues also provided the company management with "useful" information about other employees. Thus, both managers of state-owned enterprises and workmates were mostly mistrusted. In this way, family and close friends were the major source of trust. The importance of strong ties for a private and professional life of individuals is directly connected with a permanent scarcity of resources under communism (Köllermeier, 1992).

Food, clothing, medications, and means of production were among the scarcest commodities in the former socialist system. Scarce goods were obtained through family and friends and then friends of friends. In particular, strong ties that had connections to the communist administrators, that is, the so-called "nomenclatura," were of great importance, because the nomenclatura possessed resources or had access to scarce goods (Field, 2003). Many resources under communism may have been obtained by dispensing diverse favors (Ledeneva, 1998). Thus, personal networks and a system of the exchange of mutual favors played a considerable role when it came to getting hold of everyday goods and means of production. Financial capital was largely irrelevant (Ledeneva, 1998).

Social networks in the post-communist countries play a crucial role for new venture creation and performance. As mentioned above, the legal and institutional framework of entrepreneurship and small business development has not been completely established yet (Dallago, 2003). The existing law either has been changed several times or is not applied in the daily business. In addition, new venture creation and performance are hindered by the existence of considerable bureaucratic barriers (Smallbone & Welter,

2003). This situation indicates that the entrepreneurs' environment in transition economies is still unstable, non-transparent and weakly institutionalized. Therefore, strong ties are very important for individuals, in particular, because they are trustworthy and more predictable (Field, 2003). In addition, access to resources and stakeholders is more difficult in emerging market economies than in developed ones by virtue of the considerable scarcity of resources and asymmetry of market information (Lyles et al., 2004). Therefore, entrepreneurs in transition economies activate their personal contacts to mobilize resources, especially scarce financial capital, and to overcome constraints imposed by bureaucratic structures and often unfriendly officials (Smallbone & Welter, 2003).

A further feature of the transition to the market economy is the considerable continuity of social contacts from the previous socio-economic system, in particular, among individuals representing former nomenclatura (Field, 2003). Former communist administrators use their connections particularly to privatize and restructure state-owned enterprises, and to mobilize resources to develop their own businesses (Smallbone & Welter, 2003). Because the government and state-owned enterprises still are key power brokers in transition economies (Lyles et al., 2004), previous management experience in the state-owned enterprises may contribute to new venture creation and performance by the use of "old" networks and connections. In addition, these entrepreneurs mostly have high networking skills (Smallbone & Welter, 2003). It allows them to establish new connections to develop their ventures easily. We can assume that, in a transition context, close ties of a new venture to key institutions such as state-owned enterprises and government enhance the venture's survival and bring benefits to the entrepreneur.

In view of the above, the following hypotheses related to the transition context can be proposed:

Hypothesis 1. There will be a positive correlation between entrepreneur's weak and strong ties and new venture performance; however, the influence of strong ties will be stronger than weak ones.

Hypothesis 2. There will be a positive correlation between entrepreneur's management experience in the state-owned enterprise and new venture performance.

Hypothesis 3. There will be a positive correlation between close ties of the entrepreneur to key institutions and new venture performance.

4.3. Implications for Future Research: An Extended Model

The above analysis indicates the necessity of incorporating transition related variables in models of new venture performance. Before presenting a model, we have to turn our attention to some methodological aspects relevant in the transition context. By virtue of the high rate of failure of new ventures within the first year of their existence in transition economies, it is necessary to improve the understanding of causal mechanisms between the cultural and social capital and early performance of a new enterprise. Further, it requires including a time dimension into the model in order to explore founding processes better. We propose a longitudinal research design relating to new venture performance in transition economies.

Since the end of the 1980s, theorists have realized that new venture survival and growth are strongly affected by the type and quality of the founder's decisions and behaviors, such as planning, strategy formulation, and allocation of resources (Chrisman et al., 1999; Gartner, 1988). However, Shook, Priem, and McGee (2003, p. 390) point out that "perhaps the most under-researched aspect of the individual and venture creation is exploitation activities. We know very little about the role of the individual in acquiring resources and organizing the company." Therefore, both entrepreneurs' cultural and social capital and the economic activities they engage in will be the key components of the proposed model (see Fig. 1).

In the start-up phase of a new venture, there are primarily two categories of activities the entrepreneur can engage in that have an impact on performance of the start-up process, i.e., planning and organizing (Shook et al., 2003; Delmar & Shane, 2002). Planning activities can comprise preparing a business plan, estimating financial forecasts, and creating a company's strategy. Organizing activities can cover finding resources, networking, and initiation of product and service development. In transition economies, networking is a particularly widespread behavior because of the lack of resources and importance of social contacts for new venture creation and development (Lyles et al., 2004). New venture survival and growth are more likely, for example, when the entrepreneurs devote more time to establish and maintain contacts with customers and suppliers (Lyles et al., 2004; Ostgaard & Birley, 1996). Likewise, strategic planning enhances the likelihood of new venture survival and growth (Schwenk & Shrader, 1993).

Activities will be influenced by the cultural capital of entrepreneurs. For example, founders who reflect survival mentality (as work norm) mostly do not create a business plan (Shuman & Seeger, 1986). In particular, individuals in transition economies reflect a shorter-term orientation than their

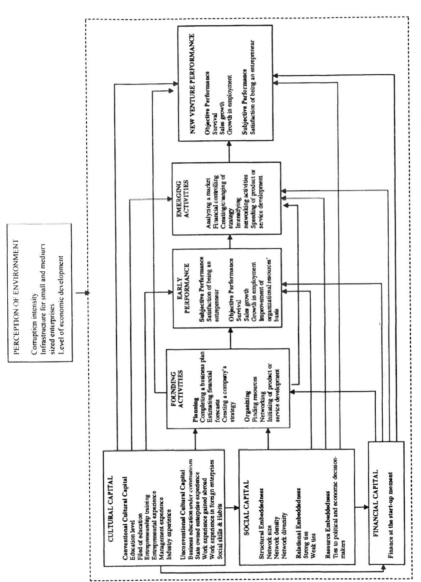

Fig. 1. Model of New Venture Performance in an Economy in Transition.

Western counterparts. It mainly reflects unstable and uncertain economic and political conditions in post-communist countries (Danis, 2003). By contrast, industry and entrepreneurial experience may positively affect creating an appropriate business plan or formulating a strategy. Considering the transition context, we distinguish between conventional and unconventional cultural capital. Conventional cultural capital will comprise variables that are usually integrated into models of new venture performance in the market economy, i.e., educational level, field of education, entrepreneurship training, entrepreneurial experience, management experience, and industry experience. Unconventional cultural capital will consist of variables related to an economy in transition, i.e., business education under communism state-owned experience, work experience gained abroad, work experience in foreign enterprises acting on emerging market economies, social skills, and individual's habits.

Social capital will also influence activities related to the establishment of a new venture. For example, entrepreneurs who have a sparse social network will have to devote more time to establishing and maintaining contacts relevant for their ventures than individuals with larger networks. Likewise, founders who have ties to the political and economic decision-makers, i.e., resourceful key institutions, can find new opportunities or exploit the existing ones easier. The model will include structural, relational, and resource embeddedness as social capital dimensions. Structural embeddedness relates to the structure of network relations and includes network size, network density, and network diversity. Relational embeddedness refers to the extent to which economic actions are affected by the quality of individuals' social relations and includes weak and strong ties of the entrepreneur. In a transition context, it is necessary to incorporate resource embeddedness, i.e., the degree to which network ties contain valuable instrumental resources (Batjargal, 2000), into the model. Resource embeddedness refers to the close ties of the entrepreneur to key institutions, such as state-owned enterprises and government.

Performance of a new venture will be predominantly affected by the entrepreneur's activities. In entrepreneurship research, various measures of new venture performance are used (Weinzimmer, Nystrom, & Freeman, 1998; Murphy, Trailer, & Hill, 1996). In the transition context, we suggest investigating both subjective and objective performance measures. We define subjective performance as an individual's satisfaction with being an entrepreneur. By virtue of high unemployment in the majority of transition economies in Europe (for example, about 19% in Poland (PEAD, 2003)), founders may be initially content with establishing a new business, even if the objective measures of performance is still low. Survival, sales growth, and growth in employment are objective measures of performance integrated into the model. Survival can be seen as the minimum criterion of successful organizational performance. Sales growth is connected with other categories of financial growth, e.g., profitability, and return on investment that usually are not announced by companies. The meta-analysis of 35 studies on measuring organizational growth conducted by Weinzimmer et al. (1998) indicates that sales growth is the most used measure of venture growth. However, sales are strongly dependent upon the type of industry and initial size of a venture. Growth in employment is of great importance for regional development by virtue of the widespread hope that new enterprises create new jobs. In a new venture context, it is also necessary to recognize that an important challenge the entrepreneur has to face in the start-up phase is to assemble and organize the needed resources to establish the new venture (Delmar & Shane, 2002). Therefore, we propose to examine the improvement of the organizational resource base as an early performance measure.

We also recommend investigating the early performance of a new venture close to the business opening, e.g., after three months after the start-up moment. In view of a low rate of venture survival in transition economies after the first operating year, we propose to investigate the subsequent performance of a new enterprise by the end of the first year after the business' opening. This research design makes it possible to accompany the founder from the start-up process and, in addition, to avoid the "survival biases."

Furthermore, we suggest investigating activities of the entrepreneur in a later phase of the first year of the venture's existence. Thus, it will be possible to provide founders with valuable postulates relating to the reduced risk of failure. These emerging activities will encompass aspects such as analyzing markets, financial controlling, creating or changing of strategy, changing of ownership structure, intensifying networking activities, and accelerating the product and service development. Emerging activities will be affected by the early performance of a new venture. For example, low sales growth and an unsatisfactory resource base can necessitate entrepreneurs to intensify their networking activities. Likewise, poor financial performance can contribute to changing the company's strategy. In the model, new venture performance will be influenced both by founding and emerging activities.

Certainly, cultural and social capital will also directly affect emerging activities as well as early and subsequent performance of a new business. Because of the variety of new ventures, it is difficult to recognize all the important activities as well as an order in which the entrepreneur engages in the activities (Delmar & Shane, 2002). In addition, financial capital of the founder will be incorporated into the model as an influence factor. A well-founded financial base of a venture helps to protect it against random shocks and increase the scope of the entrepreneur's actions (Cooper et al., 1994). In transition economies, lack of financial capital is one of the largest obstacles to small and medium-sized enterprises. In particular, it prevents the venture's growth and modernization (Dallago, 2003). Financial capital will affect new venture performance and activities (e.g., creating a strategy). The level of financial capital will be dependent upon entrepreneurs' cultural and social capital (Bourdieu, 1986). For example, individuals with a high level of education are expected to gain higher wages than their less-educated counterparts (Becker, 1993). Therefore, we can assume that well-educated founders possess higher savings than less-educated ones. Likewise, entrepreneurs who have a large social network can increase their initial financial capital by the use of informal contacts, e.g., by getting private loans from friends. Further, entrepreneurs who have a high level of cultural capital, e.g., more industry experience, may possess large networks of contacts that can be valuable in the process of new venture creation and development (Jing, Pek-hooi, & Poh-kam, 2003).

Finally, in order to reflect an unstable and uncertain nature of the environment in transition economies, it is reasonable to incorporate the entrepreneur's perception of the local business climate and the opportunities it provides into the model (Mueller & Goic, 2002). Environment will affect cultural capital of the entrepreneur, activities, and performance. We propose to examine the founder's perception of economic infrastructure for entrepreneurship and small and medium-sized enterprises and of economic development in the region. Likewise, the corrupt practices in a venture industry may determine firm performance and the entrepreneur's behavior and habits.

5. CONCLUSIONS

New ventures play an essential role in the transition process from centrally planned to market economies. In particular, they provide a counterbalance to the loss of jobs at state-owned enterprises and stimulate economic growth. However, many enterprises do not survive the first year of their existence in emerging markets. In transition economies, which are characterized by the still unstable and weak institutionalized environment and scarcity of resources, surviving the first year of operation is a main challenge to new ventures. A question that arises is what factors contribute to early survival and growth of new ventures in a transition context.

We have argued that the survival and growth of a new venture are dependent on the country's stage of economic development and its cultural factors. However, the existing models of new venture performance usually do not consider the different situations of founders who open ventures in economies with still scarce resources and a short tradition of entrepreneurship. In addition, research on new venture survival and growth in emerging market economies is under-represented. We have proposed a longitudinal model of early venture performance in a transition economy. An essential role in the entrepreneurial process in post-communist countries is played by the entrepreneur who creates a venture under conditions of high uncertainty and in an unfavorable economic environment. We have argued the necessity of incorporating transition-related variables, especially social and cultural capital of the entrepreneur, into the model.

Cultural capital of entrepreneurs in transition economies is affected by the individuals' investments in education, competences and skills, and their habits developed both under communism and in the emerging market economies. We have argued that entrepreneur's investments in business education done under communism, work experience in state-owned enterprises, and individual's habits developed in the former socio-economic system, e.g., the production-first mentality, may have a negative impact on new venture performance in an emerging market economy. By contrast, previous work experience of the founder gained abroad as well as in Western enterprises acting on the markets in transition countries may have a positive influence on new venture performance.

Social capital of entrepreneurs in post-communist countries plays a very important role for new venture creation and performance. Its relevance results from the instability of the new socio-economic system, resource scarcity, and the considerable continuity of social contacts from the communist epoch. We have argued that in an unstable, non-transparent, and weak institutionalized environment, strong ties may influence new venture performance more strongly than weak ties. Because government and state-owned enterprises are still the key power brokers in transition economies, prior management experience of entrepreneurs in these institutions may affect new venture performance positively. Likewise, entrepreneurs' close ties to these key organizations may have a positive impact on new venture performance.

By virtue of the high rate of failure in transition economies, it is required to improve the understanding of causal mechanisms between the founder's cultural and social capital and early firm performance. We have included founding and emerging activities into the model in order to better understand the role of the entrepreneur in acquiring resources and organizing the venture. Furthermore, we recommend examining the early performance of a new venture close to the business opening, and the subsequent firm performance – by the end of the first year after the business' opening. The longitudinal model makes it possible to accompany the founder from the start-up moment and to find out what factors contribute to the new venture survival and growth, and what factors cause the failure of a new venture in transition economies.

REFERENCES

Aidis, R., & Van Praag, M. (2004). Unconventional forms of human capital: Do they make a difference for business performance? Analyzing the effects of illegal entrepreneurship and travel abroad experience. *Frontiers of entrepreneurship research*. Wellesley, MA: Babson College.

Aldrich, H., & Zimmer, C. (1986). Entrepreneurship through social networks. In: D. L. Sexton & R. W. Smilor (Eds), *The art and science of entrepreneurship*. Cambridge, MA: Ballinger Publishing Company.

Barney, J. (1991). Firm resources and sustained competitive advantage. *Journal of Management, 17*(1), 99–120.

Barney, J., & Wright, M. (2001). The resources-based view of the firm: Ten years after 2001. *Journal of Management, 27*(6), 625–641.

Batjargal, B. (2000). Effects of networks on entrepreneurial performance in a transition economy: The case of Russia. *Frontiers of entrepreneurship research*. Wellesley, MA: Babson College.

Becker, G. (1993). *Human capital. A theoretical and empirical analysis with special reference to education* (3rd ed.). Chicago: The University of Chicago Press.

Bosma, N., Van Praag, M., Thurik, R., & De Wit, G. (2004). The value of human and social capital investments for the business performance of startups. *Small Business Economics, 23*, 227–236.

Bourdieu, P. (1986). The forms of capital. In: J. G. Richardson (Ed.), *Handbook of theory and research for sociology of education* (pp. 49–79). Westport, CT: Greenwood Press.

Brüderl, J., & Preisendörfer, P. (1998). Network support and the success of newly founded businesses. *Small Business Economics, 10*, 213–225.

Brüderl, J., Preisendörfer, P., & Ziegler, R. (1998). Der Erfolg neugegründeter Betriebe, 2., unveränderte Auflage, Duncker & Humblot, Berlin.

Chrisman, J. J., Bauerschmidt, A., & Hofer, C. W. (1999). The determinants of new venture performance: An extended model. *Entrepreneurship Theory & Practice, 23*(1), 5–29.

Coleman, J. S. (1991). *Grundlagen der Sozialtheorie*, Band 1, Oldenbourg Verlag, München.

Cooper, A. C., Gimeno-Gascon, F. J., & Woo, C. Y. (1994). Initial human and financial capital as predictors of new venture performance. *Journal of Business Venturing, 9*, 371–395.

Dallago, B. (2003). The importance of small and medium enterprises – transitional economies. *United Nations Chronicle*, December.

Danis, W. M. (2003). Differences in values, practices, and systems among Hungarian and Western expatriates: An organizing framework and typology. *Journal of World Business*, *38*, 224–244.

Davidsson, P., & Honig, B. (2003). The role of social and human capital among nascent entrepreneurs. *Journal of Business Venturing*, *18*, 301–331.

Davies, N. (2003) (Polish ed.). *Europe. A history*. Krakow: Wydawnictwo Znak.

De Clercq, D., & Arenius, P. (2003). Effects of human capital and social capital on entrepreneurial activity. *Frontiers of entrepreneurship research*. Wellesley, MA: Babson College.

Delmar, F., & Shane, S. (2002). What firm founders do: A longitudinal study of the start-up process. Babson entrepreneurship research conference, Pittsburgh.

Dubini, P., & Aldrich, H. (1991). Personal and extended networks are central to the entrepreneurial process. *Journal of Business Venturing*, *6*, 305–313.

Dunkelberg, W. C., Cooper, A. C., Woo, C., & Dennis, W. (1987). New firm growth and performance. *Frontiers of entrepreneurship research*. Wellesley, MA: Babson College.

European Bank for Reconstruction and Development (EBRD). (1999). *Transition report 1999: Ten years of transition*. London: EBRD.

Ferligoj, A., Prasnikar, J., & Jordan, V. (1997). Competitive advantage and human resource management in SMEs in a transitional economy. *Small Business Economic*, *9*(6), 503–514.

Field, J. (2003). *Social capital*. London: Routledge.

Garnsey, E. (1998). A theory of the early growth of the firm. *Industrial and Corporate Change*, *7*(3), 523–556.

Gartner, W. B. (1988). Who is an entrepreneur? Is the wrong question. *American Journal of Small Business*, *12*(1), 11–32.

Gerber, T. P. (2000). Membership benefits of selection effects? Why former communist party members do better in post-soviet Russia. *Social Science Research*, *29*, 25–50.

Granovetter, M. (1973). The strength of weak ties. *American Journal of Sociology*, *78*, 1360–1380.

Hisrich, R. D., & Drnovsek, M. (2002). Entrepreneurship and small business research. *Journal of Small Business and Enterprise Development*, *9*(2), 172–222.

Hoang, H., & Antoncic, B. (2003). Network-based research in entrepreneurship. A critical review. *Journal of Business Venturing*, *18*, 165–187.

Jing, Z., Pek-hooi, S., & Poh-kam, W. (2003). Human capital, competitive intensity and entrepreneur's propensity to exploit social networks in resource acquisition. *Frontiers of entrepreneruship research*, Wellesley, MA: Babson College.

Kaufmann, P., Welsh, D. H., & Bushmarin, N. V. (1995). Locus of control and entrepreneurship in the Russian Republic. *Entrepreneurship Theory and Practice*, *20*(1), 43–53.

Kennedy, J., & Drennan, J. (2001). A review of the impact of education and prior experience on new venture performance. *Entrepreneurship and Innovation*, *2*(3), 153–169.

Kenny, B., & Trick, B. (1995). Reform and management education: A case from the Czech Republic. *Journal of East-West Business*, *1*, 69–95.

Kolankiewicz, G. (1996). Social capital and social change. *British Journal of Society*, *47*(3), 427–441.

Köllermeier, T. (1992). Entrepreneurship in an economy in transition: Perspectives of the situation in the EX GDR. In: S. Birley & I. C. Macmillan (Eds), *International perspectives on entrepreneurship research*. Amsterdam: Elsevier.

Konrad, G., & Szelenyi, I. (1991). Intellectuals and domination in post-communist societies. In: P. Bourdieu & J. S. Coleman (Eds), *Social theory for a changing society*. Boulder, Oxford: Westview Press.

Kusnezova, N. (1999). Roots and philosophy of Russian entrepreneurship. *Journal for East European Management Studies*, 4(1), 45–72.

Ledeneva, A. V. (1998). *Russia's economy of favours: Blat, networking and informal exchange*. Cambridge: Cambridge University Press.

Lyles, M. A., Saxton, T., & Watson, K. (2004). Venture survival in a transitional economy. *Journal of Management*, 30(3), 351–375.

Moog, P. (2004). *Humankapital des gründers und erfolg der unternehmensgründung*. Wiesbaden: Deutscher Universität-Verlag.

Mueller, S. L., & Goic, S. (2002). Entrepreneurial potential in transition economies: A view from tomorrow's leaders. *Journal of Developmental Entrepreneurship*, 7(4), 399–414.

Mulej, M., Zenko, Z., Rebernik, M., Potocan, V., & Bucar, M. (2003). Entrepreneurship in Slovenia – a develospment economic view. Paper presented on conference "Cultural Areas" at the University of Klagenfurt, November.

Murphy, G. B., Trailer, J. W., & Hill, R. C. (1996). Measuring performance in entrepreneurship research. *Journal of Business Research*, 36(1), 15–23.

Muzyka, D. F. (1992). Critique on entrepreneurship in an economy in transition: Perspectives of the situation in the EX GDR. In: S. Birley & I. C. Macmillan (Eds), *International perspectives on entrepreneurship research*. Amsterdam: Elsevier.

Nee, V. (1989). The theory of market transition: From redistribution to markets in state socialism. *American Sociological Review*, 54, 663–681.

Orazem, P. F., & Vodopivec, M. (1997). Value of human capital in transitino to market: Evidence from slovenia. *European Economic Review*, 41, 893–903.

Ostgaard, T. A., & Birley, S. (1996). New venture growth and personal networks. *Journal of Business Research*, 36, 37–50.

Peterson, R. B. (2003). The use of expatriates and inpatriates in Central and Eastern Europe since the Wall Came Done. *Journal of World Business*, 38, 55–69.

Piasecki, B., & Rogut, A. (1993). Self-regulation of SME sector development at a more advance stage of transformation. Paper presented to the 20th annual conference of EARIE, Tel Aviv, September.

Polish Agency for Entrepreneurship Development (PEAD) (2003). *Small and medium-size enterprises in Poland in 2001–2002*. Warsaw: PEAD.

Renzulli, L. A., Aldrich, H., & Moody, J. (2000). Family matters: Gender, networks, and entrepreneurial outcomes. *Social Forces*, 79(2), 523–546.

Robinson, P. B., & Sexton, E. A. (1994). The effect of education and experience on self-employment success. *Journal of Business Venturing*, 9(2), 141–156.

Schwarz, E. J., Ehrmann, T., & Breitenecker, R. (2005). Erfolgsdeterminanten junger Unternehmen in Österreich: Eine empirische Untersuchung zum Beschäftigtenwachstum. *Zeitschrift für Betriebswirtschaft*, 11, 1077–1098.

Schwenk, C. R., & Shrader, C. B. (1993). Effects of formal strategic planning on financial performance in small firms: A meta-analysis. *Entrepreneurship: Theory and Practice*, 17(3), 53–64.

Shipley, D., Hooley, G., Cox, T., & Fonfara, F. (1998). The effects of privatization on marketing capability and activity in Poland. *International Journal of Research in Marketing*, 15, 367–381.

Shook, C. L., Priem, R. L., & McGee, J. E. (2003). Venture creation and the enterprising individual: A review and synthesis. *Journal of Management, 29*(3), 379–399.

Shuman, J. C., & Seeger, J. A. (1986). The theory and practice of strategic management in smaller rapid growth firms. *American Journal of Small Business, 11*(1), 7–18.

Smallbone, D., & Welter, F. (2003). The distinctiveness of entrepreneurship in transition economies. *Small Business Economics, 16*, 249–262.

Soulsby, A., & Clark, E. (1996). The emergence of post-communist management in the Czech Republic. *Organisation Studies, 17*, 227–247.

Stuart, R. W., & Abetti, P. A. (1990). Impact of entrepreneurial and management experience on early performance. *Journal of Business Venturing, 5*(3), 151–162.

Suutari, V., & Riusala, K. (2001). Leadership styles in Central Eastern Europe: Experiences of Finnish expatriates in the Czech Republic, Hungary and Poland. *Scandinavian Journal of Management, 17*, 249–280.

Szelenyi, I. (1988). *Socialist entrepreneurs.* Madison: University of Wisconsin Press.

Wasilczuk, J. (2000). Advantageous competence of owner/mangers to grow the firm in Poland: Empirical evidence. *Journal of Small Business Management, 38*(2), 80–94.

Weinzimmer, L. G., Nystrom, P. C., & Freeman, S. J. (1998). Measuring organizational growth: Issues, consequences and guidelines. *Journal of Management, 24*(2), 235–262.

Weiss, A. (1995). Human capital vs signalling explanations of wages. *Journal of Economic Perspectives, 9*(4), 133–154.

World Bank (2000). *Transition: The first ten years. Analysis and lessons for Eastern Europe and the former Soviet Union.* Washington: World Bank.

PART III:
ENTREPRENEURSHIP AND CRISES

DISASTERS, VULNERABILITY AND THE GLOBAL ECONOMY: IMPLICATIONS FOR LESS-DEVELOPED COUNTRIES AND POOR POPULATIONS

Charlotte Benson and Edward J. Clay

1. INTRODUCTION

1.1. Background

Two worldwide trends in recent decades are commonly noted and sometimes linked in discussing disasters. First, the reported global cost of natural disasters has risen significantly, with a 14-fold increase between the 1950s and 1990s (Munich Re, 1999). During the 1990s, major natural

Developmental Entrepreneurship: Adversity, Risk, and Isolation
International Research in the Business Disciplines, Volume 5, 115–145
Copyright © 2006 by Elsevier Ltd.
All rights of reproduction in any form reserved
ISSN: 1074-7877/doi:10.1016/S1074-7877(06)05007-0

Adapted from a paper published by the World Bank. (Benson, C and E J Clay. 2003. 'Disasters, vulnerability and the global economy'. In Kreimer, A, M Arnold and A Carlin, *Building Safer Cities: The Future of Disaster Risk*. Disaster Risk Management Series No 3. Washington, DC: World Bank)

catastrophes are reported to have resulted in economic losses averaging an estimated US$ 54 billion per annum (in 1999 prices) (*ibid*). Record losses of some US$ 198 billion were recorded in 1995, the year of the Kobe earthquake – equivalent to 0.7 percent of global gross domestic product (GDP) (*ibid*).

Second, there is an apparent steady movement toward globalization, with an increasing share of economic activity taking place across countries and regions as barriers to integration are reduced. Between 1987 and 1997 the share of international trade in total output (defined as exports plus imports relative to GDP) rose from 27 to 39 percent for developed countries and from 10 to 17 percent for developing countries (World Bank, 2000). Global foreign direct investment (FDI) flows more than tripled between 1988 and 1998 to US$ 610 billion and foreign direct investment is now the largest form of private capital flow to developing countries (*ibid*). Labor migration and financial remittances to home countries have also been of increasing importance to developing countries and poorer regions within them.

As the World Bank comments,

> globalization is one of the most charged issues of the day .... Extreme opponents charge it with impoverishing the world's poor, enriching the rich and devastating the environment, while fervent supporters see it as a high-speed elevator to universal peace and prosperity (2000, p. 1).

But what does globalization imply for vulnerability to natural hazards? Rising disaster losses have paralleled increasing globalization. But are the two trends related – and, if so, necessarily? Or are they coincidental but separate movements? And can differences in the incidence of occurrence and nature of natural hazards influence the form and level of integration of a country into the global economy?

This chapter seeks to explore the relationship between integration in the global economy and sensitivity to natural hazards – that is, to events caused by geophysical, hydrological and atmospheric forces. It takes a macroeconomic perspective and draws on both the wider literature and on evidence accumulated by the authors in a series of studies of the economic impacts of natural disasters (Benson, 1997a, b, c; 1998, 2003; Benson & Clay, 1998, 2001, 2002, 2004; Clay et al., 1999; Clay, Bohn, Blanco de Armas, Kabambe, & Tchale, 2002; ODI, 2005). This paper also presents one of these case studies, the country of Malawi in Southern Africa.

1.2. Terminology

The literature relating both to natural disasters and to globalization indicates some diversity in the use of basic terms. At the outset, it is therefore useful to define how key language is used in this chapter.

A *natural hazard* is a geophysical, atmospheric or hydrological event that has a potential to cause harm or loss. Usually these are both uncommon and extreme events in terms of the range of natural phenomena such as rainfall, tropical storms, flooding and so forth. Hence the need to determine *risk*, which is understood to be "a combination of the probability, or frequency, of occurrence of a defined hazard and the magnitude of the consequences of the occurrence" (Royal Society, 1992, p. 4).

A *natural disaster* is the occurrence of an extreme or infrequent hazard that impacts on vulnerable communities or geographical areas, causing substantial damage, disruption, perhaps casualties and leaving the affected communities unable to function normally. From an economic perspective, a disaster implies some combination of stock and flow *losses* in terms of human, physical and financial capital, and a reduction in economic activity, such as income and investment, consumption, production and employment in the 'real' economy. There may also be severe impacts in terms of financial flows, such as revenue and expenditure of public and private bodies (Benson & Clay, 1998). These stock and flow losses may be so extreme as to result in a modification in the medium to longer-term trajectory or development path of an enterprise, region or national economy as well.

Vulnerability is the potential to suffer harm or loss in terms of *sensitivity*, resilience or of the magnitude of the consequences of the potential event. Economic behavior is *sensitive to* a disaster shock. This impact is reflected at a macro or sectoral level in the deviation of economic aggregates from trends that were expected without taking into account the effects of this event. Because economic activity is sensitive to many influences, including other sources of shock, in practice it can be difficult to isolate precisely the impacts of a specific disaster or disasters. The primary objective of our studies has been to seek to isolate and understand these short-and long-term consequences of natural disasters. *Resilience* is the speed of recovery in economic activity, which may involve repair and replacement of lost and damaged capital.

The disaster management literature commonly distinguishes rapid on-set disasters, such as storm surges or earthquakes that cause immediate loss and disruption, and slow on-set events, notably drought. In our empirical investigations of economic consequences, we have found it useful to distinguish climatic hazards and related riverine and coastal hydrological hazards from geophysical hazards.

Climate-related hazards present threats of varying intensity that are usually recognized at a local or national level, and there is consequently some form of adaptation in terms of economic behavior and the technology in which capital – productive, housing and habitat or infrastructure – is embodied. The economic, and of course wider social, consequences of both individual events appear to be susceptible to investigation for most lower- and middle-income developing countries. In contrast, potentially catastrophic geophysical hazards including earthquakes, volcanic eruptions and tsunamis may be very rare in occurrence. Even in potentially high-risk geographical regions there may have been no extreme event in living memory or even within the historical record. Consequently, such hazards pose quite different problems of risk perception and economic behavior. However, a global phenomenon, satellite television and linked media information may also be changing that too.

Globalization is the process through which there is an increase in cross-border economic activities, in the form of international trade of goods and services, foreign direct investment (in turn, comprised of the financing of new investments, retained earnings of affiliates, and cross-border mergers and acquisitions), capital market flows and labor migration. It should be noted that greater globalization is not necessarily synonymous with a higher level of GDP, with increasing domestic or regional economic integration or with market liberalization, although these phenomena are commonly related.

2. BROADER IMPLICATIONS OF GLOBALIZATION FOR VULNERABILITY

2.1. International Trade

Reductions in trade barriers and transport and communications costs have resulted in a rapid growth in openness since the mid-1950s, with increasing trade in manufactures (involving more two-way trade) and a fragmentation of the production process (Martin, 2001). Developing countries typically liberalized initially to trade more slowly, with a number favoring import substitution policies instead, but since the mid-1980s developing countries have increasingly reduced barriers to trade too, often unilaterally rather than under the auspices of the World Trade Organization (WTO). Average tariff rates in developed countries are now low, although barriers remain in the two areas where developing countries have a comparative advantage: agriculture and labor-intensive manufactures (World Bank, 2002). In the case of agriculture, various exceptions have been made for export subsidy and domestic support prices schemes under successive General Agreement on Tariffs and Trade (GATT) negotiations, although negotiations are currently under way in the WTO on a new agreement on agriculture. Quotas have also remained on exports of textiles and clothing, discriminating by country. In response to such concerns, the WTO at its Doha Ministerial meeting in 2001 agreed to embark on a 'development round' of trade negotiations to be completed in 2006.

As a result of the broad process of liberalization as well as increased FDI (see the following 'External Trade' section) and a relatively high rate of accumulation of human and physical capital, many globalizing developing countries have shifted exports from agricultural to manufacturing products. In 1965, agricultural commodities accounted for about half of developing country exports and manufactures for only around 15 percent. By the late 1990s, around 80 percent of developing country exports were in the form of manufactured items, with agricultural products falling to around 10 percent by 1998 (Martin, 2001). Although there is considerable variation in the composition of exports between different developing countries with some remaining as primarily agricultural exporters, even many of these latter countries have experienced some growth in manufacturing exports. Exports of services from developing countries have also increased significantly.

Different productive activities are potentially differentially sensitive to natural hazards and, thus, any change in the composition of production could be significant in terms of the level and nature of risk. Natural hazard events may reduce the availability of particular goods and services for export (either directly or via disruptions to transport and communications networks) while simultaneously increasing imports, both to meet disaster-related domestic shortages and relief and rehabilitation requirements. Ramifications through the economy can be significant.

Depending on levels of foreign-exchange reserves and also government external borrowing policy, a deterioration in the balance of trade could result in an increase in external borrowing, with implications for future levels of debt servicing and, ultimately, economic growth. Any worsening of the balance-of-payments position could also exert pressure on the exchange rate and, thus, international competitiveness. There are also potential budgetary implications insofar as government revenue is derived from export and import duties and tariffs. Thus, it is important that a government is aware of the potential sensitivity of its various exports to natural hazards and the possible consequences of any changes in both relative and absolute composition. As liberalization encourages trade, it also encourages shifts in the composition of an economy, with implications for livelihoods, their relative security and ultimately household vulnerability to natural hazards, a theme explored in further detail below.

At first sight, diversification and the shift toward manufacturing exports would seem a positive development from natural hazards and balance of payments perspective. Renewable natural resource commodities (agriculture, forestry, fisheries) are often among the most directly affected by natural hazards. The sector is particularly susceptible to climatic hazards such as drought, excessive rainfall causing floods, and cyclones, although the extent and nature of impact depends partly on the timing of a hazard event relative to cropping cycles, as well as on the severity of the hazard itself. Moreover, it is often difficult to obtain insurance against crop losses. Natural hazards can also have indirect effects via their impact on agricultural equipment and infrastructure, such as drainage and irrigation systems, post-harvest and storage facilities and boats as well as on transport and marketing infrastructure more generally.

Primary commodity exports, including metals, minerals and oil as well as renewable natural resources, are also vulnerable to commodity price shocks. Few countries are price-setters in such markets and thus may experience coincidental contemporaneous fluctuations in international commodity prices, either offsetting or exacerbating balance of payments and inflationary impacts of disasters.

That said, there is evidence of the efforts that have sometimes been taken to dampen the impact of hazard-related falls in agricultural production. In Fiji, for instance, sugar reserves have been used to maintain export earnings and prevent loss of export markets in the aftermath of natural disasters (Benson, 1997a). There is probably less scope for using stockpiles of manufactured items to manage risk in this way. Shifts in technology and fashions make many manufactured items rapidly obsolete while modern management techniques often emphasize just-in-time production processes anyway. Moreover, most manufacturing production is in privately owned enterprises, with, by implication, little regard given to the stability of the broader external sector in undertaking production and export decisions. In contrast, stockpiling agricultural produce was often undertaken by public or quasi-public agencies, in part specifically to stabilize export earnings. Governments need to recognize this change and consider whether new ways of managing balance of payments risk – for example, encouraging international financial risk transfer mechanisms or maintaining increased foreign exchange reserves – are required.

The shift into manufacturing products also means that many developing countries are now competing against developed countries for markets. Thus, when disruptions to production occur – particularly, where just-in-time production practices are employed – contracts and future market shares may be lost. For example, the shift from agricultural to manufacturing exports and thus, at first sight, to an apparently less sensitive form of economic activity, may not in fact have reduced the potential vulnerability of Bangladesh's export earnings to natural hazards. Bangladesh faces severe global competition in the export of ready-made garments. In contrast, it was the world's primary jute producer and, as such, was a price setter on the international market. Disruption to the production of ready-made garments could result not only in the direct loss of export revenue but also in the longer-term loss of markets overseas.

The concept of vulnerability also entails potential to recover. Again, in some instances agriculture can offer certain advantages, as illustrated by banana cultivation in Dominica, but more generally manufacturing activities can often be restored faster. In the event of hazard-related damage, however, there is a possibility that a particular productive activity will not be re-established at all. Although there has been no research undertaken in this area, it is plausible that manufacturing activities, which are less geographically tied than agricultural ones, could simply be relocated elsewhere, with implied losses to the local economy and, where FDI is involved, to the national economy.

Despite these reservations, the broad shift in composition of exports experienced by many developing countries in recent years is, on balance, almost certainly a positive development from the perspective of sensitivity of exports to natural hazards. However, again from a natural hazards perspective, the fiscal implications of trade liberalization may be less beneficial, to the extent that liberalization reduces earnings from import duties. Revenue emanating from import duties is typically less sensitive to natural hazards. Import duties are also relatively easy to collect – an important point where a disaster results in administrative chaos and disruption. The precise implication of any reduction in import duties will depend on the precise structure of taxes in a country, including not only the significance of import duties but also the relative rates charged on different categories of imports (food, oil, inputs to industry, luxury items and so forth).

Finally, over the past two to three decades, growth in various service industries linked into the international economy has offered another form of risk diversification as illustrated by the case of Dominica (Benson & Clay, 2001). International financial services and tourism are probably the most significant in this regard. International financial services can be structured in such a way that performance is determined almost entirely by non-domestic factors. The growth of tourism also offers some opportunity to reduce an economy's overall sensitivity to natural hazards. However, efforts are required to ensure that the transport, communications and tourism infrastructure are hazard proofed. Tourists themselves also need to be adequately protected in the event of a disaster. It should also be borne in mind that demand is potentially highly sensitive to bad publicity. These are regionally and globally relatively footloose sectors and so investment may cluster in perceived low-risk locations.

2.2. Foreign Direct Investment

The globalization process has also involved increasing flows of FDI, as already noted, in part stimulated by a reduction in developing country restrictions on foreign investment (World Bank, 2002). The majority of FDI flows go from advanced industrial to advanced industrial countries. Advanced countries accounted for 85.3 percent of total FDI outflows between 1993 and 1997; and for 71.5 percent of FDI inflows over the period 1985–1997. However, the share of inflows to developing and transition economies is increasing, jumping from 21.8 percent in 1988–1992 to 39.8 percent in 1993–1997 (Shatz & Venables, 2000).

There are two basic forms of FDI: horizontal and vertical. Much of the intra-industrial country investment is horizontal but, relative to developed-country investment, much of the inflows to developing countries are vertical (Shatz & Venables, 2000). Both forms of FDI bring potential benefits in terms of increased supply of capital and access to technology, management expertise and markets. Each can also alter the nature of sensitivity of an economy to natural hazards.

Horizontal integration, under which a firm supplies a foreign market with its product by producing locally rather than importing, implies that domestic availability of a product may be reduced due to direct damage to the operating plant, potentially placing additional pressure on the balance of payments post-disaster. Domestic production, rather than import, of a particular item also changes the nature of demands on a country's transport network, maybe or maybe not to the firm's advantage post-disaster. Potential post-disaster slumps in an economy could also reduce demand for a particular item, perhaps with implications for demand for labor in the affected industry.

Vertical FDI involves shifting a stage of the production process to low-cost locations, on the basis of the fact that 'different parts of the production process have different input requirements and, since input prices vary across countries, it may be profitable to split production' (Shatz & Venables, 2000, p. 7). Vertical FDI offers the advantage that demand is not dependent on domestic economic circumstances and thus is immune to the consequences of any disaster-related slump, instead continuing to offer employment. However, it can be affected by temporary disruption to transportation and communications networks.

From a natural hazards perspective, both forms of FDI are also potentially significant in spreading risk, both from the perspective of individual producers, who can hold assets in more than one country, and from that of an economy, reducing relative levels of risk borne domestically. Such benefits of foreign ownership were apparent in the case of lime production in Dominica in the past. Large multinational producers involved in the production of primary commodities may be better placed to transfer risk by taking advantage of commodity futures (offering the opportunity to buy and sell forward or reserve the right to do so at a pre-agreed price) and reinsurance markets, by virtue of their greater knowledge and experience.

Foreign investors may also build factories and other buildings to company-wide building standards, which where they exist are often very high, reducing potential physical damage as a consequence of natural hazards. This is not always the case, however. In Bangladesh, for instance, inward investment in garment manufacture seeking low-cost sourcing that exploits potentially temporary tariff loopholes may be associated with low specification, poor safety designs in high-risk locations. In summary, globalization in the form of increased FDI flows will alter the nature of risk. The nature of this change will depend on individual circumstances but, on balance, in many cases probably plays a role in reducing broader economic sensitivity to natural hazards.

2.3. International Financial Markets

Financial globalization entails the integration of a country's local financial system with international financial markets and institutions. It involves an increase in cross-country capital movement, including the participation of local borrowers and lenders in international markets and widespread use of international financial intermediaries (in part via their presence, largely in the form of foreign banks, in local markets as well as use of those located overseas) (Schmukler & Zoido-Lobatón, 2001). The process of financial globalization has been significantly aided by gains in information technology, reducing the importance of geography, as well as by liberalization and privatization of public financial institutions in developing countries.

From a natural hazard perspective, such instruments offer certain advantages. First, firms and households may be able to smooth consumption and investment while meeting rehabilitation costs as they arise. International banking also enables individuals to hold funds with institutions better able to diversify risks. An extreme example of the need to diversify is the case of the Montserrat Building Society during a volcanic emergency.

> The volcanic eruption in Montserrat, which began in mid-1995, resulted in the displacement of 90 percent of residents from their homes, with over half eventually leaving the island. One of the financial casualties was the Montserrat Building Society (MBS), the country's only building society, which effectively collapsed. The MBS is largely dedicated to using savings to finance housing. The MBS estimated that prior to 1995 it had accounted for approximately 90 percent of mortgages on island as well as a high proportion of savings by residents and some non-resident migrants. However following an escalation of the crisis in August 1997, most insurance policies were suddenly cancelled by international companies that could easily give up business on an island that was a marginal part of their portfolio. The mortgaged assets held by the MBS immediately assumed a zero value, putting the Society into substantial deficit. Although the MBS remained open, following a temporary 3-week closure, depositors were initially only able to withdraw up to 35 percent of their savings while the Society remained in deficit. In early 1999, the MBS announced that savers could withdraw a further 35 percent of their savings. The contrasting behavior of international insurers and a local financial institution illustrates the ambiguities of globalization that can alter but not necessarily reduce disaster risks. (Clay et al., 1999)

Increasing international financial integration could also offer a future mechanism for the spread of risk by micro-finance institutions (MFIs). These provide financial services to the poor, extending credit and providing savings facilities. The loans they provide are typically very small, are mainly intended for productive purposes, do not require conventional forms of collateral and are extended on a non-profit-making basis. MFIs are highly vulnerable to natural hazards owing to temporary liquidity difficulties as they try to support clients through difficult periods, while also experiencing a temporary drop in flows of debt repayments. Some MFIs are therefore beginning to explore options for disaster insurance to protect themselves and enable them to respond to the additional disaster-related needs of their clients. To date, those MFIs that have established such schemes have

basically opted for self-insurance, setting some resources aside into a ca-
lamity fund for use in the event of an emergency. In the event of a disaster
seriously affecting a significant proportion of clients, however, such funds
would be grossly inadequate. The alternative – placing the risk externally –
would create additional overheads, making the cost of credit itself more
expensive. Instead, the solution could lie in some sort of international syndicate of MFIs. Good practice dictates that MFIs should not encourage a
culture of default and that, instead, borrowers should ultimately repay any
loans. Assuming this occurs and that default – as opposed to deferment –
rates are low (as evidenced in, for instance, Bangladesh and Dominica),
MFIs could benefit significantly from temporary access to additional resources to smooth fluctuations in demand relative to the availability of
funds. Such resources could be provided by other, unaffected, syndicate
members.

Globalization has also brought with it increasing possibilities for the use
of traditional and newer forms of financial risk transfer. More traditional
tools comprise insurance and reinsurance. Newer instruments, developed
over the past five years in response to dramatic increases in more traditional
ones, entail some form of hedging transaction in capital markets. Weather
derivatives involve automatic and immediate payouts (typically available
within 72 hours) upon the occurrence of a predetermined trigger event,
irrespective of the scale or nature of damage. Catastrophe bonds provide
attractive payments to investors but in the event of the specified catastrophe
event involve a reduction, and in some cases cancellation, of the principal
and/or interest on a bond.

The potential advantages of these various mechanisms include the alleviation of post-disaster pressure on fiscal and external balances; increased
government control over the financing of disasters, possibly including the
immediate and timely availability of funds; increased capacity for the relevant government to set its own priorities in the management of relief and
rehabilitation; increased transparency in the delivery of relief and reconstruction; and provision of a tool for promoting mitigation.

In developed countries, there are already well-established markets for
insurance against a wide range of natural hazards, including earthquakes,
volcanic eruptions, floods, droughts and cyclones. Newer hedging instruments are also gaining some popularity. However, insurance and capital
market instruments have played a relatively small role to date in the transfer
of risk in developing countries. Although there is thus scope for benefits of
greater financial integration to be reaped, there are also a number of practical obstacles that need to be overcome before coverage can be increased

significantly. There is a need to reform the structure and legal and regulatory framework of the insurance industry in a number of countries, including removal of barriers to entry. The cost of insurance also needs to be affordable and stable. At the same time, insurers need to remain sufficiently capitalized to bear any losses, in turn requiring detailed scientific information on current and future risks.

Despite the various potential benefits of financial integration from a natural hazard perspective, as discussed above, it should also be remembered that it carries other more general risks. Indeed, although the World Bank generally favors greater openness to trade and FDI because of its net beneficial implications for economic development and poverty reduction, it is "more cautious about liberalization of other financial or capital market flows" (World Bank, 2000, p. 2).

As Schmukler and Zoido-Lobatón (2001, p. 3) also observe, "international market imperfections, such as herding, panics and boom-bust cycles, and the fluctuating nature of capital flows can lead to crises and contagion, even in countries with good economic fundamentals." Banks and financial institutions can spread a crisis across countries, as demonstrated by the emerging-market crises in East Asia and elsewhere in 1997–1998. Natural hazards themselves could even trigger such crises. The city of Tokyo, for instance, lies in a seismically active area. It experienced a major earthquake in 1923 and volcanologists warn that another major event is 'long overdue.' As early as 1995, financial analysts were already forecasting that the next major Tokyo earthquake could result in bond and stock market crashes in the USA and a world recession as well as severe domestic economic difficulties (Hadfield, 1995). Thus there is clearly a need to balance risks from different sources and, where possible, to seek to reduce them. The World Bank (2002), for instance, calls for building up supportive domestic institutions and policies to reduce risks of financial crisis before becoming involved.

Finally, as with FDI, private capital does not flow to all countries equally. Indeed, the share of flows to low- and middle-income countries (excluding the top 12) has increased over time (Schmukler & Zoido-Lobatón, 2001), implying that many hazard-prone developing countries have yet to benefit from potential risk-spreading tools available via financial integration.

2.4. Labor Mobility

Increased labor mobility, the third aspect of globalization, allows affected people a radical and socially ambiguous way of coping with disasters.

Mobility provides a potential mechanism for spreading risk geographically via the transfer of remittances across borders. As the World Bank (2002, p. 11) states "geographic factors make it unlikely that capital flows and trade will eliminate the economic rationale for migration. Too many parts of the developing world have poor institutions and infrastructure that will not attract production; at the same time, some of the existing production networks in the North are too deeply rooted to move." Thus, labor mobility looks set to remain as a potentially significant way of reducing sensitivity to natural hazards. However, there are potential costs in terms of loss of skills to the economy.

In the case of Bangladesh, for instance, flows of external remittances provide a significant source of foreign exchange and have played an important role post-disaster. A relaxation of restrictions on out-migration, including professionals such as doctors in government hospitals and medical colleges, was one of the measures adopted in Bangladesh in response to the economic crisis associated with the 1974 floods and famine. Evidence from the 1998 flood again suggests that remittances can increase sharply during times of crisis, rising by 11.9 percent (in US dollar terms) year-on-year in 1998–1999 to US\$ 1.7 billion. Most migration is temporary, with migrants eventually expecting to return to Bangladesh (Ahmed & Chowdhury, 1998), implying that family ties are strong.

The implications of migration for broad sensitivity to natural hazards are extremely complex in sub-Saharan Africa, however, to the extent that migration is often to neighboring countries that may be simultaneously affected by drought, a problem of co-variant risk. In such circumstances, the impact is dependent upon the nature of employment of migrants – for instance, weather-sensitive agriculture or mining (a major source of migrant employment in certain southern African countries), which is relatively insensitive to water shortages.

2.5. Economic Growth

Many of those countries that have grown fastest in recent decades have also increased their participation in world trade most rapidly (e.g., Dollar & Kraay, 2000; Martin, 2001). Although the direction of causality is yet to be established, developing countries included in the latest round of globalization, begun in the early 1980s, are experiencing rapid rates of growth and catching up with more developed countries, mirroring patterns of convergence between OECD countries during earlier waves of globalization

(World Bank, 2002). This pattern basically reflects improved resource allocation, in part driven by increased competition as well as the removal of distorting tariffs and other barriers to trade that protect domestic production, and improved access to markets, with markets in turn expanding further as per capita incomes rise.

Economic growth is not necessarily synonymous with broader socioeconomic development, but higher per capita income countries also tend to be among those countries classified as more developed. Certain broad generalizations can, in turn, be made about the sensitivity of economies at different stages of development – as defined in terms of complexity of intersectoral linkages, levels of physical and human capital, the scale of secondary and tertiary sectors and so forth – to natural hazards.

In its earlier stages, development tends to alter, rather than reduce, vulnerability. Socioeconomic change associated with development can lead to the breakdown of traditional familial support, declines in traditional ways of life and associated coping measures and the increased occupation of more hazardous land, a process in part associated with urbanization. The increased provision of infrastructure and services can also alter, even increase, vulnerability. The attempt to foster rapid growth may be reflected in standards of construction unable to withstand extreme conditions. This appears to have happened in Dominica in the 20 years prior to independence. Similarly, private-sector investment in conditions of rapid technical and market change sacrifices safety and durability to short-term profitability. These are conditions in which there may be increased vulnerability to hazards, especially those regarded as extremely unlikely to occur.

At a macroeconomic level, greater domestic integration increases the multiplier effects of adverse performance in a particular sector or regional economy. For example, droughts, floods or hurricanes may impact the (larger) manufacturing as well as agricultural and livestock sectors, particularly where initial growth of the manufacturing sector is based primarily around agro-processing. A notable exception is dual economies with largely self-contained extractive sectors, which may be relatively insensitive at a macroeconomic level to climatic shocks. Examples are Botswana and Namibia.

As a country begins to develop, the structure of the financial sector is also likely to be more important in shaping the impact of a natural disaster. Intermediate economies typically have more developed economy-wide financial systems for the flow of funds, including small-scale private savings and transfers, which also diffuse impacts more widely. For example, in Zimbabwe following the 1991–1992 drought the transfer of remittances from urban to rural regions was facilitated by the well-articulated system for small savings. These transfers mitigated the impact of the drought in rural areas but also spread the effects more widely (Hicks, 1993).

In the later stages of development, evidence suggests that the relative scale of the economic impacts of disasters is likely to decline again. In part, this reflects the smaller role of the potentially particularly hazard-vulnerable agricultural sector in GDP, as a source of employment, a source of inputs to other sectors and an end-user. Other factors also contribute to reduced sensitivity, including typically higher investment in structural mitigation and proofing measures, higher building standards and maintenance practices more generally, greater use of financial risk transfer mechanisms (see 'FDI' section above), fewer foreign exchange constraints, improved environmental management and lower levels of poverty.

This framework for relating vulnerability to natural hazards to the growing complexity of the economy is a very broad brush with a variety of factors that also determines sensitivity. For example, prevailing domestic macroeconomic and sectoral policies, deliberate changes in policy resulting as a consequence of a disaster, the external policy environment, contemporaneous fluctuations in primary export and import prices, and the timing and nature of other adverse shocks can all be significant.

Nevertheless, the typology serves to remind that economic development and growth are not necessarily beneficial from a natural hazards perspective. Instead, natural hazards need to be taken into account in the determination of priorities, policies and strategies, including those relating to integration into the global economy.

2.6. Information Gathering and Exchange

Provision of various regional and global public goods – that is, goods and services that are non-rival in consumption (users do not reduce the supply available to others) and non-excludable (once provided then available to all) – can clearly benefit from improved transnational cooperation and integration. From the perspective of natural hazards, the greatest benefit has almost certainly been felt in the area of scientific monitoring and forecasting. This is most evident within meteorology and climatology (e.g. Lee & Davis, 1998; IRI, 2001).

There is a growth in regional and international cooperation in climatic forecasting for the three major climatic regions in sub-Saharan Africa, for instance. This cooperation links into and has been considerably strengthened by research and monitoring of global climatic processes such as the

El Niño Southern Oscillation phenomenon by international and industri-alized country institutions such as World Meteorological Office (WMO) and National Oceanic and Atmospheric Administration (NOAA), which have global monitoring networks and can draw on all the power of remote-sensing technologies.

Regional cooperation on water resources, which relies more directly on the political cooperation of upper-and lower-riperian states without global part-ners is less advanced. Disasters such as the devastating extreme floods in 2000 in both Mozambique and in southwestern Bangladesh have highlighted the considerable scope for progress on system modeling and flood forecast-ing. In both these cases, flows from outside the country contributed to the disaster, and these flows were influenced by the actions of public agencies responsible for water management. There were inadequate warnings to those responsible for flood response in the affected areas. A contributory factor was insufficiently precise understanding of system dynamics and links to exceptionally high rainfall (Akteer Hossain, 2001; Christie & Hanlon, 2001).

Another example of international cooperation is the global volcanology community. This is very close knit, with a small team of international ex-perts providing services around the world. The creation of this informal grouping has been greatly facilitated by improved communications and transportation. There are also major research benefits in the sense that the close cooperation has helped facilitate the building up a consolidated body of evidence from volcanoes around the world.

There are other areas where, from a natural hazard perspective, infor-mation gathering and exchange is also advantageous, such as in crop re-search, the development of building codes, the development of strategies to control pollution and the development of mechanisms for protecting the environment. For instance, in the case of the latter, as the World Bank (2002, p. 17) notes, "some environmental issues, such as global warming, are intrinsically global. They require international cooperation, and the habit of such cooperation is easier in an integrated world."

However, an emerging constraint as more information that could have important disaster reduction value is generated, is the capacity at country and regional levels to interpret and utilize these data. National meteoro-logical systems provided as a public good, for example, have to compete for recurrent expenditure with all other areas of public spending. In all the case studies undertaken by the authors, there was evidence of insufficient spend-ing. This was reflected, for instance, in inadequate operation and mainte-nance on monitoring systems. For example, there was underfunding of volcano-seismic monitoring in Dominica in 1998, at the outset of a volcanic emergency and no proper wave level monitoring even during Hurricane Lenny in 1999.

2.7. Poverty and Vulnerability

Poor and socially disadvantaged groups are usually the most vulnerable to and most affected by natural hazards, reflecting their social, cultural, economic and political environment. Disasters, in turn, are a source of transient hardship and distress and a factor contributing to persistent poverty. Indeed, at the household level, poverty is the single most important factor determining vulnerability, in part reflecting location of housing (e.g., on floodplains, riverbanks, steep slopes or contaminated land previously occupied by industrial facilities), primary types of occupation and level of access to financial and other resources. The poverty-exacerbating nature of vulnerability is attributable not only to post-disaster related damage, temporary loss of income-generating opportunities and increased indebtedness, but also to deliberate risk-averting livelihood choices that poorer households may make. For example, poorer households may choose to forego the potential benefits of higher yielding crops in favor of more hazard-tolerant ones, implying more stable and secure but, in most years, lower earnings.

The Government of Bangladesh, for instance, identifies natural hazards as one of the factors eroding the income of the poor via crisis-related expenditure and reductions in income earning capabilities. Furthermore, it recognizes that poverty alleviation cannot be achieved simply by increasing income, but instead requires a range of other measures, including the strengthening of local capacity to protect the poor against shocks (GoB, 2002).

Obviously, to the extent that globalization and related economic growth reduce poverty, they may help reduce vulnerability. Globalization tends to encourage growth and creates new job opportunities, potentially allowing people to move to better jobs. According to the World Bank (2002), in the long run, workers gain from integration, with wages growing twice as fast in the more globalized developing countries than in the less globalized ones and faster than in rich countries. However, a reduction in either poverty or vulnerability is not inevitable. Indeed, the World Bank (*ibid*, p. 1) states that although "global integration is already a powerful force for poverty reduction ... it could be even more effective." For example, skilled wages rise faster, implying that the education system needs to serve all levels of society in order to avoid increasing inequality.

In terms of vulnerability, economic growth and development may not solve problems of risk and vulnerability *per se*, as already noted. The declining importance of agriculture – potentially one of the most hazard-sensitive sectors – typically associated with globalization may reduce vulnerability, both directly and as those previously dependent on agriculture take advantage of increasing alternatives. Some 70 percent of the world's poor and food insecure people currently depend on agriculture for their incomes and food entitlements (FAO, 2001). Enhanced opportunities for diversification of household income can also help spread risk. However, traditional coping mechanisms may be simultaneously disrupted. Within the domestic economy, increased competition emanating from globalization can also imply increased entry and exit of firms, at least in the shorter term, implying greater labor market turnover. This can increase sensitivity to natural hazards and other shocks, requiring efforts to ensure that adequate social protection programs are in place. As the World Bank (2002) notes, social protection may also be crucial in encouraging poor people to take the risks involved in entrepreneurship. Those facing higher levels of risk, such as those emanating from natural hazards, may require particular encouragement and support in recasting behavior from that of risk minimization to profit maximization.

Globalization and associated growth in the manufacturing sector as well as cuts in agricultural tariffs also fuel urbanization. This process is often rapid and unplanned, by implication forcing poorer groups to live in more marginal and hazardous areas such as floodplains, riverbanks, steep slopes and reclaimed land (IFRC, 2002). Sensitive and carefully designed measures are required to help redress associated risks. However, Roberts, Buetre, and Jotzo (2002) also note that the rural non-farm sector has also been expanding and thus some labor released from farming may remain in rural areas.

2.8. Food Security

Food security is 'a situation that exists when all people, at all times, have physical, social and economic access to sufficient, safe and nutritious food that meets their dietary needs and food preferences for an active and healthy life' (FAO, 2002a).

This emphasis on people's access as the key to food security is a measure of the considerable progress made toward assuring food security at national and international levels that is partly a consequence of the liberalization of external trade and currency markets. Most, but not all developing countries are now able to acquire additional food imports to respond to temporary deficits. This is in stark contrast to the situation that prevailed in the early

1970s. For example, Bangladesh a low-income country with sometimes large, temporary additional import requirements was unable to finance food imports in the famine crisis of 1974 and was further hampered by a US embargo. Subsequently, its government responded to major disasters with a combination of massive commercial purchases and seeking, usually successfully, large-scale food aid. Finally, the private sector was allowed to cover a large part of the deficit after the floods in 1998. Small open economies, marginal to world and regional or global markets, such as Dominica, face logistical, but not access difficulties to food imports after a disaster. There are still important exceptions, countries such as Malawi, that have difficulty in financing and organizing national food security.

It is well recognized within the considerable body of literature on food security that natural hazard events, in particular droughts, are one of the principal triggers of potential transitory food insecurity for particular segments of a population. In that light, it is relevant to consider the implications of globalization, particularly agricultural trade liberalization, for sensitivity to chronic and transitory food security.

Historically, agriculture has represented a special case, with various exceptions made for domestic support price schemes under successive GATT negotiations, as already noted. However, under the present WTO Agreement on Agriculture, it was agreed that WTO member countries, other than least developed countries (LDCs), should reduce barriers to market access and market distorting forms of domestic support to agriculture. Developed countries have now implemented this agreement, while the implementation period for developing countries concluded in 2004. However, there are concerns that liberalization may not result in enhanced food security, as reflected, for instance, in "a common thread through many proposals by developing countries that staple food crops should be exempted from limits on, or reductions in, support under WTO arrangements" (Roberts et al., 2002, p. 40).

In theory, trade liberalization and associated movements in relative prices of different crops should trigger a supply response, with more rational allocation of resources. This may lead to an increase in aggregate agricultural production levels and net incomes. Such responses would be more likely to reduce chronic, poverty-related food insecurity. Furthermore, the supply response could be modified by various constraints relating to access to markets, agro-climatic factors and the level and availability of assets (including land), skills and credit. As the 2001 IFAD Rural Poverty Report (IFAD, 2001) states, "under globalization, market access becomes increasingly important as only those who have it can exploit the new opportunities.

Without market access, the potential benefits of higher product prices and lower input prices are not transmitted to poor households. Remoteness also restricts access to information about new technologies and changing prices, leaving the poor unable to respond to changes in incentives."

Moreover, even if agricultural production does increase, this does not necessarily imply an improvement in food security. Any shifts between food and non-food cash crops and between tradeables and non-tradeables could have implications for food security (FAO, 2002b). Some people may lose their livelihoods as part of the restructuring process associated with both agricultural and broader liberalization, again with potentially negative chronic food security and related poverty implications. Increased exposure to competition and world price fluctuations in countries where agricultural industries were previously protected from import competition could also expose some farmers to transitory food insecurity. Oxfam (2000), for example, asks whether small-scale farmers can compete in a liberalized environment and whether there is a need to retain some level of protection. Farmers in developing countries also typically have much more limited access to futures markets and other risk management tools (although globalization could help improve access – see section on FDI). In addition, many have few financial reserves. The two factors combined leave them more exposed to sudden price fluctuations under more liberalized conditions, potentially restricting their productive capacity the following season (Roberts et al., 2002).

Liberalization could cause increased short-run volatility in international grain markets posing difficulties for importing low-income countries. This possibility was highlighted by the severe price spike in international wheat and coarse grain markets during 1995–1996 when there was a rapid reduction in US and other stocks to low levels. Food aid levels also plummeted. They also coincided and were thought to be associated with the more liberal trade provisions of the 1995 US Farm Bill (Konandreas, Sharma, & Greenfield, 2000). These developments significantly increased, for example, the import costs for Southern African countries for coping with the 1994–1995 drought.

From the perspective of consumers, food security is to a large degree an issue of affordability, food insecurity is mainly associated with poverty and cheaper imports can be beneficial (Thompson, 1999). This is most unambiguously so for the rapidly growing numbers of poor urban consumers who are dependent almost entirely on market supply. If trade liberalization promotes economic growth and this, in turn, reduces levels of poverty then this, too, can improve food security, again by increasing access of the poor to food.

In summary, the impact of trade liberalization on food security has been broadly positive at a global level. But the short-term consequences of liberalization are less clear. Food security continues to be a highly country-specific issue, in part depending on the nature and scale of agriculture and the significance of the sector as a form of employment. There will be both winners and losers and impacts on food security are likely to vary between groups – for instance, between small-scale and commercial farmers and between farmers, rural non-farm producers and urban consumers.

In terms of implications for sensitivity to natural hazards, the impacts are, again, likely to vary between countries. From a consumer's perspective, increased access to world markets could dampen disaster-related food deficits resulting from reduced domestic production. To the extent that globalization more generally facilitates the spread of risk associated with a decline in production, it is also positive.

2.9. Environment

Finally, concerns have also been expressed about the impact of globalization on the environment. Environmental degradation, both via greenhouse gas emissions and physical destruction, has implications for the scale, frequency and extent of impact of natural hazards. There is clear evidence that a number of countries are becoming increasingly vulnerable to natural phenomena as a consequence of environmental degradation, particularly deforestation, and increased cultivation and occupation of marginal lands. Deforestation has disrupted watersheds, leading to more severe droughts and floods. It has also resulted in the siltation of riverbeds, deltas, bays and gulfs, again increasing the incidence of flooding. Meanwhile, impacts of changes in the composition of the atmosphere on the frequency and intensity of climatic hazards are predicted to vary significantly between regions and sub-regions, but there are expectations of more extreme weather variability, with associated increases in the incidence of droughts and floods, as well as sea level that rises in many parts of the world.

Globalization is widely considered to be a cause of environmental degradation. In discussing the impact of FDI more specifically, a recent WWF-UK report states that, "the past decade has ... seen all major trends of environmental degradation accelerate – for example, greenhouse gas emissions, deforestation, loss of biodiversity. Such patterns of environmental damage have been driven by increased economic activity, to which FDI is an increasingly significant contributor" (Mabey & McNally, 1998, p. 3). There is a counter argument that globalization does not necessarily directly exacerbate this process. Regarding deforestation, for instance, growth is often associated with reductions in forest area, most obviously where there is a timber export sector and land is being cleared for export-oriented production. However, the World Bank (2002) argues that particularly high rates of deforestation in some countries may not be the direct result of globalization so much as domestic factors. In discussing the more general argument that intensification of competition creates a potential for a 'race to the bottom' and 'pollution havens,' with governments perhaps trying to attain a competitive advantage by lowering their environmental standards, the World Bank (*ibid*) also argues that available evidence suggests that, in fact, this is not happening, the main reason apparently being that the costs imposed by environmental regulation are small relative to other considerations, and so their impact upon location decisions between rich and poor countries is minimal. The WWF-UK report refutes this, however, arguing that studies on which such statements are based 'have had serious flaws, and an excessive focus on site-specific environmental impacts and emissions of a few industrial pollutants' (Mabey & McNally, 1998, p. 3). The report continues on to present "ample empirical evidence that resource and pollution-intensive industries do have a locational preference for and an influence in creating, areas of low environmental standards" (*ibid*, 3).

3. DISASTERS AND THEIR IMPACT
ON GLOBALIZATION

As the World Bank (2002, p. 5) states

> while the new globalizers are beginning to catch up, much of the rest of the developing world – with about 2 billion people – is becoming marginalized. Their aggregate growth rate was actually negative in the 1990s. (World Bank, 2002, p. 5)

The direction of causality between high growth and increasing participation in world trade has yet to be established. Nevertheless, it is widely observed that these two phenomena are correlated. More open, export-orientated economies are also more successful in attracting FDI (see later discussion). Again, both affect the other, but empirical analysis by Singh and Jun (1995) suggests that, on balance, openness encourages FDI rather than vice versa. However, there are many factors, which may impact the rate of growth and participation in globalization. Natural hazards could be one of these factors, either preventing the growth benefits of globalization from being achieved or, depending on the direction of causality, preventing increasing integration into the global economy by restricting growth.

A research study undertaken by the International Institute for Applied Systems Analysis (IIASA), in conjunction with the World Bank confirms the potentially adverse long-term impact of natural disasters. The study sought to model the potential implications of natural disasters for future longer-term growth in three countries (Freeman, Martin, Mechler, & Warner, 2001). The analysis focused on their potential impact on capital accumulation and quantified the implications, in particular for growth objectives, of various policy options in dealing with disasters. The study concluded that potential catastrophes should be incorporated into economic projections for three reasons: High opportunity costs associated with the diversion of scare financial resources into post-disaster relief and reconstruction efforts; the havoc imposed by natural disasters on the already-complicated budgetary planning process; and the high demands that natural disasters place on international aid resources, diverting resources away from development uses.

There has been little empirical analysis of historical evidence on the impact of disasters on long-term growth however. Benson (2003) attempts to address this gap, examining comparative cross-sectional data on real GDP performance for 115 countries over a 34-year period from 1960 to 1993. The study involved regression analysis and an analysis of relative movements in GDP. Rather than attempting a ranking of countries according to natural hazard risk, countries were simply divided into two categories – higher and lower risk – based on evidence on the incidence of disasters over the period of analysis. Analysis was undertaken both including and excluding sub-Saharan African countries.

The results suggest that, over the past three decades, more hazard-prone low-income countries may have experienced a relatively slower rate of pace of economic growth than their less hazard-prone counterparts who had had similar levels of per capita income at the beginning of the period. However, there are fundamental problems in undertaking such analysis, in particular that less hazard-prone ones were already typically among the set of more developed countries by the latter half of the twentieth century. Thus, the results may simply reflect Quah's (1993) broader finding of polarization toward a bi-modal distribution, with countries beginning at the higher end of the income distribution likely to experience further increases in income. Moreover, a wide range of other factors also could determine rates of growth.

Nevertheless, the basic findings, if tentative, are supported by anecdotal evidence from individual countries, with poorer regions of a country also often more hazard prone. Charvériat (2000), for instance, notes that communities in the northeast part of Brazil and coastal areas of Ecuador and Peru are typically poorer than less hazard-prone parts of the same countries. In part, such patterns reflect differences in opportunities for growth and development as determined by the relative risks faced by different communities. For example, farmers in more hazard-prone regions of Vietnam have been less well placed to take advantage of higher-yielding but less hazard-tolerant strains of rice while more hazard-prone regions of the country have also received disproportionately small shares in private and public investment and external assistance (Benson, 1997b).

Disaster-related budgetary pressures can also affect a country's ability to participate in the global economy in other ways. In the aftermath of a disaster, a government will be obliged to meet potential budgetary pressures by increasing the money supply, drawing down foreign-exchange reserves or increasing levels of domestic and/or external borrowing. Foreign borrowing can result in an appreciation of the exchange rate, reducing the price of imports and increasing that of exports. In addition, it can place future strains on the economy via higher debt-servicing costs. External trade and foreign direct investment can also be affected by natural hazards (Benson & Clay, 2003, pp. 17–18).

4. A COUNTRY EXPERIENCE IN THE ERA OF GLOBALIZATION: MALAWI

4.1. Evidence of Increasing Vulnerability

The general discussion presented earlier indicates that the linkages between globalization and vulnerability to natural hazards are complex and no easily sustainable generalizations about impacts and effects can be made. Instead, the nature of the relationship is highly country specific. The following is a case study of Malawi, in Southern Africa. Parallel case studies of Bangladesh and Dominica in the Caribbean can be found in Benson and Clay (2004).

Since 1990, Malawi, as other countries in Southern Africa, seems to have experienced increased economic volatility that is linked with climatic variability (Fig. 1). This apparent increase in vulnerability has occurred during a period of many complex interacting developments in the region – some positive, such as the political reintegration of South Africa and the end to

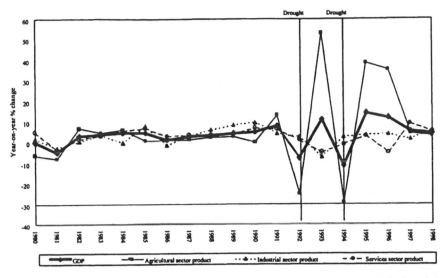

Fig. 1.   Malawi – Real Annual Fluctuations in GDP and Agricultural, Industrial and Services Sector Product, 1970–1998.

conflict in Mozambique, and others negative, such as the increasing problems of governance in Malawi, Zambia and Zimbabwe and the HIV/AIDS epidemic, which are undermining the capacity to cope with shocks. These developments are highlighted by what has happened in Malawi.

Malawi, small and landlocked, recorded a population of 10.8 million in 2000. It is one of the poorest countries in Africa, with per capita GDP of US$ 170 in 2000. Health and social indicators are also among the lowest and declining: average life expectancy fell from 43 in 1996 to 37 in 2000, and Malawi is one of the countries most severely affected by HIV/AIDS. The loss of human capital and ill health among the economically active population is likely making the country more disaster-prone.

Malawi still has a largely rural economy, with 89 percent of the economically active population classified as rural. Agriculture accounted for some 40 percent of GDP in 2000, compared with 44 percent in 1980. Its share in GDP was declining but rose again in the 1990s, with industrial stagnation and contraction in the public service sectors. Export earnings are dominated by agricultural commodities, largely rainfed tobacco, making the economy sensitive to climatic variability and commodity price shocks.

Although there has been internal liberalization and a reduction in tariffs, the Malawi economy has become relatively less open over time. Exports have declined as a proportion of GDP from 28 percent in 1980 to 24 percent in 2000. Imports fell from 43 percent to 40 percent.

The main source of natural hazard vulnerability in Malawi is climatic variability. The major food staple, rainfed maize, accounting for over 70 percent of energy intake, is extremely sensitive not only to drought or low rainfall, but to erratic rainfall within the growing season and, as the 2001 season showed, to abnormally high rainfall. There were only two clearly defined droughts in the twentieth century that satisfy the definition adopted by Dilley et al. (2005) in their global disaster risk analysis: The drought that caused a famine in 1949 and another that reduced maize production by 60 percent in 1991–1992. However, relatively unfavorable conditions such as the widely reduced and erratic rainfall of 1993–1994, extremely high rainfall as in 2001–2002 or locally erratic rainfall as in 2005 have posed increased food security threats and wider economic threats to a more vulnerable, less resilient economy.

Riverine flooding is an annual, relatively predictable hazard in lower population density southern districts. Even in 2001 flooding did not have a widespread, catastrophic impact. There are apparently no other significant forms of natural hazard.

4.2. Sources of Increasing Vulnerability

A variety of influences have interacted to make the Malawi economy and society increasingly sensitive to climatic variability, not just the extreme 'drought' events that are widely but simplistically perceived to impact on Southern Africa. These influences have included some relating to changes in the external economic environment.

Agricultural development has stalled. Demographic growth averaging 2.6 percent in the 1990s has placed increasing pressure on agricultural systems that are an adaptation of shifting cultivation. Declines in soil fertility on holdings of shrinking size are barely compensated for by increased fertilizer use and other technical improvements that could increase productivity. Liberalization of internal agricultural markets has been relatively unsuccessful. The private sector has been unable to take on and efficiently handle functions that were previously the responsibility of parastatals, especially the agricultural marketing agency, ADMARC.

Conflict in neighboring Mozambique and more recently the process of reintegration of South Africa into the regional polity and economy have contributed to the failure of industrialization or service sub-sectors such as tourism to provide alternative sources of economic growth and employment.

The relative de-industrialization of Malawi shows the need for caution in assuming that regional development will be consistent with broader global trends. The disruption to external communication because of the war in Mozambique from the late 1970s increased transport costs, reducing export parity and raising import parity prices. This favored low-input, self-provisioning rather than export-oriented agriculture, encouraging the development of small-scale manufacturing enterprises, although growth was checked by limited domestic demand. However, the more recent progressive reintegration of South Africa into the regional economy has exposed small-scale manufacture and processing of tradeables in Malawi and other 'front-line states' to a larger scale absolutely more efficient competitor. This adjustment effect amounts to de-industrialization, making the economy more exposed to agricultural sector volatility.

Malawi and some neighboring countries have been beset with problems of conflict, governance and weak public financial management. These have amplified difficulties caused by economic sensitivity to climatic variability. In 1991–1992 the economic effects of drought were intensified by the effects of an influx of displaced people from Mozambique and the halt of bilateral assistance other than emergency relief. In 1994, the effects of an agricultural sector shock were compounded by weak fiscal and monetary management in a hyper-inflationary situation. In 2000–2001 there was donor pressure to reduce parastatal debt by reducing grain stocks. Then, as the food security situation deteriorated after the 2001 harvest, there was donor reluctance to respond to aid requests from the government, which could not account for revenues from its grain marketing operations, including local currencies generated by the sale of aid commodities. It is debatable whether the food security crisis that emerged in Malawi during 2001–2002 should be categorized as the consequence of a natural hazard. Rather, climatic variability over two years within a range that had not previously been regarded as disastrously destabilizing contributed to a crisis in an economy made more vulnerable by structural changes and other developments that had reduced resilience at all levels. In 2005 Malawi again found itself beset with a severe food crisis triggered by variable rainfall rather than a full-blown drought (USAID, 2005).

5. CONCLUSIONS

The sensitivity of an economy to natural hazards is determined by a complex, dynamic set of developmental, economic and societal influences, including powerful external factors. The evidence presented in this paper suggests that increasing integration of economies around the world has significant implications for the nature of sensitivity to natural hazards. In particular, globalization has expanded opportunities for risk diversification and, for nations as a whole, it seems to be a generally positive trend. On the downside, however, globalization exposes countries to new forms of risk, possibly exacerbating the impact of natural hazards when different risk events coincide; whether globalization ultimately exacerbates or reduces sensitivity, both of particular economies and individual households, depends on specific country circumstances, including public action to reduce vulnerability.

This chapter draws upon a limited number of in-depth country studies. As such, its findings should be considered as hypotheses for wider testing. Nevertheless, it is striking to note that most of the findings confirm and elaborate conclusions and policy presumptions in the wider globalization literature, which focuses on market-related and financial risks rather than natural hazards.

The country studies also suggest that different types of natural hazard risk have a distinctive economic dynamic. Developing countries responding more successfully to the opportunities and challenges of globalization are showing some reduction in relative sensitivity (measured as a proportion of GDP or sector product) to more predictable, often relatively frequent, climatic hazards such as tropical cyclones in Dominica and extreme riverine flooding in Bangladesh. An important qualification to such trends is the highly uncertain implication of global climatic change for the frequency and severity of natural hazards.

In contrast, the exposure to geophysical hazards appears to be rising. Rapid urbanization – a process often associated with globalization – creates large concentrations of people and physical capital, mostly built with little regard for natural hazards either in choice of location or design. These geophysical hazards typically have relatively low but difficult to determine risks, less than 1 percent annually for extreme earthquake in Bangladesh or a disastrous volcanic event in Dominica. Globally, such increasing hazard exposure implies rising disaster-related losses.

The most worrying position is that of countries and even regions, such as Southern Africa, that are apparently being marginalized in the process of globalization and becoming increasingly vulnerable to natural hazards. Natural hazards may well be at least indirect compounding factors limiting opportunities and potential for globalization for some of these economies, although the precise nature of their role is complicated and, again, often highly country specific.

For those countries that are becoming more closely integrated into the global economy, risks emanating from all types of natural hazards should be considered in assessing the impacts of reductions in trade barriers and related changes in the composition of economic activity, security of livelihoods and measures taken to help protect vulnerable groups. More broadly, risks emanating from natural hazards should be taken into account in the determination of priorities, policies and strategies, with enhancement of resilience to natural hazards one of the basic objectives of government in hazard-prone countries. Opportunities for using global markets to improve risk management should also be exploited, including via insurance and other financial risk transfer mechanisms.

REFERENCES

Ahmed, K. U., & Chowdhury, H. U. (1998). The impact of migrant workers: Remittances on Bangladesh economy. *Indian Journal of Economics, 78*(311), April.

Akhter Hossain, A. N. H. (2001). Late monsoon flood in the Southwest region of Bangladesh 2000. *Engineering News*, p. 42, Dhaka.

Benson, C. (1997a). *The economic impacts of natural disasters in Fiji.* ODI Working Paper no. 97. Overseas Development Institute, London, March.

Benson, C. (1997b). *The economic impacts of natural disasters in Vietnam.* ODI Working Paper no. 98. Overseas Development Institute, London, June.

Benson, C. (1997c). *The economic impacts of natural disasters in the Philippines.* ODI Working Paper no. 99. Overseas Development Institute, London, June.

Benson, C. (1998). Drought and the Zimbabwe economy, 1980–1993. In: H. O'Neill & J. Toye (Eds), *A world without famine?* London: MacMillan.

Benson, C. (2003). *The economy-wide impact of natural disasters in developing countries.* Doctoral thesis, University of London, London.

Benson, C., & Clay, E. J. (1998). *The impact of drought on sub-Saharan African economies: A preliminary examination.* World Bank technical paper 401. World Bank, Washington, DC.

Benson, C., & Clay, E. J. (2001). *Dominica: Natural disasters and economic development in a small island state.* Disaster risk management Working Papers series no.2. World Bank, Washington, DC. Available from www.proventionconsortium.org/files/dominica.pdf

Benson, C., & Clay, E. J. (2002). *Bangladesh: Disasters and public finance. Economic and financial impacts of natural disasters: An assessment of their effects and options for mitigation.* Disaster Risk Management Series 5. World Bank, Washington, DC. Available from www.proventionconsortium.org./files/Bangladesh.pdf

Benson, C., & Clay, E. J. (2003). Disasters, vulnerability and the global economy. In: A. Kreimer, M. Arnold & A. Carlin. *Building safer cities: The future of disaster risk. Disaster risk management series 3.* Washington, DC: World Bank.

Benson, C., & Clay, E. J. (2004). *Understanding the economic and financial impacts of natural disasters. Disaster risk management series 4.* Washington, DC: World Bank.

Charvériat, C. (2000). *Natural disasters in Latin America and the Caribbean: An overview of risk.* Research department Working Paper no. 434. Inter-American Development Bank, Washington, DC, October.

Clay, E. J., Bohn, L., Blanco de Armas, E., Kabambe, S., & Tchale, H. (2002). *Climatic variability, economic performance and the uses of climatic forecasting in Malawi and Southern Africa. Economic and financial impacts of natural disasters: an assessment of their effects and options for mitigation.* Disaster Risk Management, Working Paper No. 7, World Bank, Washington, DC. Available from www.Proventionconsortium.org/files/

Clay, E. J., Borrow, C., Benson, C., Dempster, J., Kokelaar, P., Pillai, N., & Seaman, J. (1999). *An evaluation of HMG's response to the Montserrat volcanic emergency.* 2 Vols. Evaluation report EV635. Department for International Development, London.

Christie, F., & Hanlon, J. (2001). *Mozambique & the great flood of 2000. African issues.* Oxford: James Currey Publishers.

Dilley, M., Chen, R. S., Deichmann, U., Lerner-Lam, A. L., Arnold, M., Agwe, J., Buys, P., Kjekstad, O., Lyon, B., & Yetman, G. (2005). *Natural disaster hotspots: A global risk analysis.* Washington, DC: World Bank & Columbia University.

Dollar, D., & Kraay, A. (2000). *Growth is good for the poor.* Washington, DC: World Bank.

Food and Agriculture Organization (FAO) (2001). *Some issues relating to food security in the context of the WTO negotiations on agriculture. In food security in the context of the WTO negotiations on agriculture.* Geneva: Palais des Nations.

Food and Agriculture Organization (FAO) (2002a). *The state of food insecurity in the world 2001.* Rome.

Food and Agriculture Organization (FAO) (2002b). *Trade and food security: Lessons of the past 20 years. Analytical issues and framework.* Draft, Rome. ESCP, Commodities and Trade Division.

Freeman, P. K., Martin, L. A. Mechler R., & Warner, K. (2001). *Catastrophes and development: Integrating natural catastrophes into development planning: Draft.* Luxenburg: International Institute for Applied Systems Analysis, August.

Government of Bangladesh (GoB) (2002). *Bangladesh: A national strategy for economic growth and poverty reduction.* Dhaka: Economic Relations Division, Ministry of Finance.

Hadfield, P. (1995). *Sixty seconds that will change the world: How the coming Tokyo earthquake will wreak worldwide economic devastation* (2nd ed.). London: Pan Books.

Hicks, D. (1993). *An evaluation of the Zimbabwe Drought Relief Programme 1992/1993: The roles of household level response and decentralized decision making.* Harare: World Food Programme.

International Federation of the Red Cross (IFRC) (2002). World disasters report 2002: Focus on reducing risk. International Federation of the Red Cross, Geneva.

International Fund for Agricultural Development (IFAD) (2001). *Rural poverty report 2001: The challenge of ending rural poverty.* Oxford: Oxford University Press.

International Research Institute (IRI) (2001). *Coping with the climate: A way forward.* Preparatory report and full workshop report. A multi-stakeholder review of Regional Climate Outlook Forums, concluded at an international workshop, October 16–20, 2000, Pretoria, South Africa. IRI-CW/01/1. Palisades, NY: International Research Institute for Climate Prediction.

Konandreas, P., Sharma, R., & Greenfield, J. (2000). The Uruguay round, the Marrakesh decision and the role of food aid. In: E. Clay & O. Stokke (Eds), *Food and human security.* London: F Cass.

Lee, B., & Davis, I. (1998). *Forecasts and warnings: Programme overview. UK National coordination committee for the IDNDR.* London: Thomas Telford.

Mabey, N., & McNally, R. (1998). Foreign direct investment and the environment: From pollution havens to sustainable development, July. Godalming, Surrey: WWF-UK.

Martin, W. (2001). *Trade policies, developing countries, and globalization*. Development Research Group, October, Washington, DC: The World Bank.

Munich Re (1999). *A year, a century, and a millennium of natural catastrophes are all nearing their end*. Press release of 20 December. Munich: Munich Re.

Overseas Development Institute (ODI) (2005). *Aftershocks: Natural disaster risk and economic development policy*. ODI Briefing Paper, London, November.

Oxfam (2000). *Agricultural trade and the livelihoods of small farmers*. Oxford: Policy Department.

Quah, D. (1993). Empirical cross-section dynamics in economic growth. *European Economic Review, 37*, 426–434.

Roberts, I., Buetre B., & Jotzo, F. (2002). *Agricultural trade reform in the WTO: Special treatment for developing countries*. Abereconomics, September.

Royal Society (1992). *Risk: Analysis, perception and management*. London: Royal Society.

Schmukler, S. L., & Zoido-Lobatón, P. (2001). Financial globalization: Opportunities and challenges for developing countries, May. Washington, DC.: The World Bank. Available from http://www.worldbank.org/research/bios/schmucklerpdfs/Financial%20Globalization-Schmukler&Zoido-May30.pdf

Shatz, H. J., & Venables, A. J. (2000). The geography of international investment. In: G. L. Clark, M. Feldman & M. S. Gertler (Eds), *The oxford handbook of economic geography* (pp. 125–145). Oxford: Oxford University Press.

Singh, H., & Jun, K. W. (1995). *Some new evidence on determinants of foreign direct investment in developing countries*. Policy Research Working Paper 1531. The World Bank, International Economics Department, Washington, DC.

Thompson, R. L. (1999). Rural development: Challenges in the next century. Presentation prepared for the Latin American and Caribbean association of Agricultural economics, Port-of-Spain, Trinidad and Tobago, June 30–July 2. The World Bank, Rural Development Department. Washington, DC.

United States Agency for International Development (USAID) (2005). *Southern Africa: An evidence base for understanding the current food security crisis*. Available from www.fews.net/, last visited October 7, 2005.

World Bank. (2000). *What is globalization?* World Bank briefing paper. Washington, DC: PREM Economic Policy Group and Development Economics Group, The World Bank, April. Available from http://www1.worldbank.org/economicpolicy/globalization/ag01.html

World Bank (2002). *Globalization, growth and poverty: Building an inclusive world economy*. World Bank Policy Research Report, The World Bank and Oxford University Press, Washington, DC and Oxford.

DISASTERS AND ENTREPRENEURSHIP: A SHORT REVIEW

Craig S. Galbraith and Curt H. Stiles

1. INTRODUCTION

It is well recognized that disasters, whether naturally occurring or the result of human invention, affect a region on many levels. Not only are disasters felt within the painful context of human tragedy, loss of life, and physical suffering, but disasters can also destroy the immediate socio-economic fabric of the affected population as well as the ability of a region to sustain itself during the slow process of recovery and reconstruction. As Newton (1997) notes, "disasters are not isolated from the social structure within which they occur; rather, they are social phenomena" (p. 219).

Within the last decade alone, the world has seen a myriad of both natural and human-created disasters. The most publicized of the natural disasters include the tsunami disaster of December 26, 2004 that destroyed broad populated areas around the Indian Ocean, killing an estimated 310,000 individuals with the majority in the Aceh province in Sumatra, Indonesia; the 2005 Kashmir earthquake in Pakistan with a death toll estimated around 100,000, and the series of hurricanes striking the Gulf States of the U.S. in 2005 killing over 1,000 people and causing extensive damage with estimates as high as $200 billion.

Developmental Entrepreneurship: Adversity, Risk, and Isolation
International Research in the Business Disciplines, Volume 5, 147–166
Copyright © 2006 by Elsevier Ltd.
All rights of reproduction in any form reserved
ISSN: 1074-7877/doi:10.1016/S1074-7877(06)05008-2

In all of these disasters, whole communities and towns were completely obliterated or severely damaged. Other devastating disasters are less well known, even within the same time frame. For example, a 1998 tsunami drowned over 2,500 people in Papau New Guinea, the 1999 Izmit earthquake in Turkey took over 17,000 lives, and over 15,000 people died in the 1999 mudslides and flooding in Venezuela. In just the last 40 years, even worse disasters have been recorded, such as the Bhola cyclone in Bangladesh in 1970, the deadly famines in North Korea and Africa during the 1980s and 1990s, and the AIDS crises in sub-Saharan Africa where the cost of human suffering is almost immeasurable. Human-caused disasters, such as war, genocide, terrorism, fire accidents, mine explosions, and toxic chemical releases have also taken a severe toll on humanity during the last century.

In fact, statistics have shown that the reported global cost of natural disasters have jumped dramatically in the past couple of decades with recovery from some natural disasters now taking significant portions of a county's gross domestic product (Benson & Clay, 2004). During the 1980s, for example, it was estimated that approximately 147 million people were affected annually by disasters. During the decade of the 1990s this increased to approximately 211 million people per year (Van de Veen & Logtmeijer, 2005).

Inevitably, after a disaster the survivors begin to rebuild, not only on a personal level, but also structurally and economically. In general, at least in modern times, part of this rebuilding process has been assisted by a combination of humanitarian foreign and domestic relief aid. In fact, humanitarian relief aid has become an important part of the political landscape for most of the world's developed countries.

For example in the year 2003, prior to the Indian Ocean tsunami, the U.S. was the world's largest provider of humanitarian relief aid of almost $2.5 billion of government aid. On a per capita basis, the U.S. was ranked 9th in the world for direct government supported humanitarian relief aid at approximately 2.34 cents per day per person. France held the 10th place, Canada 11th place, and Germany 17th place (Development Assistance Committee, Paris, 2004). However, once private donations were included, the U.S. jumped to 3rd in the world in humanitarian aid on a per capita basis, with Norway and Sweden holding the top two spots. In addition, some countries, such as the U.S. and Australia, provide millions of dollars of direct humanitarian and relief assistance through its military, such as the large and quick response by these two countries' navies during the 2004 Indian Ocean tsunami, dollars that are not included in the official U.N. and OECD reports.[1]

Yet in spite of the tremendous effort placed by the world governments on post-disaster recovery, from an empirical point of view, the actual impact and proper focus of post-disaster recovery strategies remains somewhat unascertained. While there are certainly many dimensions that need to be considered in understanding the relationship between disasters, economic recovery, and the broader socio-political context, this paper attempts to focus on only a narrow slice of the "disaster" literature – that related to small business and the relationship between post-disaster recovery strategies and entrepreneurial efforts. Within this context, we review several streams of research.

2. DISASTERS AND THE ENTREPRENEURIAL ECONOMY

This review will focus primarily on natural disasters, but will when appropriate, also mention ideas related to human caused disasters and/or more chronic continuing disasters.

A natural disaster is commonly defined as the "impact of an extreme natural event on an exposed, vulnerable society. If impacts exceed an affected region's coping capacity thereby necessitating interregional or international help, a large disaster is said to have occurred" (Mechler, 2003, p. 10). As stated above, disaster recovery strategies are an important part of both international and domestic policy. In an early paper, Tierney (1993) defined disaster recovery as

> Longer-term efforts to (1) reconstruct and restore the disaster-stricken area, e.g, through repairing or replacing homes, businesses, public works, and other structures; (2) deal with the disruption that the disaster has caused in community life and meet the recovery-related needs of victims; and (3) mitigate future hazards (pp. 1–2).

2.1. Relief Agencies and Entrepreneurial Assistance

More and more, relief aid agencies appear to be recognizing the importance of economic recovery and rebuilding. Increasingly programs are being developed that encourage entrepreneurial activities as part of the overall recovery strategy. For example, immediately following the Indian Ocean tsunami disaster, the U.S. Agency for International Development (USAID), the principal U.S. agency responsible for disaster recovery assistance, developed a five-component reconstruction plan. The five components included direct relief, transition from "Camps to Communities," infrastructure, early warning systems, and technical assistance. Of these, the "Camps to Communities" component most directly addressed the nature of economic recovery. It included three activity areas: permanent shelter and housing programs, credit and other livelihood programs, and funding for continuing assistance, including cash-for-work programs.

The direct strategies of this program were specifically designed to facilitate the transition from temporary camps to more permanent, economically stable communities within the post-disaster environment (USAID, 2005b).

Specifically for the tsunami-impacted areas, these "livelihood activities" focused on fisheries, agribusiness, and the construction trades. It is interesting to note that the programs targeted micro-enterprise development and vocational training. In the words of the USAID,

> Many of the worst affected communities in the affected countries depended on fisheries for the bulk of their income and family consumption. In other places such as Sri Lanka and Thailand, the populations derived their income from tourism-related employment. Farmers in India have lost crops and livestock and seen their fields covered by sand and salt water. To restart the local economy of all these areas, USAID will extend cash-for-work programs begun under the relief phase and provide grants, vouchers, and credit to assist firms in replacing assets and re-establishing their businesses.

> The U.S. Peace Corps will use former volunteers, mobilized through the "Crisis Corps," to assist in re-establishing fisheries and businesses in Thailand and to support reconstruction efforts in Sri Lanka.

> USAID will support construction-related trades-people as well as provide assistance in community planning and construction site selection and preparation expertise.

> Economic recovery programs implemented through local NGOs and community-based organizations will address tsunami recovery needs and support reconciliation. (USAID, 2005a)

But while economic recovery, and perhaps the role of entrepreneurial behavior, appears to be recognized as an important component of post-disaster response in official reports, there is certainly anecdotal evidence that it still often plays a secondary role in both chronic on-going disaster intervention policies and post-natural disaster recovery strategies.

For example, it is well recognized that the economic development and reconstruction component in the immediate 2003 post-invasion period in Iraq appeared sorely lacking. As Iraq appeared to slip deeper and deeper into an uncontrolled economic and violent spiral, General Jay Garner the U.S. official in charge of the post-war recovery was fired about a month after the occupation period started. He was subsequently replaced by Paul Bremer, who also took substantial criticism for the lack of post-war economic recovery and developmental planning during the occupation.

Even in well-profiled, large disaster situations, economic programs that would appear to be critically important immediately after a disaster are often only slowly or partially implemented. For example, an "investor roadmap, the guiding tool for reforms that would promote foreign direct investment," only became available in August, 2005, over two years after Baghdad fell in April, 2003 (Kunder, 2005).

Similarly, when examining the aid and intervention strategies for disaster recovery in less-developed countries, entrepreneurial issues are only loosely addressed, if at all, within the context of more pressing aid. As Pain (2002) notes, "aid practice has been driven by simplified stories about the country reinforced through short-term humanitarian based programming that has emphasized delivery and paid little attention to learning. The result has been a monotonous landscape of interventions" (p. i).

Like the international aid literature discussed above there also appears to be a recognition regarding the general role that local small business plays in economic and social recovery after a natural disaster within developed countries (e.g., Natural Hazards Center, 2006). Newton (1997), for example, reviews the Federal disaster mitigation strategies in both the U.S. and Canada, finding that the U.S. strategies tend to be more targeted, with disaster assistance coming in the form of federal loans and grants to small business. Although it is well recognized that post-disaster economic development projects should be designed to stimulate economic growth in the post-disaster environment (see, for example, Aguirre International, 1996; Childers & Phillips, 1998; Federal Emergency Management Agency, 1997; Wachtendorf, Connell, & Tierney, 2002), and much of the professional work on disaster planning and mitigation discusses the importance of direct loans and grants to small business (e.g., Freestone & Rabb, 1998), there appears to be little comprehensive understanding as to the exact role that local entrepreneurial activity plays within the recovery effort, or in which stages small business recovery occurs.

We suggest that perhaps one reason why entrepreneurial activities appear to take a secondary role in many of the modern recovery plans, relief aid programs, and governmental efforts in a post-disaster environment is due to the general lack of research, or empirical assessment, regarding the relationships between disasters and entrepreneurial activities.

2.2. Economic Impact of Disasters: Country-Wide Studies

Economic theory suggests that governments can manage the risk of natural disasters by risk pooling within the country, at least within a somewhat efficient market argument. However, less developed or smaller countries are generally unable to assume or finance this risk, and thus must rely upon donor countries and humanitarian aid for assistance. Most of the published research tends to be somewhat theoretical in nature. Within the past decade, however, there has been an increasing amount of empirical research that attempts to examine the broad economic impact of disasters, with recognition that the economic impact of disasters includes both direct and indirect components (Otero & Marti, 1995; Mechler, 2003).

In a series of comprehensive country case analyses of the economic impact of disasters, Benson and Clay (2004) argue that major natural disasters have not only a short-run economic impact but also an increasing adverse long-term effect. It is argued that this is partly caused by the increased vulnerability and risk associated with the interrelationship and complexity of economic, political, technological, and financial components from globalization and urbanization. Freeman, Martin, Mechler, and Warner (2004) examined the impact of natural disasters on several countries, concluding that negative long-term economic effects were evident. They then developed a model of predicting economic losses based upon the indirect effects of losing capital stocks, not being able to replace these capital stocks in a timely manner, and the impacts of moving funds to relief activities. Benson (2003) performed a cross-sectional study of 115 countries from 1960 to 1993 and found that countries that had a higher number of natural disasters tended to have lower long-term economic growth.

Mechler (2003) using a simulation model examined and compared the economic impacts of natural disasters using two case examples, Honduras and Argentina, finding that disasters can have substantial impacts on GDP. Most research, in fact, has documented both short- and medium-term (three to five years) negative effects. Charveriat (2000), for example, examined 35 catastrophes in Latin America and found significant short-term GDP declines and increased debt. Crowards (2000) examined 22 hurricane events in the Caribbean and Auffret (2003) examined 16 natural disasters; both reported similar results. Other studies have also documented negative long-term impacts (i.e., Otero & Marti, 1995; Murlidharan & Shah, 2001; ECLAC, 2000).

Overall these studies of developing countries indicate that major rapid onset disasters, such as hurricanes and flooding, have the following impacts on the country's macro-economy: (a) they usually have an immediate negative impact on GDP in the short term; (b) due to increased investment and transfers, GDP may subsequent rise in following years; (c) a worsening of trade balances often occurs, continuing into the long term; and (d) country debt often increases and fiscal balances may continue to deteriorate.

The long-term effects then become a function of the magnitude and enduring nature of the disaster, the degree of resulting trade imbalances and increased debt obligation, and other economic and social conditions. It is interesting to note, however, that while these macro-economic impact studies use both capital and labor stocks as explanatory variables, few, if any, include social/human capital or entrepreneurial tendencies and statistics such as those presented in the GEM database (e.g., Crowards & Coulter, 1999; ECLAC, 2002; Rasmussen, 2004).

2.3. Economic Impact of Disasters: Developed Country Regional Studies

A number of similar empirical studies regarding macro-economic impacts in economically developed countries have also been published; however, most of these address inter-regional economic impacts often with essentially the same results (e.g, Jones & Chang, 1995). It is recognized that, since these economies can generally manage the risk internally, the overall long-term impact of a disaster is generally less within developed countries. However greater attention is currently being placed on the "unevenness" of impacts in developed countries. For example, Van de Veen and Logtmeijer (2005) develop a model examining more indirect economic impacts of natural disasters based upon the notion of "economic hot-spots" within an economy that are particularly vulnerable to disasters (e.g., Van de Veen & Logtmeijer, 2005).

This issue of unevenness of impacts can also be seen within both developed and undeveloped environments. From a socio-economic perspective, it is generally accepted that natural hazards present an even greater, if not the primary source of risk for poor countries, and for poor areas within even more developed countries (Freeman, 2000; World Bank, 2002; Rasmussen, 2004). The World Development Report 2000/2001 (World Bank, 2000) argues that the "effects of natural disasters (are) an important dimension of poverty. Low-income families typically live on marginal land, in the informal sector and have few, if any, resources with which to protect them selves."

Another stream of mostly sociological research has also examined the vulnerability and recovery potential of lower socio-economic groups within developed countries. For example, Fothergill and Peek (2004) review a number of studies that examine the vulnerability of poor people to natural disasters within the U.S., concluding that poor in the U.S. are more vulnerable to natural disasters due to such factors as place and type of residence, access to economic recovery strategies, building construction, and social exclusion.

However, in spite of a well-developed literature on both the macro-economic and socio-economic impact from disasters, the vast majority of this literature tends to ignore entrepreneurial and small business activities as they related to disaster vulnerability, speed of recovery (typically the first year after a disaster), and breadth of reconstruction.

2.4. Livelihood Analysis and Food Economies: Slow Onset Disasters

While the focus of this short review is primarily on natural disasters, the literature examining the impact and recovery of other types of disasters can also provide a useful background. For example, the literature of disaster management tends to distinguish between two different types of disasters, those that arrive suddenly with little warning, such as hurricanes or earth-quakes (rapid onset), and those that are more gradual in nature, such as starvation from crop failure (slow onset).

There are various types of slow onset disasters. One of the most common is drought and the associated crop failures. Another type of slow onset disaster has been described as situations of chronic conflict and political instability (SCCPI). Characteristics of SCCPI include a strong parallel economy, high incidences of violence, forced displacement, poverty, very weak institutions, and economies that are highly vulnerable to shocks (Schafer, 2002). Unlike disasters that have one particular event, such as a tsunami, a slow onset disaster environment represents one of continuous change.

One increasingly common analytical framework for examining potential intervention strategies in disaster situations, particularly slow onset disasters in chronically impoverished economies, has been labeled a "food economy analytical framework." This framework starts from the concept of a "live-lihood analysis." Livelihood analysis is a well-established methodology which models both the required assets and use patterns of these assets to understand how people survive (Carney et al., 1999; Longley & Maxwell, 2003; Farrington et al., 2002).

The food economy analysis expands on this by "linking livelihood ana-lysis to an analysis of the effects of change" (Boudreau & Coutts, 2002, p. 1), by modeling the economic components and trading boundaries of the com-plete food chain, including both cash and barter markets, within an eco-nomy. It can be used not only to examine the underlying economic changes in slow onset disasters but also to provide an early warning system for slow onset disasters as well as developing baselines to analyze the impact of recovery policies. During the past decade, a food economy analysis has been used extensively to examine the economic impacts of various types of crop failure economies, SCCPI, sub-national conflicts, and conflict recovery.

The basic livelihood approaches to understanding disasters, whether chronic or rapid onset in nature, has as a fundamental intervention strategy to assist households in expanding a household productive asset base with the longer-term object of avoiding future basic aid requirements (Lautze, 1997; Wood & Salway, 2000; Longley & Maxwell, 2003). While there are different approaches to livelihood analysis, many of the actual policies and interventions developed under the livelihood perspective recognize the need to re-establish pre-existing small business economic transactions by developing strategies to lower the ultimate transaction cost of recovery (Carney et al., 1999). These intervention strategies, however, are often communal economic efforts, such as a small town communally assisting in repairing individual fisherman nets. This may be due to the lack of institutional oversight, risk management strategies, and insurance markets in these chronic disaster environments. Another common approach is to address the "dependency" syndrome by developing analytical skills for self-reliance, a strategy that often results in training in specific job and productive skills, but little or no education in entrepreneurial functions.

Assessing the effectiveness of these livelihood interventions, particularly as they relate to small business development or increased entrepreneurial activity, is difficult at best. Most assessment studies are small case studies of specifically targeted programs and pilot studies, but the opinion to date suggests that a sustainable livelihood approach of interventions does appear to assist development within chronic disaster situations (e.g., Booth et al., 2006; Ashley, 2005; Archibald & Richards, 1999, 2002; Ashley & Carney, 1999).

While certainly dominant in the many sectors of disaster aid proactive, livelihood analysis, while focusing specifically on enhancing household livelihood, very rarely examines the broader context of entrepreneurial behavior or the foundations, such as institutions, property rights, intellectual capital, and social networks, that appear to stimulate entrepreneurial economies. For example, Longley and Maxell (2003) summarize that "embedded in a livelihoods approach are assumptions about working in solidarity with communities, building their capacity, strengthening their access to resources, etc., that clearly go beyond either just the alleviation of short term suffering or a strong application of classic humanitarian principles" (p. 31) – with no reference to the role of local entrepreneurs.

This non-entrepreneurial orientation of current aid interventions and analytical techniques, such as livelihood methodologies, may in part be due to their grounding in political economy theories rather than industrial economics, strategic management, and entrepreneurship theory. However, developmental entrepreneurship thought, particularly in cases of slow onset disasters such as drought, crop failures, and SCCPI, may find important foundations in the livelihood and food economy stream of literature.

2.5. Shadow Economies, Aid, and Institutions in Slow-Onset Disasters

There have been several recent empirical thrusts that examine recovery from slow-onset disasters, such as starvation and chronic poverty, that have possible parallel applications to the topic of natural disaster recovery and entrepreneurial activity.

First is the recognition of the importance of the "shadow" economy or "extra-legal" market, particularly in very poor regions. The shadow economy can be described in two different ways, (a) as a "hidden economy" that is simply not recorded in official statistics, or (b) as a behavioral phenomenon where the members of the economy circumvent the set of institutional rules and regulations. It is now recognized that in poor countries, the shadow economy can account for a substantial percentage of the economy, and over the past two decades there have been numerous macro-economic attempts to estimate the size of this economy in almost every part of the world (see Tanzi, 1999, for a good summary). More important to our subject, however, are the recent empirical attempts to understand the nature, motivations, structure, and entrepreneurial drive of the micro-enterprises that often constitute these shadow economies (e.g., de Soto, 1989, 2000). In particular, it has been suggested that the micro-enterprises of the shadow economy should be directly addressed in aid/micro loan programs, that aid policies directed to encourage and rebuild the micro-enterprises of the shadow economy should be different than those firms that operate in the legal economy (Kaufmann & Parlmeyer, 2006), that the shadow economy accounts for significant portions of cross-border trade in poor countries (MaCamo, 1998; Peberdy & Crush, 2001) and that the shadow economy may respond much quicker after natural disasters, such as the 2000/2001 floods in Mozambique (Peberdy & Crush, 2001). This suggests that an important dimension of post-disaster recovery might be found in the micro-enterprises within an impacted region's shadow economy.

The second relevant thrust of research examines the relationship between aid, economic growth, and poverty. While a number of researchers have argued that there is substantial evidence that aid has a positive impact on reducing poverty (see Dollar & Kraay, 2002; Kraay, 2005 for reviews), this is still a hotly debated topic (e.g., Easterly, 2001; Dollar & Easterly, 1999; Smith, 2005), and it is likely that aid only explains a relatively small portion of economic growth. This suggests that there are several non-aid determinants of poverty reduction. Research has generally indicated that good institutional governance, low corruption, and property rights are positively related to poverty reduction and economic growth (e.g., Islam & Kaufmann, 1999; Devarajan et al., 2001; Burnside & Dollar, 2000, 2004; Dollar & Levin, 2005). From the perspective of natural disasters and entrepreneurial behavior, this might suggest that future disaster recovery research might investigate the more micro-relationships between post-disaster institutional governance/property rights and entrepreneurial activity and recovery in the post-disaster period.

Finally, an important line of macro-economic research has focused on the ideas of "poverty traps." According to Kraay (2005), poverty traps occur as, "self-reinforcing mechanisms whereby countries, or individuals, that start out poor might remain poor. If saving rates, or technology, or other positive forces for growth are low precisely because countries are poor, then countries may find themselves trapped at low levels of development." (p. 15). In these situations, good governance and institutions may not be sufficient to pull the country out of its poverty cycle (Sachs et al., 2004). While there is substantial debate as to the source of poverty traps, or whether poverty traps actually exist, it does suggest an interesting line of future research – in "poverty trap" conditions, is there a different relationship between aid strategies, natural disasters, and entrepreneurial recovery?

2.6. Recovery Strategies: Rapid Onset Disasters

While livelihood methodologies and strategies tend to frame much of the intervention and recovery strategies in slow onset disasters, there is also an expanding body of literature addressing fast onset disasters such as natural or technological disasters. Within this respect, the literature can be divided into two areas: recovery strategies for poor economic environments such as the tsunami strike on Indonesia in 2004 (which are also often framed within a livelihood perspective) and recovery strategies in more economically developed regions, such as the 2005 Hurricane Katrina landfall in

Mississippi and Louisiana. Within this literature, most of the empirical research has focused on case studies.

For example, following the 2000 and 2001 floods in Mozambique, Wiles, Selvester, and Fidalgo (2005) examined the lessons learned from the recovery strategy. Mozambique is one of the world's poorest countries, ranking in the bottom 5% in the UN Human Development Index (HDI). During a period of internal conflict, it is estimated that approximately one-third of its population was displaced. After the peace agreement in 1992, the country stabilized. In 2000, flooding from severe tropical storms killed over 700 people, with another 650,000 displaced. In 2001 flooding displaced another 223,000. From an entrepreneurial perspective, the major findings were that the recovery success was grounded in the rehabilitation and reconstruction of damaged infrastructure and the protection of larger capital assets. The conclusions found that the use of local entrepreneurs, such as construction contractors, rather than international contactors, assisted in the recovery. Another conclusion was that recovery strategies should not just rebuild the infrastructure but also use the opportunity to expand infrastructure to encourage future economic development. Approximately 23% of the aid money was dedicated to development of the productive sectors, such as fisheries and agriculture.

Similar studies of recovery strategies have been conducted by the World Bank. For example, Beck (2005) studied recovery following the 1998 floods in Bangladesh, while Telford et al. (2004) examined recovery strategies after Hurricane Mitch struck Honduras in October 1998 and found similar results. From an entrepreneurial perspective, the aid-based replacement of lost capital assets from individual businesses tended to force a new communal business entrepreneurial activity upon an existing, more family or individual business culture (Wiles et al., 2005). This communal process was due to a combination of an economic scarcity in asset replacements (such as one fishing boat donated to a community to replace five family-owned boats that were lost, forcing a communal use of the donated asset) or a planned strategy of communal behavior, such as community receipt of assets at a distribution center, or forcing communal ownership of farm animals even when the replacement asset is somewhat abundant. Although in most cases it was recognized that the communal economy was at odds with the local economies, there is little evidence as to whether the resulting communal entrepreneurial elements will be long lasting or economically productive, or that a community might return to its more individual entrepreneurial economy after a period of time.

Within these studies it is interesting to also note that often the only reference to entrepreneurs is within a negative context, such as entrepreneurs taking advantage of the credit situation to charge high interest, or "entrepreneurs may take advantage of the poor" (Benson, 2003).

In a somewhat related theme, Deare (2004) argues that disaster recovery strategies have overemphasized the reconstruction of infrastructure, and not examined closely enough the mitigation issues related to social structure. In this analysis, Deare (2004) is suggesting certain social differences (in this case, gender) be incorporated into both assessment models and intervention strategies. While not specifically examining entrepreneurial behavior, Deare (2004) does suggest that response activity among the local affected population does vary significantly by certain social and gender characteristics. The same argument can be made for entrepreneurial propensities.

In addition, these studies recognize the importance of credit for economic recovery, noting that in most cases in spite of widespread networks of microfinance institutions and donor gifts, there appeared to be chronic shortages of credit available in the recovery periods.

3. IMPACT AND RECOVERY OF SMALL BUSINESS

Most of the literature reviewed above only tangentially discusses entrepreneurial or small business activity, either in terms of the impact a disaster has upon small business or the role that entrepreneurs can play in recovery and reconstruction. There is, however, a small, but expanding literature examining the behavior and failures of small business in a post-disaster environment. The vast majority of this literature has focused on small business within the U.S.

In a comprehensive survey and empirical analysis of business recovery after various natural disasters in the U.S. between 1992 and 2000 (two hurricanes, one earthquake, one wildfire, one tornado, and eight flooding events), Alesch, Holly, Mittler, and Nagy (2001) found that marginal businesses prior to the disaster event were much more likely to not reopen after the disaster even when the disaster event was not catastrophic – "we were unable to establish a statistical relationship between the amount of structural damage businesses experienced and business survival" (p. 8). The authors note that the traditional precautions aimed at protecting life and property within a disaster area were not correlated with post-disaster business survival. Those marginal organizations that did reopen, often subsequently failed. Stronger businesses, typically lost market share in regional and national markets. The authors offer several interesting recommendations for "managerial mitigation" including lease provisions for disasters and diversification of a firm's customer or locational base, and recognition that business interruption insurance can not reestablish a pre-event marginal business. This study built upon findings from previous empirical research by the authors (Alesch & Holly, 1996, 1997) following the 1994 Northridge-Resda earthquake.

Another similar line of research by the Delaware Disaster Research Center includes surveys and case examination of businesses after the 1993 floods within the Midwestern states of the U.S. (Tierney, Nigg, & Dahlhamer, 1996) and the Northridge earthquake (Dahlhamer & Tierney, 1998; Tierney, 1997). Much of this research is focused on developing a post-disaster small business firm survival model, with an emphasis on four components of small business survival: firm characteristics, direct and indirect disaster impacts, loss containment measures taken, and previous disaster experience. Webb, Tierney, and Dahlhamer (2000, 2003) provides a summary of this stream of research, focusing on three major areas: factors influencing business disaster preparedness, disaster-related sources of business disruption and financial loss, and factors that affect the ability of businesses to recover following major disaster events. A number of conclusions are offered, such as that business owners tended to use personal assets to cover disaster losses and that the success of small business recovery may be more a function of the larger regional economy than disaster-related factors.

Using an inertia theory application, Faircloth and Bronson (2001) found that small businesses tend not to alter their business strategy in a post-natural disaster environment. Following the 1997 Grand Forks Flood, a survey found that the majority never altered their strategies related to target markets, product offering pricing, promotional strategies, or distribution network. This appears consistent with research investigating SBA loan activities in a post-disaster environment.

Other notable research include Kroll, Landis, Shen, and Stryker (1991) who surveyed businesses following the 1989 Loma Prieta earthquake in Oakland, CA and Alesch, Taylor, Ghanty, and Nagy (1993) who created a small business post-disaster financial bankruptcy prediction model based on financial ratios.

4. CONCULSIONS

The scholarly literature that examines impact of disasters on small business and the role that entrepreneurial activities play in post-disaster recovery and reconstruction is sparse at best. While there appears to be several distinct streams of literature that examine natural disasters from a macro-economic point of view, most of this empirical research tends to examine the issue of entrepreneurship and small business only in a tangential manner. Distinct literatures appear to exist in the areas of (a) appropriate relief aid management, (b) the impact of disasters on both short- and long-term economic development, (c) hazard and natural disaster risk management, and (d) the relationship between disasters and socio-economic condition, such as poverty and gender. Within these literatures there appears to be a general recognition regarding the importance of small business development as it related to disaster management. Only the literature that empirically examines the impact of natural disasters on small business, and the strategies that these businesses employ to recover from disasters, appears to directly address the topic. And even this literature is relatively small, tends to be focused on natural disasters within well-developed countries, such as the U.S., and often approaches the problem more from a sociological perspective than an economic perspective.

There are several ways in which entrepreneurial enterprise might play into the issue of disaster management. First, a strong entrepreneurial foundation may act as a mitigating buffer to reduce a community's vulnerability to disasters. Second, policies that emphasize small business development may offer an effective intervention strategy for countries suffering from chronic violence or slow onset disasters. Third, while the evidence points to both short- and long-term negative economic impacts from disasters, the entrepreneurial propensity within an affected economy may mitigate some of these structural economic problems. Fourth, entrepreneurial solutions may assist to mitigate some of the apparent unevenness of natural disasters on certain socio-economic groups of people. And finally, disasters clearly have a negative impact on local small business, yet the evidence suggests that the impact may be more fundamental in nature. Understanding how small firms successfully respond within a post-disaster environment may be critical in framing future relief efforts targeted toward the local business community.

No doubt the recent world disasters such as the Indian Ocean tsunami in 2004, Hurricane Katrina in 2005, the 2005 Kashmir earthquake in Pakistan, and the multiple chronic problems within sub-Saharan Africa will provide the impetus for a closer look at the role of entrepreneurship in mitigating disaster vulnerability and providing a vehicle for improving post-disaster recovery and reconstruction.

NOTES

1. In this discussion, it is important to note that humanitarian or relief aid is different from the much broader foreign aid, which is often reported as official development assistance (ODA) by the OECD. While the U.S. rates relatively low in per capita ODA, the ODA does not capture the majority of actual U.S. foreign aid which includes private donations, direct aid provided by the military, private transfers to individuals, forgiveness of non-aid designated debt, volunteer time, grants to foreign students, delivery costs, aid to "part II" countries, and direct individual transfers. In addition, much of the world's foreign aid may ultimately fuel corruption in the recipient countries, with a rousing debate as to whether foreign aid actually has much impact on real economic development (e.g., Easterly, 2001; Dollar & Easterly, 1999; Smith, 2005; Kraay, 2005). Humanitarian or relief aid, however, tends to be more directly applied.

REFERENCES

Aguiree International. (1996). *EDA's post-disaster assistance program after Hurricane Andrew: Final report*. Washington, DC: U.S. Department of Commerce.

Alesch, D., & Holly, J. (1996). How to survive the next natural disaster: Lessons for small business from Northridge victims and survivors. *Proceedings of the pan pacific hazards conference*, Vancouver, British Columbia, Canada, July 29–August 2.

Alesch, D., & Holly, J. (1997). Small business failure, survival, and recovery lessons from the January 1994 Northridge Earthquake. *Proceedings of the CURee conference on findings from Northridge Earthquake Research*. Los Angeles, CA, June.

Alesch, D., Holly, J., Mittler, E., & Nagy, R. (2001). *Organizations at risk: What happens when small business and not-for-profits encounter natural disasters?* Technical Report. Public Entity Risk Institute, Fairfax, VA.

Alesch, D., Taylor, C., Ghanty, A., & Nagy, R. (1993). Earthquake risk reduction and small business. In: K. Tierney & J. Nigg (Eds), *1993 National earthquake conference monograph, no. 5: Socioeconomic impacts*. Memphis, TN: Central United States Earthquake Consortium.

Archibald, S., & Richards, P. (2002). Seeds and rights: New approaches to post-war agricultural rehabilitation in Sierra Leone. *Disasters, 26*(4), 356–367.

Ashley, C. (2005). *Facilitating pro-poor tourism with the private sector: Lessons learned from pro-poor tourism pilots in southern Africa*. Working paper 256. Overseas Development Institute, London.

Ashley, C., & Carney, D. (1999). *Sustainable livelihoods: Lessons from early experience*. London: Department for International Development.

Auffret, P. (2003). *Catastrophe insurance market in the Caribbean region: Market failures and recommendations for public sector interventions*. World Bank Policy Research Working Paper 2963, Washington, World Bank, http://econ.worldbank.org/view.php?topic=16&type=5&id=23420.

Beck, T. (2005). *Learning lessons from disaster recovery: The case of Bangladesh*. Working Paper Series 11. World Bank, Hazard Management Unit, Washington, DC.

Benson, C. (2003). *Catastrophic risk financing: A comprehensive model*. World Bank Presentation, http://www.info.worldbank.org/etools/docs/library/201226/Lester_CatRiskFinancing.ppt

Benson, C., & Clay, E. (2004). *Understanding the economic and financial impacts of natural disasters*. Disaster Risk Management Series, no. 4. World Bank, Washington, DC.

Booth, D., Cammack, D., Harringan, J., Kanyongolo, N., Mataure, M., & Ngwira, N. (2006). *Drivers of change and development in Malawi*. Working paper 261. Overseas Development Institute, London.

Boudreau, T., & Coutts, P. (2002). Food economy in situations of chronic political instability. In: C. Longley & K. Hussein (Eds), *Livelihoods and chronic conflict working paper series*. London: Overseas Development Institute.

Burnside, C., & Dollar, D. (2000). Aid, policies, and growth. *American Economic Review, 90*(4), 847–868.

Burnside, C., & Dollar, D. (2004). Aid, policies, and growth: Reply. *American Economic Review, 94*(3), 781–784.

Carney, D., Drinkwater, M., Rusinow, T., Neefjes, K., Wanmali, S., & Singh, N. (1999). *Livelihood approaches compared: A brief comparison of the livelihood approaches of the UK Department of International Development, CARE, Oxfam and the United Nations Development Programme*. London: Department for International Development.

Charveriat, C. (2000). *Natural disasters in Latin America and the Caribbean: An overview of risk*. Working paper 434. Inter-American Development Bank, Washington, DC.

Childers, C., & Phillips, B. (1998). *Sustainable development or transformative development? Arkadelphia, Arkansas after the tornado*. Quick response research report #109. Boulder, CO, Natural Hazards Research and Applications Information Center.

Crowards, T. (2000). *Comparative vulnerability to natural disasters in the Caribbean*. Working Paper no. 1/00. Caribbean Development Bank, Barbardos.

Crowards, T., & Coulter, W. (1999). Measuring the comparative economic vulnerability in the Caribbean. *Journal of Eastern Caribbean Studies, 24*(3), 41–80.

Dahlhamer, J., & Tierney, K. (1998). Rebounding from disruptive events: Business recovery following the Northridge Earthquake. *Sociological Spectrum, 18*, 121–141.

De Soto, H. (1989). *The other path*. New York: Basic Books.

De Soto, H. (2000). *The mystery of capital*. New York: Basic Books.

Deare, F. (2004). *A methodological approach to gender analysis in natural disaster assessment: A guide for the Caribbean*. Manual Series, no. 31. Mexico City: ECLAC.

Devarajan, S., Dollar, D., & Holmgren, T. (Eds) (2001). *Aid and reform in Africa*. Washington, DC: The World Bank.

Development Assistance Committee (2004). *Development cooperation 2004*. Report, OECD, Paris.

Dollar, D., & Easterly, W. (1999). The search for the key: Aid, investment and policies in Africa. *Journal of African Studies, 8*(4), 546–577.

Dollar, D., & Kraay, A. (2002). Growth is good for the poor. *Journal of Economic Growth, 7*, 195–225.

Dollar, D., & Levin, V. (2005). *Sowing and reaping: Institutional quality and project outcomes in developing countries*. Washington: World Bank.

Easterly, W. (2001). *The elusive quest for growth: Economists' adventures and misadventures in the tropics*. New York: MIT Press.

Economic Commission for Latin America and Caribbean (ECLAC) (2000). A matter of development to reduce vulnerability in the face of natural disasters. Seminar, "confronting natural disasters: A matter of development." New Orleans, March 25–26.

Economic Commission for Latin America and Caribbean (ECLAC). (2002). *Handbook for estimating socio-economic and environmental effects of disasters.* Mexico City, MX: Economic Commission for Latin America and Caribbean.

Faircloth, J., & Bronson, J. (2001). A preliminary examination of why small businesses don't adapt marketing practices following a natural disaster: An inertia theory explanation. Paper presented to the 2001 USASBE/SBIDA national conference.

Farrington, J., Ramasut, T., & Walker, J. (2002). *Sustainable livelihoods approaches in urban areas: General lessons with illustrations from Indian cases.* Stockholm: Swedish International Development Cooperation Agency.

Federal Emergency Management Agency. (1997). *Report on costs and benefits of natural hazard mitigation.* Washington, DC: Federal Emergency Management Agency.

Fothergill, A., & Peek, L. (2004). Poverty and disasters in the United States: A review of the sociological literature. *Natural Hazards, 32,* 89–110.

Freeman, P. (2000). Infrastructure, natural disasters and poverty. In: A. Kreimer & M. Arnold, (Eds), *Managing disaster risk in emerging economies* (pp. 23–29). Disaster Risk Management Series No. 2. Washington, DC: World Bank.

Freeman, P., Martin, L., Mechler, R., & Warner, K. (2004). A methodology for incorporating natural catastrophes into macroeconomic projections. *Disaster Prevention and Management, 13*(4), 337–342.

Freestone, J., & Raab, R. (1998). *Disaster preparedness.* Menlo Park, CA: CRISP Publications.

Isham, J., & Kaufmann, D. (1999). The forgotten rationale for policy reform: The performance of investment projects. *Quarterly Journal of Economics, 114*(1), 149–184.

Jones, B., & Chang, S. (1995). Economic aspects of urban vulnerability and disaster mitigation. In: F. Cheng & M. Sheu (Eds), *Urban disaster mitigation: The role of engineering and technology* (pp. 311–320). Oxford, England: Elsevier Science.

Kaufmann, R., & Parlmeyer, W. (2006). The dilemma of small business in Mozambique: A research note. In: C. Galbraith & C. Stiles (Eds), *Developmental entrepreneurship: Adversity, risk and isolation* (pp. 207–219). London: Elsevier.

Kraay, A. (2005). Aid, growth, and poverty. Paper presented to the IMF seminar on foreign aid and macroeconomic management, Maputo, Mozambique, March.

Kroll, C., Landis, A. Shen, Q., & Stryker, S. (1991). *Economic impacts of the Loma Prieta Earthquake: A focus on small business.* Working paper 91–187. University of California Transportation Center and the Center for Real Estate and Economics, Berkeley.

Kunder, J. (2005). Testimony before the subcommittee on foreign operations, export financing and related programs, committee on appropriations, U.S. house of representatives. Washington, DC, 9/7/2005.

Lautze, S. (1997). *Saving lives and livelihoods: The fundamentals of a livelihoods strategy.* Tufts University, Boston: Feinstein International Famine Center.

Longley, C., & Maxwell, D. (2003). Livelihoods, chronic conflict and humanitarian response: A synthesis of current practice. In: C. Longley & K. Hussein (Eds), *Livelihoods and chronic conflict working paper series.* London: Overseas Development Institute.

MaCamo, J. (1998). *Estimates of unrecorded cross-border trade between Mozambique and her neighbors: Implications for food security.* Report for the regional economic support office for eastern and Southern Africa: USAID, Washington, DC.

Mechler, D. (2003). *Natural disaster risk management and financing disaster losses in developing countries.* Doctoral dissertation. Universitat Fridericiana zu Karlsruhe.

Murlidharan, T., & Shah, H. (2001). Catastrohpes and macro-economic risk factors: An empirical study. *Proceedings 1st annual IIASA-DPRI conference on integrated disaster risk management*.

Natural Hazards Center (2006). *Holistic disaster recovery: Ideas for building local sustainability after a natural disaster*. Boulder, CO: University of Colorado, Natural Hazards Center.

Newton, J. (1997). Federal legislation for disaster mitigation: A comparative assessment between Canada and the United States. *Natural Hazards, 16*, 219–241.

Otero, R., & Marti, Z. (1995). The impacts of natural disasters on developing economies: Implications for the international development and disaster community. In: M. Munasinghe & C. Clarke (Eds), *Disaster prevention for sustainable development economic and policy issues*. Washington, DC: World Bank.

Pain, A. (2002). Understanding and monitoring livelihoods under conditions of chronic conflict: Lessons from Afghanistan. In: C. Longley & K. Hussein (Eds), *Livelihoods and chronic conflict working paper series*. London: Overseas Development Institute.

Peberdy, S., & Crush, J. (2001). Invisible trade, invisible travellers: The Maputo Corridor spatial development initiative and informal cross-border trading. *South African Geographical Journal, 83*(20), 115–123.

Rasmussen, T. (2004). *Macroeconomic implications of natural disasters in the Caribbean*. IMF Working Paper. New York: International Monetary Fund.

Sachs, J., McArthur, J., Schmidt-Traub, G., Kruk, M., Bahadur, C., Faye, M., & McCord, G. (2004). *Ending Africa's poverty trap*. Brookings Papers on Economic Activity, #1.

Schafer, J. (2002). Supporting livelihoods situations of chronic conflict: Overview of conceptual issues. In: C. Longley & K. Hussein (Eds), *Livelihoods and chronic conflict working paper series*. London: Overseas Development Institute.

Smith, J. (2005). *Economic democracy. The political struggle for the 21st century.* Bloomington, IN: J.W. Smith, 1st Books.

Tanzi, V. (1999). Uses and abuses of estimates of the underground economy. *The Economic Journal, 109*, 338–347.

Telford, J., Arnold, M., & Harth, A. (2004). *Learning lessons from disaster recovery: The case of Honduras*. Washington, DC: World Bank.

Tierney, K. (1993). *Disaster preparedness and response: Research findings and guidance from the social science literature*. Research paper #193. University of Delaware Disaster Research Centre, Delaware.

Tierney, K. (1997). Business impacts of the Northridge earthquake. *Journal of Contingencies and Crises Management, 5*, 87–97.

Tierney, K. Nigg, M., & Dahlhamer, J. (1996). The impact of the 1993 Midwest Floods: Business vulnerability and disruption in Des Moines. In: R. Sylves & W. Waugh (Eds), *Disaster management in the U.S. and Canada* (2nd ed., pp. 214–233). Springfield, MA: Charles C. Thomas.

USAID (2005a). Tsunami reconstruction plan, press release 2005–09, 6/23/05, http://www.usaid.gov/press/releases/2005/pr050623.html, accessed 2/6/06.

USAID (2005b). Asia and the near east tsunami reconstruction: Update – December, 2, 2005. http://www.usaid.gov/locations/asia_near_east/tsunami/pdf/tsunami_update_120205.pdf

Van de Veen, A., & Logtmeijer, C. (2005). Economic hotspots: Visualizing vulnerability to flooding. *Natural Hazards, 36*, 65–80.

Wachtendorf, T., Connell, R., & Tierney, K. (2002). *Disaster resistant communities initiative: Assessment of the Pilot Phase – Year 3*. Disaster Research Center. University of Delaware, Newark, DE.

Webb, G., Tierney, K., & Dahlhamer, J. (2000). Businesses and disasters: Empirical patterns and unanswered questions. *Natural Hazards Review, 1*, 83–90.

Webb, G., Tierney, K., & Dahlhamer, J. (2003). Predicting long-term business recovery from disaster: A comparison of the Loma Prieta earthquake and Hurricane Andrew. *Environmental Hazards, 4*, 45–58.

Wiles, P., Selvester, K., & Fidalgo, L. (2005). *Learning lessons from disaster recovery: The case of Mozambique*. Working Paper Series 12. World Bank, Hazard Management Unit, Washington, DC.

Wood, G., & Salway, S. (2000). Introduction: Securing livelihoods in Dhaka slums. *Journal of International Development, 12*, 669–688.

World Bank (2000). *World development report 2000/2001*. World Bank: Washington, http://povlibrary.worldbank.org/library/view/10059

World Bank. (2002). *Poverty reduction and the world bank: Progress in operationalizing the WDR 2000/2001*. World Bank: Washington, DC.

HIV/AIDS, CRIME AND SMALL BUSINESS IN SOUTH AFRICA

Eslyn Isaacs and Christian Friedrich

1. INTRODUCTION

The Republic of South Africa is located on the southern most part of Africa and stretches latitudinally from 22° to 35° South and longitudinally from 17° to 33° East. Its surface area is 1,219,090 km². It has a population exceeding 44 million and 11 official languages namely English, Afrikaans, isiNdebele, isiXhosa, isiZulu, Sepedi, Sesotho, Setswana, siSwati, Tshivenda and Xitsonga (Burger, 2004). Since becoming a democracy in 1994 it has embarked on an ambitious process of political, economic, social and legal reforms to improve the quality of life of the people of South Africa.

The Government's social and economic development programme, referred to as the Reconstruction and Development Programme (RDP) and the Growth, Employment and Redistribution (GEAR) programme was developed to ensure a stable macro environment and contribute to accelerated growth. These programmes assisted in decreasing the inflation rate from 15% in the 1990s to below 1% in 2004. The economic growth rate for the last 10 years has been about 2.8% (Department of Trade and Industry, 2003b).

Although the Government believes that it has achieved many of its goals, unemployment remains a chronic problem, decreasing marginally from 28.4% in September 2003 to 27.8% in March 2004 (Burger, 2004). The economic workforce increased from 11.7 million in September 2003 to just less than

Developmental Entrepreneurship: Adversity, Risk, and Isolation
International Research in the Business Disciplines, Volume 5, 167–183
Copyright © 2006 by Elsevier Ltd.
ISSN: 1074-7877/doi:10.1016/S1074-7877(06)05009-4

12 million in March 2004 (Burger, 2004). Despite the increase in the work-force, it was reported that "75% of this year's matriculants (learners who have successfully completed grade 12) will not progress to tertiary education despite having a matriculation certificate (matriculation certificate gives learners access to study at a tertiary institution, that is, technical university or university), according to the National Professional Teachers Organization of South Africa (Naptosa)" (Staff Reporter, 2003, p. 1; Kassiem, 2003, p. 1).

Mining, agriculture, forestry and fishing, manufacturing, construction, electricity and water (24%) and the service sector (20%) are the main contributors to the gross domestic product of South Africa (Werkmans Attorneys, 2005).

Despite all its natural resources (gold, copper, coal, iron ore, manganese, etc.), good infrastructure (roads, rail, air, water, networks), a strong agricultural sector and a skilled and unskilled labour pool, South Africa still imports a large percentage of basic items, such as low-priced clothing, toys, and electronic items from various countries outside of Africa. As a result, recently a number of clothing manufacturers were forced to close or scale down operations, resulting in large numbers of people being released from employed.

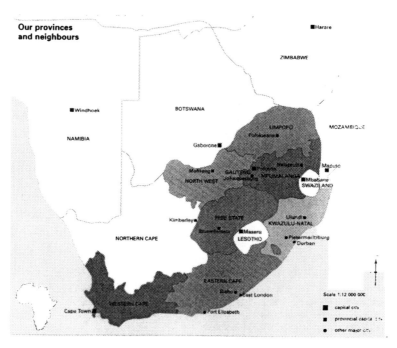

1.1. Province of Western Cape

South Africa is divided into nine provinces, namely Gauteng, Kwazulu-Natal, Western Cape, Eastern Cape, North West, Free State, Mpumalanga, Limpopo and Northern Cape. Twenty-seven percent of South Africa's population lives in the Western Cape, the third biggest province in terms of population. Fifty-four percent of the population of the Western Cape is referred to as Coloureds, while Blacks constitute 27%, Whites 18% and Indians/Asians only 1% (Department of Trade and Industry, 2003a). The Western Cape economy has grown at an average rate of 3.3%, higher than the national growth rate (Burger, 2004). The per capita GDP of the Western Cape and Gauteng is in excess of $3,000 per annum; the only two provinces whose percentage of GDP is greater than their share of the country's population. These two provinces jointly employ more than 56% of the total workforce of the country; and are the only two provinces where more than 30% of the population is employed (Department of Trade and Industry, 2003a).

It was for this reason that during the Apartheid era it was referred to as a "Coloured job preferential area." During this period this group was dominant in the building, fishing and clothing sectors. However, with the current economic slump in these sectors, there has recently been substantial unemployment, with its related social problems. For this reason, recently a number of individuals from all ethnic groups, Coloured, Blacks, Whites and Indians, who were innovative and had financial resources have ventured into starting their own businesses to mitigate against these unemployment problems.

1.2. Small, Medium and Micro Enterprise

The South African government has identified the small, medium and micro enterprise (SMME) as an important sector, hence its continued support in the institutional framework (Department of Trade and Industry, 2005). In 1995 the government produced the National Strategy for the Development and Promotion of Small Business in South Africa (Department of Trade and Industry, 1995), and in 1996 the Small Business Act. These two documents provided the necessary institutional frameworks for SMME development in South Africa. These documents were produced because the government believed that the SMME sector can add much-needed jobs and contribute to poverty alleviation. In the National Strategy document it identified five specific objectives to create an enabling small business environment. These objectives are listed below:

1. facilitating greater equalization of income, wealth and economic opportunities;
2. creating long-term jobs;
3. stimulating economic growth;
4. strengthening the cohesion between small enterprises; and
5. levelling the playing fields between big and small business.

In addition, the institutional framework for SMME support and development is discussed in the National Strategy document and is indicated in Fig. 1.

It is clear that the structures which the government has implemented are bearing fruit. In 1995, there were about 800,000 SMMEs (Department of Trade and Industry, 1995). Currently, it is estimated that there are between 1.8 million and 2.5 million SMMEs in South Africa, with a growth rate of about 150,000 firms per annum (Department of Trade and Industry, 2004).

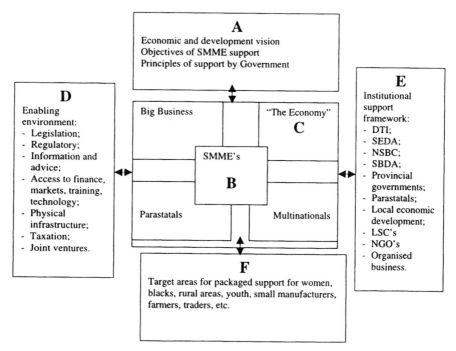

Fig. 1. The National SMME Support Strategy in Perspective. *Source:* Department of Trade and Industry (1995). National Strategy for the Development and Promotion of Small Business in South Africa, p. 51.

In South Africa SMMEs are defined in terms of total number of full-time employees, sales turnover per annum and gross asset value, but excluding the value of fixed property. A micro enterprise normally employs less than five people, has a sales turnover not exceeding $30,000 and an asset value not exceeding $15,000; small enterprise employs between 6 and 50 people, its sales turnover should not exceed $2,000,000 and has an investment in asset value not exceeding $750,000 and medium enterprises are those which employ between 51 and 200 employees, its sales turnover should not exceed $7,500,000 and the value of its assets should not exceed $3,000,000 (National Small Business Amendment Bill, 2003).

Table 1 gives the provincial breakdown of Gross Domestic Product, percentage of all enterprises and percentage of SMMEs.

The importance of SMMEs to the economy has grown. In 1995, SMMEs contributed 32.7% to the Gross Domestic Product, while in 2001 it rose to 36.1%. The contribution to employment was 44% in 1995 and 53.9% in 2001 (State of Small Business Development in South Africa, 2002).

While this sector plays an important role in the economy of South Africa, a high prevalence of HIV/AIDS and crime also appears to affect this sector. This has prompted researchers to start examining perceptions of HIV/AIDS and crime for this sector and the impact it has upon small business. A good resource to investigate this problem is the government's partners in the Western Cape. These include organizations which the government selected to provide training, consultation and research to the SMME sector such as Ntsika Enterprise Promotion Agency, Khula Enterprise Finance Limited and Namac Trust.

Table 1. Provincial Breakdown of Population, Percentage of GDP, Number of SMMEs and Percentage of SMMEs.

Province	% of Population	% of GDP	Number of SMMEs	% of SMMEs
Gauteng	18.0	38.0	414,166	38.3
Kwazulu-Natal	20.7	16.0	199,749	18.4
Western Cape	9.6	15.0	144,594	13.4
Eastern Cape	15.8	8.0	94,253	8.7
Mpumalanga	7.0	7.0	53,636	5.0
Free State	6.4	6.0	49,335	4.6
North West	8.3	5.0	56,117	5.2
Limpopo	12.2	3.0	49,985	4.6
Northern Cape	2.0	2.0	19,791	1.7
Total	100.0	100.0	1,079,726	100.0

Source: Department of Trade and Industry (2003a).

2. HIV/AIDS, CRIME AND ECONOMIC GROWTH

Crime and HIV/AIDS are a worldwide phenomenon. Estimations by the World Bank indicate that as of July 2004, 37.8 million people were living with HIV/AIDS. Some researchers believe that the long-term impact on economies is greater than anticipated and could even cause a collapse of some economies, like that of South Africa (World Bank, 2005). Despite the investment in anti-retroviral drugs, only 7% of people living in low- and middle-income countries have been receiving treatment (World Bank, 2005).

The International Labour Office (2005) projects that by 2005, 28 million workers globally will be lost; this will increase to 48 million by 2010 and 74 million by 2015. The loss for Africa is estimated to be 20 million by 2005, 34 million by 2010 and 50 million by 2015. This translates to almost 68% of the labour force losses will be in Africa. It is evident from research (Trebilcock, 1989; World Bank, 2005; Conyers, 2004; International Labour Office, 2005) that HIV/AIDS is threatening economic growth, reducing the workforce, decreasing productivity and increasing social insurance costs (Fraser, Grant, Mwanza, & Naidoo, 2002; Connelly & Rosen, 2003; Lehohla, 2003).

Another issue not commonly researched in the context of small business is crime. In the United Kingdom, for example, it is estimated that business crime will cost about £19 million annually (Axa Insurance, 2003). According to Wilson (2003) although police statistics show a decrease, the perception of the general population is that crime has increased. In Australia, Taylor (2002) and Department of Justice (1999) were adamant that crime is causing small businesses to operate at higher risk levels. Other researchers are starting to examine the important relationships between crime, small business and economic development in developing countries. For example, Ortega-Alvarez (2002) discusses crime and small business in Venezuela, while Mfaume and Leonard (2004) examine the negative impact of crime on business in Tanzania.

3. RESEARCH METHODOLOGY

3.1. Questionnaire

A questionnaire was sent to organizations providing training, consulting/counselling services and research among SMMEs in the Western Cape of South Africa. These are commonly referred to as service providers or business support organizations. A questionnaire consisting of 25 items covering (1) the profile of the organization, year started, mission and objectives; (2) the conducive environment – objectives of the National Strategy for the promotion of small business and factors inhibiting growth and development; (3) the service providers – the use, knowledge and quality of service delivery by the different service providers; and (4) an understanding of issues such as crime and HIV/AIDS and its impact on the small, medium and micro sector. This chapter discusses the results regarding service providers' perception on issues such as crime and HIV/AIDS, and how these issues affect the small, medium and micro business sectors in the Western Cape.

3.2. Pilot Sample

Prior to using the questionnaire a pilot study was undertaken after which the questionnaire was adapted and used. The questionnaire was e-mailed and/or faxed or personally delivered to the participants. Some participants completed and returned it by e-mail or postal mail; the researcher collected others personally. This resulted in 40 usable questionnaires.

The Department of Trade and Industry has compiled a database with the names and addresses of those service providers in South Africa that they were able to locate. The list provided the names and addresses by province. In addition, the service providers were probed for names and addresses of other service providers with (1) whom they are familiar with, (2) with whom they are working or have worked before, or (3) who they are aware are providing similar services to the SMMEs.

The initial list contained the names and other details of 67 service providers. Additional names of service providers were provided which added another 40 organizations. The questionnaire was therefore send to 107 service providers in the Province of the Western Cape. These 107 service providers were rendering their services to SMMEs in urban and rural areas as well as addressing the needs of advantaged and disadvantaged communities.

3.3. Research Results

3.3.1. Profile of the Survey Respondents
Based on the type of service provided, the organizations were divided into the following categories: Management and Consulting services, financial institutions, non-governmental organizations, information providers

Table 2.   Profile of the Service Providers.

Type of Organization	Total per Category	Number of Respondents	Percentage
Managerial and consulting services	21	3	14
Financial institutions	7	2	29
Non-governmental organizations	51	26	51
Provincial and local governments	4	3	75
Tertiary institutions	17	2	12
Research institutions	7	4	57
Total	107	40	37

(libraries and newspapers focusing on SMMEs), provincial and local governments, tertiary institutions (colleges, technical universities and universities), and research institutions (see Table 2).

It is clear from this table that there may be a response bias, with non-government-related agencies having a much greater response rate and sample representation than other groups. In spite of a potential response bias, the results provide an interesting picture of the perceptions regarding the effect of crime and HIV/AIDS on small, medium and micro business enterprises.

3.3.2. Success Factors

The first set of questions examined, in a general sense, factors that inhibit success development of the small business sector in the Western Cape Region. It is clear from the Table 3 that (i) "people starting a business out of necessity" is the biggest inhibiting factor, followed by (ii) "unemployment drives starting a business," and (iii) "lack of previous experience in managing a business."

In addition to these 13 factors a number of other factors were also identified. These factors are lack of an entrepreneurial culture, lack of business skills, lack of affordable mentorship, access to information to properly prepare business plans or other documentation required by financial institutions or government organizations, the high rates on loans but low interest on investments, lack of ability to plan ahead lack of affordable infrastructure in close proximity to markets or residential areas, and high crime rate.

Ueckermann (2004) also reports that the regulatory framework is negatively impacting on the establishment and performance of SMMEs in South Africa. Ueckermann, for example, reports that it takes about 38 days to register a business. According to Djankov, La Porta, Lopez-de-Silanes, and Shleifer (2001) the registration of a business in South Africa includes

Table 3.   Factors Inhibiting Success.

Factors	Mean Values
People start businesses out of necessity	4.17
Unemployment drives starting a business	4.05
Lack of previous experience in managing a business	3.8
Lack of motivation among small business people	3.55
Inability of informal businesses to become part of mainstream	3.55
Lack of access to finance below $10,000	3.53
Lack of aggressiveness	3.47
Lack of achievement-oriented	3.47
Lack of pro-activeness	3.47
Low educational qualifications	3.43
Inability to meet stringent government/legal requirements	3.4
Lack of risk-taking	3.2
Lack of transport, premises and water (infrastructure)	3.15

about nine procedures and 26 days to register a business. In comparison, in Australia there are only two procedures and takes two days to register a business. These procedural delays are a particular problem in many poorer countries (Djankov et al., 2001). According to the South African Registrar of Companies the process is unduly delayed because entrepreneurs often select a name which already exists or is inappropriate for the type of business that they intend registering (Registrar of Companies, 2005).

Despite the criticisms Ueckermann (2004) reports the following achievements for year ending June 2004 for South Africa:

1. Ntsika Enterprise Promotion Agency supported 15,000 small and medium enterprises.
2. Khula Enterprise Finance has provided 628 credit guarantees valuing $30 million and $15 million in loans.
3. Namac Trust has provided support to 2,000 manufacturing businesses. Through this process 1,744 new jobs were created and 14,726 were retained.

3.3.3. Department of Trade and Industry's Partners

The Department of Trade and Industry is partnering with a number of institutions in service delivery such as Ntsika Enterprise Promotion Agency, Khula Enterprise Finance Limited and Namac Trust. Despite the effort of these organizations, it appears that the service providers who took part in the research were not always positive about their performances (Isaacs &

Friedrich, 2005). The Ntsika and Namac Trust were dissolved on 31st March 2005 and the Small Enterprise Development Agency (SEDA) was established.

It is clear from our research that most of the service providers had reasonable knowledge of the organizations, but their perception in terms of the quality of service delivery was not positive. Based on the statistical analysis Khula and Ntsika in particular did not have a good reputation in terms of the service providers' perception of the service delivery (Isaacs & Friedrich, 2005).

It is further reported that 62% of the respondents were adamant that the Government is not doing enough to help small and medium enterprises, and 70% of these respondents are of the opinion that the government does not adequately promote the available assistance. This corresponds with the study conducted by Orford, Wood, Herrington, and Wood (2004).

3.3.4. HIV/AIDS

The National Government has certainly realized the impact of HIV/AIDS, increasing its expenditure from about $5 million in 1994 to more than $50 million in 2001/2002 (Burger, 2004). In 1999, approximately 22.4% of the population was HIV/AIDS prevalent; this increased to 24.5% in 2000, 24.8% in 2001 and 26.5% in 2002 (Noble, 2004). The percentage of HIV/AIDS prevalence in the Western Cape was much lower than the national figure, namely 7.1% in 1999, 8.7% in 2000 and 8.6% in 2001. However, this increased dramatically in 2002 to 12.4%. It was hoped that with all the prevention campaigns and the increase in drug supply to the HIV/AIDS-infected citizens these percentages would start to decrease, but there is little evidence of this to date. In addition, HIV/AIDS does have negative consequences for SMME sector as shown in Table 4.

Eighty-eight percent of the respondents in our sample reported that HIV/AIDS has a negative impact on small businesses. The respondents identified two consequences: (a) reducing the workforce (54.3%), and (b) reducing the purchasing power (45.7%). Other consequences mentioned were demotivating other employees, increasing absenteeism and inability to offer quality service to clients. A small percentage (12.5%) of the respondents believed that HIV/AIDS did not have a negative impact on small businesses. They are, however, of the opinion that while it does reduce the purchasing power of the employees, HIV/AIDS-infected individuals can still work and therefore can be productive employees.

Table 4. Consequences of HIV/AIDS.

Is HIV/AIDS Affecting SMMEs	Consequences			
	Reducing the Workforce	Reducing Spending Power	People can Still be Productive	Total
Yes	19	16	0	35
% of SMMEs being affected by HIV/AIDS	54.3	45.7	0.0	100.0
No	0	3	2	5
% of SMMEs not being affected by HIV/AIDS	0.0	60.0	40.0	100.0
Total	19	19	2	40
% of SMMEs being affected by HIV/AIDS	100.0	84.2	0.0	87.5

Interestingly, our results are somewhat in contrast to another by Grant Thornton (Ueckermann, 2005) which reports that only 26% of South African businesses believe that HIV/AIDS will negatively affect the operations of their businesses over the next five years. This study included 6,000 businesses from 24 countries.

Regarding treatment policies, about 13% of the respondents believed it can be prevented but the government with its policy of providing $120 to HIV/AIDS sufferers is not contributing to solving the problem, but rather providing an incentive to engage in acts which might increase the problem. Table 5 provides the responses as to what solutions were suggested by our sample of service providers to assist in managing the HIV/AIDS problem.

It is clear from the statistics reflected in Tables 4 and 5 that HIV/AIDS has a negative impact on SMMEs. This corresponds to the research conducted by Fraser et al. (2002) and McDonald (2003). McDonald (2003), for example, mentioned that although 9% of the companies surveyed indicated that HIV/AIDS already had a significant adverse impact on their business, 43% expected a significant impact in five years time.

Similar to our conclusions, Lehohla (2003) and Fraser et al. (2002), also argue that since micro enterprises are typically operated by individuals with a higher prevalence of HIV/AIDS, it is this sector that is most likely to be affected first, and with the greatest impact. Fraser et al. (2002), McDonald (2003), Lehohla (2003), Head (2005) and van der Merwe and Gouws (2005) all report the negative effect of HIV/AIDS on SMMEs. For the SMME

Table 5. Ideas to Deal with HIV/AIDS.

Is HIV/AIDS Affecting SMMEs	What Can be Done?				
	More Awareness Programmes	Treatment Programmes	Can be Prevented	Don't Know	Total
Yes	19	8	1	7	35
% of SMMEs being affected by HIV/AIDS	54.3	22.9	2.9	20	100
No	0	0	4	1	5
% of SMMEs not being affected by HIV/AIDS	0	0	80	20	100
Total	19	8	5	8	40
% of SMMEs being affected by HIV/AIDS	100	100	20	87.5	87.5

sector, they report an increase in absenteeism, a decrease in the morale of employees, a lowering of productivity, higher employee benefits, higher labour turnover rates, higher recruitment and training costs, loss of workforce experience, loss of workplace cohesion and increased overall burden on management (Conyers, 2004).

In addition to the ideas mentioned above to overcome HIV/AIDS, Fraser et al. (2002) believe SMMEs could take a more aggressive role and provide literature and posters on the effects of HIV/AIDS, facilitate group discussions, hosting workshops presented by external practitioners, have condom distribution points in strategic positions and provide condom education. Fraser et al. (2002) and McDonald (2003) also believe that SMMEs should have an explicit HIV/AIDS policy in place. McDonald (2003) further supports the idea that businesses request employees to be voluntary tested and provide anti-retroviral therapy in the workplace.

3.3.5. Crime

Crime is a social issue. Poverty is a contributing factor. The government is focusing on a range of programmes to address poverty alleviation (Burger, 2004). Various programmes are currently in progress but the problem remains severe. The business fraternity experiences a significant portion of this crime.

Table 6.   Crime in the Western Cape.

Type of Crime	Percentage Change from 1996 to 2000	
	Western Cape	South Africa
Burglary at business premises	12.4	4.8
Stock theft (inventory)	0.3	−1.0
Shoplifting	23.4	8.7
Malicious damage to property	25.3	6.7
Hijacking of trucks	394.2	29.1
Robbery of cash in transit	−10.5	−42.1
Bank robbery	33.3	−30.4
All fraud, forgeries, misappropriations, embezzlements and other related crimes	−9.5	9.2
Total	15.0	6.2
Total crime activities		
1996	56,306	389,124
2000	64,776	413,538

Source: Lehohla (2004).

For example, Lehohla (2004) reported that in South Africa all types of crime have increased annually by 5% from 1996 to 2000, while the crime in the Western Cape increased by an average of 8% over the same period. Business-related crimes in for South Africa increased by 6.2% from 1996 to 2000, while in the Western Cape it increased by 15.0%. Business related crimes are shown in Table 6.

Our survey, however, indicated that the perception of the service providers is that the crime situation for the business community is not too serious, and that the major contributing factors are unemployment (60%), low self-esteem due to unsuccessful primary or secondary schooling (15%) and lack of sensitivity (2.5%). The respondents are adamant that through job creation (30%), increased police visibility (30%), introducing youth programmes (22.5%) and improved prosecution system (17.5%), the crime rate can be reduced. Crime necessitates that entrepreneurs need to invest money in burglar bars, alarm systems and security companies to ensure that their property and products are well protected. The result of crime is that insurance premiums increase and thus decrease the profit. It might negatively impact on its sustainability and success (Business Gazette, 2005) or even cause business closure (Truter, 1998; Wilson, 2003; Alton, 2004; Head, 2005). According to Smit (2001) crime is rated the second most important factor which impacts upon the business confidence index. It is evident that there are different views about the impact of crime on businesses and is therefore an area that could be further researched.

4. SUMMARY AND CONCLUSIONS

HIV/AIDS and crime are realities. In South Africa, it is affecting not only the lives of many people, but also various sectors within the business fraternity.

With respect to HIV/AIDS, there are apparently two schools of thought, the service providers/business community and the government. While the empirical literature on the topic is relatively small, the existing research appears to indicate that HIV/AIDS is negatively impacting the economy, and most probably the small and micro enterprise of the economy disproportionately. Several studies, including ours of service providers, indicate that either of these problems can result in increased absenteeism, decreased morale of employees, lower productivity, higher employee benefits, higher labour turnover rates, higher recruitment and training costs, loss of workforce experience, and loss of workplace cohesion.

A general feeling, however, is that the South African government, while recognizing the serious problem of both HIV/AIDS tends not to also see the large impact it might also have on the country's SMME economy (e.g., Burger, 2004). There appears to be a consensus among researchers that countries with a serious HIV/AIDS problem should also have an HIV/AIDS policy as part of its economic policy. These would include working with the SMME sector, developing policies related to voluntary counselling and testing, providing anti-retroviral therapy, providing HIV/AIDS literature and posters at business sites, allow group discussions, facilitate workshops by external practitioners, ensure condom distribution points are strategically placed and provide or facilitate condom or sex education.

With respect to crime, again although various researchers (Axa Insurance, 2003; Wilson, 2003; Head, 2005; Business Gazette, 2005) have shown that it has a negative impact on SMMEs, there is a general belief that government does not understand the impact that crime has upon the SMME business sector. Crime increases costs, reduces profitability and causes uncertainty among the business community.

Both the HIV/AIDS and crime problems can also impact negatively on the business confidence index, which could reduce the likelihood of further foreign investment in South Africa, and discourage potential foreign investors from starting and operating small and medium enterprises in South Africa.

Crime therefore has both a direct and indirect impact on SMMEs in South Africa.

While South Africa's competitiveness improved slightly from being 49th in 2004 and 46th in 2005 (Garelli, 2005), its low fluctuating entrepreneurial activity index (9.4 in 2001, 6.5 in 2002, 4.3 in 2003 and 5.4 in 2004) (Zoltan, Arenius, Hay, & Minniti, 2005) plus its HIV/AIDS pandemic and crime situation are definitely factors for business failures among small, medium, and micro enterprises.

Scholars need to closely and empirically examine the impact that disease and crime have upon the economy of developing countries, particularly those in sub-Saharan Africa that struggle with high infection rates of HIV/AIDS, chronic violence and poverty and where micro-enterprise plays an important role in economic development and cross-border trade.

REFERENCES

Alton. (2004). Research study shows impact of cyber crime on SMEs. http://www.ictworld.co. za/EditorialEdit.asp

Axa Insurance (2003). One million small businesses are unprepared for a rising tide of crime. *News Release*, Monday 28 April, http://www.prnewswire.co.uk/cgi/news, 15/08/2005.

Burger, D. (2004). *South Africa yearbook 2004/05* (12th ed.). Yeoville: Government Communications (GCIS).

Business Gazette (2005). Region has its own business crimebuster. Monday 1 August, Cumbria's Premier Business Site. (Online): http://www.businessgazette.co.uk, 15/08/2005.

Connelly, P., & Rosen, S. (2003). *The provision of HIV/AIDS services to small and medium sized enterprises in South Africa*. Centre for International Health and Development, Boston, Boston University.

Conyers, L. (2004). Expanding understanding of HIV/AIDS and employment: Perspectives of focus groups. *Rehabilitation Consulting Bulletin, 48*(1), 5–18.

Department of Justice. (1999). *Crime and small business*. Melbourne: Crime Prevention Victoria.

Department of Trade and Industry (1995). *National strategy for the development and promotion of small business in South Africa*. White Paper on small business, February.

Department of Trade and Industry (2003a). *State of small business development in South Africa: Annual review 2002–2003*. Ntsika Enterprise Promotion Agency.

Department of Trade and Industry (2003b). *Towards a ten year review – synthesis report on implementation of government programmes*. Policy Co-ordinating and Advisory Services, The Presidency, A Discussion document.

Department of Trade and Industry (2004). *Review of ten years of small-business support in South Africa 1994 to 2004*. Pretoria: Government Printers.

Department of Trade and Industry (2005). *Integrated small-enterprise development strategy – unlocking the potential of South African entrepreneurs*. Pretoria, January.

Djankov, S., La Porta, R., Lopez-de-Silanes, F., & Shleifer, A. (2001). The regulatory entry. *Quarterly Journal of Economics, CXVII*, 1–37.

Fraser, E., Grant, W., Mwanza, P., & Naidoo, V. (2002). The impact of HIV/AIDS on small and medium enterprises in South Africa. *South African Journal of Economics*, *70*(7), 1–2.

Garelli, S. (2005). The world competitiveness landscape in 2005: A higher degree of risk. April 26. http://www01.imd.ch

Head, C. (2005). Crimes forces business out of business, 11 February, http://an.newbusiness.co.uk/cgi-bin/newsdesk, 15/08/2005.

International Labour Office. (2005). *HIV/AIDS and employment. Fifth item on the agenda. Governing body*. Geneva: Committee on Employment and Social Policy.

Isaacs, E. B. H., & Friedrich, C. (2005). Small, medium and micro service providers in the Western Cape: Service or disservice. *5th International entrepreneurship forum (IEF), international conference*. Graduate School of Business, University of Cape Town, Cape Town, South Africa, 7–9 September.

Kassiem, A. (2003). 75% of matriculants won't get jobs or further education. *Cape Times*, December 24, http://www.capetimes.co.za/index.php

Lehohla, P. (2003). AIDS leads to poverty, July 1, http://www.lesotho.gov.ls, 17/08/2005.

Lehohla, P. (2004). *Provincial profile 1999 – Western Cape*. Report no. 00-91-01. Statistics South Africa, Pretoria.

McDonald, L. (2003). *SA businesses already hit by adverse impact of HIV/AIDS. Bureau for economic research*. Report to the Board of Governors of the South African Business Coalition on HIV/AIDS, December 10.

Mfaume, R., & Leonard, W. (2004). *Small business entrepreneurship in Dar es salaam – Tanzania: Exploring problems and prospects for future development*. African Development and Poverty Reduction: The Macro–Micro Linkage. Forum Paper. Somerset West, October 13–15.

National Small Business Amendment Bill (2003). *Government Gazette no. 24628*. Republic of South Africa.

Noble, R. (2004). South Africa HIV/AIDS statistics. http://www.avert.org/safricastats.htm

Orford, J., Wood, H. M., & Wood, E. (2004). *Global entrepreneurship monitor – South African report 2004*. Cape Town: Graduate School of Business.

Ortega-Alvarez, D. (2002). *Crime and entrepreneurship*. Venezuela: Office of Economic and Financial Advisors to the National Assembly.

Registrar of Companies. (2005). Registration procedure. http://www.cipro.co.za/products_services/co_regist_doc.asp

Smit, B. (2001). *RMB/BER business confidence index for the fourth quarter of 2001*. Johannesburg: Bureau for Economic Research.

Staff Reporter (2003). Matrics face jobs battle. *Cape Argus*, December 29, http://www.capeargus.co.za/index.php, 17/08/2005.

Taylor, N. (2002). *Reporting on crime against small retail businesses*. Report no. 242. Australian Institute of Criminology, Canberra, December.

Trebilcock, A. (1989). Aids and the workplace – some policy pointers from international labour standards. *International Labour Review*, *128*(1), 29–45.

Truter. (1998). SA fraud alarmingly high. Disptach Online, July, http://www.dispatch.co.za/1998/07/16/business/FRAUD.HTM

Ueckermann, H. (2004). *Staat moet hulp aan kleintjies uitbasuin*. Sake-Rapport, Rapport, 25 Julie.

Ueckermann, H. (2005). *Min sake is bang vir vigs*. Rapport Loopbane, Rapport, 22 Mei, p. 1.

van der Merwe, A., & Gouws, S. (2005). HIV/AIDS and institutions of higher education. *South African Journal of Higher Education, 19*(1), 45–58.

Werkmans Attorneys (2005). Business Guide to South Africa, www.werkmans.co.za/sabus-guide.part_01.htm, 18/08/2005.

Wilson, R. (2003). *Crime: Its extent, impact and consequences for business. Institute of Directors Policy Paper*. London: Business Policy Executive.

World Bank (2005). World Bank intensifies action against HIV/AIDS: At a glance. http://web.worldbank.org/wbsite/external/topics, 15/08/2005.

Zoltan, J., Arenius, P., Hay, M., & Minniti, M. (2005). *Global entrepreneurship monitor – 2004 executive report*. London: Business School and Babson College.

PART IV:
POVERTY TRAPS,
ENTREPRENEURSHIP AND
DEVELOPMENT: THE CASE
OF MOZAMBIQUE

POVERTY, DEVELOPING ENTREPRENEURSHIP AND AID ECONOMICS IN MOZAMBIQUE: A REVIEW OF EMPIRICAL RESEARCH

Leo Paul Dana and Craig S. Galbraith

1. INTRODUCTION

Located in South-eastern Africa, between South Africa and Tanzania, Mozambique (population 19,000,000) is currently one of the poorest countries in the world with only a $1,300 gross domestic product per capita (purchasing power parity, CIA World Factbook, 2005). In spite of its rich natural resources, because of the chronic history of violence, dire poverty, HIV/AIDS (12.2% adult infection rate) and diseases related to pollution and natural disasters, Mozambique also has one of the lowest life expectancies in the world at 40.32 years (CIA World Factbook, 2005). The recent 2000 Mozambican floods alone displaced a quarter million residents into emergency camps, with the affected population reaching 1 million residents. In overall human and social development, Mozambique currently ranks

Developmental Entrepreneurship: Adversity, Risk, and Isolation
International Research in the Business Disciplines, Volume 5, 187–201
Copyright © 2006 by Elsevier Ltd.
ISSN: 1074-7877/doi:10.1016/S1074-7877(06)05010-0

168th out of 177 countries in the U.N.'s Human Development Index (2003 HDI, U.N. Human Development Reports), and 96th among 103 developing countries in the U.N.'s human poverty index (2003 HPI-1, U.N. Human Development Reports).

To many scholars, Mozambique would be classified as an economic "poverty trap." According to Kraay (2005), poverty traps occur as, "self-reinforcing mechanisms whereby countries, or individuals, that start out poor might remain poor. If saving rates, or technology or other positive forces for growth are low precisely because countries are poor, then countries may find themselves trapped at low levels of development." (p. 15). In these situations, good governance and institutions may not be sufficient to pull the country out of its poverty cycle (Sachs et al., 2004).

The focus of this paper is to review the small body of empirical literature that examines components of the small business and entrepreneurial process in Mozambique. In particular, we will examine empirical studies that explore issues related to the importance of micro-enterprises and the shadow economy, the policies and functions of micro-loan institutions, the role of Mozambican labour unions, the successes of international efforts to support micro-enterprise development, and micro-enterprise cross-border exchanges.

2. ECONOMIC OVERVIEW

The economic history of Mozambique is quite unique. It was originally colonised by the Portuguese in the early 16th century. In 1885, there was sufficient Portuguese immigration to form the region into a formal colony named Portuguese East Africa. Many of these early settlers were part of the "prazo" system of the 17th and 18th century which encouraged European immigrants, including many felons, ex-soldiers, and destitute Portuguese government officials to seize land in the country (Henriksen, 1978; Newitt, 1996).

During the years following World War II, over half a million indigenous families in Mozambique were producing cotton (Pitcher, 1993). This allowed Portugal to rely on its colonies for 96% of its cotton needs. During this time there were often forced labour events. In the early 1950s, for example, the Portuguese ordered many indigenous Mozambicans to leave their farms and villages to clear more land for forced cotton growing. Cassava and sorghum were also raised. Immigrants from Asia, however, were exempt from forced labour, and were allowed to operate private small businesses. Where cotton could not grow, farmers were made to grow groundnuts and/or rice. Subsequently, in addition to cotton, cashew nuts became one of Mozambique's major exports. The people of Mozambique, however, relied on the Union of South Africa for energy and basic foods including fish, maize, onions, potatoes and other vegetables through cross-border trade. By 1960, approximately 250,000 Portuguese settlers and their descendants were living Mozambique.

To use Acemoglu, Robinson, and Johnson's (2001, 2004) terminology, the economy during this colonial time was primarily "extractive," with little or no effort by the Portuguese settlers to establish workable economic institutions based on European models, or control the country politically (Westfall, 1984), a situation resulting in depressed economic development.

The guerrilla war for independence began in earnest in the early 1960s, with sporadic outburst of significant violence (Westfall, 1984). Mozambique ultimately gained its independence from Portugal in June 1975 with the new governing Front for the Liberation of Mozambique (FRELIMO) adopting rigid Marxist policies and aligning itself with Soviet Union. At the same time, most of the white population left Mozambique, abandoning their enterprises, farms, and administrative positions (Pitcher, 1993) – currently, only a few thousand Europeans live in Mozambique.

A difficult and chronic period of civil war violence ensued during the years 1977–1992, in which the economy worsened even further. During this time it is estimated that up to 1 million people were killed, 1.7 million became refugees, and another 3.2 million people were displaced (Hanlon, 1996). As a response to the impending disaster, in 1987 the FRELIMO government implemented several macro-economic reforms targeted to stabilise the economy. Concurrent with these policies, Mozambique started to receive substantial donor assistance, not only in direct aid from donor organisations from Europe, the U.S., the IMF, the World Bank, and the U.N., but also assistance, such as training programs and education, by several religious, private and semi-government aid organisations. These transfers and aid programs often came with strict conditions, such as reducing government expenditures, phasing out protective tariffs, relaxing minimum labour standards, and control of corruption (Newitt, 1996; Pitcher, 2002). These measures did not come without controversy, however (e.g., Hanlon, 1996).

The ruling FRELIMO, under Joaquim Chissano, formally abandoned Marxism in 1989, and a new constitution was established which called for multi-party elections. Some state-owned enterprises were privatised. A U.N. brokered cease-fire between FRELIMO and the rebel Mozambique

National Resistance (RENAMO) was implemented in 1992, and in 1994 multi-party elections were held under U.N. peacekeeping force supervision. Joaquim Chissano was subsequently elected to office (see Wood, 1999). By 1995 many of the refugees from the civil war era had repatriated back to their native regions within Mozambique. Elections were held in 1999, and Joaquim Chissano was re-elected; although there were protests regarding the legitimacy of the 1999 elections (U.S. State Department, 2001). Typical of many emerging democracies, subsequent public opinion surveys in Mozambique suggest a wide range of opinions regarding the notion of democracy and freedom (Pereira, Davids, & Mattes, 2002).

The combination of these events (progress towards democracy, movement towards a market-based economy, and controls tied to aid funds) appeared to substantially improve the Mozambican economy (Wood, 1999), resulting in positive economic growth with growth rates in the late 1990s estimated at close to 10% (Economist Intelligence Unit, 2000). Currently, GDP is estimated to grow at about 7.0%, with industrial production growth rates estimated at 3.4% (CIA World Factbook, 2005). However, it must be remembered that the economic statistical base for these growth statistics remains relatively small. In addition, inflation was controlled at single-digit levels for much of the 1990s, but had started to climb to the low-teens by 2003.

In spite of this, the vast majority of the population is still involved with subsistence agriculture and small micro-businesses within the cities. Foreign aid remains a major component of the Mozambican economy with some estimates reporting that foreign aid constitutes around 75% of the state budget. In addition, much of the foreign debt for Mozambique has been either forgiven or rescheduled. In December of 2004, President Chissano stepped down without seeking a third term and Mozambique made the transition to a new government under his FRELIMO successor, Amrando Emilio Guebuza.

This historical chronic unrest, combined with several severe droughts and floods during the last decade, has encouraged migration of the rural population to the urban centres, such as the capital Maputo. This, in turn, has created substantial environmental problems, such as significant pollution of surface and coastal waters. Reports of governmental human right violations continue in Mozambique, although a number of groups including the Catholic Church (Commissão Católica de Justiça e Paz), Protestant Churches (Conselho Cristão de Moçambique), universities, and international organisations such as the U.N. are working hard to control these violations (Fry, 2006).

3. REVIEW OF EMPIRICAL LITERATURE: BUSINESS IN MOZAMBIQUE

While there are a number of macro-economic studies that examine economic growth in sub-Saharan Africa including Mozambique, the empirical literature examining business activities at the micro-level in Mozambique is sparse, at best. This review explores some of the important studies that examine critical issues related to entrepreneurial activity in the post-civil war and post-Marxist era of Mozambique. These studies focus on the importance of micro-enterprises and the shadow economy, the policies and functions of micro-loan institutions, the role of Mozambican labour unions, the successes of international efforts to support micro-enterprise development, and micro-enterprise cross-border exchanges. The theme behind this review is that it is difficult, if not impossible, to implement effective macro-economic policies and targeted poverty reducing programs without having a base of empirical knowledge regarding how the small business sector works, and what strategies appear most effective at the individual firm and sector level.

3.1. The Importance of the Shadow Economy: An Ethnographic Study

Dana (1996) performed an ethnographic case study of Mozambican small business and economic conditions in 1995, immediately following the first elections in 1994. Ethnographic research in business research focuses on immersion and close field observation of a socio-economic phenomenon. From an institutional and infrastructure perspective, Dana noted that travel by roads was problematic due to piracy, and in some cases unexploded land mines left over from the civil wars. Violent crime was prevalent, and general anarchy prevailed. Public transportation was weak, and communication and power grids were often reported down. Dana also estimated that about 10% pilferage was occurring at the Port of Maputo, in spite of a well-organised private guard. Most government buildings in the major cities were in poor condition, remnants of the previous Marxist economy. Dana also remarks that many signs were hand-painted, with previous Marxist or Communist references or names crossed out, or simply missing.

From a government and banking perspective, Dana reported that profits from all legal business entities were still being taxed at 50%, and it appeared difficult to obtain a business loan from the local banks without paying bribes. In addition, developing new ventures within the legal sector was difficult due to bureaucracy, petitions, forms, and taxes. This obviously encouraged the development of a shadow, extra-legal economy. At the time of Dana's report, the government had made efforts to decrease the shadow economy by passing legislation that required all business activities to be withdrawn from residential houses.

At this time formal unemployment ran over 80%. From an entrepreneurial perspective, it is clear from Dana's study that the vast majority of Mozambicans participated in the shadow economy. He noted that crime was an established business activity, with car thefts ranking high. In fact, a Mercado Estrela, or "Thieves Market" was openly operating in Maputo where stolen goods were sold and bought. It should also be noted that Mozambique is now regarded as the primary South African transit point for South Asian hashish and heroin, and a major transit point for South American cocaine destined for European markets (CIA World Factbook, 2005).

In spite of the dangerous streets, Dana (1996, p. 69) also observed that the marketplaces were a "bastion of small enterprise, where traditional remedies and potions are sold alongside animal tails, shells, and snake heads, as well as live sheep, mangoes, and wood. Among the countless dealers are some selling cooling oil in Canada Dry bottles. Others sell gasoline in Russian Coca-Cola bottles ... " (see Photos 1 and 2).

Photograph 1.   Shadow Market Economy, Female Vendors in Mozambique (1995).
Source: Leo Paul Dana.

Photograph 2.   Selling Fuel in Soda Bottle: Mozambique (1995). *Source:* Leo Paul Dana.

Dana indicated that a number of entrepreneurs provided services parallel to the formal governmental services, such as private busses competing with public transportation and local small private security companies competing with the police force. For example, he reported approximately 3,000 "mercenaries" had been hired to protect local entrepreneurs.

Several important small business assistance programs in Mozambique were discussed by Dana. First, was the Trust Fund for the Development of Small Industry, which due to required paperwork, did not appear to be very effective. Another was the U.N.'s Urban Micro-Enterprise Support Fund. Approximately $2 million funds were distributed to almost 300 micro-enterprises (<10 employees), with a reported creation of approximately 2000 jobs. Most of the entrepreneurs were fishermen, confectioners, and construction-related firms. Dana did not report on the longevity of these firms, or whether the micro-loans were ever repaid.

Dana concluded from his study that supplying credit was not enough and that despite the government's official policy to support small enterprise, misguided economic policies survived immediately following the transition to a market economy, which hindered small-scale firms. Dana argued that in contrast to the republic of South Africa, where informal enterprise was encouraged, in the immediate post-election era (1995) municipalities in Mozambique actively persecuted street vendors, although these were performing an important economic function, and vigorously attempted to reduce the informal economy by enacting "residential restriction" laws.

3.2. The Effectiveness of Micro-Enterprise Business Assistance Programs

A study by Kaufmann and Parlmeyer (2006) involved a sample of 1,037 PAPIR Mozambican client firms in 1998 and 1999. PAPIR, or Projecto de Apoio as Pequenas Industrias Rurais, was designed to support small-scale manufacturers in the post-war period. The firms studied were clients of the Danish PAPIR project in Sofala Province, Mozambique. PAPIR provided a number of micro-finance and consulting services, including training. The details of this study are provided in another chapter of this volume, but the results indicated that the major barriers were lack of capital and access to credit, and that the failure rate was very high. In addition, the study indicated that formal training did not appear to contribute to success in the micro-enterprises interviewed (see Kaufmann & Parlmeyer, 2006). The key policy recommendation was that the Mozambican government, and other countries in similar impoverished development stages, need to develop different programs targeted to the informal sector versus the formal sector.

3.3. Strategies of Micro-Loan Institutions

Van de Ruit (2001) examined micro-finance and donor roles in Mozambique, with her primary empirical research taking place in 2001. She found approximately 30 institutions serving 16,000 clients in Mozambique. This effort was part of the 2001 Mozambique Structural Adjustment Program which focused on agricultural small businesses and micro-finance; however, she noted that most rural areas did not have access to these institutions. Van de Ruit (2001) also found that the attrition of these institutions was high, with 10 institutions closing in the previous five years. The major donors to the institutions were the EC member states, the Canadian International Development Agency (CIDA), the UK Department for International Development (DFID), and the U.S. Agency for International Development (USAID). She argued that historically, micro-finance efforts in Mozambique had not been very effective, partly due to claims of fraud and corruption. She noted, however, that current (2001) micro-loan efforts were (a) focused on urban centres with the argument that successful economic growth must first start in the urban centres, and the opportunities are greater in urban centres; (b) offering financial products based upon a "group solidarity lending model" (c) since financial sustainability was now an objective of many micro-loan institutions, these loans were not reaching the "ultra-poor" (d) donors had become much more aggressive in demanding financial sustainability; (e) few of the micro-finance institutions were managed by native Mozambicans, instead relying on foreign expertise; and (f) the Mozambique government had done little in this sector, or provided policies that assist in its implementation.

Van de Ruit (2001) concluded that overall, the "minimalist" model of credit had been largely unsuccessful in Mozambique, that micro-loan programs with a primary poverty alleviation strategy was somewhat at conflict with the notion of sustainability, and that future loan programs and financial products needed to be more specific to the notion of "livelihood" ideas. In addition, the study raised important issues about collateral for loans as it related to rural land titles. De Vletter (1999) also provides a good summary of microfinance strategies in Mozambique during the post-Marxist transition period.

3.4. The Role of Mozambican Labour Unions

Labour unions played a critical role in supporting the war for independence, and later became a dominant political power within the FRELIMO Marxist dictatorship (Westfall, 1984). After the 1994 elections, labour unions in Mozambique still retained substantial power, which included calling for a number of labour stoppages in the post-1994 period (U.S. State Department, 2001).

Webster, Wood, and Brookes (2004) performed the first systematic attempt to empirically examine the effect of liberalisation of industrial relation practices at the firm level in Mozambique. In their study, the authors noted that there were currently 21 unions in Mozambique, grouped into two federations, the OTM and the CONSILMO. The OTM (Organisation of Mozambican Workers), which had ties to the pre-liberalisation Marxist FRELIMO government, had approximately 90,000 members. Since the early 1990s, however, the OTM generally had "become a persistent critic of the government's (current) economic policies" (Webster et al., (2004, p. 9), see also Pitcher, 2002). The CONASILMO (Confederation of Free and Independent Trade Unions) was formed in 1998 by union groups that broke away from the OTM.

Webster et al. (2004) surveyed 177 commercial firms in Mozambique using a stratified sample of different geographical locations. The average firm size was 267 employees, with many firms being much smaller. Most of the sample firms were in construction, transportation, and manufacturing. Thirty-six percent of the firms had no union representation, while 64% had some or complete union representation. Overall the results indicated that only 22% of the firms had formal employee relations training, and about one-third indicated that they do not honour labour agreements. About 69% of the firms indicated that job training was by shadowing.

The major conclusions of the study were that; (a) unions in Mozambique appeared to have diminishing effect on enterprise due to the emergence of the large non-formal, shadow economy and the strategy of many smaller firms to use casual labour defined under Mozambique labour rules; (b) that Mozambican unions had little effect reaching marginal, low paid workers; (c) that even if a collective agreement was in place, many firms did not abide by the agreement; and (d) that within the formal economy, employment practices still appear to be based upon "informalism and autocratic managerialism," that may have its roots in Mozambique's "historical legacies."

Other useful studies or reports cited by the authors regarding labour practices in Mozambique, and the Southern region in Africa in general, included Kimenia (2000), Wood and Els (2000), Levy (2003), and Gumende (1999).

3.5. Micro-Cross Border Trade: The Role of Small Entrepreneurs

The informal economy in most chronically depressed countries involves more than micro-enterprises simply serving a small, localised market. These informal and shadow sectors often expand to the exporting and importing of products through cross-border trade. While there appears to be interest by many policy makers and donor agencies in understanding the impact of micro-enterprises on poverty reduction and economic development, particularly as they relate to the development of successful micro-loan institutions and strategies, the importance of these micro-enterprises in cross-border trade, or technically the import and export markets, is often overlooked.

Peberdy (2000) argues that part of this oversight is due to lack of empirical data. Likewise Ackello-Ogutu (1996) observes that cross-border trade is often ignored and recommends collection techniques such as selecting appropriate border observation sites and using a 12-month duration of border observation for tracking goods to quantify cross-border trade and fit specific circumstances that prevail in Eastern and Southern Africa. Similarly, Little, Teka, and Azeze (1998) examine appropriate research methods for cross-boarder trade in the Horn of Africa.

In fact, in an early study, the USAID estimated the nature and economic value of the informal cross-border trade sector between Mozambique and other neighbouring countries (e.g., MaCamo, 1998), concluding that the informal sector exceeded the formal sector in trade value and volume. Peberdy (2000) concludes that these studies suggest that, "the informal sector cross-border trade plays a significant role in regional trade relationships and is a significant part of small, micro and medium enterprise activity in Mozambique" (p. 362), and thus provides a motivation for additional empirical research in this area.

In addition, there is a growing literature examining the role that borders have with respect to the entrepreneurial activities of migrants and immigrants (e.g., Portes & Sensenbrenner, 1993; Light, 2004; Galbraith, Stiles, & Benitez-Bertheau, 2004) as well as whether or not the movement of immigrants, capital, and goods at a informal and micro-level represents an overall "globalisation" trend of trade barrier reduction, and the potential homogenisation of localised culture (e.g., Basch, Schiller, & Blanc, 1994; Peberdy & Rogerson, 2000).

Thus while Dana's (1996) study focused on the micro-enterprise and the informal economic sector within Mozambique, the empirical study reported in Peberdy (2000), Peberdy and Rogerson (2000) and Peberdy and Crush (2001) examined the active cross-border trade between South Africa and Mozambique. Peberdy and her colleagues interviewed 101 cross-border traders and 40 formal sector shops in late 1999 and early 2000. Interestingly, the results indicated that "cross-border trade between South Africa and Mozambique was dominated by women traders" (2000, p. 364), particularly Mozambican women from Maputo. While many of the women traders were unmarried (52.4%), the traders generally supported families (average three children per trader), and other dependents (average 2.37 other dependents than children).

Perberdy noted that while other studies of African borders appear to indicate that cross-border traders tend to be more educated, the Mozambican traders were seen to be uneducated and poor, although they did appear to have higher literacy rates than the general Mozambique population – a conclusion that might indicate that although micro-enterprise informal sector entrepreneurs may have less formal education and be poor (which may limit their entry into the formal economy), there appears to be some possible socio-economic characteristics (such as high literacy, support of large families) that might characterise this type of entrepreneurial behaviour.

One of the key findings of the Perberdy study was the difficulty in separating the informal sector from the formal sector. For example, an "extra-legal" cross-border sourced product from South Africa may be sold in a formal sector retail shop in Mozambique – Perberdy reported about 25% of goods may take this form. Another finding was the mobility of this sector, that informal traders often travelled between a number of neighbouring states.

In terms of economic goods transported, the pattern of informal cross-border trade appeared to mirror the formal sector statistics, that is, clothing, textiles, household goods, and food products tended to be imported into Mozambique (many which find their way into the Mozambican market places) while food products were the major informal export to South Africa. Perberdy (2000) estimated the value of goods transported generally above the US$400 level. While this appears low, it is actually double the estimated average monthly income of Mozambicans. Profit margins were estimated in the 15–30% range.

Two important points made in the Perberdy study were that the informal trade process recovered rapidly, within only a couple of months, after the devastating 2000 floods, and that most of the traders (61.4% of Mozambican respondents) interviewed indicated they employed other people in their enterprises.

The important conclusions of the Peberby study are; (a) that it was difficult to separate the informal sector from the formal sector; (b) that the entrepreneurs tended to network around the formal border barriers; (c) that the cross-border entrepreneurial activities from these micro-enterprises were vibrant, active, and provided substantial cross-border economic activity; and (d) these entrepreneurs tended to respond quickly to opportunity, such as the quick recovery of trade seen after the 2000 floods in Mozambique. Peberdy (2002) offered several policy recommendations in light of these findings.

4. CONCLUSIONS

Throughout its history, Mozambique has suffered a multitude of devastating events. From a 400-year extractive colonial economy, to tragic floods and droughts, violent civil wars, a brutal Marxist dictatorship, the HIV/AIDS pandemic and even unexploded land mines that limit travel in certain areas, Mozambique appears to be stuck in a classic economic "poverty trap." It is not surprising that there is considerable interest in finding mechanisms to help pull Mozambique out of its poverty cycle. In fact, there are literally hundreds of internationally sponsored programs, development agencies, and donor organisations all targeted to Mozambique.

Clearly, it is recognised that aid and assistance that targets the small business and micro-enterprise entrepreneurial level of the economy is critical for economic development (e.g., De Vletter, 1999). However, in spite of the *Report on the Millennium Development Goals for Mozambique's* (U.N., 2002) assessment that shows "strong" support for reducing extreme poverty in Mozambique the vast majority of discussions on how to accomplish this tend to be overly broad-brushed and non-specific. And the fact remains that, in spite of innumerable reports, suggestions, programs, and aid dollars, it appears that only a little progress has been made over the years in Mozambique.

One reason for this failure is perhaps the lack of real empirical data at the micro-level of the economy. Without a real understanding of the true nature of entrepreneurial activity at the micro-level, and its critical role in economic development within chronically impoverished nations, it is difficult, at best, to develop more macro-economic strategies or aid assistance programs.

This short review attempts to shed a little empirical light on several important elements of the Mozambican economy, particularly at the small enterprise level. This includes the importance of micro-enterprises and their related shadow economy, the policies and functions of micro-loan institutions, the role of Mozambican labour unions, efforts to provide direction and advice to micro-enterprise development, and micro-enterprise cross-border exchanges between Mozambique and its neighbours.

REFERENCES

Acemoglu, D., Johnson, S., & Robinson, J. (2001). The colonial origins of comparative development: An empirical investigation. *American Economic Review, 91*, 1369–1401.

Accmoglu, D., Robinson, J., & Johnson, S. (2004). *Institutions as the fundamental cause of long-run growth.* NBER Working Paper #10481.

Ackello-Oguto, C. (1996). *Methodologies for estimating informal crossborder trade in Eastern and Southern Africa: Kenya/Uganda Border, Tanzania and its neighbours, Malawi and its neighbors, Mozambique and its neighbors.* Technical Paper #29, office of sustainable development, USAID, Washington, DC.

Basch, L., Schiller, N., & Blanc, C. (1994). *Nations unbound: Transnational projects, post colonial predicaments and deterritorialized nation states.* Basel: Gordon and Breach Science Publishers.

CIA (2005). *Mozambique country report.* CIA World Factbook.

Dana, L. (1996). Small business in Mozambique after the war. *Journal of Small Business Research, 34*(4), 67–71.

De Vletter, F. (1999). The evolution of microfinance in a successful post-conflict transition: The case study of Mozambique. Paper presented for the Joint International Labour

Office/UN High Commissioner for Refugees Workshop: Microfinance in Post-Conflict Countries, September, Retrieved from http://www.ilo.org/public/english/employment/ finance/papers/mozamb.htm

Economist Intelligence Unit (2000). *Mozambique Malawi Country Report*. London: Economist Intelligence Unit.

Fry, P. (2006). *The status of human rights organizations in sub-Saharan Africa: Mozambique*. University of Minnesota Human Rights Library, http://www1.umn.edu/humanrts/ africa/mozambiq.htm, accessed February 20, 2006.

Galbraith, C., Stiles, C., & Benitez-Bertheau, J. (2004). The embryonic development of an ethnic neighbourhood: A longitudinal case study of entrepreneurial activity. In: C. Stiles & C. Galbraith (Eds), *Ethnic entrepreneurship: Structure and process* (pp. 95–114). Elsevier: London.

Gumende, A. (1999). *Industrial relations in a restructuring economy: Implications for corporate strategy and human resource management in Mozambique*. Unpublished MBA dissertation, Nottingham Trent University, Nottingham, June.

Hanlon, J. (1996). *Peace without profit: How the IMF blocks rebuilding in Mozambique*. Oxford: James Currey.

Henriksen, T. (1978). *Mozambique: A history*. Southampton, England: The Camelot Press.

Kimemia, P. (2000). An overview of the performance of the East African economies since 1985: Implications for the new initiate on East African Cooperation. *African Sociological Review, 4*(1), 119–137.

Kraay, A. (2005). Aid, growth, and poverty. Paper presented to the IMF Seminar on Foreign Aid and Macroeconomic Management, Maputo, Mozambique, March.

Levy, S. (2003). *The legal and administrative framework for labor relations in Mozambique*. Report, SAL Consultoria e Investimentos, Maputo.

Light, I. (2004). The ethnic ownership economy. In: C. Stiles & C. Galbraith (Eds), *Ethnic entrepreneurship: Structure and process* (pp. 3–44). London: Elsevier.

Little, P., Teka, T., & Azeze, A. (1998). *Research methods on cross-border trade in the Horn of Africa: Further observations*. Research Paper. Organization for Social Science Research in eastern and Southern Africa (OSSREA), Addis Ababa, Ethiopia.

MaCamo, J. (1998). *Estimates of unrecorded cross-border trade between Mozambique and her neighbors: Implications for food security*. Report for the regional economic support office for Eastern and Southern Africa. USAID, Washington, DC.

Newitt, M. (1996). *A history of Mozambique*. London: Hirst.

Peberdy, S. (2000). Border crossings: Small entrepreneurs and cross-border trade between South Africa and Mozambique. *Tijdschrift voor Economishe en SocialeGeografie, 91*(4), 361–378.

Perberdy, S. (2002). Hurdles to trade? South African's immigration policy and informal sector cross-border traders in the SADC. Paper presented at the SAMP/LHR/HSRC workshop on regional integration, poverty and South Africa's proposed migration policy,pretoria, South Africa, April.

Peberdy, S., & Crush, J. (2001). Invisible trade, invisible travellers: The Maputo Corridor spatial development initiative and informal cross-border trading. *South African Geographical Journal, 83*(20), 115–123.

Peberdy, S., & Rogerson, C. (2000). Transnationalism and non-South African entrepreneurs in South Africa's small, medium and micro-enterprise (SMME) economy. *Canadian Journal of African Studies, 34*, 20–40.

Pereira, J., Davids, Y., & Mattes, R. (2002). *Mozambicans' views of democracy and political reform: A comparative perspective.* Afrobarometer Paper #22, Institute for Democracy in South Africa (IDASA), Cape Town, South Africa.

Pitcher, A. (1993). *Politics in the Portuguese empire: The state, industry, and cotton.* Oxford: Oxford Press.

Pitcher, A. (2002). *Transforming Mozambique: The politics of privatization.* Cambridge: Cambridge University Press.

Portes, A., & Sensenbrenner, J. (1993). Embeddedness and immigration: Notes on the social determination of economic action. *American Journal of Sociology, 98*(6), 1320–1350.

Sachs, J., McArthur, J., Schmidt-Traub, G., Kruk, M., Bahadur, C., Faye, M., & McCord, G. (2004). Ending Africa's poverty trap. *Brookings Papers on Economic Activity, 1,* 117–216.

United Nations (2002). *Report on the millennium development goals: Republic of Mozambique.* United Nations Development Programme (http://www.undp.org.mz/anmviewer. asp?a = 4, accessed February (1), 11720, 2006).

United States State Department (2001). *Mozambique: Country reports on human rights practices.* Washington, DC: U.S. State Department, Bureau of Democracy, Human Rights, and Labor.

Van de Ruit, C. (2001). *Micro-finance, donor roles and influence and the pro-poor agenda: The cases of South Africa and Mozambique.* Draft Working Paper, University of Kwazulu-Natal, South Africa.

Webster, E., Wood, G., & Brookes, M. (2004). International homogenization or the persistence of national practices?: The remaking on industrial relations in Mozambique. Paper presented at the 2004 society for the advancement of socio-economics, Washington, DC, July.

Westfall, W. (1984). *Mozambique – Insurgency against Portugal, 1963–1975.* Quantico, Virginia: U.S. Marine Corps Command and Staff College.

Wood, G. (1999). Democratization in Mozambique: Trends and practices. *Democratization, 6,* 156–170.

Wood, G., & Els, C. (2000). The making and remaking of HRM: The practice of managing people in the Eastern Cape Province, South Africa. *International Journal of Human Resource Management, 11,* 112–125.

THE DILEMMA OF SMALL BUSINESS IN MOZAMBIQUE: A RESEARCH NOTE

Friedrich Kaufmann and Wilhelm Parlmeyer

1. INTRODUCTION

A vast portion of the economic activity in Mozambique consists of small businesses. Moreover, these business activities are often either informal or unrecorded in official sources (Dana, 1996; Fialho, 1996; Fungulane, 1999). Not surprising, the accuracy of the statistical coverage is poor and uneven.[1] For example, calculations of the economic contribution of the informal sector by the Instituto Nacional de Estatistica (INE) and the Italian Government Co-operation Agency suggest that the real GDP is underestimated by some 79% (Economist Intelligence Unit, 1998). Abreu and Abreu (1996), of the Central Bank in Mozambique, using a monetarist approach, have estimated that the informal sector accounts for at least 33% of the Mozambican GNP. In Beira, the second largest city in Mozambique, Navaia and Kaufmann (1999) estimate that at least 60% of the firms are informal businesses.

The latest approved *Industrial Strategy Policy* of the Mozambican government (a new policy document is currently under discussion) has officially recognised the importance of small businesses and stressed the need for the "inclusion of the informal sector" (República de Moçambique, 1997, p. 32). Also the new Mozambican National Poverty Reduction Strategy

Developmental Entrepreneurship: Adversity, Risk, and Isolation
International Research in the Business Disciplines, Volume 5, 203–214
Copyright © 2006 by Elsevier Ltd.
ISSN: 1074-7877/doi:10.1016/S1074-7877(06)05011-2

(PARPA II) emphasizes the importance of the private sector for poverty reduction and social development.

Within this context our empirical study defines firms as "micro," or "small," when they have no more than 10 employees. This broad definition implies that small firms can be both formal and informal. In Mozambique, the so-called "empresas informais" and the "empresas registadas (3rd categoria)" fulfill these criteria. The "third category" firms have up to 10 employees and are administered by the local authorities, just like the "informal businesses," which have to pay fees to the city council. These companies are supposed to register, but do not need a licence to operate (SAL, ACIS, 2005).

Like anywhere, small business in Mozambique varies substantially in economic activity (Fafchamps, 1994; Dana, 1996; Correiro & Reis, 1996; Kaufmann & Navaia, 1999). They are actively engaged in production (agricultural, non-agricultural, craftsmen, petty producers), trade (food, drinks, agricultural products, manufactured goods, firewood, charcoal, etc.) and/or many service-related sectors (repair, hair-cutting, food stalls, etc.).

2. ENTREPRENEURSHIP IN MOZAMBIQUE: A BACKGROUND

Small firms are not only the fastest growing sector in Africa (de Vletter, 1996), but they are also considered an important outlet for indigenous entrepreneurship. Usually, the owners of small firms in Africa migrate from within the small-firm sector itself; few have learned their productive skills within larger firms.

Many previously colonial African countries, like Mozambique, actually have somewhat of a dual economic structure (Todaro, 1997; Biggs, Nasir, & Fisman, 1999). On the one hand, the country has inherited a number of large and relatively modern enterprises from the colonial rule period, while the local indigenous firms mainly use older, less sophisticated production techniques. This sort of duality still remains across many sectors and regions in Mozambique. This dual economy is often reinforced by the ongoing privatisations of previous nationalised "colonial" enterprises, which rely mainly on foreign direct investment.

The level of formal education in Mozambican enterprise is modest. Most productive skills have been acquired through traditional apprenticeship or by employment within other small firms (Billetoft, 1998). Nevertheless, most small businessmen lack extensive training in financial management, marketing, business organisation and cost assessment.

In addition, most Mozambican small firms do not have access to formal financial institutions, and often the overvalued real-interest rates discourage investments (e.g., International Finance Corporation, 1996). Hence, business investments are typically financed by personal risk capital like savings, loans, assistance from relatives, pensions or the selling of an asset. Typically, the initial capital for a start-up is low (< 100 US$) and the capital stock required is generally modest. Nevertheless, the growing number of NGO-Micro-Enterprise financing schemes provides, at least for some small firms, new ways of financing (de Vletter, 1997; KFW, 2003).

It has been frequently pointed out that small, micro-enterprise firms provide many of the consumer goods demanded by the lower-income population. However, Billetoft (1998) reports that some micro-firms have been able to shift away from inferior goods for the lower-income consumer, and successfully operate in broader, segmented markets.

Empirical studies in sub-Saharan Africa also indicate that there is a strong positive correlation between local income and the demand for small-scale products (e.g., Liedholm, 1992). Not surprising many small firms are established, and subsequently operate near income-generating large businesses, like the Mozambican sugar industry.

Typically the barriers for small, micro-enterprises in poor nations like Mozambique include (Nathan Associates, 2004; Roberts, 2003; Kaufmann, 2005) inefficient markets, implying high transaction costs; lack of trust and honesty in the business culture (no culture of risk-sharing); inefficient, old-fashioned legal system (enforcement problems); red tape, high legal requirements, rigid bureaucratic regulations; corruption; lack of managerial skills/entrepreneurship; lack of information of the advantages of formality; social status; lack of transparency and information in the market for sub-contracting; and public procurement problems.

3. SOME EMPIRICAL EVIDENCE FROM MOZAMBIQUE

The Projecto de Apoio às Pequenas Industrias Rurais (PAPIR) sample we have used in our study is based on internal registration documents of the PAPIR clients. The Danish PAPIR project in Sofala was designed to support small firms, especially small-scale manufacturers, in the post-war period, with technical assistance and, later on, with credits. In 1998, this project ended after 10 years of activities. In the beginning of the PAPIR project, firm assistance served as a means to help refugees and alleviate

Table 1. Sectors of Activity and Number of Surviving Small Businesses (PAPIR).

Sector	PAPIR Clients 1987–1997		1998		1999	
Petty manufacturers	497	47.9%	217	35.8%	155	36.3%
Petty trade	242	23.3%	217	35.8%	159	37.2%
Service	298	28.7%	172	28.4%	113	26.5%
Total	1037		606		427	

poverty. Later on, it focussed primarily on business growth. Nevertheless, this strategy was never clearly defined (see Cotter, 1996).

While the registration documents were not designed for research purposes, the interviews and the updates allow us to apprehend some of the characteristics of Mozambican small firms, as well as some of the reasons for their existence. The updates also make it possible to demonstrate the high volatility of small businesses and highlight some important correlations.

3.1. How Many Firms Survived?

The small-business sector in Mozambique is highly volatile. Out of a total of 1,037 PAPIR small-business clients (1987–1997), 58.4% (606) had survived by 1998. The latest update, in 1999, showed that only 427 (41.1%) had survived, which indicates a high attrition rate of these firms. Between 1998 and 1999, 29.5% of the sample firms have closed (see Table 1).

3.2. The Informal Economy

By 1998, 58.1% of these small firms could be considered informal businesses in that they were not officially registered and did not pay taxes on a regular basis (Navaia & Kaufmann, 1999). Interestingly, the 1999 update indicated that, out of the surviving firms, 64.4% were informal businesses. This higher survival rate for informal firms appears to indicate that the informal economy (without regular taxes, checks, etc.) might be an easier path. Sixty-two percent of the small firms did not have a bank account, which directly correlates with the percentage of informality.

3.3. Firm Growth

The 1999 update did not indicate any significant growth. The average number of people employed decreased from 2.0 to 1.6 employees per small

Table 2. Number of Workers Employed and Investment.

No. of Workers	Equipment 1998				Equipment 1999			
	≤80 US$		>80 US$		≤80 US$		>80 US$	
0	44	65.7%	23	34.3%	63	70.8%	26	29.2%
1	60	62.5%	36	37.5%	35	53.0%	31	47.0%
2	45	49.5%	46	50.5%	20	44.4%	25	55.6%
3	23	34.3%	44	65.7%	14	35.0%	26	65.0%
4	13	48.1%	14	51.9%	3	13.6%	19	86.4%
5–10	4	10.5%	34	89.5%	1	10.0%	9	90.0%
≥11			11	100.0%			7	100.0%
Total	189	47.6%	208	52.4%	136	48.7%	143	51.3%

Note: Significance = 99.9%, Pearson's $R = 0.342$ (1998); significance = 99.9%, Pearson's $R = 0.396$ (1999).

firm. The average monthly income also decreased to less than 40 US$ per month for over 73.0% of the PAPIR small firms versus only 52.0% in 1998.

In addition, the amount of capital invested did not show any increase in our sample. Over one-half of the small firms still operated on investments under 80 US$. Eighty percent indicated they had no access to energy sources, and around 40% had no stable fixed location of business. Almost all the sample worked in very labour-intensive operations.

However, the few small firms that have made larger investments showed a strong positive correlation with an increase in the number of employees (Table 2).

It appears from the sample that the firms were not replacing labour for capital. Instead, they needed capital as a complement, in order to prevent a decrease in productivity and to grow.

3.4. Identified Problems

Lack of capital and access to credit were identified as the main problem of doing business. Two-thirds of the sample indicated having missed opportunities because of lack of funding. On the other hand, access to tools and raw materials, which used to be a problem in earlier post-war periods, was no longer identified as a serious issue. The firms identified that competition has risen significantly, which might be interpreted as a sign of overall economic growth and more efficient (informal) markets. The lack of capital and the rising competition may explain why the sample did not expand in small firms. The less successful firms displayed more passive strategies of cost reduction rather than expanding or approaching the market in a more aggressive manner.

Given the high rate of informality in the sample, it is not surprising that the problems associated with formality (e.g., taxation) were not often mentioned.

3.5. Successes

Success, in terms of income, is positively correlated with having a bank account, having a formal licence and with the amount invested. However, this relationship appears to only hold for a minority of more permanent businesses.

3.6. Monthly Income

Maintaining relations with the formal banking system seem to be a necessary condition for growth and income increase. By 1999, over 90% of the firms with a monthly income over 80 US$ were "formal businesses," in the sense that they had bank accounts (see Tables 3 and 4).

Apparently, unregistered firms are necessarily small, since growth and success typically render them more public, and subject to legal enforcement. Hence, at least indicated from our sample, formalisation might be an inevitable step in the process of firm growth and success.

In the labour-intensive small-business sector, the amount invested shows a significant correlation with an increase in monthly income (see Table 5).

According to other authors (Elkan, 1995), it is doubtful whether there are positive returns from training. In our sample this appeared, indeed, to be the case. No significant relationships between firm income and training were found. There seems to be evidence that training as a condition for access to finance is not very effective (see Table 6).

Table 3. Monthly Income and Bank Account.

Minimum Income	Bank Account 1998				Bank Account 1999			
	Yes		No		Yes		No	
≤40 US$	86	27.8%	223	72.2%	90	28.8%	222	71.2%
>40 US$≤80 US$	81	45.5%	97	54.5%	52	63.4%	30	36.6%
>80 US$	55	51.4%	52	48.6%	30	90.9%	3	9.1%
Total	222	37.4%	372	62.6%	172	40.3%	255	59.7%

Note: Significance = 99.9%, Pearson's $R = 0.2$ (1998); significance = 99.9%, Pearson's $R = 0.4$ (1999).

Table 4. Monthly Income and Licence.

Minimum Income	Licenced 1998				Licenced 1999			
	Yes		No		Yes		No	
< 40 US$	94	30.4%	215	69.6%	82	26.3%	230	73.7%
> 40 US$ ⩽ US$	95	53.4%	83	46.6%	40	48.8%	42	51.2%
> 80 US$	59	55.1%	48	44.9%	30	90.9%	3	9.1%
Total	248	41.8%	346	58.2%	152	35.6%	275	64.4%

Note: Significance = 99.9%, Pearson's $R = -0.22$ (1998); significance = 99.9%, Pearson's $R = -0.37$ (1999).

Table 5. Monthly Income and Equipment.

Minimum Income	Equipment 1998				Equipment 1999			
	⩽ 80 US$		> 80 US$		⩽ 80 US$		> 80 US$	
⩽ 40 US$	142	63.4%	82	36.6%	115	57.8%	84	42.2%
> 40 US$ ⩽ 80 US$	32	33.7%	63	66.3%	19	32.8%	39	67.2%
> 80 US$	10	15.2%	56	84.8%	2	9.1%	20	90.9%
Total	184	47.8%	201	52.2%	136	48.7%	143	51.3%

Note: Significance = 99.9%, Pearson's $R = 0.384$ (1998); significance = 99.9%, Pearson's $R = 0.307$ (1999).

Table 6. Monthly Income and Training Courses.

Minimum Income	Professional Training 1998				Professional Training 1999			
	Yes		No		Yes		No	
⩽ 40 US$	48	15.5%	261	84.5%	42	13.5%	270	86.5%
> 40 US$ ⩽ 80US $	31	17.4%	147	82.6%	19	23.2%	63	76.8%
> 80 US$	18	16.8%	89	83.2%	10	30.3%	23	69.7%
Total	97	16.3%	497	83.7%	71	16.6%	356	83.4%

Note: Significance = 14.6%, Pearson's $R = -0.018$ (1998); significance = 15.1%, Pearson's $R = -0.147$ (1999).

3.7. Labour Force

As previously mentioned, growth in the informal sector appears possible only up to a certain limit. The larger a firm grows, the greater the need to

Table 7. Number of Workers Employed and Licence.

No. of Workers	Licenced 1998				Licenced 1999			
	Yes		No		Yes		No	
0	24	23.8%	77	76.2%	14	12.0%	103	88.0%
1	45	29.8%	106	70.2%	25	23.1%	83	76.9%
2	67	43.8%	86	56.2%	38	36.2%	67	63.8%
3	50	50.5%	49	49.5%	35	66.0%	18	34.0%
4	22	51.2%	21	48.8%	21	84.0%	4	16.0%
5–10	36	75.0%	12	25.0%	12	100.0%		
≥11	10	90.9%	1	9.1%	7	100.0%		
Total	254	41.9%	352	58.1%	152	35.6%	275	64.4%

Note: Significance = 99.9%, Pearson's $R = -0.306$ (1998); significance = 99.9%, Pearson's $R = -0.513$ (1999).

Table 8. Number of Workers Employed and Bank Account.

No. of Workers	Bank Account 1998				Bank Account 1999			
	Yes		No		Yes		No	
0	32	31.7%	69	68.3%	25	21.4%	92	78.6%
1	45	29.8%	106	70.2%	34	31.5%	74	68.5%
2	57	37.3%	96	62.7%	36	34.3%	69	65.7%
3	31	31.3%	68	68.7%	37	69.8%	16	30.2%
4	23	53.5%	20	46.5%	23	92.0%	2	8.0%
5–10	32	66.7%	16	33.3%	11	91.7%	1	8.3%
≥11	7	63.6%	4	36.4%	6	85.7%	1	14.3%
Total	227	37.5%	379	62.5%	172	40.3%	255	59.7%

Note: Significance = 99.9%, Pearson's $R = 0.187$ (1998); significance = 99.9%, Pearson's $R = 0.421$ (1999).

formalise the business. By 1999, all firms in our sample employing over five workers were formal, legal enterprises (Table 7).

The number of workers employed and the degree of participation in the formal banking system appeared positively correlated with income. This is not only due to the access to credit but also to reputation improvement, which may be an important success factor (Table 8).

Similar to income, professional training does not seem to have any significant correlation with the number of employees. Thus, training again does not appear as an important success factor, in terms of either growth or income (Table 9).

Table 9. Number of Workers Employed and Professional Training.

No. of Workers	Professional Training 1999			
	Sim		Não	
0	22	18.8%	95	81.2%
1	14	13.0%	94	87.0%
2	18	17.1%	87	82.9%
3	6	11.3%	47	88.7%
4	5	20.0%	20	80.0%
5–10	2	16.7%	10	83.3%
≥11	4	57.1%	3	42.9%
Total	71	16.6%	356	83.4%

Note: Significance = 43%, Pearson's $R = -0.040$ (1999).

4. SUMMARY AND CONCLUSION

Operating a small business in Mozambique, even in the presence of assistance from NGOs like PAPIR, is a highly risky activity. Many assisted firms from our sample of PAPIR had already closed only a few years after assistance. For those that survived, the performance of many small firms has been quite poor. Most of these firms work in very labour-intensive operations, they participate in the informal economy and they do not have access to any energy source or a fixed location. The growing competition was also indicated as a possible source for the failures by the sample firms (although certainly there are positive aspects to competition from a consumers' point of view).

Although most small-business entrepreneurs earn a minimum monthly salary of at least 35 US$, survival is the main concern for most of them. For the very small micro-enterprises, the chances of firm survival seem to be directly correlated to the strategy of cost reduction and remaining informal. They do not have a vision or clear business objectives; they live by short-term opportunities.

On the other hand, there were a few successful and growing small firms (according to the 1999 update, about 5% of the total sample). They can be characterised as permanent specialised firms that have been able to over-come the small-business dilemma. For these firms, informality is no longer a condition for survival, they have other competitive advantages. In fact, they appeared to maintain stable relations with the formal banking system and most of them had obtained licences and tried to complement their capital investments with an increase in the number of employees and productivity.

Reflecting upon development policy and the instruments for the development of small business, it is clear that these two groups of small firms require different approaches. The large group of temporary informal businesses need policies aimed at reducing poverty and increasing purchasing power in order to stabilize their business activities. They are, and probably will stay, short-term opportunity takers. On the other hand, the few growing small businesses that expand through the formal sector need more traditional, long-term strategies tied to financial stability and market information.

In any case, especially for micro-, small- and medium-sized enterprises in Mozambique, it is urgent to improve the business environment as a whole. Unfortunately, in this area, little progress has been made (Dana & Galbraith, 2006). The barriers to business and especially formal business are – despite of some improvements in the last years – still too high and costly and among the worst in Africa (World Bank, 2006). Transaction costs are sometimes prohibitive, competitiveness is low, and a sound dialogue between private sector and public administration is needed to improve and create a level playing field for the economic agents (UNDP, 2004).[2]

A systematic, coordinated, inter-ministerial SMME approach for a sustainable development in Mozambique, and in other similar sub-Saharan African nations, should be on the political agenda.

NOTES

1. Unfortunately there is no "official" definition of enterprise size. For example, the Ministry of Industry and Trade (MIC) uses other size definitions as the National Statistics Institute (INE).
2. See, Kaufmann (2005) and Kaufmann and Tesfayohannes (1997).

REFERENCES

Abreu, S., & Abreu, A. (1996). *Sector informal em Moçambique: Uma abordagem monetária.* Staff Paper no. 5, Banco de Moçambique, Maputo.

Biggs, T., Nasir, J., & Fisman, R. (1999). *Structure and performance of manufacturing in Mozambique.* PRED Paper no. 107, Regional Program on Enterprise Development, World Bank, Maputo.

Billetoft, J. (1998). *Coping with uncertainty – petty producers in post-war Mozambique.* Working Paper 98, Center for Development Research (CDR), Copenhagen.

Correiro, J. J., & Reis, E. (1996). Culturas empresariais na África Lusófona. *Economia Global e Gestão, 2,* 7–20.

Cotter, J. (1996). Distinguishing between poverty alleviation and business growth. *Small Firm Development*, 7(2), 49–52.

Dana, L. (1996). Small business in Mozambique after the war. *Journal of Small Business Management*, 34(4), 67–71.

Dana, L., & Galbraith, C. (2006). Poverty, entrepreneurship and aid economics in Mozambique: A review of empirical research. In: C. Galbraith & S. Stiles (Eds), *Development entrepreneurship: Adversity, risk and isolation*. Oxford: Elsevier.

de Vletter, F. (1996). *Study on the informal sector in Mozambique*. Maputo: Ministry of Planning and Finance.

de Vletter, F. (1997). Money for nothing and the kits are free: A critical look at the evolution of credit policy and the role of the informal sector. In: D. Sogge (Ed.), *Mozambique – perspectives on aid and the civil sector* (pp. 149–175). Amsterdam: Gemeenschappelijk Overleg Medefinacierig.

Economist Intelligence Unit (1998). *Country profile Mozambique 1998–1999*. London: Economist Intelligence Unit.

Elkan, W. (1995). *An introduction to development economics*. London: Harvester Wheatsheaf.

Fafchamps, M. (1994). Industrial structure and micro-enterprises in Africa. *The Journal of Developing Areas*, 29, 1–30.

Fialho, J. (1996). Empresários em Moçambique: percursos 1983/93. *Economia Global e Gestão*, 2, 23–44.

Fungulane, B. (1999). *Mercado informal na Beira*. Beira: UCM.

International Finance Corporation (IFC) (1996). *Mozambique – administrative barriers to investment: The red tape analysis*. Washington, DC: The World Bank.

Kaufmann, F. (2005). Enabling environment for the private sector – GTZ Program: Economic reform and market systems development. In: GTZ (Ed.), *Promoting the business and investment climate* (pp. 27–40). Eschborn, Germany: GTZ.

Kaufmann, F., & Tesfayohannes, M. (1997). Una politica de promoción efectiva de las PYME como un Elemento de Re-orientación económica en Paises en Desarrollo. In: *Contribuciones, Fundación Konrad-Adenauer/CIEDLA* (No. 1, pp. 167–184). Buenos Aires.

Kaufmann, F., & Navaia, E. (1999). *Pequena industria, Relatorio da 2 actualização dos clientes do PAPIR, UCM-GEA*. Consult Paper no. 5, UCM-GEA, Beira.

KFW (German Development Bank) (2003). *Cooperacao com Mocambique, Outubro*. Frankfurt: KFW.

Liedholm, C. (1992). Small-scale industries in Africa: Dynamic issues and the role of policy. In: F. Stewart, S. Lall & S. Wangwe (Eds), *Alternative development strategies in sub Saharan Africa* (pp. 185–212). London: Macmillan.

Nathan Associates (2004). *Removing obstacles to economic growth in Mozambique. A diagnostic trade integration study* (Vol. 2, Main Report, Part 1). Washington, DC: USAID.

Navaia, E., & Kaufmann, F. (1999). *Abordagem sobre Pequenas Empresas em Sofala, UCM-GEA*. Consult Paper no. 1, UCM, Beira.

Republica de Moçambique (1997). *Industrial policy strategy, bulletin of the republic* (No. 33(2) Supplement). Maputo: Republica de Moçambique.

Roberts, B. (2003). *Small and medium enterprise (SME) mapping Mozambique*. Maputo: World Bank Group Small and Medium Enterprise Department.

SAL; ACIS (2005). *O Quadro Legal Sobre a Constituição de Sociedades Comerciais em Moç ambique*. Consultoria e Investimentos Lda (SAL) and Associação Comercial e Industrial de Sofala (ACIS), Maputo.

Todaro, M. (1997). *Economic development*. London: Addison-Wesley.

United Nations Development Programme (UNDP) (2004). *Unleashing entrepreneurship: Making business work for the poor*. New York: U.N. Commission on the Private Sector and Development.

World Bank (2006). *Doing business in 2006*. Washington, DC: World Bank.

PART V:
ISOLATION AND WEALTH DEVELOPMENT: THE CASE OF ICELAND

ISOLATION AS A SOURCE OF ENTREPRENEURIAL OPPORTUNITIES: OVERCOMING THE LIMITATIONS OF ISOLATED MICRO-STATES

Örn D. Jónsson and Rögnvaldur J. Saemundsson

1. INTRODUCTION

Within entrepreneurship research there is an increased interest in investigating the nexus between venture opportunities and enterprising individuals (Venkataraman, 1997; Shane & Venkataraman, 2000; Eckhardt & Shane, 2003; Sarasvathy, Dew, Velamuri, & Venkataraman, 2003). The move is towards the understanding of why and when opportunities emerge, why only some individuals identify and exploit these opportunities, and how different conditions influence the means of their exploitation.

A common objective of government policy makers has been to stimulate innovation and entrepreneurial activity. The rationale behind this objective is usually the belief that innovation and entrepreneurial activities are important factors for ensuring economic development and growth (e.g., European Commission, 2003). In order to stimulate innovation and entrepreneurial activity, policy makers create and implement different kinds of specific policies

Developmental Entrepreneurship: Adversity, Risk, and Isolation
International Research in the Business Disciplines, Volume 5, 217–233
Copyright © 2006 by Elsevier Ltd.
All rights of reproduction in any form reserved
ISSN: 1074-7877/doi:10.1016/S1074-7877(06)05012-4

and government/regionally sponsored support programs complementing general economic and social measures that are associated with both regulation and deregulation. Thus, governments influence entrepreneurial activity in many ways, often in a very complex and unintended manner.

In the last decade, Icelandic entrepreneurs belonging to an isolated island in the middle of the North Atlantic and populated by less than 300,000 inhabitants, have managed to identify and exploit international business opportunities in such diverse fields as aviation, retail, biotechnology, banking and medical instruments around the world. From being a very isolated and poverty ridden economy in the beginning of the 20th century, the number of foreign employees in companies owned and managed by Icelandic entrepreneurs abroad is currently on par with the total working population of the country. Iceland now consistently ranks in the top 10 nations in the world in the various measures of human development index (HDI), infrastructure development (IMD International), income per capita (GNI), gender empowerment (GEM) and life expectancy.

In Iceland it is possible to detect 4 distinct phases of government involvement that have influenced the opportunities available to individual entrepreneurs. Each has their own internal rationality bounded in the process towards modernization. The development is continuous yet disrupted both due to outside influences or outright attacks, as well as the changing national context within Iceland. In one sentence, the modernization process in Iceland has been a move from a paternalistic guidance of a poverty ridden population towards the creation of an outward reaching and uncertain global business environment, definably risky at times, but as yet, extraordinarily successful.

The purpose of this paper is to contribute to our knowledge of why and when entrepreneurial opportunities emerge within the context of an isolated economy, and the role that government can play within the process. Through historical analysis of four different entrepreneurship regimes in Iceland, we argue that the changing nature of government involvement has created sources of international opportunities based on the country's isolation. We show government interventions to (a) create unforeseen opportunities stressing the importance of creating a cohort of alert entrepreneurs to encourage discovery and exploitation, and (b) creating a favorable institutional environment, especially a functioning and globally connected education system.

The paper is structured in the following manner. First, the frame of reference for the historical analysis is presented. This framework is based on the current opportunity-based view on entrepreneurship combined with evolutionary economics. Second, the historical analysis is presented. Finally, the paper is concluded.

2. FRAME OF REFERENCE

The central focus in the current opportunity-based view on entrepreneurship is the nexus of opportunities and enterprising individuals. The concept of opportunity is used to bridge environmental conditions that are favorable for the creation of economic value and the individuals who are able to recognize or influence these conditions and harvest at least some of this value through a profitable process of exploitation.

Despite the agreement on putting the concept of opportunity in the center, there has been a considerable debate on its meaning, more precisely, the relationship with the actor(s) and their environment over time. In this paper we use the concept of opportunity in a rather broad sense to include all opportunities for profits, including both the creative acts of innovation as defined by Schumpeter (1934) or price differences discovered by Kirzner's (1997) alert entrepreneurs. In line with Shackle (1955) we see opportunities as a set of beliefs about an uncertain future that can only be validated through action. Hence, opportunities may turn out to be wrong, both in the sense that environmental conditions do not support the expected value-creation and appropriation, as well as in the sense of being ineffectively pursued.

When understanding the sources of opportunities it is instructive to use Burt's (1992) concept of 'structural holes.' As opportunities are cognitive phenomena, their identification is based on the knowledge endowments of the entrepreneurs as well as the information they have access to. Weak connections between groups represent structural holes in the social structure of the market. Individuals bridging these holes have not only access to more information on environmental conditions than participants in each of the weakly connected groups, but this information is also scarce. The existence of structural holes is therefore a source of opportunities for profit which only individuals who bridge those holes are being able to identify and pursue, given that their "attitude is one which is always ready to be surprised, always ready to take the steps needed to profit by such surprises" (Kirzner, 1997, p. 72).

But the existence of weak connections and alertness is not sufficient for the successful exploitation of opportunities. Resources are also needed. Both the identification and exploitation of opportunities requires access to complementary human, physical and financial resources (Teece, 1986). Environments differ in their resource capacity (Aldrich, 1979), the types of actors providing resources and the available mechanisms for mobilizing actors (Freeman, 1991). As weak connections are the source of value added, network closure may turn out to be critical for gaining access to the necessary complementary resources (Burt, 2001).

But sources of opportunities are dynamic and changing. Just as environmental conditions are changing (such as natural resources, institutional setup, knowledge and the dispersion of knowledge), so are the information channels which then gives rise to exploitable structural holes. We take an evolutionary approach to these changes in the sense that there is no equilibrium to which the changes gravitate. Rather the development is a natural and evolving sequence, partly endogenous and partly subject to exogenous shocks (Schumpeter, 1934; Nelson & Winter, 1982). Structural holes therefore emerge and vanish in an unpredictable manner. Unless they are bridged by alert entrepreneurs with access to sufficient resources they are unlikely to be of any economic value.

3. ENTREPRENEURSHIP REGIMES IN 20TH CENTURY ICELAND

In this section a historical analysis will be presented of four successive entrepreneurship regimes in 20th century Iceland. We argue that these regimes provide a path dependent development of modernity in Iceland leading to the current regime of heroic international entrepreneurship where entrepreneurs exploit international business opportunities. The successive development of regimes has built up a crowd of alert entrepreneurs taking advantage of opportunities emerging from historical development and geographic isolation.

3.1. Collective Agrarian Entrepreneurship (1910–1939)

Iceland, a late developer, currently populated by less than 300,000 inhabitants, is situated in the North Atlantic midways between the USA and Europe. Iceland is noticeably influenced by various ideological, economic as well as technological-diffusion processes attained from the neighbouring countries, especially the Nordic regions, Great Britain and the USA, and later, the Mediterranean countries and Asia. Although a Danish colony until 1944, Icelanders gained authority over all decisive matters in 1918. Between 1918 and 1944, only foreign policy was controlled by the Danish Government due to extreme poverty and topographic isolation of Iceland at the time.

It was in the wake of World War I that the basic political, social and economic institutions were formed in Iceland. Political advocates emerged from the three classes, farmers, workers and property owners, in that order

(Jonsson, 1984). The social structure was basically rural, a society with a few scattered fishing ports located around the country close to the most important and rich fishing grounds. The few signs of the drift towards modernization were halted by the Great Depression that arrived in Iceland in 1930 and was prolonged because of the Spanish Civil War (1933–1939) as Spain was the main market for Iceland's primary export, salted cod. In 1930, for example, approximately 60% of exports were salted cod, with 35% of all exports being sent to Spain. In comparison, in 1936, only 3% of exports went to Spain (National Economic Institute, 2001).

Under these conditions, the relative power of the farmer's party was strengthened by an alliance with the Social Democrats, or the labor party. The governance of such coalitions was dominant in all the Nordic countries, but in Iceland the farmers created an early advantage because of the early establishment of various cooperatives (Co-ops), which operated simultaneously as distribution and production collectives, and then ventured into fisheries and industrial production in the early 1950s. The farmer's ideology was generally based on the belief that it was possible to steer the ragged route to modernity by empowering the population through education and allowing the small farmer, local fisherman or craftsman to pave their own route to prosperity, not unlike the populist movement in the United States (Canovan, 1981), a movement that appeared somewhat at conflict with scale arguments being made by corporations at the time. The basic idea was that the cooperatives, or the workers collectives, would protect the vulnerable small entrepreneur, or the allied workers organizations, by rationalizing production and distribution through the non-profit seeking co-ops, local authorities and the state. They regarded themselves as 'collective entrepreneurs' empowered by the governance of most of the basic routes of economic, political and social implementation (Connel, 1999). The building of power plants, schools, theaters and even swimming pools were given the same entrepreneurial significance, in a consciously steered move towards a better life for all.

The advocates of a more market-orientated society often criticized this "green and red" coalition for stifling the true entrepreneurial spirit of the capitalist (Kristinsson, 1991) and correctly so, as there were numerous examples of hindering the market-orientated entrepreneurs to pursue their goals. In industry as well as commerce, the economics of scale and the advantages of location were often ruled out by law. For example, between 1930 and 1932, there was fierce debate on this very issue in the Icelandic parliament built around the notion that products should have the same price at the producers' door irrespective of location, that the cost of transportation should be public. Within this framework, the cooperatives also had a competitive tax and cost advantage since they were regarded as non-profit organizations. Under the conditions of severe poverty and few opportunities to export goods the governance of a paternalistic alliance appeared justifiable to many, and despite totalitarian leanings, they were never devotees of communism. Instead they adhered to a version of agrarian socialism, staging the farmer in centre, "reaping the benefits of land" (Fridriksson, 1991). The farmers, or the small-scale entrepreneurs, were regarded as the movers of history instead of a state owned or totalitarian restructuring of society by building gargantuan industrial or agricultural facilities as was the case under the Stalin regime (Wegren, 1990).

This was the Iceland society of 'practical man' (Hansen & Serin, 1997) or a substance economy, (Polanyi, 1957/1992) transparent and fully rational seen in the light of the set and concrete goals, a populist or pastoral ideal of living in accordance with the laws of nature, but enlightened by the benefits of modernity.

The basic difference between the situation of 'practical man' in comparison with those acting under market conditions is that the only opportunity for enrichment was to extend the working hour and/or use the state or collectives, such as the cooperatives, as facilities or aides for collective action. At this point in Icelandic history, capital for individual initiatives was generally absent, while "working time" was abundant.

The first steps towards modernity were thus guided ones, but without pecuniary means. The government emphasized the importance of work for everyone at "affordable" wages. Education, or the combination of useful work and enlightenment of education, was perceived as the social capital that eventually would lead the Icelanders to the promised good society. An emphasis was on 'positive liberty' (Berlin, 2003), or creating opportunities for the collective to take control over its own life in order to realize common fundamental objectives, rather than removing obstacles for individual self-realization. The entrepreneur was largely viewed as a social person, a society builder; those who compete survive (in a Darwinian sense), those who win are the ones that work together as the 'collective entrepreneur'.

3.2. Government Entrepreneurship (1940–1960)

The advent of World War II in 1939 altered the situation dramatically. The paternalistic rule that overshadowed the first path towards modernity became concurrently obsolete and, to a large extent, ineffective. In May 1940, Iceland was occupied by the Allies whose first task was to build or amend the basic infrastructure; build functional airports, roads and telecommunications with the outside world. The demand for food, in Icelandic context, fish and mutton, became abundant. Fish exports doubled in value between 1939 and 1940 and quadrupled between 1939 and 1945 (National Economic Institute, 2001). The previous isolation was broken both socially and politically, but the institutional settings created under the earlier phase had surprising endurance.

The Americans replaced the British in 1941. The 'Yankees' brought with them visions of the New World; modern effective machinery, consumer culture, entertainment and a new kind of optimism. To many, this was viewed as "manna from heaven," despite the fears and dangers of the War. In 1944, Icelanders claimed independence from the Danes, who at that time were occupied by the Germans. For the first time, and with the support of the Americans, Icelanders believed they were in an economic position to be capable of pursing sovereignty, a move that was met with little international resistance.

After World War II, in 1949, Iceland became a charter member of NATO; and then signed a treaty with the United States in 1951 for the defense of Iceland. One of the priorities of the newly established partnership was to continue the modernization of the infrastructure and facilities of the country as a part of the overall strategy to defend the West against the increasing threats envisioned in the Cold War.

A clear sign of the backwardness of the Icelandic economy at that time was how the Marshall-aid was utilized. The basic objective of the Marshall-aid was to rejuvenate the destroyed production structure of Europe after the War, but in Iceland it was used to provide the basic means of economic development, e.g. to erect a fertilizer plant, a cement factory, and increasing the catching and processing capacity in the fishing sector. The use of the Marshall-aid also signified the most enduring alliance in the post-war period, that of the increasingly influential Independence Party supported by industrialists and property owners, with the historically strong Farmers Party. This coalition had strong focus on creating a stronger industrial structure, where all significant organizations, private or public, were heavily dependent or subordinated under state rule and belonging to the sphere of influence of either party.

During the period, rich fishing grounds around Iceland were generally controlled by Icelanders through the extension of territorial waters. The fishing grounds had previously been exploited by foreign fleets, primarily from the UK and France. In 1952, the limit was set at 4 miles from the coast, in 1958 it became 12 miles, 50 miles in 1972 and finally, 200 miles in 1979. At the same time the financial capital accumulated by government from supplying food to the Allies during the war was channeled through government initiatives to construct a modern fishing fleet, with processing and freezing plants in a number of villages around the country. This, in turn, opened up doors to the emerging and affluent market of the United States, resulting in a shift from exporting salted cod to the Mediterranean to supplying the United State's emerging fast food chains and pubic institutions such as hospitals, schools and prisons with, what was regarded as, a healthy meal. In 1940, for example, less than 14% of Icelandic goods were exported to the US, but in 1975 the percentage had increased to 29%. In 1940, only 8% of all exports were frozen fish. In 1951, the percentage was 25% and in 1975, frozen fish exports had risen to 38%. At the same time (between 1940 and 1975), the total value of exported goods increased more than 350% measured in 2001 prices (National Economic Institute, 2001), with the value of frozen fish exports increasing more than 1000-fold in this period.

This was the second phase of modernization characterized by the transparent needs to master the art of sovereignty, build an independent nation state and exploit the rich fishing grounds. In this task all the major players were united, despite political disputes. Even the most fervent advocates of free market policy saw the need for the government's guiding hand in utilizing the Marshall-aid and subsequently building up the basic infrastructure and production facilities. In the highly regulated international markets after World War II, governmental and diplomatic activities were also important for identifying and exploiting international business opportunities.

The seeds of the knowledge society were admittedly planted earlier, but the prolonged crises of the Second World War, and the subsequent Cold War environment, generally meant that the emphasis on general education focused mainly on the primary and secondary levels along with the emphasis on the crafts. The national university was primarily focused on the functionaries (professional areas) that were needed during the infrastructure build-up, such as medicine and law (i.e. public service), and in the arts, the cultural aspects of nation building, the Icelandic language, religion and history (i.e. education and identity).

The shift from a local agricultural society, which was close to a subsistence level and governed by a complex redistribution system, to fisheries geared for export represents a shift from collective entrepreneurship to a more government-based entrepreneurship. Owing to the backwardness of the Icelandic economy, diplomatic activity during and after the war, as well as the financial resources accumulated during the war, the Icelandic government came to take an active role in expanding the necessary infrastructure for the fisheries as well as to ensure access to foreign markets, particularly in the US. Not only did these activities help identify and exploit business opportunities during the period, but they also opened up Iceland for more lasting ties with businesses around the world, cumulating into experiences that could later be utilized in fields outside the fisheries.

3.3. Corporate Local Entrepreneurship (1960–1995)

In the period after the war up until the 1960s, recurring downturns in fish catches, such as the disappearance of the Norwegian-Icelandic herring in 1968, convinced politicians as well as the Icelandic public in general, that more solid economic foundations were needed, although politicians often debated about the appropriate route towards prosperity (Kristjansson, 1979, 2004).

The increasing wealth creation of the fisheries, along with a increasingly more powerful private sector, especially in commerce and some aspects of the productive sectors, undermined the political, as well as the structural power of the Farmers party and ultimately led to an alliance of the Independent Party and the Social Democrats, a new alliance, that lasted over 10 years (1960–1971). This alliance aimed to create a strong mixed economy, along the Nordic "social" model, which combines "an extensive social insurance system with labor market policies that promote full employment, equal opportunity and an equitable distribution of wealth" (Vogel, 1998).

Another important watershed was the decision to join the European Free Trade Agreement (EFTA) in 1970. During this period, and up until the 1980s, Iceland could be regarded as a volatile, but rapidly growing economy, soon to be ranked among the ten most affluent countries in the world as measured by the GNP per capita (National Economic Institute, 2001), mainly due to a controlled use of the natural resource of the rich fishing grounds surrounding the country and an emphasis on equalitarian welfare policy.

The institutional settings from the 1960s onwards, thus were molded in the manner of the Nordic welfare states (Denmark, Iceland, Finland, Norway and Sweden) and the opening of the economy by membership in EFTA. The coalition between the Independent Party and the Social Democrats emphasized a more market-orientated economy adjoined by highlighting the education system, health, pension funds, infrastructural facilities and other aspects of the Nordic Welfare State; a mixed economy in a literal sense.

The earlier consensus between the Farmers Party and the more conservative Independent Party tended to divide certain spheres of the economy between them (public banking, industrial enterprises, commerce and insurance) and was basically divided between rural areas and the towns as two parallel organizational systems. In the new political alliance, the entrepreneurial activity was still governed by the 'practical man' up until the early Seventies, but the role of the 'collective entrepreneur' (Jonsson & Jonsson, 1987) was gradually overtaken by the more individualistic 'businessman' as in most other westernized societies. The labor movement tended to confine its activities to wage issues as the basic preconditions of modernization in Iceland. However, the entrepreneurial activities of the businessman, in the Icelandic context, was still very much dependent on political influence as the resources available for exploitation were controlled by organizations managed by the ruling government, such as financial institutions and banks.

What divided the entrepreneurial approach from the 'agrarian' understanding of 'practical man' and the more social democratic view of 'industrial man' or the 'modern laborer' was the role of work and, especially, the importance of the relationship between minimum wages and productivity. According to the agrarian populist approach it was better to do something than to do nothing and this was true even if the work offered could only support wages that were near subsistence level (Chayanov, 1986).

The key for Iceland at this point was that the Social Democrats and the advocates of the labor-movement concluded that it was the responsibility of the state or local authorities to provide work for everyone if the private sector was unable to offer sufficient work paying acceptable wages. During this time this approach was especially strong in all of the Nordic countries, as well as in Germany. However, the stagflation (i.e. simultaneous occurrence of inflation and structural unemployment) of the early 1980s into the mid-1990s forced an evolution into a system of "job creation" in order to avoid enduring and threatening labor disputes. In essence, the national government or local authorities were prepared to subsidize the construction of new industries to support employment and wages. In Iceland, this was interpreted as providing structural facilities, such as power plants, to attract foreign industries, such as aluminum companies. This strategy appeared partly successful as three major energy intensive firms were established in the period (one aluminum plant, one producing ferro cilicium and one silicium facility). However, the dependency on this policy showed its weaknesses when the failing interest of more foreign companies to invest in Iceland led to periodic economic downturns during this time, with slow or even decreasing GDP (National Economic Institute, 2001).

The ongoing problem of what came to be called 'structural unemployment' (OECD, 2000) led to the creation and support of semi-public supported organizations within Iceland and other Nordic countries. These organizations could be general in nature, such as various Centers of Technological Expertise and Development, or highly specialized, such as "The Welding Institute" in

Denmark. Accompanying the government funding of these support institutes, the state or the local government often supplied grants or "soft money" for individual projects and firms.

In many Nordic countries, this system ultimately grew into an inflated grant system. At first the system, a Social Democratic project at its core, was thought of as encouraging entrepreneurship and innovation in small- and medium-sized enterprises (SMEs) through targeted measures, but soon developed into knowledge centers assisting small firms on a technology level in their start-up phases. Over time, however, these Nordic institutes failed to be equal partners with the increasingly knowledge-intensive and global firms, on the one hand owing to the increasing capabilities of SMEs to develop their own technologies, but also because of highly specific needs that could be primarily diffused through company networks, local or global. Thus, entrepreneurial and innovative activities of SMEs were becoming less dependent on government support for knowledge transfer and development, and more based on market exchange or strategic alliances with other firms.

In Iceland, however, the development was somewhat different from other Nordic countries, although it could be seen as a variation of the Nordic theme. The basic difference was that Iceland was heavily dependent on fisheries, a resource that was subject to significant fluctuations, and Iceland had only a few industrial sectors, with a need of specific or tacit knowledge characterized by each sector. Thus it was somewhat easier to focus on appropriate technology transfer schemes.

The historic Icelandic belief of the vast responsibilities of the strong and often paternalistic/ bureaucratic state was additionally undermined by more market orientated arguments of the "New Right" or Thatcherism/Reaganism at the time. In the case of Iceland, it can be argued that two other decisive steps were taken during this time, the enlargement of the surrounding fishing grounds, stepwise to a 200-mile limit, and subsidized graduate education abroad. In particular, nationalizing the fishing grounds within the 200 miles limits was done in a semi-privatized manner creating a system of transferable fishing quotas. And subsidizing higher education for Icelandic students abroad appeared to pave the way for a more open market-orientated society.

Despite the general acceptance of these strategies within the Independent Party, Farmers Party and the Social Democrats, the move towards a more market oriented society was a cautious one, partly because politicians are not apt to loose their grip freely and partly because of the wide-spread, often cited, "indigenous" fear that a more open economy would lead to an influx of foreign investors and lost control over the natural resources, such as fishing grounds and land. The fear was ultimately unfounded as foreign companies were, in most cases, less than interested in investing in Iceland apart from the utilization of semi-public electric plants that were being erected for energy-intensive industries, such as aluminum smelting (Martinek & Orland, 2000).

An orientation towards a more market-oriented society clearly reduced the government's role in identifying and exploiting business opportunities. Instead, the government focused on encouraging entrepreneurial activities with the creation of semi-public support institutions for knowledge development and dissemination.

Despite these changes, this period had many of the institutional characteristics inherited from the former regimes. Strong government, where a large sphere of the economy (such as banks, insurance companies, transportation companies and industrial firms) was still politically influenced, often resulting in a strong influence as to where new business opportunities could be exploited. In addition, much of this political influence was mainly local in focus.

3.4. Heroic International Entrepreneurship (1995–2005)

The economic downturn at the end of the 1980s and the early 1990s was also a phase of stabilization, reducing the economic fluctuations that periodically led to hyperinflation. The turmoil, and fear of a prolonged downturn resulted in an overall agreement between the main actors in the economy (government, labor movements and industry) to aim towards an even more open and market-oriented economy, a move that had earlier on been a cautious one. The more radical measures that followed, such as becoming a member of the European Economic Area (EEA) 1994), privatization of government-owned firms and banks during the late 1990s and gradual pension reform, led to fundamental changes to the economy and the nature of entrepreneurial activities from the period before. Instead of being local due to political influence over resources, it has become increasingly international and has lead to individual wealth accumulation never experienced before.

The decisive step was the privatization of the state owned banks, which started in 1997. The banks had played a central role in the earlier regimes. Before World War II banks were often seen as simply redistribution institutions, according to what the politicians deemed publicly necessary. After World War II the banks functioned more or less as rational redistribution systems to individual, regional authorities and private firms and guaranteeing foreign loans, both to get more favorable rates and amend the destructive effects of continuous inflation. At times this led to a more or less openly political nepotism, especially under the conditions where the raging inflation meant that you did not need to pay the granted loans back.

Following privatization, the size of the banking system has increased substantially, both in terms of their capital assets and market value as well as becoming increasingly international. Between 1998 and 2002, the capital assets of the five largest banks had almost quadrupled while their market value had tripled. Since 2002, the banks have grown even larger through the acquisition of foreign banks in the Nordic countries and Britain. This expansion of the banking sector has not only provided more resources for exploiting opportunities for individual entrepreneurs, but also helped the wealth of the nation, broadly defined (Mokyr, 1990), which was becoming constrained by the lack of national investment opportunities, to identify and exploit international investment opportunities. A case in point would be the investments made in Britain by Baugur (a dominant retail company in Iceland) and Bakkavor (a fresh food manufacturer) in cooperation with KB bank (currently one of the three largest banks in Iceland).

The second decisive, and largely entrepreneurial, factor has been the increased inflow of people returning to Iceland from abroad. These people bring back new and innovative ideas inspired by their education and newly found contacts around the world (Jonsson, 2006). Many years of subsidizing education for Icelandic students abroad in many of the most prestigious universities around the world appears to have resulted in an accumulated and ever-increasing group of highly educated people. Most of these people continued to work abroad, but many are willing to return, or visit allowing for a substantial opportunity for technology transfer. For example, the US venture capital industry funded the genomics firm DeCode, founded by an Icelandic earning his Ph.D. degree from Harvard School of Medicine. When he founded the operation in Iceland in the late 1990s, it attracted many highly educated Icelanders working abroad.

But Icelanders were not only returning after completing advanced education abroad. One 'small historical event' as W. Brian Arthur (1989) would phrase it, in the life of a small group of three entrepreneurs was the move of a defunct bottling factory from Iceland to Leningrad (now St. Petersburg) in the beginning of the 1990s. The entrepreneurs behind this enterprise were among the pioneers of foreign investors to operate a privatized company in the turmoil of the Soviet regime's downfall. Less than ten years later, in 2002, the company they had established (Bravo) had gained a significant size of St. Petersburg's beer/soft-drink market. The entrepreneurs decided to sell the factory to a major beverage company (Heineken) for over $300 million. They brought their capital back to Iceland and invested in several local companies as well as buying a majority holding in Landsbankinn, one of the three largest banks in Iceland, in 2002. In the following years they used the bank as a basis for further investments, among them a pharmaceutical company (Pharmaco) and an aviation group (Atlanta). One of the entrepreneurs concentrates on running the bank and is now definably one of the central players in the Icelandic business world, another continued to invest in the former Eastern Block and is now ranked among the 400 richest individuals by Forbes. The third focused on the aviation business, and his company has become the largest wet-lease company worldwide.

Although the new generation of entrepreneurs can be seen as quite different individuals or groupings, certain common traits can be detected. The older business elite who reigned from World War II onwards were focused on guarding their position within Iceland and reaping the benefits of the economy's rapid growth. Export was more or less confined to fish, and the understanding of the outer world economic environment was in the hands of the semi-monopolized fisheries export companies, the importers of foreign goods who worked under strict regulations and the diplomats stationed in a handful of countries. The second generation of this group tended to become risk evasive and relatively content with their, seemingly, secure holdings.

From one point of view the recent development and the occurring power shift can be seen as a process of 'creative destruction' (Schumpeter, 1942/ 1976) but that would probably be a limited or restricted view. A broader approach would be to take into account the overall changes in the world economy and the increasing impact of immigrant flows. The disembedded and rapidly increasing (institutional) wealth such as pension funds, as well as the detachable "concretized" wealth could be utilized to turn the 'down to earth experience' of a relatively few young entrepreneurs that had lived abroad for a considerable time with their business or diplomatic parents to abundant wealth by any measure. In addition, the widespread knowledge gained from fisheries exports around the world combined with innovative organizational settings (ISO and traceability) opened up 'windows of opportunities,' especially in the UK and the former Eastern Block and the other Nordic countries. This was clearly the case of Bakkavor, presently UK's biggest supplier of fresh ready-made meals, and partly the case in the innovative development of the outward reaching financial sector.

The new generation of alert entrepreneurs often gained detailed branch related knowledge (or 'sticky' information as von Hippel, 1998 would term it) through their fathers occupations, combined with a global education abroad and subsequently accessed the new availability of investment capital with Iceland. This has led to an entrepreneurial explosion within Iceland.

Similar situations have been seen in history. The Newly Rich, or the pecuniary class as Veblen would describe them, have risen, often rapidly, from the beginnings of the industrial revolution and is definably part of the rooted belief of the individual's freedom to seek fortune in new frontiers. What is probably distinctive for this new entrepreneurialism is the swiftness of these movements, especially across national borders. In a case of a micro-economy, such as Iceland, such a situation can manifest itself in appalling over investment nationally.

But it would be unadvisable to seek explanations in the unique Icelandic National Character, as was fashionable during the amazing growth and modernization of Japan in the 1980s. A more sober approach would be a broader Schumpeterian explanation, that of a push situation, where abundant financial capital developed into outward leanings.

4. CONCLUSIONS

In retrospect, it is possible to explain the development of the Icelandic economy, how one phase leads to another. Such a view could in a sense, undermine the role of the entrepreneurs and how they seized opportunities at any given time, individually or collectively. What is of crucial importance, and separates the development into phases, are the different rationalities that are the basis for each of these phases.

First is the rationality of the bottom-up approach where small-scale entrepreneurs try collectively to make the most out of the limited, somewhat fixed, resources they have access to. Second is the rationality of trying to obtain economies of scale through industrialization and access to larger markets. Third is the rationality of obtaining economic stability facing the cyclic nature of the fishing stocks. Fourth is the rationality of the open and out-reaching economy, where opportunities and resources are abundant for the alert and talented entrepreneur. These different rationalities give rise to different forms of entrepreneurship in a path-dependent way. Different means are used to bridge structural holes for identifying opportunities and different means are used to reach network closure in order to gain access to resources for their exploitation. Isolation and small size, such as in Iceland, increases the vulnerability of the country, but at the same time provide incentives to reach out for opportunities.

To generalize, three underlying factors seem to be crucial to explain the Iceland phenomenon. First, World War II opened up the economy in a radical manner, a step Icelanders had been aiming at for a long time although inhibited by the isolationistic interests of the farming sector. Second, Iceland's imitation of the Nordic "welfare state" only became possible due to the window of opportunity created by the combination of the micro-size character of the society and its location. Education abroad opened up networks that could be utilized later by the emerging crowd of alert entrepreneurs. Last but not least, what characterizes the fourth phase of the development is the changing relationship between the means, financial as well as technological in comparison with the earlier ones.

The case of Iceland demonstrates the path dependency of government intervention as well as how unforeseen opportunities are created along the path. The nature of this development shows the importance of creating a favorable institutional environment grounded in a globally connected education system. Such conditions have, in recent years, resulted in a crowd of alert Icelandic entrepreneurs able to discover unforeseen opportunities and having access to the means for exploiting them. It can be expected that in less than five years from the time of this writing the number of employees of Icelandic firms abroad will exceed the ones employed in Iceland. This opens up questions of volatility of the microstate and to what extent it is meaningful to regard the nation state as the operating area for the contemporary entrepreneur.

REFERENCES

Aldrich, H. (1979). *Organizations and environments.* Englewood Cliffs, NJ: Prentice-Hall.

Arthur, W. (1989). Competing technologies and lock-in by historical small events. *Economic Journal, 99*(March), 116–131.

Berlin, I. (2003). *The proper study of mankind.* London: Farrar, Straus and Giroux.

Burt, R. (1992). *Structural holes.* Cambridge, MA: Harvard University Press.

Burt, R. (2001). Structural holes versus network closure as social capital. In: N. Lin, K. Cook & R. Burt (Eds), *Social capital: Theory and research.* New York: Aldine de Gruyter.

Canovan, M. (1981). *Populism.* London: Junction Books.

Chayanov, A. (1986). *The theory of peasant economy.* Manchester: Manchester University Press.

Connell, D. (1999). *Collective entrepreneurship: In search of meaning.* Unpublished paper (http://www.djconnell.ca/articles/CollEntrep.pdf, accessed August 25, 2005).

Eckhardt, J., & Shane, S. (2003). Opportunities and entrepreneurship. *Journal of Management, 29*(3), 333–349.

European Commission. (2003). *Entrepreneurship in Europe (green paper).* Brussels: Enterprise Directorate-General, European Commission.

Freeman, C. (1991). Network of innovators: A synthesis of research issues. *Research Policy, 20,* 499–514.

Fridriksson, G. (1991). *The history of Jonas Jonsson from Hrifla.* Reykjavik: Idunn, Reykjavik.

Hansen, P., & Serin, G. (1997). Will low technology products disappear? The hidden innovation processes in low technology industries. *Technological Forecasting and Social Change, 55,* 179–191.

Jonsson, I., & Jonsson, F. (1987). *Internationalization of west-nordic innovations systems-fisheries technology and innovations.* Unpublished report.

Jonsson, O. (1984). *The populist economy.* Roskilde: Roskilde University Centre.

Jonsson, O. (2006). *Innovation systems, the icelandic version, microstates and meaningful nodes.* Unpublished paper.

Kirzner, I. (1997). Entrepreneurial discovery and the competitive market process: An Austrian approach. *Journal of Economic Literature, 35*(1), 60–85.

Kristinsson, G. (1991). *Farmers' parties. A study in electoral adaptation.* Reykjavik: Felagsvisindastofnun.

Kristjansson, S. (1979). The electoral basis of the Icelandic independence party 1929–1944. *Scandinavian Political Studies, 2*(1), 31–57.

Kristjansson, S. (2004). Iceland, OECD and the trade liberalisation of the 1950s. *Scandinavian Economic History Review, 51*(2–3), 62–84.

Martinek, J., & Orlando, M. (2002). *Do primary energy resources influence industry location?* Kansas City: Federal Reserve Bank of Kansas City.

Mokyr, J. (1990). *The lever of riches. Technological creativity and economic progress.* New York: Oxford University Press.

National Economic Institute (2001). Historcial econometric overview. reykjavik: National economic institute (http://www.ths.is/rit/sogulegt/index.htm, accessed August 25 2005, in Icelandic).

Nelson, R., & Winter, S. (1982). *An evolutionary theory of economic change.* Cambridge, MA: Harvard University Press.

Organisation for Economic Cooperation and Development (OECD). (2000). *Revised OECD measures of structural unemployment.* Paris: OECD Outlook.

Polanyi, K. (1957/1992). The economy as instituted process. In: M. Granovetter & R. Swedberg (Eds), *The sociology of economic life* (pp. 29–52). Westview Press.

Sarasvathy, S. D., Dew, N., Velamuri, S. R., & Venkataraman, S. (2003). Three views of entrepreneurial opportunity. In: Z. J. Acs & D. Audretsch (Eds), *Handbook of entrepreneurship research: An interdisciplinary survey and introduction* (pp. 141–160). New York: Kluwer.

Schumpeter, J. A. (1934). *The theory of economic development.* Cambridge, MA: Harvard University Press.

Schumpeter, J. A. (1942/1976). *Capitalism, socialism and democracy.* London: Routledge.

Shackle, G. L. S. (1955). *Uncertainty in economics and other reflections.* Cambridge: Cambridge University Press.

Shane, S., & Venkataraman, S. (2000). The promise of entrepreneurship as a field of research. *Academy of Management Review, 25*(1), 217–226.

Teece, D. J. (1986). Profiting from technological innovation: Implications for integration, collaboration, licensing and public policy. *Research Policy, 15*, 285–305.

Venkatraman, S. (1997). The distinctive domain of entrepreneurship research. In: J. A. Katz (Ed.), *Advances in entrepreneurship, firm emergence, and growth* (pp. 119–138). Greenwich, CT: JAI Press.

Vogel, J. (1998). *Three types of European society.* Internet: Nordic news network (http://www.nnn.se/n-model/europe3/europe3.htm, accessed August 25 2005).

von Hippel, E. (1998). Economics of product development by users: The impact "Sticky" local information. *Management Science, 44*(5), 629–644.

Wegren, S. T. (1990). From Stalin to Gorbachev: The role of the Soviet communist party in the implementation of agricultural policy. *Studies in Comparative Communism, 23*(2), 177–190.

PORTRAIT OF AN ENTREPRENEURIAL TRADE MISSION: ICELAND GOES TO CHINA

Porlákur Karlsson, Michael R. Luthy and Katrín Ólafsdóttir

1. INTRODUCTION

"No man is an island, entire of itself" (Donne, 1624). When the British metaphysical poet John Donne (1572–1631) wrote that, concepts such as entrepreneurship, marketing, tourism, and world trade were either not known or rudimentarily conceived. The scope and implications of these business forces for the health of countries would not be more fully realized for centuries to come. While Donne was not speaking directly to the issues of this research, it is significant, given the central focus of marketing on exchange, that what Donne wrote about in the context of human relations and the need of people to exist in interaction with one another has a connective interpretation to commerce. By extension, individual companies or organizations are not islands unto themselves as they face the make-or-buy and outsourcing decisions, industries are not islands as they must exchange for raw materials and labor, and countries are not metaphorical islands given the uneven distribution of raw materials around the planet. The

Developmental Entrepreneurship: Adversity, Risk, and Isolation
International Research in the Business Disciplines, Volume 5, 235–249
ISSN: 1074-7877/doi:10.1016/S1074-7877(06)05013-6

relative geographic isolation of Iceland (2 hours by airplane from Great Britain), a small population base of approximately 300,000, and a location near the Arctic Circle underscores the need for trade and interaction with other countries as a means of creating and maintaining a vibrant economy.

Within this context, the authors investigate through an exploratory study, the role of the modern, large-scale mission to a foreign country. This joining of forces of private entrepreneurs with governmental entities for the purpose of establishing the nurturing connections between the peoples and institutions of two countries is an area ripe for investigation.

In May 2005, a large delegation of individuals including entrepreneurs from Icelandic businesses, the President of Iceland, officials and staff from several governmental Ministries as well as leaders from education, scientific, and civic institutions in Iceland flew to the People's Republic of China. The overarching goal of this mission was to initiate and strengthen ties that would lead to increased commerce for Icelandic companies. The current paper focuses on the expectations of those traveling on the mission from Iceland, both before and after this initial contact. While the actual outcomes of the trade mission will not be known for many months or years to come, the authors will track changes in the participants' expectations and actions in future research in order to better understand the dynamics and outcomes of this type of entrepreneurial activity.

2. PEOPLE'S REPUBLIC OF CHINA

Economic growth has been very robust in China in recent years and the outlook is for continued growth in the future, although perhaps at a slower pace. Economic growth during the last decade has been over 8% per year on average and is expected to remain in that range this year and the next (IMF, 2005). Consequently, China's GDP per capita has risen rapidly. According to the *Economist*, it increased by 30% between 2000 and 2003 (Economist.com, 2005). Although still far behind the level of other developed countries, the gap is getting smaller. Thus, the standard of living has risen considerably in China in recent years, although by varying degrees depending on the location.

The partnership of Iceland and China is an unlikely one considering the differences between the two countries (see Table 1). The difference in size of population is enormous, with over 4,400 times more people living in China than in Iceland. The geographical distance between Reykjavik and Beijing is vast at just under 4,900 miles (7,900 km); however, there are also significant

Table 1. Country Comparison.

	China	Iceland
Population	1,300,000,000	294,000
Workforce	744,000,000	156,000
GDP per capita (USD)	$5,400	$32,400

Source: National Bureau of Statistics of China (2004), Statistics Iceland (2005), and IMD, World Competitiveness Yearbook (2005).

differences in cultural and political environments. Iceland's culture and politics is a mix of what prevails in Europe and North America, while China's culture is distinctively Asian in nature.

As time passes, China's role in the world economy will certainly expand. There are 1.3 billion people in China (National Bureau of Statistics of China, 2004) and as the standard of living improves and disposable income increases, the prospect is for China becoming the largest market in the world for a multitude of goods and services. China's share in the world economy is currently 13% in terms of GDP, while 21% of the world's population lives there. Thus, the growth potential is quite large. Also China currently accounts for 6% of all exports in the world (IMF, 2005) and as China's trade process opens up, this share is only going to increase. Iceland's markets are by nature tiny in comparison and to benefit from economies of scale will be required to break into other markets – with China representing a strong candidate.

China joined the World Trade Organization (WTO) at the end of 2001. With the joining, China agreed to the obligations dictated by the WTO, i.e. to help trade of goods and services flow freely between member countries. This implies opening Chinese markets to direct foreign competition. That includes lowering tariffs and eliminating import quotas for various products as well as changing the domestic legal framework in various ways to conform to WTO's rules (OECD, 2002).

3. REPUBLIC OF ICELAND

Iceland is a founding member of the WTO and a member of its predecessor, the General Agreement on Tariffs and Trade (GATT) since 1968. Furthermore, Iceland and China recently signed an agreement to explore the possibilities of a free trade agreement between the two countries. With

China joining the WTO and with a possible free trade agreement, increased levels of commerce between the two countries should grow.

The advantages for Iceland having increased trade with China are both on the demand side and the supply side. On the demand side, China is quickly growing into the largest market on earth. On the supply side, the price of labor in many parts of China is still relatively low. Per capita disposable income of urban households is over three times higher than that of rural households. The Chinese labor market has 744 million people (National Bureau of Statistics of China, 2004), which suggest the opportunity to produce labor-intensive products in China at a competitive cost.

4. ENTREPRENEURSHIP

Recent research in entrepreneurship suggests a strong positive link between entrepreneurship and economic growth with entrepreneurship stimulating and generating growth (Audretsch, 2002). This stands in contrast to traditional theory, which holds that entrepreneurship would retard economic growth. In the traditional theory, static efficiency dictates economic growth. The new theories, on the other hand, are dynamic in nature and emphasize the role of knowledge. However, there are no unique measurements of entrepreneurship and there are several ways to measure economic performance. According to Audretsch (2002, p. 13) "The positive relationship between entrepreneurship and performance has been found to hold not just for a single measure of performance, but rather across a broad spectrum of performance measures, such as employment creation, growth, firm survival, innovation and technological change, productivity increases, and exports. This link has proven to be robust across multiple units of observation, ranging from individuals, to establishments, enterprises, industries, geographic clusters, regions and even countries. Just as importantly, the positive relationships between entrepreneurship and the various measures of economic performance have been found to hold not just in the context of one country, but consistently for different countries in Europe and North America."

Thus policies supporting entrepreneurship are likely to promote growth (Audretsch, 2002). As a general rule (and putting aside political reasons), the theoretical reasons for governmental intervention is to manage various market failures or inefficiencies. In this case of Iceland, a highly isolated island country, these may be identified as network externalities, knowledge externalities, and learning externalities (Audretsch, 2002).

5. METHOD

5.1. Participants

The respondents were from a population of approximately 150 Icelandic delegates who went on the trade mission from Iceland to China with the Trade Council of Iceland and the President of Iceland in 2005. Most of the population were CEOs and managers of businesses located in Iceland. The main business sectors represented included representatives of seafood, biotechnology, and other technology-based products which have export potential to China; and representatives of businesses potentially seeking import, services, or investment from China such as aviation, shipping, tourism, banking, finance, and construction. Other delegates were deans and directors of business schools in Iceland, representatives from trade associations, central government, and the president's office. Twenty-one individuals responded to the survey prior to visiting China and 60 responses were obtained after the completion of the mission. The majority of the respondents were CEOs and managers of businesses (20 pre-China and 46 post-China). Eighteen males and three females were respondents to the pre-China survey. For the post-China survey, 49 males and 11 females responded.

5.2. Measures

Two survey instruments were used in this research. One was administered on the way to China, asking in general about each individual's expectation of what the trade mission would yield, and the other after meeting with Chinese officials and business people, asking about opportunities people saw in China. The survey utilized multiple Likert 7-point scales and several open-ended questions.

The pre-China visit questionnaire consisted of 11 items. The first two concerned how optimistic the delegates were about opportunities for the country of Iceland (Q1) and for the delegate's particular business or organization (Q2) on particular dimensions. The third item was on how likely respondents thought they would pursue opportunities in China within the next 24 months (Q3). It was followed by two open-ended questions on the objectives of their organization for the trip (Q4) and the potential difficulties they foresaw that could interfere with accomplishing these objectives (Q5). The next four items addressed the respondent's knowledge and experience with China and other countries outside the US and Europe. Finally, there were two background questions on gender and organizational affiliation.

The post-China visit questionnaire incorporated 15 items, many identical to those in the first questionnaire. The first was again on how optimistic people were about opportunities for Iceland, but now after they had been in China. Question 2 asked about the same six areas of delegates' business or organization as in the first survey, but now how successful they were in China (in the first survey they were asked about how optimistic they were). The third question was as before on how likely people thought they would pursue opportunities in China within the next two years. In four open-ended questions people were asked what they accomplished during the trip, difficulties accomplishing the trip's objectives, surprises in China, and what was obtained through the face-to-face mission that could not have been accomplished with mere e-mails or telephone calls. One question inquired about how pleased delegates were with the trip (not in the first question-naire). Finally, the post-visit questionnaire had the same items on knowl-edge and experience with China and countries outside Europe and North America as well as the two background questions on gender and affiliation, and a question on whether people answered the first survey.

5.3. Procedure

The first questionnaire was administered on the air flight to China on May 15, 2005. It was a pencil and paper survey. Twenty-one of approximately 150 attendees returned their questionnaire upon leaving the plane. The second questionnaire was administered after the trade mission visit. Respondents were invited to complete the survey three days after return-ing to Iceland via a web survey.

6. RESULTS

6.1. Pre-China Visit Results

As only 21 responses were obtained from the sample on the way to China, one has to look at the results in a qualitative way. They are not to be viewed as a reliable result for the whole population. On the other hand, several aspects of the results give us a better intuitive grasp of the expectations of the members of the trade mission held before arriving in China. Table 2 shows descriptive statistics for the closed questions of the survey on the way to China.

It can be observed from the responses that respondents were some what optimistic about the trade mission, particularly in "learning" about

Table 2. Descriptive Results of Closed Questions on Pre-China Trip Survey.

	n	Minimum	Maximum	Mean	Standard Deviation
Q1. Optimistic for Iceland about					
(a) Diplomacy	19	2	6	4.3	1.1
(b) Scientific exchange	19	2	7	4.1	1.0
(c) Education	19	2	7	4.5	1.3
(d) Culture	20	1	7	4.4	1.5
(e) Business/entrepreneurship	21	3	7	5.4	1.0
Average for a–e	19	2.6	6.2	4.5	0.9
Q2. Optimistic for organization about					
(a) Learning about the general culture of China	21	2	7	4.7	1.6
(b) Learning about the business culture of China	21	2	7	5.0	1.6
(c) Learning about the governmental culture of China	20	1	6	4.0	1.4
(d) Establishing professional contacts with other business people that will be beneficial in the future	20	2	7	4.9	1.3
(e) Establishing professional contacts with government officials that will be beneficial in the future	20	1	6	3.5	1.5
(f) Initiate collaboration	20	1	7	3.8	1.5
Average for a–f	20	1.5	5.8	4.3	1.0
Q3. Likely to pursue opportunities in China in the next two years?	21	2	7	5.0	1.5
Q6. Knowledge of China	20	2	7	4.2	1.6
Q7. Experience with China in terms of contacts, visiting, and staying in China	20	1	7	3.2	2.1
Q8. Knowledge of countries outside Europe and North America, other than China	20	3	6	4.8	1.0
Q12. Experience with countries outside Europe and North America, other than China, in terms of contacts, visiting, and staying in there	20	1	7	3.9	1.8

China – there was, however, substantial variability in the answers. Examining the frequency tables (not presented) it was apparent that there was a
good spread of answers over most of the seven response options of each
question. The group was a little less optimistic on establishing or initiating
contacts or collaboration, particularly with government officials. However,
this group was more optimistic on how likely they were to pursue opportunities in China within the next two years (Q3, mean 5.0), again with
substantial variability in the responses. The item on knowledge and
experience with China and other countries outside the US and Europe
tended to indicate a wide range of knowledge and experience.

6.2. Relationships among Variables

Several noteworthy relationships exist between answers to different questions,
which serve as a basis for future hypotheses and research. Those who were
optimistic in general about opportunities in China for Iceland also tended to
be optimistic about opportunities for their company or organization
($r = 0.536$). Also, the more knowledgeable people reported being about
China, the more likely they thought they could pursue opportunities in China
within the next two years ($r = 0.541$). A similar relationship was present for
experience with China ($r = 0.455$). A relatively high negative correlation,
however, was found between knowledge and experience with China on one
hand and how pessimistic people were about learning and understanding the
general, business, and governmental culture of China on the other (bivariate
correlations between -0.383 and -0.557). Finally, those who reported extensive knowledge and experience with China also tended to report extensive
knowledge and experience with other countries outside the US and Europe.

6.3. Open-Ended Questions

Responses to the two open-ended questions in the pre-China visit survey
revealed very general views on the objectives the delegates hoped to
accomplish for their organization and the potential difficulties they saw that
could interfere in accomplishing those objectives. A few respondents said
they hoped to either obtain new contacts or strengthen the already made
contacts. Others hoped to achieve more knowledge about China. Words
such as "learn," "understand," "know," and "experience" were mentioned
in that context frequently.

7. POST-CHINA TRIP

7.1. Descriptive Results

Table 3 provides the descriptive statistics of the post-China visit survey. The table contains the same or similar questions as in Table 2 in addition to a question on how pleased delegates were with the trade mission to China (Q8). In the second survey, people were asked whether they had answered the first survey. Fifteen people answered both. There is no significant difference between those 15 who answered both the surveys and the 45 who answered only the second survey. Therefore, it is reasonably appropriate to compare the answers between the two surveys and draw inferences based on attitude change generated by the trade mission experience itself.

The statistical means for the question of how optimistic people were about the opportunities Iceland has in China (Q1a–e) were slightly higher post-China mission (Table 3) than pre-China (Table 2). Females were more optimistic (5.4) than males (4.4) concerning opportunities Iceland has in China in terms of education ($p < 0.05$). The delegates working in the technology sector, investment, and finance were more optimistic about possibilities for the country of Iceland than those in seafood exporting, importing from China, transportation, and tourism sectors – in terms of both education (5.0 vs. 4.1, $p < 0.05$) and business/entrepreneurship (5.9 vs. 5.1, $p < 0.05$). Non-business delegates were significantly more optimistic (4.8) than business people in the delegation (4.0) with respect to opportunities in culture in China for the country of Iceland.

There was a slight change in wording of question 2 between the surveys. The pre-China survey asked about assessing the opportunities of the business or organization of the respondents in six areas. After the trip the question asked how successful people were in the trade mission in the same areas. On the average, the means for these six areas in question 2 (a–f in Table 2) were slightly lower after the trip than on the way to China, although none were statistically significant. This might indicate that expectations were not quite fulfilled on the average with respect to learning about Chinese culture and initiating business contact and collaboration. Males thought the trade mission was more successful (3.9) than females (2.9) in terms of learning about and understanding the business culture in China ($p < 0.05$).

Despite the evidence that delegates' expectations were not fully realized during the trade mission to China, overall they thought it was more likely that they would pursue opportunities in China in the next two years after the

Table 3. Descriptive Results of Closed Questions from Post-China Trip
Survey.

	n	Minimum	Maximum	Mean	Standard Deviation
Q1. Optimistic for Iceland about					
(a) Diplomacy	58	2	7	4.8	1.1
(b) Scientific exchange	58	2	6	4.3	1.1
(c) Education	58	2	7	4.6	1.3
(d) Culture	58	1	7	4.3	1.1
(e) Business/entrepreneurship	60	2	7	5.5	1.0
Average for a–e	57	2.8	6	4.7	0.7
Q2. Success of mission for organization about					
(a) Learning about the general culture of China	59	2	7	4.6	1.5
(b) Learning about the business culture of China	59	2	7	4.8	1.5
(c) Learning about the governmental culture of China	59	1	7	3.7	1.3
(d) Establishing professional contacts with other business people that will be beneficial in the future	58	1	7	4.3	1.7
(e) Establishing professional contacts with government officials that will be beneficial in the future	57	1	7	3.1	1.6
(f) Initiate collaboration	59	2	7	3.9	1.5
Average for a–f	56	1.8	6.2	4.1	0.9
Q3. Likely to pursue opportunities in China in the next two years	60	1	7	5.7	1.6
Q8. Pleased with trip to China	60	4	7	6.1	0.9
Q9. Knowledge of China	59	2	7	4.1	1.2
Q10. Experience with China in terms of contacts, visiting, and staying in China	60	1	7	4.5	1.6
Q11. Knowledge of countries outside Europe and North America, other than China	60	1	7	4.3	1.4
Q12. Experience with countries outside Europe and North America, other than China, in terms of contacts, visiting, and staying in there	60	1	7	3.9	1.8

trade mission ($p < 0.10$). Overall, the delegates reported being "fairly pleased" with the trade mission, a mean of 6.1.

It is not surprising to see that the delegates reported more experience with China after the trip (4.5 in Table 3, a scale of 1–7, where 1 is very little experience and 7 extensive experience) than prior (3.2 in Table 2). On the other hand, there was no change in what people thought they knew about China. The delegates reported less knowledge and less experience about other countries outside the US and Europe after the trip than prior – a difference of 0.5 and 0.8, respectively (see Tables 2 and 3). In general, males reported more knowledge and experience than females with both China and other countries outside the US and Europe. The difference was significant when asked about knowledge about China, where males had the mean of 4.3 and females 3.3 ($p < 0.01$).

7.2. Scale Response Questions

Regression analysis was performed on how likely people were to pursue opportunities in China within the next two years as a dependent variable (Q3). Respondents' assessments of the opportunities in China for Iceland (Q1a–e), views on how successful the trip was for the business/organization (Q2a–f), and knowledge and experience of China and other countries outside the US and Europe (Q9–12) were used as predictors (i.e. independent variables). The total model ($F[5, 51] = 9.466$; $p < 0.001$), containing five predictor variables ($p < 0.10$), explained about 48% ($R^2 = 0.481$) of the variance in how likely delegates felt they would pursue opportunities in China within two years.

These final predictor variables were assessments of the opportunities for Iceland in China in terms of culture (Q1d) and business/entrepreneurship (Q1e), and education (Q1c). The first two were positively related to the dependent variable, that is, the more optimistic about opportunities in culture and business/entrepreneurship, the more likely respondents felt they would pursue opportunities in China within the next two years. The third, however, was negatively related, that is, the more optimistic about opportunities for Iceland in China in education, the less likely people thought they would pursue opportunities in China within the next two years. The fourth significant predictor was how successful the trip was for the business/ organization in terms of initiating collaboration (Q2f) and was positively related to the dependent variable. The fifth and final significant predictor was the respondents' report on their knowledge of countries outside the US and Europe, that is, the more knowledge, the more likely people thought they would pursue opportunities in China within the next two years.

Another regression was performed on how pleased people were with the mission to China (Q8) as a dependent variable using the same predictors as in the prior regression analysis. Three predictors were significant ($F[3, 52] = 9.015$; $p < 0.001$, total model), explaining statistically about 34% ($R^2 = 0.342$) of the variance in how likely people thought they would pursue opportunities in China within the next two years. The predictors were all positively related to how pleased people were with the trip. The first was the assessment of the opportunities for Iceland in China in terms of culture (Q1d). The second and third were how successful the trip was for the business/organization in respect to learning about and understanding the business culture in China (Q2b) and with respect to establishing professional contacts with government officials (Q2e).

7.3. Open-Ended Questions

For the post-China mission survey, four open-ended questions were asked. The first one dealt with what the delegates accomplished in the trip (Q4). Almost 50 out of the 60 delegates responded to the question and most of them in a general way. Over 20 delegates mentioned that they accomplished meeting people and initiated contacts. Almost the same number said they accomplished knowledge or an understanding or a feeling of China or of the markets in China. Only five delegates indicated that they signed an agreement or a letter of interest, and four said that they strengthened existing contacts. Two delegates mentioned that they accomplished introducing products from Iceland; two got to know the competition better. One mentioned each of the following accomplishments: trade more with China, got in contact with a Chinese-speaking person who will assist him in the future, and increased goodwill.

Approximately, 40 delegates reported that they experienced significant difficulties in accomplishing their objectives (Q5). Fourteen of them experienced language difficulties; they were surprised how little English the Chinese people they met understood and some said they were not sure whether the Chinese in the meetings understood what the Icelanders said. The delegates ran into several other difficulties, a few mentioned by each. Four thought that some difficulties were due to last-minute changes before the trip.

The following difficulties were mentioned by two delegates each: too short a time in China and too strict a schedule; pre-arranged business seminars were not practical; bad Chinese consultant services; and few Chinese contacts. Finally, the following difficulties were mentioned by one delegate each: Chinese companies did not show up for meetings, not finding the right person or official for correct information, could not set meetings through Chinese contacts, not enough information at the beginning about Chinese businesses, poor Chinese Trade Council, and unfortunate geographical location of the contact firm, so no meeting could be arranged. Only six delegates reported that they ran across no difficulties.

Several different responses were given by about 40 delegates on what surprised them in the trade mission (Q6). About 10 different "pleasant surprises" were mentioned by about 30 delegates, and four different "unpleasant surprises" were mentioned by about seven delegates. The "pleasant surprises" were indicated by answers related to how modern China was, westernized, fast development, and a lot of growth (14 delegates), positive attitude or hospitality of the Chinese people (7), the emphasis on business in China (6), the ease of doing business or readiness of going directly into negotiating prices (5), how many Icelanders are doing business in China (2), good preparation of the Icelandic Trade Council (1), quality of products (1), increasing numbers attending universities in the next few years (1) and just "China" (1).

The "unpleasant surprises," on the other hand, were language problems (3), few contacts or ill-prepared meetings (2), difficulties in finding what people needed (1), and the corruption in China due to lack of property rights (1).

The last open-ended question asked what the delegates' business or organization gained on the trip that could not have been accomplished with a telephone call or an e-mail (Q7). About 50 out of the 60 delegates answered. Almost 30 said that it was necessary to have a face-to-face meeting with business partners in China, direct contact, eye-to-eye, personal contact, or direct feedback. Approximately, 10 mentioned that they needed to "feel" the culture, understand it, or experience it. Five delegates mentioned that they were able to get unplanned contacts and four said things like visibility of the delegation committee, meet top Chinese personnel, or the presence of the President of Iceland. Each of the following was mentioned by one delegate each: see facilities of potential partners, the trip focused the search, necessary for writing an agreement, get to know public Chinese business representatives, and trust. One delegate noted that there was nothing that the business got out of the trip that could not have been done by a telephone call or an e-mail.

8. DISCUSSION

On the average, prior to the state-trade mission to China, delegates had moderate expectations concerning the creation of business opportunities during their stay in China. After the experience, respondents rated their success during the visit in the same areas as moderate. The mean of how likely respondents thought they and/or their organizations would pursue opportunities in China within two years was 5.0 (pre-China) and 5.7 (post-China) – both indicating that respondents thought it was more likely than not.

This increase in how likely the delegates would pursue opportunities in China might be interpreted as the trade mission was more successful than expected. However, reviewing what the delegates said after the mission on what they accomplished, only a handful reported they actually signed an agreement. A large group (over 40%) said they initiated contacts or "met people" and about 40% said they got to know markets in China better. These agreements are important for future business so more of them would have been better.

To Iceland, was the trip worth the money and time spent? It has been established that entrepreneurship is related to economic growth (Audretsch, 2002), and the entrepreneurship of seeking opportunities in foreign markets should be no exception. China is certainly a huge, growing market and is expected to continue to grow (IMF, 2005). These facts alone make it necessary to visit China. The stay appeared to be a positive experience for most of the delegates.

With the end of the Cold War and the defusing of major potential hostilities among nation states, the climate for increased trade has improved. For nations such as Iceland, which are relatively remote, the need for trade is paramount. When coupled with a small population base, it should not be surprising that an active entrepreneurial effort, involving individuals, governmental entities, and representatives of multiple sectors of the economy would collaborate. Such are the circumstances that culminated in this large trade mission to China.

REFERENCES

Audretsch, D. (2002). *Entrepreneurship: A survey of the literature prepared for the European Commission.* Enterprise Directorate General, July.
Donne, J. (1624). *Devotions upon emergent occasions and death's duel.* Vintage Spiritual Classics, 1999.
Economist.com (2005). Country briefings: China, economic data. Webpage accessed March 3, http://www.economist.com/countries/China/profile.cfm?folder = Profile%2DEconomic%20Data
IMD (2005). *World competitiveness yearbook.* Lausanne, Switzerland: IMD International.
International Monetary Fund (IMF) (2005). *World economic outlook,* April.

National Bureau of Statistics of China (2004). China statistical yearbook. Website acce-
    ssed March 6, 2005, http://www.stats.gov.cn/english/statisticaldata/yearlydata/yb2004-e/
    indexeh.htm
Organization for Economic Cooperation and Development (OECD) (2002). *China in the World
    economy: The domestic policy challenges.* OECD: Paris.
Statistics Iceland (2005). Webpage accessed March 5, http://www.hagstofa.is/template21.
    asp?PageID=218

PART VI:
ENTREPRENEURSHIP AND
HISTORICAL DISADVANTAGES

INDIGENOUS ENTREPRENEURSHIP RESEARCH: THEMES AND VARIATIONS

Ana María Peredo and Robert B. Anderson

1. INTRODUCTION

The concept of entrepreneurship is a long-standing pillar of economic theory. From the beginning, the entrepreneurial notion represented forces of economic change that introduce new energy into systems of exchange and allowed these systems to produce the surpluses that contribute to one important aspect of human well-being. Beyond the well-being associated with economic surplus, other benefits are seen to flow from entrepreneurship. Blawatt (1998), for example, sees the following gains in entrepreneurial venture:

- Entrepreneurs drive the economy, creating new concepts, innovations, new ventures, employment, and national wealth.
- Entrepreneurs bring a balance to a nation's economic system, offsetting concentrations of power, increasing competitiveness.
- Entrepreneurship serves the community and society first by providing an improved standard of living, social responsiveness, and sustainable industry. It adds to the social and psychological well-being of the community by providing an outlet for creative action.
- Entrepreneurship ... offers third world countries the opportunity to become first world countries (Blawatt, 1998, p. 21)

Developmental Entrepreneurship: Adversity, Risk, and Isolation
International Research in the Business Disciplines, Volume 5, 253–273
Copyright © 2006 by Elsevier Ltd.
All rights of reproduction in any form reserved
ISSN: 1074-7877/doi:10.1016/S1074-7877(06)05014-8

Early on it was recognized that this broad concept of entrepreneurship could be used to understand and improve the condition of particular disadvantaged populations; the so-called "under-developed" communities and regions (e.g. Danson, 1995). Only recently, however, has the notion been applied by scholars of entrepreneurship to a particular sector within this category, to the indigenous populations of the world.

It is the purpose of this paper to give an overview of this relatively new, but vital, field of enquiry. Indigenous entrepreneurship is a growth area of scholarship not just because it appears to be a distinguishable subject, with its own characteristics and invitations to research, but also because it addresses an urgent problem – how to improve the lot of a chronically disadvantaged segment of the world's population.

This paper identifies the principal themes that have emerged in studies of indigenous entrepreneurship, beginning with how the field is identified. It then outlines some main themes in the discussions concerning indigenous entrepreneurship, especially the fundamental issue of the relation between entrepreneurship and cultural values. The paper attempts to sketch where scholars have found themselves coming together, and where they have differed in direction and outcomes. Comment is offered on where the most urgent lines of enquiry appear to lie, and where the most promising directions of research seem to be located. The paper closes with an indication of the journals most given to publishing material concerning indigenous entrepreneurship.

2. CHARACTERIZING THE FIELD

One set of issues in any emerging subject area concerns the delineation of the area itself. Scholars attempting to describe the field of indigenous entrepreneurship face a pair of obvious questions: (1) who are the indigenous people of the world? and (2) what is indigenous entrepreneurship? On both points, there is a contention among those working in this emerging field. Both questions are complicated by a distinction that is theoretically clear but in practice quite untidy – the distinction between the way a field is delimited by definition, and the characterizations that emerge from empirical observation.

2.1. The Concept of "Indigenous"

Several authors offer explicit definitions or near-definitions of the term "indigenous," ranging from the relatively simple to the complex. All seek to delineate sub-populations that are found worldwide, which differ in many respects but have one thing in common and that is their *"indigenousness."* The simplest approach to identifying the indigenous is an "accepted self-identification" criterion. On this view, an indigenous person is one who identifies himself or herself as "indigenous," and whose self-identification is accepted by the indigenous community in which the person claims membership (e.g. Hindle & Lansdowne, 2005).

Foley (2003) expands the "accepted self-identification" definition with an explicit mention of an original connection with the land. Within this context, Lindsay (2005) writes, "an indigenous person is regarded as an individual who is an original owner of a country's resources or a descendent of such a person and which, in either case, the individual regards himself or herself as Indigenous and the Indigenous community in which they live accepts them as Indigenous" (Lindsay, 2005, p. 1).

Dana's (2006) concise definition employs an "ancient connection" criterion. He writes, "Indigenous nations are people whose ancestors were living in an area prior to colonisation, or within a nation-state, prior to the formation of a nation-state" (Dana, 2006, p. 1).

Other approaches tend to provide more specific criteria. For example, the United Nations, in a 1995 resolution states,

> Indigenous or aboriginal peoples are so-called because they were living on their lands before settlers came from elsewhere; they are the descendants ... of those who inhabited a country or a geographical region at the time when people of different cultures or ethnic origins arrived, the new arrivals later becoming dominant through conquest, occupation, settlement or other means (General Assembly the United Nations, 1995).

Peredo, Anderson, Galbraith, Benson, and Dana (2004) provide the most detailed review of relevant characteristics. They review a number of definitions used for indigenous peoples, including those by the International Labour Organization (1991), the United Nations, the World Bank (2001), the Asian Development Bank (2000), and other writers and researchers. The authors suggest that there are six key, or common elements relevant to the concept of indigenous entrepreneurship: (1) descent from inhabitants of a land prior to later inhabitants, (2) some form of domination by the later inhabitants, (3) maintenance of distinguishing socio-cultural norms and institutions by the indigenous group, (4) an attachment to ancestral lands and resources, (5) often, but not always, subsistence economic arrangements, and (6) an association with distinctive languages. Not all elements are present in all cases, but in many cases of modern indigenous cultures, all six characteristics are present. In general, these characteristics, or some significant combination of them, serve to set apart indigenous people from those populations that came later.

Dana and Anderson (2006a) also note that indigenous people display remarkable heterogeneity across nations and even within particular communities. Governing myths, family, and community organization, values concerning work, play, sexual roles and relations, are among the many matters where different indigenous groups exhibit striking differences. As Peredo et al. (2004) note, between 250 and 300 million people are estimated by the UN (General Assembly The United Nations, 1995) to fit the definition of indigenous. By any definition, indigenous are found on all populated continents and range from traditional hunter-gatherers and subsistence farmers to expert professionals in industrialized societies.

In addition, there is wide agreement that indigenous populations are generally poor and otherwise disadvantaged in terms of various economic measures. The World Bank (2001), for example, opens its "Draft Operational Policy Concerning Indigenous People" with the acknowledgment that, "indigenous peoples are commonly among the poorest and most vulnerable segments of society" (World Bank, 2001, p. 1), an assessment echoed by all scholars of indigenous entrepreneurship (e.g. Peredo, 2001; Anderson, 2004a, b; Berkes & Adhikari, 2005).

Scholars point out that indigenous people are, typically, not only poor but also severely disadvantaged in terms of broader socio-political measures. Indeed it is this broadly defined, disadvantaged position that is commonly given as a reason for focusing on indigenous entrepreneurship. To many scholars, indigenous leaders and politicians, entrepreneurial activity is seen as a potential instrument of relief within these chronically impoverished indigenous communities. As Galbraith, Rodriguez, and Stiles (2006) note, "indigenous entrepreneurial activities are often cited as the 'second wave' of economic development, with the first wave of economic development being direct governmental support and wealth transfer policies" (p. 3).

2.2. Collective Social and Economic Organization

Beyond being disadvantaged, other commonalities emerge among indigenous people in spite of their diversity. In particular, two general tendencies have attracted comments and debates within the indigenous entrepreneurship literature. One of these is the recurring theme of communal or collective patterns of social organization, including property arrangements and distribution of resources. Dana (1995, 1996), for example, draws attention to "the Eskimo preference for a communal form of organization" (p. 65) in one indigenous community he studied in the sub-Arctic, and to "the traditional values of these people, working collectively and sharing collectively, while disliking the concept of competition" (p. 78) in another, quite distinct, indigenous community.

Bewayo (1999) refers to "the communalistic culture known to be prevalent in black Africa" (p. 2), while Peredo and Chrisman (2006) employ the concept of "community orientation" to describe the social organization of several indigenous communities in the Andes. "The more 'community-oriented' a society is, the more its members experience their membership as resembling the life of parts of an organism; the more they will feel their status and well-being is a function of the reciprocated contributions they make to their community" (Peredo & Chrisman, 2006, p. 313). They maintain that "community orientation" in this sense is a prominent feature of the indigenous communities they study.

Perhaps the most elaborate and generalized argument for this view is presented by Redpath and Nielsen (1997), using Hofstede's (1980) "cultural dimension" of individualism/collectivism. Redpath and Nielsen (1997) take this dimension to indicate the extent to which members of a society value individual over collective needs. In their view, "this dimension is the key to many core cultural differences between Native and non-Native cultures (and between indigenous and non-indigenous cultures throughout the world)" (Redpath & Nielsen, 1997, p. 329). They sharply contrast the individualistic emphasis of non-indigenous societies, especially those in North America, and the distinctly collectivist orientation they see in indigenous communities. Indeed they argue that the difference on this dimension underlies other cultural differences, such as "power distance" (acceptance of unequal distributions of power and wealth), and is the basis of organizational structure and behaviour of indigenous groups (Redpath & Nielsen, 1997, p. 336).

While there is widespread agreement on this tendency in indigenous communities, there is a fundamental controversy on its origins and depth. The scholars cited above, and others (e.g. Tully, 1995; Bishop, 1999) take the view that indigenous cultures are, or tend to be, "communal" or "collective" with respect to property and social arrangements, and see this tendency as deeply rooted in the cultural heritage of indigenous peoples. However, a number of other scholars disagree with this assessment.

Galbraith et al. (2006), for example, mount a spirited attack on that basic assumption. Citing a range of historical and anthropological scholarship, they argue that pre-Colonial populations, in North America at least, possessed a strong sense of private property, and lacked only the standardized economic institutions of later Europeans necessary to make them full participants in the economic activity that is standard today. Essentially, they argue that without the institutions, common language, and contractual characteristics required to sustain an organization of non-related individuals (such as employees and investors), the indigenous populations needed to access social capital through the networks of related "clan" members in order to lower the economic costs of economic transactions and productive activities. And whenever possible, particularly when the economics of production changed, as when indigenous populations adopted the horse and firearm, pre-reservation trade and property ownership was generally done on an individual or family basis.

Galbraith et al. (2006) do not deny that many current indigenous communities exhibit "collective" inclinations with respect to property and economic arrangements. But they hold that it is not a cultural characteristic, but rather a comparatively recent phenomenon, born of either the forced reservation system and its collective land-tenure arrangements in many developed countries or the weak institutional structures commonly seen in "less developed countries" (e.g. Galbraith & Stiles, 2003). Similar arguments have been made by other scholars of indigenous economics (e.g. Anderson, 1997; Miller, 2001; Anderson, Benson, & Flanagan, 2006).

As Galbraith et al. (2006) themselves argue, one's view on this matter of the cultural rootedness of collective and communal arrangements has powerful implications for one's view about how to foster and encourage indigenous entrepreneurship. It should be expected that this will prove to be an important strand in research concerning indigenous entrepreneurship.

The second cultural tendency that has drawn comment from some scholars is the inclination toward forms of social organization built around kinship rather than economic or other functional factors. In their summary of a reference work on indigenous entrepreneurship, Dana and Anderson (2006a) observe that, "Social organisation among indigenous people is often based on kinship ties, and not created in response to market needs" (p. 6). Berkes and Adhikari (2005), investigating a number of indigenous entrepreneurial ventures involving integrated conservation and development in Central and South America, also note that many of these ventures are social enterprises, and involve networks of family members directly and indirectly. The kin-based social organization of many indigenous communities is another factor, which may be expected to have implications for understanding and promoting entrepreneurial ventures among these communities.

2.3. The Concept of "Entrepreneurship"

What is meant by the term "entrepreneurship" within the concept of indigenous entrepreneurship? It is fair to say that there is no consensus among management scholars as to what, precisely, constitutes entrepreneurship (Venkataraman, 1997, p. 120). It is therefore not surprising that treatments of indigenous entrepreneurship tend also to show considerable variety in the definitions, explicit or implicit, of the entrepreneurial element in the concept. The "minimalist" definition of entrepreneurship, according to which it is simply the operation of a commercial enterprise (as in Siropolis (1977, pp. 23–24) is cited by Dana (1996), and echoed in several other publications) Hindle and Lansdowne (2005), for instance, define "indigenous entrepreneurship" as "the creation, management and development of new ventures by indigenous people ..." (2005, p. 133). Dana (2006), who in one place subscribes (with minor reservations) to Casson's (1982) definition of an entrepreneur as someone who specializes in taking judgemental decisions about the coordination of scarce resources, also tends to take a similar "minimalist" approach in other publications regarding indigenous populations. Anderson (2004b), citing Drucker (1985), supplements the minimalist notion within the context of indigenous entrepreneurship with the idea of recognizing opportunity and the employment of technology to exploit opportunity by creating an enterprise. A still broader concept of entrepreneurship (in the indigenous setting and elsewhere) is offered by Peredo (2004), who adds not only the recognition and exploitation of opportunity but also innovation, risk-acceptance, and resourcefulness.

For purposes of discussing entrepreneurship in its indigenous forms, as in discussing the concept of the indigenous itself, many scholars tend to move beyond the definitional to an empirical grounding. Dana (1996), for instance, elaborates entrepreneurial possibilities with the identification of at least seven sub-kinds of entrepreneur ("Cantillonian," "Weberian," "Schumpeterian," "Barthian," "McClelland," "the Displacee," and the "Kirznerian"), all arguably species of the genus "entrepreneur" identified empirically.

It seems obvious that disparities in what is considered entrepreneurship will have an impact on scholarship concerning indigenous entrepreneurship. The need for an accepted concept of entrepreneurship is well recognized in entrepreneurship scholarship generally, and applies with at least equal urgency to the subject of indigenous entrepreneurship. It is to be expected that the refinement of this fundamental notion in its indigenous environment will be an important line of research in this emergent area.

2.4. Indigenous Entrepreneurship: Two Paths

Given the differences in opinion regarding both the fundamental nature of "entrepreneurship" and the critical elements that constitute the notion of "indigenous," it is not surprising that there are different opinions regarding the term, "indigenous entrepreneurship." The indigenous entrepreneurship literature tends to fall into two camps on matters concerning the location and/or the objectives of this form of enterprise. One approach – in some ways the most obvious – is to think of indigenous entrepreneurship as what goes on wherever people who are indigenous happen to be engaged in entrepreneurial activities. In discussing the challenges to indigenous entrepreneurship with respect to gaming-related reservation economies, Galbraith and Stiles (2003) for instance, consider the number of business start-ups by indigenous people, whether individually or collectively, on or off reserves. Dana and Anderson (2006a) appear to take a similar view. On this account, indigenous entrepreneurship is basically entrepreneurial activity conducted by indigenous people.

The contrary view is that indigenous entrepreneurship differs conceptually in its situational context and/or its ultimate objects or goals. It must be admitted that here as elsewhere the boundary between conceptual boundaries and empirical generalization is not rigorously observed. But there is a clear tendency on the part of many scholars to consider entrepreneurship (however that is understood) that is indigenous to be restricted to certain contexts. One restriction is to location, another is to its ultimate objective, and a third is to its form or organization.

For example, Peredo et al. (2004) indicate clearly that in their consideration of indigenous entrepreneurship they are counting only indigenous ventures in certain territories or locations. Here indigenous entrepreneurship is necessarily undertaken as something identifiable within an indigenous territory. Thus indigenous entrepreneurs, "may or may not be located in native homelands – many have been displaced or relocated. But they are situated in communities of indigenous people with the shared social, economic, and cultural patterns that qualify them as indigenous populations" (Peredo et al., 2004, p. 12).

Indigenous entrepreneurship can also be viewed in terms of its goals, objectives, or mission, such as self-determination. For example, Lindsay (2005) argues that indigenous entrepreneurship is undertaken "for the benefit of indigenous people." He continues by connecting this with the "holistic" aims of indigenous entrepreneurship at furthering self-determination on the part of indigenous communities, the preservation of heritage, and other distinct social aims. Underlying many of these concepts is the often implicit notion that this form of venture is, almost by definition, organized in a certain way, that is, collectively. This is intimately connected with the idea that goals are communal rather than individual. The connection is explicit in Lindsay and others, who identify indigenous entrepreneurship as incorporating "entrepreneurial strategies originating in and controlled by the community, and the sanction of Indigenous culture" (Lindsay, 2005, p. 1).

The divergence may have considerable significance for the way in which indigenous entrepreneurship is characterized empirically and should therefore attract some concentrated discussion. Research themes mentioned later in this paper (e.g. compatibility with indigenous culture, and the tendency to land-based ventures and partnership arrangements) are likely to be influenced significantly in their findings by assumptions made restricting the concept of indigenous entrepreneurship in any of the ways just mentioned.

3. DOMINANT RESEARCH THEMES

Even though the field of indigenous entrepreneurship is still in comparative infancy, a number of research themes have emerged in the literature.

3.1. Indigenous Entrepreneurship and Culture

By far, the dominant theme in indigenous entrepreneurship research to date is the relationship between indigenous entrepreneurship and indigenous culture. The nest of sub-themes located under this heading are captured in a symposium addressing indigenous entrepreneurship presented during the 2004 Academy of Management Annual Meeting. The symposium introduction read,

> Is there such a thing as "Indigenous Entrepreneurship?" If so, what distinguishes it from other forms of entrepreneurship? Or is entrepreneurship universal, and must all accommodate themselves to its essential requirements? If this is so, what are these essential requirements and what implications do they have for indigenous entrepreneurship and enterprise? To come full circle, if an irreducible set of essential entrepreneurship requirements exist, in satisfying these in ways consistent with their particular culture, history and objectives, are various Indigenous Peoples around the world developing differing models of entrepreneurship and enterprise development, or is a common approach emerging? (Anderson, 2004a, p. 5)

As we have seen, while there is a great diversity of opinion as to what constitutes indigenous entrepreneurship it is arguable that the majority of scholars working in this area believe that "indigenous entrepreneurship," clearly exists in some form (Peredo et al., 2004). The question of what it is that distinguishes indigenous from other forms of entrepreneurship is one of the richest areas of discussion and research. There are those, however, who appear to suggest that the requirements of entrepreneurship are universal in a way that makes it difficult if not impossible to reconcile with at least some indigenous cultural traditions. Other scholars (e.g. Dana, 1996; Peredo, 2001), however, hold that the activity of entrepreneurship should be understood more broadly, admitting many forms and adapting itself to different cultural and social settings. The continuum of opinions between the "universalist" and "relativistic" views of entrepreneurship forms one of the most engaging areas of debate in indigenous entrepreneurship.

In this symposium, Stiles (2004) approached this issue via the question of whether indigenous peoples "can opt in to the process of global development on their own terms," and if so, whether that implies "a uniquely indigenous form of entrepreneurship in order to address the imperatives of Schumpeterian style economy building?" (p. 1). He argued that there are historical reasons to be sceptical about the possibility of an indigenous entrepreneurship, which succeeds both entrepreneurially and culturally. For example, he rhetorically asked, "how well have indigenous peoples in the past adapted to Schumpeterian style intrusions?" According to Stiles (2004), "in the case of virtually all people indigenous to the Americas, the answer is 'not well.' In fact the totality of their failure must be the focus of all that we say" (Stiles, 2004, p. 1). Stiles argued that the indigenous of North America quickly recognized the advantages of such European novelties as firearms, but failed to appreciate, "that European economic and social methods were also superior" (Stiles, 2004, p. 1). Stiles' contention that the failure to adopt the social systems needed to produce and/or acquire the goods they came to value, clearly suggests that the cultural endowments of the indigenous were, and presumably still are, difficult to reconcile with the "Schumpeterian intrusions" that might have rescued them. The implication is that the requirements of entrepreneurship are universal, and successful entrepreneurial responses require that indigenous people leave behind, or at least adapt, those features of culture, which are incompatible. A truly indigenous form of entrepreneurship seems bound to fail.

The approach taken by Galbraith (2004), and later by Galbraith et al. (2006) somewhat resembles these approaches but differs in some important respects. Galbraith et al. (2006) state that, "not surprisingly, individual entrepreneurial activity among tribal members has been an abysmal failure" (p. 27). The authors refer to elders' reports that "the more entrepreneurial indigenous individuals and families had moved off the reservations to start businesses in the cities" (Galbraith et al., 2006, p. 24). This might be taken as *prima facie* evidence for the conclusion, once again, that entrepreneurship has its objective demands, and indigenous cultural values tend to conflict with them. But as noted earlier, Galbraith et al. (2006) also argue that the "reservation culture" is, to a large extent, a recent and artificial overlay. Precolonial indigenous populations were, they contend, highly entrepreneurial. Their disadvantage was the lack of standardized legal, contractual, and linguistic institutions to support a more fully developed economic system. And that lack was frozen in place by the collective land-tenure system that came with reservations. On this view, then, the cultural adaptation needed to foster indigenous entrepreneurship is largely the shedding of the alien property system enforced by reservations, together with the acceptance of regularized social and legal patterns demanded by developed economic exchanges. The suggestion remains that entrepreneurship objectively requires certain detailed responses, but the idea that indigenous culture is basically antithetical to those requirements is less evident.

Mitchell (2004), however, employed the apparatus of "transaction cognition" theory to argue for universal requirements in entrepreneurship. Arguing that the theory permits the identification of universal elements in entrepreneurship (see, e.g., Mitchell, Smith, Seawright, Peredo, & McKenzie, 2002), Mitchell contended that "on-reserve" transactions (where, presumably, cultural forces are fully in play) require more than three times the cognitions called for by "off-reserve" exchanges.

All three of the positions just described in the 2004 symposium tend to see entrepreneurship as embodying a set of demands that are largely universal in their scope, and they emphasize the tension between those demands and the cultural environments of the Indigenous. The conclusion drawn, or implied, is that if indigenous entrepreneurship is possible, it is likely to require significant cultural adaptation. The outlook furthest removed from this position is one that accepts the tension between entrepreneurship *as standardly conceived* and indigenous culture but goes on to argue that this merely calls on us to enlarge the standard conception of what entrepreneurship is. Entrepreneurship, on this view, is highly elastic in what it requires.

Dana (1995) and Dana and Anderson (2006a) are perhaps the most emphatic in their insistence that indigenous entrepreneurship takes place, but that it has markedly different characteristics from the non-indigenous varieties. They maintain that, "cultural values of indigenous peoples are often incompatible with the basic assumptions of mainstream theories" (Dana & Anderson, 2006a, p. 4), a position also argued by the Lockean scholar philosopher John Bishop (1999) and others (e.g. Tully, 1995). This approach tends also to undermine the "universality" of mainstream characterizations of entrepreneurship. For example, entrepreneurial activity need not even involve transactions, as in the case of "internal subsistence activity" (Dana & Anderson, 2006a, p. 8), but wealth is created and so entrepreneurship takes place. Similarly, Lindsay (2005) employs the language of "cultural value dimensions" to emphasize the contrast between indigenous entrepreneurship and non-indigenous.

Likewise Peredo (2004), who believes something recognizably entrepreneurial is common in indigenous societies, cites Polanyi (1944) in challenging the universality of economic assumptions underlying standard theories of entrepreneurship. Berkes and Adhikari (2005) concur with Peredo and Chrisman (2006) in arguing that indigenous entrepreneurship may in fact be an instrument for maintaining cultural values, and that entrepreneurship may be conducted in a different way in keeping with those values, including "a community emphasis, consensus decision-making, and a focus on sharing and cooperation, instead of competition" (Berkes & Adhikari, 2005, p. 12). And while Morris (2004), in his study of two sub-cultures in "relatively modernized" societies (South African and Hawaiian), is perhaps closest to the "universalist requirements" position, concluding that there is no need for different models of entrepreneurship to accommodate cultural differences, he also finds significant differences in the values leading to entrepreneurial undertakings and their goals among indigenous peoples.

What emerges from this sketch is the idea that responses to the general question of the relation between indigenous entrepreneurship and culture are formed in large part by how one conceives of entrepreneurship. This is not just a matter of definition, but rather how one conceives of venturing in relation to economic systems, and economic systems in relation to social arrangements, culture, and values. The ongoing search for an account of what entrepreneurship is, and what its social, cultural, and psychological requirements might be, therefore takes on an added urgency in the context of the study of indigenous entrepreneurship. The indigenous context particularly requires that the search be conducted in a way which addresses those large questions of the cultural boundedness of our conceptions of the values pursued entrepreneurially, the way that economic and other transactions are socially contained, and the conditions that give rise to recognizing and exploiting opportunities to create "value."

3.2. Distinguishing Features of Indigenous Entrepreneurship

Among those who agree that entrepreneurship is, to some degree at least, a flexible concept, and that indigenous forms of entrepreneurship exploit this flexibility to create distinctive kinds of venturing, there is a stimulating variety of proposals as to what distinguishes the phenomenon.

Scholars of indigenous entrepreneurship who are inclined to see it as an adaptation of entrepreneurship to indigenous environment almost universally comment on the inclusion, even the superordination, of social aims in the goal-structures of indigenous entrepreneurship. Morris (2004), as noted above, tends to argue that entrepreneurship takes similar forms across cultures. Nevertheless, he observes that in the two cases he studied closely, "neither of the two samples placed much emphasis on wealth generation" (p. 2). Anderson (2004b), on the basis of his study of indigenous people pursuing development in the Canadian context, comments, "Their goal is not economic development alone, but economic development as part of the larger agenda of rebuilding their communities and nations and reasserting their control over their traditional territories" (p. 2).

3.2.1. Community-Based Development Goals

Peredo (2004), whose work on "Community-Based Enterprises" includes indigenous populations in the Andes, goes even further. "The goals of these Community-Based Enterprises are broad: they include at least social, cultural, political as well as economic aims. In fact economic goals are generally a means to social ends" (Peredo, 2004, p. 3). Berkes and Adhikari (2005), who surveyed 42 cases of indigenous enterprise in the "Equator Initiative" database, note that "the nature of community benefits strongly suggests that indigenous entrepreneurships tend to focus on social, community-based development" (p. 18). Lindsay (2005) does not hesitate to generalize the point, "Indigenous entrepreneurship is more holistic than non-Indigenous entrepreneurship; it focuses on both economic and non-economic goals" (p. 1).

The extent to which it is true that indigenous entrepreneurship is characteristically different from non-indigenous entrepreneurship in its goal structures deserves a close study. The results will depend on, among other things, what one counts as indigenous entrepreneurship. The earlier division of opinion as to whether indigenous entrepreneurship is necessarily or typically conducted collectively and in indigenous communities, or may be undertaken by indigenous individuals wherever they happen to be, will have a major impact on these findings. But the outcomes are of major importance to those who wish to understand and foster indigenous entrepreneurship in its various settings.

3.2.2. Collective Organization

A second characteristic singled out by many scholars is the "collective" or "communal" nature of much indigenous entrepreneurship. Anderson's studies (1995, 1996, 1999) of indigenous development in Canada remarked that the foundation of that approach was predominately collective, based in individual First Nations. Lindsay (2005) cites the work of Redpath and Nielsen (1997), referred to earlier, in support of the view that indigenous entrepreneurship can be expected, generally, to be collective in its approach. Berkes and Adhikari (2005), in their review of more than 40 indigenous projects in Central and South America, refer repeatedly to communally owned lands, tool banks, and stocks of natural resources. The markedly collective nature of the indigenous enterprises encountered by Peredo in the Andes led her to see one of the distinguishing features of that enterprise as the "basic unit of entrepreneurship." She argues that, "the entrepreneurial agent is not some individual but the indigenous community as a group" (Peredo, 2004, p. 3; see also Peredo & Chrisman, 2006).

3.2.3. Environmental Sustainability

A closely related feature often associated with indigenous entrepreneurship is a connection with the land, especially with ancestral lands; a feature which we have seen plays an important part in specifying who the Indigenous are. Berkes and Adhikari (2005) address the question, "Does indigenous entrepreneurship have distinctive features?" by remarking that "One of the ways in which many indigenous groups are distinguishable from other rural groups is their attachment to their ancestral lands and natural resources" (p. 1). Berkes and Adhikari (2005) echo Anderson (1999) and others in noting that a conspicuous aim of many indigenous peoples is the recovery of their traditional lands.

It is perhaps part of this sense of connection with the land that the indigenous are frequently said to demonstrate a strong environmental concern in their operations. Peredo (2001) emphasizes the inherent sustainability of indigenous use of the land among Quechuas and Aymaras. In summarizing a considerable body of research on indigenous entrepreneurship, Dana and Anderson (2006a) comment that, "Indigenous enterprise is often environmentally sustainable." (p. 3) Berkes and Adhikari (2005) refer throughout their review of indigenous projects reported in the Equator Initiative database to the environmental sensitivity of the enterprises and their widespread success in recovering and as well as preserving the natural habitat. This environmental awareness is taken by many to be a hallmark of an indigenous enterprise. This concern for the environment is frequently linked with two other features ascribed to many or most indigenous undertakings: the use of "traditional knowledge" and the idea that the indigenous inherit a sense of a "spiritual" connection with the land.

Berkes and Adhikari (2005) note that indigenous enterprises often rely on traditional knowledge, defined by Berkes (1999) as "knowledge, practice and belief, evolving by adaptive processes and handed down through generations by cultural transmission, about the relationship of living things (including humans) with one another and with their environment" (p. 27). They emphasize the additional resources available in that knowledge, and the requirement of indigenous political control over their assets in order to capitalize on those resources. Dana (2006) echoes the importance of traditional knowledge and its connection with ecological awareness.

The sense of a spiritual connection with the land is often seen as connected with traditional knowledge. In his discussion of traditional knowledge, Dana (2006) quotes McGregor (2004) in including within indigenous knowledge "principles and values such as respect, and recognition of relationships among all of Creation" (McGregor, 2004, p. 389). Jacob and Suderman (1994) make a clear connection between this sense of spiritual connection and environmental sensitivity.

> Perhaps the salient characteristic of the native worldview, and the one which has the greatest relevance to sustainability, is that of a sacred perspective on the nature of the universe. The spiritual point of view possesses the potential to inhibit a cavalier approach to the use of the earth's resources. (Jacob & Suderman, 1994, p. 5)

3.2.4. The Debate Regarding Cultural or Economic Forces

Whether or not this concern for the environment is a typical feature of Indigenous – and this deserves further study – its roots in indigenous culture and tradition has been hotly contested. Several authors (e.g. Anderson, 1997; Miller, 2001; Galbraith et al., 2006) take an opposing point of view, and argue that the perceived "environmental sustainability" or "ecological awareness" among indigenous populations is simply good management of what are seen to be valuable, scarce, and non-imitable resources. When natural assets were viewed as plentiful or abundant, they argue, indigenous populations had little concern for environmental maintenance. These scholars contend that until scarcity made itself felt, indigenous people were as exploitative as other populations in their attitude to natural resources. Galbraith et al. (2006) are not just bent on correcting what they take to be a romantic myth. They argue that the "tradition of indigenous overkill continues into modern times on reservation land where tribal members are not restricted by state environmental laws regarding the number or size of animals that can be hunted" (Galbraith et al., 2006, p. 14).

Galbraith et al. (2006), in fact, argue that the commonly cited cultural "philosophy of environmental protectionism" and the proposal that its spiritual connection exceeds other religions (see Galbraith, 2004) is simply a modern, romantic myth. They note that, "this is not to suggest that indigenous people were more or less environmentally destructive that other cultures, but only that indigenous people tended to be influenced by the same incentives of economic scarcity or abundance" (Galbraith et al., 2006, p. 11). This contention plays a part in their argument that (re-)instituting individual property rights is an essential step in promoting viable indigenous entrepreneurship, a theme also presented in economist Terry Anderson's research (Anderson, 1997; Anderson et al., 2006).

3.2.5. Indigenous Entrepreneurship and Partnerships

Another common theme in indigenous entrepreneurship is the role of partnerships in developing vigorous and effective indigenous enterprises. In developing their "research paradigm" for indigenous entrepreneurship, Hindle and Lansdowne (2005) conducted interviews with a number of indigenous people in Australia and the United States. Among the dominant themes that emerged (along with the degree of indigenous "content" necessary to qualify something as indigenous entrepreneurship, and the issue of individuality versus collectivity) was the issue of how to manage partnerships between indigenous and non-indigenous members of an enterprise.

This requires recognition that indigenous entrepreneurship often takes place in a setting where non-indigenous individuals and corporations often collaborate with indigenous people in an entrepreneurial undertaking. Anderson (1996) highlighted the prominent role of partnerships, largely between collectively owned indigenous groups and non-indigenous corporations, in the development of indigenous entrepreneurship in Canada. Anderson (1996) also drew attention to advantages for both indigenous groups and non-indigenous businesses in these partnerships, while Hindle and Lansdowne's (2005) study suggested some of the questions that must be faced in exploring this form of enterprise. Berkes and Adhikari (2005) also explore the importance of partnerships among the indigenous enterprises they studied. Many indigenous enterprises, they discovered, had partnerships at several levels of organization. Some of these partnerships were with non-government organizations (NGOs), others with government and/or funding agencies. The importance of these partnerships, from fund-raising to training and technical support, was explicit. However, there was less detail regarding the partnerships between indigenous and non-indigenous businesses – possibly due to the nature of the indigenous populations Berkes and Adhikari (2005) studied. Differences in these partnership relationships, such as patterns of ownership and governance, the role of cultural differences, and the differences between corporations and not-for-profit organizations will need further investigation.

4. RESOURCES

Indigenous entrepreneurship is clearly an emergent field. As the discussion in this paper reveals, it is also a field that invites interdisciplinary research, as the resources of sociology and anthropology, as well as economics, politics, history, philosophy, and religious studies interact with management scholarship in investigating the phenomenon of indigenous entrepreneurship. It can be expected, therefore, that relevant material may be published in a wide variety of journals, including several that are not usually consulted by entrepreneurship scholars. It is nevertheless worth identifying several that have, at least to date and a certain extent, been the principal source of discussions concerning indigenous entrepreneurship. These include the *Journal of Aboriginal Economic Development, Canadian Journal of Native Studies, Journal of Developmental Entrepreneurship, American Indian Quarterly, Journal of Small Business and Entrepreneurship, Canadian Journal of Administrative Sciences*, and *International Journal of Entrepreneurship and Small Business.* In addition, there are a number of recent edited volumes that are dedicated to indigenous economic development and entrepreneurship. Most recently these include Anderson, Benson and Flanagan's (2006), *Self-Determination: The Other Path for Native Americans* and Dana and Anderson's (2006b) *Handbook of Research on Indigenous Entrepreneurship.*

5. SUMMARY

The purpose of this paper has been to offer an overview of the current study of indigenous entrepreneurship. From the existent literature on the topic, the following appear to be some of the major themes and questions that have emerged.

First, while there is broad agreement on the application of the term "indigenous," there are differences of emphasis and outright controversies about empirical description of indigenous people, especially concerning the role of ownership and private property in their culture and traditions.

Second, the concept of entrepreneurship is as controversial in this field as elsewhere in management studies. What lends urgency to the question of its definition and its empirical features is the range of opinion as to how compatible the demands of entrepreneurship are with the cultural heritage of the indigenous populations of the world. There are fundamental disagreements as to how flexible the requirements of entrepreneurship are, and whether true indigenous entrepreneurship can transform entrepreneurship into an authentic and distinctive form.

Third, the concept of indigenous entrepreneurship as a total concept is open to debate and discussion. Not only does it inherit the question of whether the notion of entrepreneurship can be culturally transformed, there is also a difference of approach concerning the location and ultimate goals of indigenous entrepreneurship. While some scholars appear willing to accept any kind of entrepreneurship involving indigenous people as "indigenous entrepreneurship," other scholars are inclined to restrict the concept to undertakings within indigenous territories and/or directed toward the communal goals of the indigenous population under study.

Fourth, there are a number of critical discussion points related to indigenous populations, and, in turn, their relationship to entrepreneurial activities and enterprises. These include, but are not limited to, the pursuit of multiple goals, including social objectives; the notion of collective organization, ownership and outcomes; and a population's association with the land, characteristically leading to a high degree of environmental sensitivity, drawing on traditional knowledge and fostered by a sense of spiritual connection with the land and its resources.

Finally, the theme of partnerships involving indigenous enterprises with other indigenous enterprises and non-indigenous bodies, including NGOs, government agencies, funding organizations, and non-indigenous individuals and corporations, is recognized as a vital topic demanding further attention.

ACKNOWLEDGMENT

The authors acknowledge the editorial assistance of Murdith McLean, of the Centre for Studies in Religion and Society, University of Victoria, with an earlier draft of this paper.

REFERENCES

Anderson, R. (1995). The business economy of the first nations in Saskatchewan: A contingency perspective. *The Canadian Journal of Native Studies, 15*(2).

Anderson, R. (1996). Corporate/indigenous partnerships in economic development. *World Development, 25*(9), 1483–1503.

Anderson, R. (1999). *Economic development among the aboriginal peoples of Canada: Hope for the future.* Toronto: Captus University Press.

Anderson, R. (2004a). Indigenous entrepreneurship: Is it, and if so what is it? (panel symposium proposal). *Annual Meeting of the Academy of Management.* New Orleans, LA, USA.

Anderson, R. (2004b). Indigenous entrepreneurship: The 5 w's. *Annual Meeting of the Academy of Management.* New Orleans, LA, USA.

Anderson, T. (1997). Conservation – native American style. *The Quarterly Review of Economics and Finance, 37,* 769–785.

Anderson, T., Benson, B., & Flanagan, T. (2006). *Self-determination: The other path for native Americans.* Stanford, CA: Stanford University Press.

Asian Development Bank (2000). Policy on indigenous peoples. Retrieved 15 June, 2004, from www.adb.org/Documents/Policies/Indigenous_Peoples/ippp-002.asp?p = policies

Berkes, F. (1999). *Sacred ecology: Traditional ecological knowledge and resource management.* Philadelphia, PA: Taylor and Francis.

Berkes, F., & Adhikari, T. (2005). Development and conservation: Indigenous businesses and UNDP equator initiative. In: L. Dana (Ed.), *Ethnic minorities in entrepreneurship.* London: Edward Elgar.

Bewayo, E. (1999). Will entrepreneurship lead to national development in Africa? *Proceedings of the small business institute directors' association, Feb. 10–13.* Retrieved 26 July, 2005, from http://www.sbaer.uca.edu/research/sbida/1999/31.pdf

Bishop, J. (1999). The Lockean basis of Iroquoian land ownership. *Journal of Aboriginal Economic Development, 1,* 35–43.

Blawatt, K. (1998). *Entrepreneurship: Process and management.* Carborough, Canada: Prentice-Hall.

Casson, M. (1982). *The entrepreneur: An economic theory.* London: Gregg Revivals.

Dana, L. (1995). Entrepreneurship in a remote sub-arctic community. *Entrepreneurship Theory and Practice, 20*(1), 57–73.

Dana, L. (1996). Self-employment in the Canadian sub-arctic: An exploratory study. *Canadian Journal of Administrative Sciences, 13*(1), 65–81.

Dana, L. (2006). Toward a definition of indigenous entrepreneurship. In: L. Dana & R. Anderson (Eds), *International handbook of research on indigenous entrepreneurship.* Cheltenham, UK: Edward Elgar (in press).

Dana, L., & Anderson, R. (2006a). A multidisciplinary theory of entrepreneurship as a function of cultural perceptions of opportunity. In: *International handbook of indigenous entrepreneurship* (in press). Cheltenham, UK: Edward Elgar.

Dana, L., & Anderson, R. (Eds) (2006b). *International handbook of research on indigenous entrepreneurship.* Cheltenham, UK: Edward Elgar.

Danson, M. (Ed.) (1995). *Small firm formation and regional economic development.* London: Routledge.

Drucker, P. (1985). *Innovation and entrepreneurship.* New York: Harper & Row Publishers.

Foley, D. (2003). An examination of indigenous Australian entrepreneurs. *Journal of Development Entrepreneurship, 8*(2), 133–151.

Galbraith, C. (2004). The myths of indigenous entrepreneurship. *Annual Meeting of the Academy of Management.* New Orleans, LA, USA.

Galbraith, C., Rodriguez, C., & Stiles, C. (2006). False myths and indigenous entrepreneurial strategies. *Journal of Small Business and Entrepreneurship, 8*(2), 1–20.

Galbraith, C., & Stiles, C. (2003). Expectations of Indian reservation gaming: Entrepreneurial activity within a context of traditional land tenure and wealth acquisition. *Journal of Developmental Entrepreneurship, 8*(2), 93–112.

General Assembly The United Nations (1995). Fact sheet no. 9 (rev.1), the rights of indigenous peoples. Retrieved 9 June, 2004, from http://www.unhchr.ch/html/menu6/2/fs9.htm

Hindle, K., & Lansdowne, M. (2005). Brave spirits on new paths: Toward a globally relevant paradigm of indigenous entrepreneurship research. *Journal of Small Business and Entrepreneurship, 18*(2), 131–142.

Hofstede, G. (1980). *Culture's consequences – international differences in work-related values.* Beverly Hills, London: Sage.

International Labour Organisation (1991). Convention (no. 169) concerning indigenous and tribal peoples in independent countries. Retrieved 9 June, 2004, from http://www1.umn.edu/humanrts/instree/r1citp.htm

Jacob, J., & Suderman, B. (1994). Alternative visions of progress: The multiple meanings of sustainable development. Paper presented at the sustainable development in the 21st century Americas: Alternative visions of progress, university of Calgary, Canada.

Lindsay, N. (2005). Toward a cultural model of indigenous entrepreneurial attitude. *Academy of Marketing Science Review.* Retrieved 12 July, 2005, from www.amsreview.org/articles/lindsay05-2005.pdf

McGregor, D. (2004). Coming full circle: Indigenous knowledge, environment, and our future. *American Indian Quarterly, 28*(3/4), 385–410.

Miller, R. (2001). Economic development in Indian country: Will capitalism or socialism succeed. *Oregon Law Review, 80,* 757–859.

Mitchell, R. (2004). Issues of indigenous entrepreneurship. *Annual Meeting of the Academy of Management.* New Orleans, LA, USA.

Mitchell, R., Smith, B., Seawright, K., Peredo, A. M., & McKenzie, B. (2002). Are entrepreneurial cognitions universal? Assessing entrepreneurial cognitions across cultures. *Entrepreneurship theory and practice, 26*(4), 9–32.

Morris, M. H. (2004). Is entrepreneurship universal: A values perspective. *Annual Meeting of the Academy of Management.* New Orleans, LA, USA.

Peredo, A. M. (2001). *Communal enterprises, sustainable development and the alleviation of poverty in rural Andean communities.* Unpublished Doctoral dissertation. University of Calgary, Calgary.

Peredo, A. M. (2004). Entrepreneurship and diversity. *Annual Meeting of the Academy of Management.* New Orleans, LA, USA.

Peredo, A. M., Anderson, R., Galbraith, C., Benson, H., & Dana, L. (2004). Towards a theory of indigenous entrepreneurship. *International Journal of Entrepreneurship and Small Business, 1*(1/2), 1–20.

Peredo, A. M., & Chrisman, J. (2006). Toward a theory of community-based enterprise. *Academy of Management Review, 31*(2), 309–328.

Polanyi, K. (1944). *The great transformation.* New York, Toronto: Farrar & Rinehart inc.

Redpath, L., & Nielsen, M. (1997). A comparison of native culture, non-native culture and new management ideology. *Canadian Journal of Administrative Sciences, 14*(3), 327–339.

Siropolis, N. (1977). *Small business management*. Cambridge, MA: Houghton Mifflin.

Stiles, C. (2004). Failures of indigenous adaptation: A historic case study. *Annual Meeting of the Academy of Management*. New Orleans, LA, USA.

Tully, J. (1995). Property, self-government and consent. *Canadian Journal of Political Science*, *23*, 105–133.

Venkataraman, S. (1997). The distinctive domain of entrepreneurship research: An editor's perspective. In: J. Katz & R. Brockhaus (Eds), *Advances in entrepreneurship, firm emergence, and growth* (Vol. III, pp. 119–138). Greenwich, CT: JAI.

World Bank (2001). Draft operational policies (op 4.10), indigenous peoples. Retrieved 9 June, 2004, from http://lnweb18.worldbank.org/ESSD/sdvext.nsf/63ByDocName/ PoliciesDraftOP410March232001

GENDER DIFFERENCES IN MINORITY SMALL BUSINESS HIRING PRACTICES AND CUSTOMER PATRONAGE: AN EXPLORATORY STUDY

Pat Roberson-Saunders and Raymond D. Smith

1. INTRODUCTION

Recent statistics indicate that the number of minority-owned and women-owned firms in the United States continues to rise. Indeed, the number has risen substantially since the last census count; from 2.3 million minority businesses in 1992 to over 3 million in 1997 – a 30 percent increase. During this same period, the receipts of minority businesses increased 60 percent – from $369 billion to $591 billion. At the same time, the number of firms in which women held majority ownership (51 percent or more) increased 16 percent – from 6.4 million to 7.4 million. The receipts of predominantly women-owned firms increased 33 percent – from $1.2 trillion to $1.6 trillion (when data are adjusted for comparability of 1992 and 1997 statistics – see U.S. Department of Commerce, 1992a, b, 1997a, b, c).

Not only do minority-owned and women-owned firms account for a significant portion of the revenue base of the nation, but a substantial amount

Developmental Entrepreneurship: Adversity, Risk, and Isolation
International Research in the Business Disciplines, Volume 5, 275–295
Copyright © 2006 by Elsevier Ltd.
All rights of reproduction in any form reserved
ISSN: 1074-7877/doi:10.1016/S1074-7877(06)05015-X

of the employment of the country is generated by their activities as well. Cumulatively, minority firms employed more than 4.5 million people in 1997; while women-owned firms employed almost 7.1 million persons – representing, respectively, 4.4 percent and 6.8 percent of total U.S. non-farm employment (U.S. Department of Commerce, 1992a, b, 1997a, b, c).

Minority women represent a pairing of race and gender – two variables that have received increasing attention in the literature over the last few years. Even so, just a cursory analysis of the most recent census statistics reveals that the performance portrait of firms owned by minority women is substantially unlike that of the two broader groups to which these firms belong: minorities and women. Minority women owned almost a million firms, roughly 33 percent of all minority firms and 13 percent of all women-owned firms. However, the receipts of minority women-owned firms totaled $85.8 billion – roughly 15 percent of total minority business receipts and only 5 percent of the receipts of all firms in which women held majority ownership. Thus, on average, firms owned by minority women had lower revenues than firms owned by minority men and White women. Further, of the 4.5 million persons employed by minority firms, minority men employed approximately 3 million (67 percent), while minority women employed 778,000 (roughly 18 percent), the remainder being employed by firms equally owned by men and women. Minority women-owned firms employed only 11 percent of all persons employed by women-owned firms.

Clearly, at the performance level, there are significant differences between firms owned by minority men and minority women and between firms owned by minority women and non-minority women. Therefore, implicitly subsuming the discussion of minority women entrepreneurs under the broader labels of "minority entrepreneurs" or "women entrepreneurs" can contribute to the overlooking of a segment of both groups that might share certain characteristics with each but also be distinctively different from both in measurable ways.

From a psychological/demographic perspective, Shane, Vereid, and West-head (1991) suggested that, across cultures, women entrepreneurs appear to be the same and to hold similar values. However, DeCarlo and Lyons (1979) found non-minority and minority women entrepreneurs to be different on some values; non-minority women scored higher on needs for achievement and independence than minority women while minority women scored higher on conformity and benevolence. Indeed, some years ago, Stevenson (1986, p. 33), in her description of characteristics of female entrepreneurs, observed that the profile of the "typical female entrepreneur ... would not fit the description of black [sic] or Hispanic women entrepreneurs."

In a longitudinal study of self-employed minorities, Bates (1988) found that gender alone explained a significant amount of the difference in earnings between minority males and females. A logical question would then be what, if any, systematic differences exist among self-employed minority women. Yet, to date, while the amount of research on women entrepreneurs seems to be increasing (see overview in Smith-Hunter, 2004), there remains a surprising paucity of literature on the various subgroups of minority women entrepreneurs (Butler & Greene, 2000; Roberson-Saunders, 2001). However, a noteworthy exception is found in a fairly recent exploratory study by Shim and Eastlick (1998), who compared Hispanic male and female entrepreneurs on a variety of business-related factors and called for research on "gender as a differentiating factor" for other groups of ethnic business owners.

In response to the call of Shim and Eastlick (1998), this paper presents the results of an exploratory study of the profile of employees and customers of minority firms on the basis of race/ethnicity and gender of firm owner. The choice was made to focus on employees and customers, because, regardless of owner background, industry type, or other relevant factors, firm growth usually requires the hiring of employees to produce the products and/or services of the enterprise. Moreover, all firms must have customers or clients as a *sine qua non* of firm existence.

As is the case for most of the entrepreneurship literature, the research on minority entrepreneurship has been largely predicated on male samples (Roberson-Saunders, 2001). Nonetheless, from this literature we will cite relevant findings on co-racial/ethnic employment and customers and use the concept of enclaves as our point of departure for further exploration of the topic as relates to women.

1.1. Co-Racial/Ethnic Employment

Milliken and Martins (1996) stated that groups and organizations act systematically to force out those who are different from the group or organizational majority. Clearly, such practices can serve to ensure a predictable degree of employee homogeneity within such groups and organizations, even in the face of increasing diversity in the population-at-large. However, homogeneity can be ensured not only by ferreting out persons who are unlike the majority but also by limiting initial entry into the organization. Indeed, previous research has indicated that entrepreneurs, in general, tend to hire co-racials and co-ethnics. Bates (1994) found that Black entrepreneurs tend not to hire Whites but to hire co-racial/ethnic minorities, whether the firms are large or small or are located within or outside minority communities. Bates also found that Whites predominantly hire Whites. He describes this as a "world of network hiring" governed by race.

Study of ethnic communities supports Bates' conclusion. Ethnic groups, such as Asians and Hispanics, draw employees from their respective co-racial/ethnic enclaves (Aldrich & Waldinger, 1990; Greene, 1997; Butler & Greene, 2000). Enclaves are said to serve as a basis for co-racial hiring among Blacks as well (Fratoe, 1999). Newman (1995) even called for inner-city Black business owners to develop employment consortia. These would serve as networking pipelines in which quality low-wage (secondary market) employees could be afforded opportunities for upward mobility within higher-paying (primary market) organizations. Implicit in this suggestion is the acceptance of the prevalence of co-racial hiring practices.

In a consistent finding, Gudmundson and Hartenian (2000) found that firms owned by minorities had more minority employees than those owned by non-minorities. Additionally, firms owned by younger entrepreneurs were more diverse than those owned by older entrepreneurs. However, contrary to expectations, firms owned by women tended to be less diverse than those owned by men. Gudmundson and Hartenian's (2000) sample of owner/managers was composed of male and female non-minorities as well as the four major racial/ethnic subgroups of minorities; however, the data was analyzed at a level that did not provide results on minority females.

Unfortunately, a review of the literature revealed no specific coverage of the topic of gender with respect to hiring practices and operations within ethnic enclaves. Thus, it is not known whether the subgroups of minority females (Blacks, Hispanics, Asians, and Native Americans/Alaska Natives) show a similar tendency to look to the enclave as the primary source of employees. Likewise, even if it is found that co-racial/ethnic hiring practices are common among minority female entrepreneurs, it is still unclear whether minority female entrepreneurs (or minority male entrepreneurs, for that matter) predominantly hire "minorities" or if the tendency is to hire "co-racial/ethnic minorities," as Bates (1994) has suggested.

1.2. Co-Racial/Ethnic Customers

Ethnic enclaves are said to provide a base of employees and customers for co-racial/ethnic start-up ventures (see Butler & Greene, 2000; Aldrich & Waldinger, 1990). These readily available sources of support are critical to the survival of these new, often fledgling, enterprises. Shared language, customs and values make it easy to establish relationships that sustain the enclave. Moreover, minority ventures tend to serve predominantly niche markets targeted toward co-racials/ethnics (cf., Lee, 1999; Light, Bernard, & Kim, 1999). Bates and Williams (1993) further found a sort of racial enclave effect in the increased likelihood of success among Blacks whose businesses were located in areas where Blacks dominated in local government. However, Aldrich and Waldinger (1990) indicate that over-reliance on co-racial/ ethnic patronage will limit the potential for growth of minority ventures.

Donthu and Cherian (1994) found that Hispanic Americans who reported strong identification with their ethnic group were more likely to patronize Hispanic (co-ethnic) businesses than were Hispanic Americans with weak identity ties. Shim and Eastlick (1998), however, found no difference in the type of business or customers targeted in their exploratory study of Hispanic male and female entrepreneurs, but unfortunately, there was no indication of the race or ethnicity of customers in their study.

Dyer and Ross (2000) found that Blacks reported experiencing a mixed relationship with co-racial patrons. On the one hand, many perceived co-racials as supportive; on the other hand, many perceived negative overtones that reflected a somewhat ambivalent orientation of customers regarding the success of the co-racial business owner. Similarly, Campbell (1968) and Omg (1981) disagree as to whether Blacks tend to patronize Black businesses.

Asians, in general, have a long history of patronizing each other's businesses (Wong, 1987; Geoffrey, 1988; Light & Bonacich, 1988; Zhou, 1992). However, surprisingly little is known about Asian women in the context of business. For example, in a case study of a 100-year-old firm in Osaka City, Japan, Lee (1981) noted that the attempt to employ females in sales positions was met with resistance from customers who were accustomed to and desirous of continuing relations with male salespersons. While this finding sheds no light on the orientation toward patronizing businesses owned by Asian women, it does suggest a question as to whether the reactions represent a location-specific resistance of customers to Asian women employees or are also typical of Asian women's experiences as business owners in America. Indeed, who are the customers of Asian women?

Finally, and unfortunately, very little is known about the Native American/Alaska native with respect to customer patronage. This study hopes to provide at least some preliminary insight into this issue.

As was the case with hiring practices, there was no record of research that has specifically addressed whether owner gender influences customer patronage among minority subgroups. As Butler and Greene (2000, p. 276) observed, "Very little attention is paid to ethnic women in the literature ...."

Butler and Greene (2000, p. 276) go so far as to say that "... the ethnic business literature [is] mostly 'gender blind'."

1.3. Research Questions

From the foregoing discussion, it is apparent that some gaps exist in the literature, specifically with respect to hiring practices and customer patronage of firms owned by minority females. It is important that at least some preliminary steps are taken toward resolving these gaps so that discussions of minority entrepreneurship with respect to these issues can be undertaken with an eye toward inclusion of females.

Thus, this paper seeks to explore three questions: (1) Are there significant differences between minority women and men entrepreneurs of the same race/ethnicity with respect to hiring practices and customer patronage? (2) Are there significant differences between the various racial/ethnic subgroups of minority female entrepreneurs with respect to hiring practices and customer patronage; and, (3) With respect to mainstream customers and clientele, are there overall significant differences, and specifically are there gender differences in hiring practices and customer patronage of minority firms as a function of firm age and size? The third question is offered as a preliminary test of the Aldrich and Waldinger (1990) thesis on firm growth in the context of gender.

2. METHOD

The study employed a convenience sample of minority men and women entrepreneurs who participated in government-sponsored executive education programs planned and managed by the senior author in Anchorage, AK, Dorado, PR, Oklahoma City, OK; and Washington, DC. A total of 128 men and 66 women completed a questionnaire that provided *demographic data* (gender, race/ethnicity, age at founding of the business and current age); *firm performance data* (firm age as measured by years in business and firm size as measured by gross revenues, as well as net earnings), and *customer and employee race/ethnicity profiles* measured on both rank-ordered and Likert-type scales. Additional questions directly related to the concepts under scrutiny sought to determine the entrepreneur's levels of satisfaction with the entrepreneurial role. Table 1 provides a summary of the demographic profile of the sample. Table 2 lists the variables used in the study along with a description of each.

Table 1. Frequencies.

Race	Gender		Total
	Men	Women	
Blacks	52	32	84
Hispanics	28	11	39
Asians	27	12	39
NA/AN	21	11	32
Total	128	66	194

Table 2. List of Variables.

Variable	Description
RACE	Race or ethnicity
SEX	Gender
AGE	Current age
STARTAGE	Age upon founding of the business
GROSSREV	Last year's gross revenues
NETEARN	Last year's net earnings
CAUCCUST	Caucasian customers
BLACKCUST	Black customers
HISPCUST	Hispanic customers
ASIANCUST	Asian customers
PICUST	Pacific Islander customers
NACUST	Native American customers
ANCUST	Alaska native customers
CAUEMP	Caucasian employees
BLACKEMP	Black employees
HISPEMP	Hispanic employees
ASIANEMP	Asian employees
PIEMP	Pacific Islander employees
NAEMP	Native American employees
ANEMP	Alaska native employees
RACEHELP	Race or ethnicity contributed to business success
SAMERACE	Members of own race/ethnicity are predominant customers
SUCCPROF	Define success in terms of profitability of the business
AGAIN	Would start own business again
RACEHURT	Race or ethnicity hindered business success
SREMP	Members of own race/ethnicity are predominant employees
STARTSAM	Would start same type of business again
SUCCNP	Define success in terms other than profitability of the business

Use of the convenience sample was considered an acceptable method of data collection for this exploratory study, as it allowed the rare opportunity for inclusion of male and female entrepreneurs from all four major subgroups of minority entrepreneurs. Clearly, future research, which draws upon a random sample of these groups would contribute to verifying the extent to which the results reported here may be confidently generalized.

The research questions were explored by utilizing an analysis of variance model (ANOVA) to determine which variables were significantly different across the various categories of race/ethnicity and gender. With almost 200 observations and dependent variables that had five or more categories or were of a continuous nature, it was clear that the distribution was appropriate for the use of ANOVA, and the resulting F-test, as opposed to the less precise χ^2 statistic (Kervin, 1992, p. 578). As confirmation, the tests were duplicated using standardized scores and the results were the same for all variables in terms of significance. Additionally, the directionality of the differences was determined by analyzing the associated means. Only results with an alpha confidence level of 0.05 or lower are discussed.

3. RESULTS AND DISCUSSION

All 3 research questions appear to have been answered in the affirmative (see Tables 3, 4, and 5 for a summary of significant results.

A discussion of results related to each research question follows.

3.1. Within-Race Gender Effects

The first research question focused on whether minority men and women of the same race/ethnicity are different with respect to hiring practices and customer patronage. The results of this study are mixed. Differences were found between Black men and women and between Native American men and women but not between male and female Asians and Hispanics (see Table 5). Black men and women entrepreneurs in this sample are different with respect to their tendency to have co-racial/ethnic customers, while Native American men and women entrepreneurs show a different propensity to hire persons of their own race/ethnicity. The Asian and Hispanic men and women entrepreneurs in this sample principally hire and are patronized by persons of their own race/ethnicity.

Table 3. ANOVA Across Race Women Only.

		Sum of Squares	df	Mean Square	F	Significance
Zscore(STARTAGE) * Race	Between groups (Combined)	8.073	3	2.691	2.69	0.055
	Within groups	55.019	55	1		
	Total	63.092	58			
Zscore(GROSSREV) * Race	Between groups (Combined)	1.827	3	0.609	2.665	0.059
	Within groups	10.281	45	0.228		
	Total	12.108	48			
Zscore(HISPCUST) * Race	Between groups (Combined)	5.729	3	1.91	4.313	0.02
	Within groups	7.527	17	0.443		
	Total	13.256	20			
Zscore(BLACKEMP) * Race	Between groups (Combined)	18.442	3	6.147	16.77	0
	Within groups	16.862	46	0.367		
	Total	35.304	49			
Zscore(HISPEMP) * Race	Between groups (Combined)	10.502	3	3.501	4.963	0.011
	Within groups	12.696	18	0.705		
	Total	23.198	21			
Zscore(ASIANEMP) * Race	Between groups (Combined)	11.897	3	3.966	9.474	0.001
	Within groups	6.279	5	0.419		
	Total	18.176	8			
Zscore(SREMP) * Race	Between groups (Combined)	10.669	3	3.556	4.136	0.01
	Within groups	47.287	55	0.86		
	Total	57.956	58			

Table 4.	ANOVA Men Only Across Race.

		Sum of Squares	df	Mean Square	F	Significance
Zscore(GROSSREV)	Between groups	16.629	3	5.543	4.478	0.005
	Within groups	139.873	113	1.238		
	Total	156.503	116			
Zscore(NETEARN)	Between groups	22.291	3	7.43	6.395	0.001
	Within groups	109.223	94	1.162		
	Total	131.513	97			
Zscore(CAUCCUST)	Between groups	9.768	3	3.256	3.02	0.034
	Within groups	97.043	90	1.078		
	Total	106.811	93			
Zscore(BLACKCUS)	Between groups	16.159	3	5.386	12.747	0.000
	Within groups	19.86	47	0.423		
	Total	36.019	50			
Zscore(HISPCUST)	Between groups	34.714	3	11.571	26.627	0.000
	Within groups	19.121	44	0.435		
	Total	53.835	47			
Zscore(ASIANCUS)	Between groups	14.14	3	4.713	7.228	0.001
	Within groups	18.91	29	0.652		
	Total	33.05	32			
Zscore(ANCUST)	Between groups	11.693	3	3.898	6.919	0.003
	Within groups	10.14	18	0.563		
	Total	21.833	21			
Zscore(BLACKEMP)	Between groups	31.193	3	10.398	19.688	0.000
	Within groups	34.855	66	0.528		
	Total	66.048	69			
Zscore(HISPEMP)	Between groups	31.677	3	10.559	37.274	0.000
	Within groups	13.031	46	0.283		
	Total	44.708	49			
Zscore(ASIANEMP)	Between groups	18.772	3	6.257	12.934	0.000
	Within groups	15.481	32	0.484		
	Total	34.253	35			
Zscore(NAEMP)	Between groups	10.12	3	3.373	3.599	0.037
	Within groups	14.996	16	0.937		
	Total	25.116	19			
Zscore(RACEHELP)	Between groups	9.687	3	3.229	3.131	0.028
	Within groups	116.525	113	1.031		
	Total	126.212	116			

Table 4. (*Continued*)

		Sum of Squares	*df*	Mean Square	*F*	Significance
Zscore(SAMERACE)	Between groups	10.925	3	3.642	4.223	0.007
	Within groups	95.72	111	0.862		
	Total	106.645	114			
Zscore(AGAIN)	Between groups	16.049	3	5.35	8.399	0.000
	Within groups	68.79	108	0.637		
	Total	84.839	111			
Zscore(SREMP)	Between groups	15.454	3	5.151	5.896	0.001
	Within groups	95.236	109	0.874		
	Total	110.69	112			
Zscore(STARTSAM)	Between groups	8.308	3	2.769	2.739	0.047
	Within groups	110.215	109	1.011		
	Total	118.523	112			

Gudmundson and Hartenian (2000, p. 32) defined "diversity" as the "mix of non-minority and minority employees in the workforce." Contrary to their findings for women, the minority women in this sample showed more of a tendency than minority men to have a diverse workforce.

Further, consistent with prior research and theory (cf., Bates, 1994; Light & Bonacich, 1988; Donthu & Cherian, 1994), half of the subgroups (Asians and Hispanics) showed the pattern of co-racial/ethnic solidarity as evidenced by both hiring practices and customer patronage. This pattern was most pronounced among Asians (see, again, Tables 5 and 6).

Among the races, Blacks and Hispanics were more likely to hire each other and patronize each other's businesses than were any other groups. For Blacks and Hispanics, then, these results suggest inclusion of other minorities rather than exclusion of all who are not of the same-race/ethnicity, as appears to have been suggested by Bates (1994). And, while there was little evidence of interaction between Hispanic women and Native Americans with respect to hiring and customer patronage, a clear pattern emerged between Hispanic women and Alaska Natives. Specifically, next to Native American/Alaska Native men, Hispanic women were the predominant beneficiaries of Alaska Native customer patronage, and they were the second most likely to employ Alaska Natives. Thus, contrary to the findings of Shim and Eastlick (1998), Hispanic men and women in this study were, indeed, different with respect to their total customer base. However, it is important to note that, while Shim and Eastlick (1998) found no differences, they also did not explore the profile of customers patronizing the firms

Table 5. ANOVA Tables by Race Across Gender.

		Sum of Squares	df	Mean Square	F	Significance
Blacks						
Zscore(PACCUST) * SEX	Between groups (Combined)	2.382	1	2.382	5.419	0.059
	Within groups	2.638	6	0.44		
	Total	5.02	7			
Zscore(NACUST) * SEX	Between groups (Combined)	2.796	1	2.796	6.667	0.027
	Within groups	4.194	10	0.419		
	Total	6.991	11			
Zscore(ANCUST) * SEX	Between groups (Combined)	2.228	1	2.228	17.286	0.009
	Within groups	0.644	5	0.129		
	Total	2.872	6			
Zscore(RACEHELP) * SEX	Between groups (Combined)	3.433	1	3.433	3.958	0.05
	Within groups	67.661	78	0.867		
	Total	71.094	79			
Zscore(SAMERACE) * SEX	Between groups (Combined)	9.257	1	9.257	8.543	0.005
	Within groups	83.432	77	1.084		
	Total	92.689	78			

		Sum of squares	df	Mean square	F	Sig.
Zscore(AGAIN) * SEX	Between groups (Combined)	8.067	1	8.067	9.756	0.003
	Within groups	62.842	76	0.827		
	Total	70.909	77			
Hispanics						
Zscore(AGAIN) * SEX	Between groups (Combined)	1.919	1	1.919	3.784	0.06
	Within groups	18.253	36	0.507		
	Total	20.172	37			
Zscore(STARTSAM) * SEX	Between groups (Combined)	7.308	1	7.308	9.534	0.004
	Within groups	27.593	36	0.766		
	Total	34.9	37			
Asians						
Note: None Significant at 0.05						
Native Americans						
Zscore(SREMP)	Between groups	4.689	1	4.689	5.966	0.022
	Within groups	19.648	25	0.786		
	Total	24.337	26			

sampled. So it is possible that they, too, would have found such differences had their research included this dimension.

Native American men and Black women received the highest reported patronage of Native American customers, while Native American men and Asian women reported roughly equal incidences of having hired Native American employees. Native American women also showed a tendency to hire Native Americans but to a lesser extent than they hired Caucasians. Further, Black women and Asian men reported the highest incidence of Pacific Islander customers and employees.

Hispanics and Native Americans/Alaska Natives reported having more Caucasian employees than either Blacks or Asians. Further, Hispanic and Native American/Alaska Native women entrepreneurs reported having more Caucasian employees than any other group.

Of all racial/ethnic groups, Asians were least likely to have Caucasian customers and employees; although Asian women were consistently more likely than Asian men to have Caucasian customers and less likely than Asian men to have Caucasian employees. This finding is particularly interesting in that it runs counter to Aldrich and Waldinger's (1990) claims that over-reliance on an ethnic market (or conversely, failure to cultivate or penetrate the mainstream market) will limit minority firm growth. For some time, Asians have – on a national level – had the largest share of receipts of minority firms, and the results reported here suggest that they might have accomplished this without significant reliance on mainstream (predominantly Caucasian) customers.

Another interesting finding was that there was a discernible inconsistency among Asians in the rank-ordered responses as compared to Likert-scale responses regarding the race/ethnicity of their employees. Specifically, when asked to indicate the degree of representation of each race/ethnicity among their employees (1 = highest representation), the mean ranking of Asians was – at 1.70 – fundamentally similar to that of the other minority groups. However, Asians had the lowest mean score (2.31) when asked directly to indicate on a Likert scale (1 = strongly disagree to 5 = strongly agree) their degree of agreement with the statement that their employees were predominantly of their same race or ethnicity. When asked directly, Hispanic and Native American/Alaska Native women entrepreneurs, as well as Asians of both sexes, were least likely to have reported hiring employees of their same race. The results for the former groups (non-Asians) were consistent with their previous rank-orderings. Black and Hispanic men and Black women were most likely to have reported hiring employees of their own race/ethnicity.

These findings suggest that, at least for some groups, self-reports of employee racial/ethnic profiles might require additional verification. It is also possible that direct questions of this nature might inspire self-report biases that conceal a preference for (or even a bias against) co-racials/ethnics. In this latter regard, it is also possible that, for some, the concern might well be one of the legality of demonstrating such bias in hiring. Future research that seeks to replicate this finding and explore the underlying causes might prove beneficial in enhancing understanding of the motivations and strategies of minority entrepreneurs with respect to human resource management practices. On a general level, there are far too few studies of the organizational management practices of minority ventures (Roberson-Saunders, 2001).

3.2. Across-Race Gender Effects

The second research question focused on whether there are gender differences across race/ethnicity with respect to hiring practices and customer patronage. The results of this study indicate that, while there are some significant differences between the various racial/ethnic subgroups of women entrepreneurs with respect to hiring practices and customer patronage, on the whole there are fewer differences between minority women entrepreneurs than between minority men entrepreneurs.

There were 5 significant differences found among women entrepreneurs with respect to hiring practices and customer patronage and 16 significant differences found among minority men entrepreneurs (see Tables 4 and 5). This finding seems to provide support at the organizational management level for the psychological/demographic finding of Shane et al. (1991) that women entrepreneurs are fundamentally similar across cultures.

For all racial/ethnic groups except Blacks, women entrepreneurs were significantly more likely to report having Caucasian customers than were men entrepreneurs. Further, regarding the issue of racial/ethnic contrasts within gender, the measures gross revenue and net earnings were significant for men and not women due to the large revenues reported by Native American/Alaska Native men. They reported mean revenues of $6.527 million, whereas the next highest group, Black men, reported revenues of $1.659 million. Further, nearly all of the customer measures differed significantly by race among men but not among women. The results indicate, therefore, a tendency for men to *both* employ co-racials and have co-racials as customers.

3.3. Hiring of and Patronage by Caucasians as a Function of Firm Age and Size

The final research question related to whether, among minority firms and across gender, age and size of the venture had a differential impact on hiring practices and customer patronage (particularly as relates to Caucasians). For all minority firms combined, there was a decided absence of either an age effect in the hiring of Caucasians ($F = 0.470$; $p = <0.495$) or a size effect ($F = 1.439$; $p = <0.233$). Similar results were obtained for women (age: $F = 1.961$; $p = <0.175$; size: $F = 0.538$; $p = <0.471$), as well as for men with respect to firm size ($F = 1.655$; $p = <0.203$). However, firm age was inversely and significantly correlated with the tendency of minority men-owned firms to hire Caucasians ($F = 7.537$; $p = <0.008$). Thus, the results indicate that, among minority firms, overall, as well as among firms owned by women, there are no differences in the tendency to hire Caucasian employees, as a function of firm age or size. However, among minority men-owned firms, while there are no size-related differences, younger firms tend to have more Caucasian employees than older firms.

A test of the Aldrich and Waldinger (1990) thesis that over-reliance on co-ethnic patronage limits firm growth potential was undertaken by segmenting firms on the basis of size (revenues) and then determining whether there were significant differences in their customer profiles. The operating thesis was that larger minority firms would have significantly more reliance on mainstream (Caucasian) customers/clientele than would smaller minority firms. Moreover, as age and size are generally viewed as companion variables with respect to firm growth, a similar segmentation of firms based on a mean split on the variable age was also undertaken. Here, the expectation was that older firms would have higher revenues than younger firms and those larger, older firms would show more reliance on a Caucasian customer base than would either smaller, older firms or younger firms.

The results reveal that age was inversely related to Caucasian patronage while size was positively related (see Table 6). Larger, younger firms were most reliant on Caucasian patronage while smaller, older firms were least reliant, resulting in significant age and size effects as well as an interaction effect (see Table 7). Strikingly, all of the larger, younger firms ranked Caucasian customers as their predominant customers. Larger, older firms were also more reliant on Caucasian customers. Together, these results provide support for the Aldrich and Waldinger (1990) thesis that developing clientele outside the enclave (or in the mainstream) increases minority firm growth potential.

Table 6. Means for CAUCCUST by Firm, Age, and Size.

YEARSCAT	REVCAT	Mean	N	Standard Deviation
1	1	1.0833	60	0.2787
	2	1	20	0
	Total	1.0625	80	0.2436
2	1	1.7	20	1.1743
	2	1.1111	9	0.3333
	Total	1.5172	29	1.0219
Total	1	1.2375	80	0.6796
	2	1.0345	29	0.1857
	Total	1.1835	109	0.5957

Table 7. ANOVA by Size and Age for CAUCCUST.

Source	Type III Sum of Squares	df	Mean Square	F	Significance
Corrected Model	6.658(a)	3	2.219	7.358	0
Intercept	105.171	1	105.171	348.663	0
REVCAT	1.984	1	1.984	6.577	0.012
YEARSCAT	2.325	1	2.325	7.709	0.007
REVCAT * YEARSCAT	1.122	1	1.122	3.72	0.056

When owner gender was considered in the context of firm age and size, it was found that women and men were distinctly different with respect to patronage by Caucasian customers (see Table 8). Indeed, the findings for men mirror (and, thus, apparently account for) the age, size and interaction effects previously shown for all minority firms.

Finally, some additional (rank-ordered) questions were posed to the entrepreneurs to ascertain their comparative levels of satisfaction with owning their own businesses as well as their assessments as to whether their race/ ethnicity had been beneficial or detrimental to their business. Men had more disparate responses by race to the questions as to whether their race has helped them, whether they would start a business again, and whether they would start the same business again (see again Tables 4 and 5). The higher means for Native American/Alaska Native men (at 3.3) seem to be driving the result regarding their race being a help, with the next highest group being Blacks, with a mean of 2.62. Regarding the willingness to start again measures, the differences between Black and Asian men appear to be responsible for the resulting significant difference, with Asians reporting more

Table 8.   ANOVA for Cauccust Individuals.

	Dependent Variable: CAUCCUST				
Source	Type III Sum of Squares	df	Mean Square	F	Significance
Men					
Corrected model	9.179(a)	3	3.06	8.704	0
Intercept	91.634	1	91.634	260.681	0
REVCAT	2.677	1	2.677	7.615	0.007
YEARSCAT	3.315	1	3.315	9.43	0.003
REVCAT * YEARSCAT	1.668	1	1.668	4.746	0.032
Error	27.418	78	0.352		
Total	161	82			
Corrected total	36.598	81			
Women					
Corrected model	2.179E–02(a)	3	7.26E-03	0.177	0.911
Intercept	15.084	1	15.084	368.614	0
REVCAT	3.17E–03	1	3.17E-03	0.077	0.783
YEARSCAT	3.17E–03	1	3.17E-03	0.077	0.783
REVCAT * YEARSCAT	3.17E–03	1	3.17E-03	0.077	0.783
Error	0.941	23	4.09E-02		
Total	30	27			
Corrected total	0.963	26			

willingness to start again. Unfortunately, however, no explanations were solicited so as to provide additional insight into the reasons for such disparities.

4. DIRECTIONS FOR FUTURE RESEARCH

The results reported here indicate that some racial/ethnic subgroups of minority men and women entrepreneurs do seem to hire predominantly within their own race and benefit from co-racial/ethnic patronage, while others do not. In the future, it will be important to verify for minority women entrepreneurs these and the other findings of this study with a random, nationwide study design that will allow for the making of definitive and generalizable conclusions.

Additionally, future research should seek to determine whether the inter-minority group hiring and patronage patterns identified here were simply the result of this non-random design or, indeed, a reflection of a replicable pattern. If so, it will be worthwhile to determine why the patterns have emerged. One might speculate that location of the business in an area that would attract customers from another minority group (e.g., a Black business in a Hispanic community) could contribute to such results. However, does this possibility in its antithesis explain why Black and Asian women have so few Caucasian customers? A greater understanding of the patronage characteristics of minority ventures is clearly needed.

An equally compelling question arises with respect to the contradictory responses of both male and female Asian entrepreneurs with regard to their tendency to hire Asians. Is there really some discernible basis for their seeming unwillingness to admit that they predominantly hire other Asians?

Further, it is noteworthy that, on a conceptual level, all of the variables identified among the females were replicated among the males. This suggests the possibility that the minority entrepreneurship literature's historical research on men might, nonetheless, have resulted in findings that capture – but, perhaps, overstate – differences among minority female entrepreneurs. Additional research needs to be conducted on a variety of variables, especially utilizing random samples, to ascertain whether cross-gender generalizations may be confidently undertaken.

Additional efforts to explicate the operational experiences of minority entrepreneurs with respect to human resource management and marketing, as well as other aspects of organizational management, are very much needed.

Finally, the results presented here indicate the possible existence of racial/ethnic differences among men regarding overall satisfaction with business ownership as well as beliefs about the impact of their race/ethnicity on their level of business success. These are topics worthy of additional research. Such research possibly could contribute toward increased understanding of the differential rates of business formation and failure among minority entrepreneurs.

ACKNOWLEDGMENT

The authors wish to thank Dr. Frank Hoy of the University of Texas-El Paso for his helpful comments on this paper.

REFERENCES

Aldrich, H., & Waldinger, R. (1990). Ethnicity and entrepreneurship. *Annual Review of Sociology, 16,* 111–135.

Bates, T. (1988). *An analysis of income differentials among self-employed minorities.* Los Angeles: UCLA Center for Afro-American Studies.

Bates, T. (1994). Utilization of minority employees in small business: A comparison of non-minority and Black-owned enterprises. *The Review of Black Political Economy, 23*(1), 113–121.

Bates, T., & Williams, D. (1993). Racial politics: Does it pay? *Social Science Quarterly, 74*(3), 507–522.

Butler, J., & Greene, P. (2000). Ethnic entrepreneurship: The continuous rebirth of American enterprise. In: D. Sexton & R. Smilor (Eds), *Entrepreneurship 2000.* Chicago: Upstart Publishing Company.

Campbell, A. (1968). *Racial attitudes in fifteen American cities.* Ann Arbor: University of Michigan Survey Research Center/Institute for Social Research.

DeCarlo, J., & Lyons, P. (1979). A comparison of selected personal characteristics of minority and non-minority female entrepreneurs. *Journal of Small Business Management, 17*(4), 22–29.

Donthu, N., & Cherian, J. (1994). Impact of strength of ethnic identification on Hispanic shopping behavior. *Journal of Retailing, 70*(4), 383–393.

Dyer, L., & Ross, C. (2000). Ethnic enterprises and their clientele. *Journal of Small Business Management, 38*(2), 48–66.

Fratoe, F. (1999). Social capital and Black business owners. In: J. Walker (Ed.), *Encyclopedia of African American business history.* Westport, CT: Greenwood Press.

Geoffrey, B. (1988). *Neighborhoods in transition: The making of San Francisco's ethnic and nonconformist communities.* Berkeley: University of California Press.

Greene, P. (1997). A resource-based approach to ethnic business sponsorship: A consideration of Israeli-Pakistani immigrants. *Journal of Small Business Management, 35*(4), 58–71.

Gudmundson, D., & Hartenian, L. (2000). Workforce diversity in small business: An empirical investigation. *Journal of Small Business Management, 38*(3), 27–36.

Kervin, J. (1992). *Methods for business research.* New York: Harper-Collins.

Lee, J. (1999). Retail niche domination among African American, Jewish and Korean entrepreneurs: Competition, co-ethnic advantage and disadvantage. *American Behavioral Scientist, 42*(9), 1398–1416.

Lee, M. (1981). Changing personnel management practices: A case study of a Japanese firm. *Journal of Small Business Management, 19*(2), 83–86.

Light, I., Bernard, R., & Kim, R. (1999). Immigrant incorporation in the garment industry of Los Angeles. *International Migration Review, 33*(1), 5–25.

Light, I., & Bonacich, E. (1988). *Immigrant entrepreneurs.* Berkeley: University of California Press.

Milliken, E., & Martins, L. (1996). Searching for common threads: Understanding the multiple effects of diversity and organizational groups. *Academy of Management Review, 21*(2), 402–433.

Newman, K. (1995). Dead-end jobs: A way out? *The Brookings Review, 13*(4), 24–28.

Omg, P. (1981). Factors influencing the size of the Black business community. *The Review of Black Political Economy, 11*(3), 313–319.

Roberson-Saunders, P. (2001). Minority and female entrepreneurship. In: G. Libecap (Ed.), *Entrepreneurial inputs and outcomes* (Vol. 13). Oxford: Elsevier Science, Ltd.

Shane, S., Vereid, L., & Westhead, P. (1991). An exploratory examination of the reasons leading to new firm formation across country and gender. *Journal of Business Venturing, 6*(6), 431–446.

Shim, S., & Eastlick, M. (1998). Characteristics of Hispanic female business owners: An exploratory study. *Journal of Small Business Management, 36*(3), 18–34.

Smith-Hunter, A. (2004). Women entrepreneurship across racial lines: Current status, critical issues and future implications. *Journal of Hispanic Higher Education, 3*(4), 363–381.

Stevenson, L. (1986). Against all odds: The entrepreneurship of women. *Journal of Small Business Management, 24*(4), 30–36.

U.S. Department of Commerce. (1992a). *1992 Economic censuses: Survey of minority-owned business enterprises – summary.* Washington, DC: Bureau of the Census, Economics and Statistics Administration.

U.S. Department of Commerce. (1992b). *1992 Economic censuses: Women-owned businesses – WB92-1.* Washington, DC: Bureau of the Census.

U.S. Department of Commerce. (1997a). *1997 Economic censuses: Survey of minority-owned business enterprises, MB97-1 – Black.* Washington, DC: Bureau of the Census, Economics and Statistics Administration.

U.S. Department of Commerce. (1997b). *1997 Economic censuses: Survey of minority-owned business enterprises, MB97-2 – Hispanic* Washington, DC: Bureau of the Census, Economics and Statistics Administration.

U.S. Department of Commerce. (1997c). *1997. Economic Censuses: Women-Owned Businesses – WB97-1.* Washington, DC: Bureau of the Census.

Wong, B. (1987). The Chinese: New immigrants in New York's Chinatown. In: N. Foner (Ed.), *New immigrants in New York.* New York: Columbia University Press.

Zhou, M. (1992). *Chinatown: The socioeconomic potential of an urban enclave.* Philadelphia: Temple University Press.

IMMIGRANTS AND ENTREPRENEURS IN SÃO PAULO, BRAZIL: ECONOMIC DEVELOPMENT IN THE BRAZILIAN 'MELTING POT'

José Renato de Campos Araújo, Odair da Cruz Paiva and Carlos L. Rodriguez

1. INTRODUCTION

When examining anecdotal evidence of migration processes, from historical and geographical perspectives, stories of individual immigrants that became successful entrepreneurs in the host country are commonplace. These narratives help individualize and romanticize the usually crude statistics of the increasingly common population movements across political borders. They also serve a number of purposes within the ethnic community, most of them associated with the creation and nurturing of the group's *social capital*. This critical ethnic resource has been consistently shown to provide significant benefits to immigrant communities, particularly in environments with higher levels of perceived risk (e.g., Portes, 1998; Martes & Rodriguez, 2004).

Those of us who live in large metropolises such as São Paulo, Buenos Aires, and perhaps especially New York and London, have almost certainly

Developmental Entrepreneurship: Adversity, Risk, and Isolation
International Research in the Business Disciplines, Volume 5, 297–322
Copyright © 2006 by Elsevier Ltd.
ISSN: 1074-7877/doi:10.1016/S1074-7877(06)05016-1

heard stories of immigrants, of the most diverse ethnic origins, who succeeded as professionals or entrepreneurs in their countries of adoption. The ethnicities that provide the actors to these narratives may change, but the scripts are in most cases strikingly similar. They usually start with descriptions of the hardships immigrants faced in the home country and of the always-long trips to the 'chosen' destiny.[1] These are followed by depictions of the uncertainties associated with life in the adopted country, with emphasis on the unfamiliarity with the new language, culture, and basic aspects of daily life. Communicating with people in the host country can be a complex endeavor, which limits integration into the host society and reinforces the yearning toward the now distant motherland. The first years are always difficult from a financial perspective, and work, usually in menial jobs, is hard and long. Immigration success stories also commonly mention the participation of family and friends in the business initiatives, and conclude in many cases with some form of praise for the personal efforts of the immigrant entrepreneur and for what these individuals are said to have given back to the community. These accounts are often based on the individual achievements of a few members of the group, and represent, to the eyes of the immigrant community, the ideal of victory of individual effort against all odds, also providing the group with elements of a common culture and identity. In those large, cosmopolitan metropolises, all of them with sizeable and in some cases still growing ethnic communities, one commonly hears discourses that value multicultural diversity as a mechanism for the creation of richer social experiences. However, these narratives are often presented side by side with biased and prejudiced comments against foreigners in general, or directed toward a specific ethnic group.

In spite of the fruitful potential of an examination of these individual trajectories, the main goal of this chapter is to shed light on the broad connections between immigration and entrepreneurship. It also emphasizes the support that immigration, as a collective phenomenon, provides to the initiatives of individual entrepreneurs by means of the social capital developed within the ethnic communities to which they belong. This analysis is done on the basis of historic information about immigration to an area of the world that has received relatively little attention from researchers in the field: the state of São Paulo, in Southeastern Brazil, and especially the state's capital, the city of the same name, the now largest metropolis in South America. We hope to provide evidence of the extraordinary importance of the role of immigrant entrepreneurs for the broader economic development of the region. While their initiatives were based and supported by their ethnic communities, they transcended the small immigrant group and became the main engine of economic development for the region as a whole.

The examination of the initiatives of immigrant entrepreneurs in three groups, which were an important element in the economic development of São Paulo, will be made with the consideration of historic and social variables of their ethnic communities. By doing this, we attempt to provide a more detailed picture of the institutional and cultural structures that influence the individuals who discover, evaluate, and exploit entrepreneurial opportunities. The type of analysis presented in this paper is part of an effort to provide more contextualized perspectives to the examination of entrepreneurial initiatives that occur across political borders or within immigrant communities (e.g., Baker, Gedajlovic, & Lubatkin, 2005).

The development of this paper will proceed as follows. In the next section we make a brief review of the sociology, ethnic economy, and entrepreneurship literatures to examine the theoretical foundations for the relationship between social capital, entrepreneurship, and ethnic entrepreneurship. Next we present data on the city of São Paulo, with a description of the immigrant groups and the reasons for their impact on regional development. Following that, findings and relationships are proposed and discussed. The conclusion indicates the limitations of the analysis and suggests directions for future research.

2. IMMIGRATION, SOCIAL CAPITAL, AND ENTREPRENEURSHIP

The view of entrepreneurial opportunity recognition in foreign environments as a purely objective phenomenon, without consideration of the institutional and cultural contexts of the host society (e.g., Shane & Venkataraman, 2000) has been criticized for providing an under-socialized, incomplete view of the issue (Baker et al., 2005). This perspective is said to be based on strong and unrealistic behavioral assumptions of hyper rationality by utility-maximizing individuals. A more adequately contextualized view of the two important social phenomena – immigration and immigrant entrepreneurship – needs to recognize the similarities and the connections between the nature of individuals as immigrants and entrepreneurs. If entrepreneurs have been described in the literature as those individuals that uncover, create, take advantage, or simply make sense, ahead of others, of business opportunities in the face of uncertainty (e.g., Schumpeter, 1934), a rather similar description can be applied to immigrants. Indeed, analyses of migration processes indicate that, in many cases, the driving force behind the initiative to start life again in countries that may be far away culturally and geographically from one's own has a number of common elements with the entrepreneurial process (Martes, 2000). This analysis attempts to shed light on two main aspects: the similarities between the developmental paths of entrepreneurs and immigrants, and the advantages brought to the initiatives of immigrant entrepreneurs by their shared immigrant identities and by their communities' pool of ethnic resources, especially social capital. Regarding the latter topic, we also emphasize the reality commonly found in immigrant communities, where individuals are sometimes forced to engage in entrepreneurial initiatives due to the restricted opportunities available to them in the labor markets – an aspect often ignored in analyses of entrepreneurial development based on pure economic or managerial motivations (Light & Gold, 2000).

Our discussion uses the city of São Paulo, Brazil, as its scenario. We hope to demonstrate that the histories of the waves of immigrants that settled in that region and of the process of regional economic development are intertwined, and can only be explained by the joint consideration of the phenomena of immigration and entrepreneurship. The history of South America's largest urban agglomeration will tell the story of how immigration created professional and entrepreneurial niches that contributed decisively to the creation of wealth and economic development in the city.

Research on entrepreneurship in immigrant communities has the potential for shedding light on a number of key questions in various fields of investigation, including strategy and economic sociology. Immigrant entrepreneurs face various sorts of hardships, starting possibly with the relatively unfamiliar and thus, from their perspective, relatively unstructured environment in which they operate or plan to start doing so. The few resources they can draw from are likely to originate from the community to which they belong, and from their network of relationships and support (Portes & Sensenbrenner, 1993). Higher rates of entrepreneurship in those environments have also been associated with faster rates of social mobility and advancement, and as such there is great interest in studying the processes by which businesses are started in immigrant communities (Wilson & Portes, 1980; Halter, 1995; Light & Gold, 2000).

Owing to the basic characteristics of the phenomenon of immigrant entrepreneurship, there is increasing interest in the examination of the processes of creation and growth of businesses by immigrant entrepreneurs, and how this process can contribute to a broader analysis of economic development, particularly in isolated and higher-risk areas. This is one of the main motivations behind the present volume. Research on immigrant entrepreneurship can contribute to the examination of the key questions of the field of entrepreneurship, i.e., the creation, discovery, and modes of exploiting business opportunities.

However, this type of analysis cannot be properly conducted without the examination of the role of social capital and of the contribution of support networks in its creation and, as a consequence, on the process of business development. A number of studies have been conducted about the impact of various types of support networks in the creation and growth of social capital (e.g., Light, 1972; Portes, 1987; Light & Bonacich, 1988; Putnam, 1993).

2.1. Social Capital

The concept of social capital has been in the literature of sociology since the late 1970s (Portes, 1998), and has been used in analogy to other types of resources or capital that individuals need for personal improvement and that firms must possess if they are to survive and grow. It is considered to be among the most influential concepts in the social sciences to appear in recent years and has been used in a diverse range of fields in social theory and economic development studies (Woolcock, 1998). Recent scholarly treatments from a macro-perspective have come mostly from comparative studies of national institutions and their effects on economic development, and from a micro-perspective, from the strategy, entrepreneurship, and immigrant entrepreneurship literatures. In the macro perspective, interest on the theme is said to arise from the incomplete explanation that traditional economic theory provides to the differences in national rates of economic development and reduction of social inequality (Portes & Landolt, 2000). From a micro perspective, the embeddedness of firms in networks, and the impacts of network support on firm creation and performance are topics of increasing interest (Greene, 1997; Shane & Cable, 2000).

Definitions of the concept revolve around the ideas of networks of relationships, trust, and reciprocity. Social capital is usually described as an asset, a capability, or a resource, whose possession is associated with positive outcomes (see, e.g., Bourdieu, 1985; Coleman, 1988, 1990; Burt, 1992; Putnam, 1993; Fukuyama, 1995; Portes, 1998). Common to most definitions of social capital is the idea that it comprises two elements: the network of relationships that enables access to resources and opportunities, and the sets of resources and opportunities themselves. In the case of immigrant communities, for example, stable relationships and recurring interaction among individuals sharing a common language and similar immigration experiences may increase trust. In turn, trust is likely to improve access to information leading to business opportunities and thus function as a "lubricant" of the network, by reducing the transaction costs of exploiting those opportunities. Common costs of transacting cited in the literature are those related to negotiating, monitoring, and enforcing contracts (e.g., Williamson, 1975), activities that can be conducted more efficiently in a high-trust environment. Among the benefits of social capital are improved coordination, facilitation of actions, preferential access to opportunities, information and resources, greater visibility and legitimacy, and efficiency (e.g., Nahapiet & Ghoshal, 1998; Portes & Landolt, 2000).

2.2. Social Capital and Entrepreneurship

Empirical studies and conceptual analyses of social capital in the management, sociology, and entrepreneurship literatures provide evidence of a positive relationship between social capital and entrepreneurial success, as well as between the growth of entrepreneurial firms and economic development (see, e.g., Fukuyama, 2001). Entrepreneurs who possess a high level of social capital have been found to have privileged access to information about opportunities and resource acquisition possibilities, and facilitated cooperation for business development and growth. They were also better positioned to reap the benefits of higher levels of trust, e.g., reduced opportunism and lower costs of doing business (e.g., Fukuyama, 1995; Nahapiet & Ghoshal, 1998). In recent empirical studies, it was shown that high-social capital entrepreneurs had better chances at gaining access to people important for the success of their ventures (Baron & Markman, 2003) and at finding sources of venture capital for their projects (Shane & Cable, 2000; Shane & Stuart, 2002). At the firm level, social capital has been proposed as a key element in the creation and successful exploitation of intellectual capital, which in turn is an important source of competitive advantage (Bolino, Turnley, & Bloodgood, 2002). It was also shown to increase information interchange and product innovation (Tsai & Ghoshal, 1998), and foster network formation in ways that increased the stability of start-zups and their chances of survival (Walker, Kogut, & Shan, 1997). At the individual level, social capital has been identified as a source of job opportunities and career advancement (Podolny & Baron, 1997; Seibert, Kraimer, & Liden, 2001).

The emerging literature on immigrant entrepreneurship generally supports the connection between the possession of social capital and economic and business success (Light, 1972, 1998; Bonacich & Modell, 1980; Light & Gold, 2000). If immigrant entrepreneurship is seen, as suggested by

Waldinger, Aldrich, and Ward (1990), as the "set of connections and regular patterns of interaction among people sharing common national background or immigration experience" (p. 33), it can be expected that the more abundant social capital is in the ethnic community, the higher the chances of survival of businesses that draw their resources from the community. This happens primarily because ethnic-based trust is considered to be more efficient than legalistic forms of trust to reduce transaction costs. As such, social capital developed within immigrant communities has the potential to lower costs of doing business, at least for the transactions conducted among co-ethnics (Fukuyama, 2001).

According to Light (1998), the key connection between social capital and entrepreneurship is the efficient use of ethnic resources to support the creation and survival of businesses. Ethnic resources are derived from the ethnic group's particular characteristics, and include things such as values, knowledge, skills, information, solidarity, and work ethic. They empower the immigrant group in general, and immigrant entrepreneurs in particular, to take advantage of opportunities and to avoid or neutralize possible risks. Ethnic resources are also the basis upon which immigrant communities build networking mechanisms such as rotating credit associations. These associations, which are essentially based upon the principles of "enforceable trust" (Portes & Sensenbrenner, 1993), have helped business formation in a number of U.S. immigrant communities. Business initiatives of immigrant entrepreneurs can also draw from the stable pool of low-wage workers that have few alternatives outside the community, and from the sources of venture capital represented by mechanisms such as the credit associations. Ethnic resources create mechanisms of social control that reduce costs of doing business and leverage their potential to raise the level of trust and solidarity. In sum, ethnic resources derived from social capital in the immigrant community are expected to help immigrant entrepreneurs find loyal customers for their products and services, reliable suppliers for intermediate goods, relatively inexpensive sources of investment capital, hard-working employees, and partners that are likely to share their goals and expectations.

3. MIGRATION AND ENTREPRENEURSHIP IN SÃO PAULO, BRAZIL

The city of São Paulo started receiving immigrants around 1850, by that time mostly from European countries such as Italy, Portugal, and Spain.

The first decades of the last century witnessed the arrival of immigrants from the Middle and Far East, in the latter case especially from Japan. Domestic migration, particularly since the start of the industrialization process in the years after World War II, has been and continues to be important to the region. Populations from impoverished Northeastern states have been moving to the city since the early 1960s, in waves that swell after each of the large periodical droughts that occur in that part of Brazil. It is worth noting that from the early 16th century – when the first European populations started arriving in South America[2] – until the early 1990s, Brazil was a net receiver of immigrants, and indeed received a diverse influx of groups from various parts of the world (Levy, 1974). It was only recently that the country became a net issuer of immigrants, with the bulk of this movement going to countries such as the U.S. and Japan, and in smaller numbers to Europe (Fausto, 1991).

Migration to the state of São Paulo was a direct consequence of the process, initiated by mid-19th century, of substitution of slaves with free workers in the large, labor-intensive coffee plantations that were the dominant economic activity in that region – and, in fact, in the whole country – until recently. This process accelerated around 1870, due to the increasing restrictions on slave trade, and gained even greater momentum with the abolition of slavery in 1888. As a historical phenomenon, it needs to be understood together with the development of the coffee industry, which for a number of years had its most important center in the state of São Paulo, mainly in the city of São Paulo and the state port, Santos.[3] The two concomitant historical developments, i.e., the elimination of slave labor and the growing importance of coffee in the Brazilian economy, created the adequate conditions for initiatives, both public and private, regarding the introduction of immigrant work. Economic activities developed around this product, including not only those at the plantations, but also processing and exporting, comprised the most important sector of the economies of São Paulo and Brazil until the end of the 1930s. Industrial production and urbanization already had economic relevance at the end of the 19th century in Brazil, but were secondary in importance to the coffee agri-business complex until the beginning of World War II.

During the period 1880–1940, the state of São Paulo received approximately three million immigrants, mostly from European countries. Other countries from Asia (especially Japan) and the Middle East were also significant issuers of immigrants to the region.[4] The capital of the state of São Paulo, due to its geographic location, immediately became the center of the growing number of activities related to the coffee economy. At the edge of the great plains that cover a significant part of that region, the city of São Paulo was located close to one of South America's best ports, Santos, with a significant infrastructure to serve shipments to Europe and North America. São Paulo was also at the center of a large network of railroads that connected the areas of coffee production with the coast. The city soon became the first required stop for immigrants that arrived in Santos, bound to the coffee plantations in the interior of the state.

Until the 1920s, São Paulo witnessed almost uninterrupted economic growth, based mainly on the creation of support activities to the coffee production and export industries, such as banks to finance production and commerce enterprises to assist trade. By this time, it was already Brazil's second largest city, after Rio de Janeiro, the country capital until the early 1960s. São Paulo grew rapidly in population and urban development, which was accompanied by the creation of a large infrastructure of transportation and urban services. The vast majority of the coffee agri-business was under the control of a local elite, which through its connections with foreign capital occupied the most important positions in Brazil's economic and political worlds, and which derived its wealth from the sizeable profitability of the coffee business. These factors slowly opened opportunities for an increasing number of immigrants to take over occupations that were considered secondary in importance and potential for rent-generation, or that were simply off the radar and interests of the representatives of the local elite and of the large foreign organizations. From this perspective, the same process of social stratification that prevented immigrants from having access to the most attractive businesses made them particularly well positioned to take advantage of economic opportunities in other sectors.

Assimilation of immigrants into the growing number of economic activities needed to support São Paulo's urban and economic development occurred in two ways: as workforce in established businesses and as entrepreneurs in commercial and industrial activities. From any perspective, by the end of the 19th century, immigrants were already a dynamic and significant presence in the economy of the state of São Paulo in general, and its capital in particular, as shown by the profile of the city's workforce (Table 1).

3.1. Ethnicities and Economic Activities in São Paulo

Some of the numerous immigrant groups that settled in the city of São Paulo established economic profiles that became forever marked, in the

Table 1. Domestic and Foreign Workforce per Economic Sector in São Paulo (1893).

Sector of Activity	Domestic Workers	Foreign Workers	Total
Transportation and related	1,998 (18.98%)	8,527 (81.02%)	10,525
Artistic (crafts)	1,481 (14.46%)	8,760 (85.54%)	10,241
Commercial	2,680 (28.34%)	6,776 (71.66%)	9,456
Manufacturing	774 (21.11%)	2,893 (78.89%)	3,667
Total	6,933 (20.6%)	26,956 (79.54%)	33,889

Source: Santos (1998).

memory of the city's population, as inseparable characteristics of these groups' identities. This is particularly true in the cases where they acquired some level of dominance over specific professions or sectors of activity. There is also a physical relationship between these groups and certain parts of the city where large numbers of their members settled, forming a continuum between economic activity and spatial insertion. Part of the identity of belonging to the Italian community in São Paulo in the first decades of the last century, for example, meant working in a factory and living in the area called *Mooca*. However, in most cases, in spite of the spatial concentration, these areas did not represent ethnic economies in the way these are usually defined. While comprising a significant percentage of the local population, immigrants did not control large sectors of the local economy, nor did their patterns of exchange generate benefits from quasi-vertical integration that would significantly reduce transaction costs. Thus, instead of forming an ethnic enclave, these communities would be more properly called 'ethnic neighborhoods', as suggested, in other cases, by Portes and Rumbaut (1990).

Similarly to what happened in a number of cities of the new world, São Paulo offered diverse and multiform possibilities of insertion, into its social fabric, to the immigrant groups it received. The next sections of this paper will briefly analyze three immigrant groups that left permanent marks in the history and development of the city: the Syrian/Lebanese, the Armenian, and the Korean. We will discuss their connections with specific areas of economic activity, to provide a more complete picture of these groups' ethnic and economic identities. We will also mention a fourth ethnicity that migrated in significant numbers to the region, the Spanish group, in order to present a case where the link among the elements of business, identity, and spatial concentration did *not* occur. The case of the Spanish migration is identified as an exception, which by emphasizing characteristics and trends of the other groups may help us have a better understanding of their profiles.

3.1.1. Syrian/Lebanese Immigrants and Entrepreneurs

According to Truzzi (1991), while relatively small in numbers,[5] Syrian and Lebanese immigrants to the city of São Paulo had a marked presence in the city's economic life. In fact, internal divisions in the community – owing to cultural and religious reasons, the discussion of which is not in the scope of this work – prevented them from using a unified identity to even more strongly impose their presence in the urban scenario. In the years between the end of the 19th century and the early decades of the 20th century, the area in the city of São Paulo surrounding the *25 de Março* street had approximately 500 commercial establishments owned by Syrian/Lebanese entrepreneurs, of which close to 80 percent were retail stores selling fabrics and miscellaneous sewing items. The concentration was so significant that this part of the city was called 'Turkish territory.'[6] The relationship of the immigrant Syrian/Lebanese community with specific areas of the city of São Paulo acquired a structure that is common in immigrant communities in other parts of the world. The first to arrive settled in the area around *25 de Março* street, and later waves of arrivals found advantageous to use the connections that were already in place to develop the relationship between residence and workplace in the same urban space.

In order to understand the successful insertion of Syrian/Lebanese immigrants in the sectors where their presence was more significant (also including traveling salesmen activities), three characteristics of these groups have to be briefly mentioned. The first is an identity strongly related to a shared religion (in the case, Roman Catholicism) and a common regional origin. These elements contributed to the creation of social capital in the group, which allowed the assimilation of the constant stream of new arrivals. These links also reinforced group identity via the integration of relatives, friends, and fellow countrymen, and made possible the creation of an endogenous type of sociability, which with time developed schools, clubs, associations, and charities to serve the needs of the community.

The second characteristic is the pattern of marriage adopted by the members of the 'Turkish' immigrant community. According to Truzzi (1991), compared to other ethnicities that settled in the area around the same time, Syrian and Lebanese married essentially within the group. This happened in spite of a large imbalance between the numbers of males and females in the first years of immigration, when the first arrivals were mostly male. To solve this problem, it was usual for the immigrants to go back to their countries of origin when time came for them to get married, to find a spouse from the same culture and religion, and hopefully from the same village. This pattern, that reinforced a highly introverted sociability among the early members of the community, is said to derive from the patriarchal nature of these countries' cultures (Truzzi, 1991). The practice of returning to Syria or Lebanon to find a wife only started to slowly decline after 1920. In the Demographic Census of 1927, the percentage of same-culture marriage in the Syrian community was still higher than 50 percent, while among Italian immigrants it had already decreased to around 20 percent.

The third aspect was the highly defined profile of the members of this immigrant group. They were, in the vast majority, young, single males who had come to Brazil to work hard, accumulate resources and hopefully monetary wealth, and return permanently to their country of origin as soon these goals had been achieved. The interest of these immigrants for the activity of traveling salesmen can be explained by some of the advantages offered by this type of commerce, e.g., the independent and essentially entrepreneurial nature of the work, the dependence upon individual effort, and the possibility of relatively rapid financial returns.

The patterns under which social capital developed within this community produced a hierarchical structure based on seniority, under which the elders provided the newly arrived (or 'invited' new members, e.g., those that joined the community by marriage) with financial and social capital. Credit was extended in the form of merchandise that only had to be paid for after sale. Other forms of general support were also common, including a ritual of introductions to the ethnic network that legitimized the trustworthiness of new members and provided them with the needed social capital. Similarly to what happened as a consequence of intra-community marriages, endogenous economic relationships developed within the community that supported and reinforced the identity links derived from the common cultural heritage. According to Truzzi (1991)

... those circumstances should not be underestimated, since they created alternatives for the growth of businesses that otherwise would have been restricted to the labor capacity of the nuclear family. The immigrant community could grow and become stronger, and with this provide increasing possibilities of role differentiation. With this, the elders who had been in business for longer periods of time could reach strategic positions in retail or manufacturing in the community (p. 66).

3.1.2. Armenian Immigrants and Entrepreneurs

The Armenians arrived in Brazil more recently, and their numbers are smaller compared to the other ethnicities mentioned in this work. There were basically two groups: the first, having settled in São Paulo by the end of the 19th century, engaged mostly in traveling salesmen activities. Similar to the Syrian/Lebanese community, some Armenians started businesses in textile manufacturing. A few were extremely successful, creating family fortunes that have survived to the present day. A second, larger group, numbering about 25,000 immigrants, arrived in the years around 1920, having fled their country after the massacre of 1915 under the Ottoman Empire. This second wave settled in the areas of the city of São Paulo with concentrations of members and descendants of the first immigrants, known in the community as *pioneers*. These were located mostly around the *Municipal Market, Florencio de Abreu* street, and in the districts of *Santana* and *Imirim*, in the northern part of the city. A few went to the neighboring cities of *Santo Andre* and *Osasco*, in the region of *Presidente Altino*. Spatial concentration also occurred in the case of this community, in the usual process designed to leverage the available, sometimes scarce amount of social capital.

The *pioneers* established social networks and community associations, connected generally to the Apostolic Church, and their leaders formed the *Council of the Forty*. This group became the main source of support for the newly arrived and for their integration into the established community From this perspective, they linked the goals of the two groups – power and respect for the elders, solidarity and capital (financial and social) for the newcomers.

The second wave of Armenian immigrants to São Paulo adopted a new functional specialization, rapidly occupying niches in activities related to shoe manufacturing and retail. However, according to some authors (e.g., Grun, 1992), the occupation by Armenian immigrants of important positions in this sector of activity in a sense transcended the usual patterns of dominance of particular trades by certain ethnic groups. In this view, the relationship between this group and the sector of activity where they chose to specialize had the role of providing them with a common identity, creating a link with past times in the country of origin via the symbolic repetition, in the present, of activities performed by their ancestors. Or, in other words, by developing this amount of symbolic capital, with the re-creation of the links with the motherland and its national culture, the group was attempting to strengthen the social capital needed to assist them in the new environment.

Research by Grun (1992) revealed the mechanisms through which the Armenian immigrant community maintained its dominance over the shoe manufacturing and retail businesses

> Part of the compensation paid to Armenian workers that were employed in Armenian units of (that) sector was in the form of used molds from previous collections and raw materials that had not passed quality control. In this business, the possession of the molds was the main barrier to entry, which in this case was facilitated to the co-ethnics. In the case of other raw materials, they were provided mostly by a store called 'Casa da Boia', owned by a Lebanese immigrant who had married an Armenian. They provided inputs and credit, easing the entry of newcomers into the business (pp. 46–48).

The initial accumulation of resources was thus facilitated by the network of relationships and mutual assistance that existed in the community, in a process similar to the one that had developed among the Syrian/Lebanese. Within the Armenian community, a clear hierarchical structure could also be noted, particularly in the issue of the initial capital for business initiatives. The senior group had control over the associations responsible for the distribution of resources (including social capital), and thus possessed significant power over the newcomers. While the provision of (outdated) molds represented some level of support, it also presented technical challenges to those that were required to work with them. The amount of effort needed to be successful with these molds helped develop the required occupational skills, and in this sense reinforced the functional specialization of the group.

3.1.3. Korean Immigrants and Entrepreneurs

While a small group of Koreans, fleeing the Korean War, arrived in Rio de Janeiro in 1954, Korean immigration to Brazil is considered to have started officially in 1963, with continuous flows coming to the country until the early 1990s, by then mostly to São Paulo. By the early years of the last decade, approximately 43,000 Koreans were living in Brazil. While small compared to the 1.2 million Korean immigrants who went to the U.S. in the same period (Freitas, 2004), Brazil is still the fourth largest recipient of immigrants from that country.

Most Koreans settled in the city of São Paulo, which between 1960 and 1980 was still presenting very high rates of economic growth. This period, called the Brazilian "Economic Miracle", marked the creation and development of the auto industry in Brazil, which was highly concentrated in the Greater São Paulo Metropolitan area. A number of Koreans obtained jobs as specialized technicians in auto manufacturing and related industries, while others decided to open their own businesses, mostly in food distribution-related areas: small food markets, coffee shops, and wholesale produce sales. Large supermarket chains, currently a dominant force in this sector, particularly in the city of São Paulo, only came to control food distribution in the late 1970s. The barriers to entry in the business, in the form of economies of scale, remained low until then, making possible the temporary survival of small firms.

By the end of that decade, with competitive rivalry in the food distribution sector becoming increasingly intense, a few Korean entrepreneurs started investing in textile manufacturing and apparel. They opened the first small units in the *Liberdade* district, interestingly known as the 'Japanese' sector of the city. They were essentially family businesses, with very little or no employees outside the members of the nuclear family, and that executed all stages of production. The Koreans soon developed functional expertise in textile manufacturing and apparel, and these activities grew significantly in importance for the community. By the late 1990s, 72 percent of Koreans had jobs or businesses in these sectors.

An interesting phenomenon involving the relationships between two ethnic groups in São Paulo, the Jewish and the Korean communities, occurred because of the involvement of these two groups in the textile business. The Jewish community traditionally had a significant presence in textile manufacturing, represented by a spatial concentration of businesses in the *Bom Retiro* district. By the 1970s, younger generations of this group, already born in Brazil, were becoming increasingly assimilated into the broader host society. Larger numbers of families could afford sending their children to higher education, and a slow process of functional diversification occurred in the community. Korean immigrants, who had occupied until then a subordinate position to Jewish interests in the textile manufacturing business, took advantage of the opportunity to occupy the economic niche left open by the increasing numbers of descendants of Jewish immigrants that had transitioned to other areas of activity. As the younger members of the Jewish community lost interest in running the family businesses, a number of Korean immigrants who had started as employees in textile plants owned by the first Jewish immigrants ended up acquiring the companies.

According to Freitas (2004), the Christian churches of the Korean community had an important role in the assimilation of this group into the larger Brazilian society. They created networks of support, collecting contributions from the families of the first arrivals, and coordinating a structure that provided not only social but also legal and financial assistance to the newcomers. Especially important was the role of these networks in the provision of documents, translation, and legal services to the immigrants who entered the country illegally or who had problems with the Brazilian judicial system.

Similar to what happened in the case of the other two groups described in the previous sections, the local Korean Christian churches and their related institutions had a fundamental role in the creation and maintenance of the cultural, social, and economic links that provided the community with its identity in the new country. One example of this role, described by Freitas (2004), is their support to the formation and development of informal rotating credit associations. Considering the difficulties members of the community had obtaining credit in local banks, these associations, called *kye*, supplied immigrant entrepreneurs with working capital for their initiatives. The costs of these funds were considerably lower than the interest charged by local banks. In addition, the churches served as places for socialization, especially after the weekend services, providing the environment where potential entrepreneurs discussed business, met potential clients and partners, and obtained funds.

These endogenous mechanisms created by the Korean community had a key role in maintaining group unity and growing its pool of social capital. As a consequence, this is the only group among those mentioned so far that still shows vitality and group cohesion – obviously also a consequence of the fact that this group was the last to arrive in São Paulo. The success of the community's entrepreneurs in the textile manufacturing industry transformed the environment of the *Bom Retiro* district, where most of them had settled. The 'Jewish' district has now become the 'Korean' district, with a concentration of manufacturing and retail units in the clothing industry that has been growing in importance in Brazil's economy.

The textile business in São Paulo has been showing, for over two decades already, an interesting trend of hierarchical involvement of the ethnicities that arrived successively in the area. First, Korean immigrants learned the trade from Jewish business owners as their employees, and took over some of the businesses when the second and third generations of Jewish immigrants diversified into other activities. Now, Korean immigrant entrepreneurs, the new business owners, are increasingly using the labor of the last wave of immigrants to arrive in São Paulo. Mostly from South American countries, particularly from Bolivia and Peru, these groups are the new low-cost labor force. This is already allowing Korean entrepreneurs to move to other economic niches, as evidenced by the growing number of Korean restaurants and food markets in many parts of the city. These new areas of activity have the additional benefit of allowing the assimilation of the continuous flow of Korean immigrants that is still moving to Brazil.

3.1.4. Spanish Immigrants

Spanish immigration to Brazil has been occurring since the late 19th century. It is the third largest immigrant group in the country, only behind the Portuguese and the Italians, with around 750,000 immigrants arriving in the period 1888–1958. Having settled mostly in the state of São Paulo, they represent approximately 22 percent of all immigrants in Brazil. Spanish immigrants are perhaps the group most closely related to the process of substitution of slaves by salaried workers that occurred after the emancipation proclamation of 1888 – coincidentally the year they started arriving in larger numbers. The profile of the group, particularly of those that arrived in Brazil before the Second World War, had the essential characteristics of family immigration; the number of single males, for example, was never higher than 18 percent. Approximately two-thirds were illiterate, and almost 80 percent were agricultural workers in Spain.

The spatial dispersion of the group, however, was a distinctive characteristic of the Spanish immigration to São Paulo. According to Klein (1994), Spanish settlers seem to have preferred smaller urban centers in the state of São Paulo to the large capital city. By doing this, they gave up some of the potential benefits they could have derived from their large numbers, such as scale economies, which are particularly important for entrepreneurial business initiatives. This tendency may also explain the relatively small percentage that Spanish workers represent in the few available historical statistics about the state's foreign workforce (Klein, 1994).

Another important feature of the Spanish immigration to São Paulo, with important consequences to its assimilation into the new society, was their exogamy or outmarriage. While Syrian/Lebanese, Armenian, and Korean – the latter at a smaller proportion – married mostly within their own ethnic communities, the vast majority of Spanish immigrants found their spouses among native Brazilians or, in a few cases, in other immigrant groups. Statistics of the Demographic Census of 1926 cited in Klein (1994), for example, show that among the 4,093 persons of Spanish origin that were married in São Paulo state in that year, only 24 percent married another co-ethnic. Also cited in Klein (1994) is the total number of marriages of persons of Spanish origin in the period 1934–1946, a time of relatively slow immigration: of the 5,232 marriages, the endogamy index was just 12 percent, with only 20 percent of Spanish males and 30 percent of females marrying a co-ethnic.

The endogamy and the spatial dispersion of the Spanish community in the state of São Paulo are possible evidence of relatively low levels of social capital and ethnic resources among the members of that immigrant group. These factors negatively impacted their economic significance for the city of São Paulo, in comparison to the other immigrant communities. According to the São Paulo State Industrial Census of 1934, there were only 275 manufacturing and commercial units owned by individuals of Spanish origin, concentrated basically in small retail operations and shops, restaurants, and small shoe factories. In the first years after the Second World War, individuals of Spanish origin owned only seven percent of all industrial units in the state, mostly in textiles and small manufacturing equipment.

There is also evidence that the Spanish community – compared to other groups such as the Italian and the Portuguese – created a relatively small number of community associations such as hospitals, schools, and clubs, and that most of those had a relatively short existence. In the city of São Paulo, there are no regions with distinctive signs of the presence of the Spanish community, and the marks of the Spanish immigration can only be observed today in a few private schools and restaurants.

3.2. Entrepreneurs, Ethnicity, and Immigration in São Paulo

Any analysis of the phenomena of immigration, ethnicity, and entrepreneurship in São Paulo is likely to be seen as incomplete if it does not mention some centrally important members of the city's immigrant communities, who also became crucial figures in its business and economic life. A significant majority of the family names that proudly adorn company letterheads and the marquees of some of the city's tallest skyscrapers are of Italian, Syrian/Lebanese, Jewish, or Japanese origin. São Paulo received the substantive part of immigration to Brazil,[7] and this is reflected in the genealogies of most of the city's middle and upper classes.

From a historical perspective, São Paulo's fast pace of economic growth, especially after the Second World War, can be directly associated with the phenomenon of immigration. Before that period, the city's development was a direct consequence of the capital generated by the coffee sector, then Brazil's main export. And, as mentioned earlier, the growth itself of this segment of the country's economy, after the end of slavery, is fundamentally connected to the arrival of the immigrant workforce from Europe and Asia (Cano, 1983; Dean, 1971).

An important thesis of this paper, related to the essential role of immigrants as entrepreneurs in the city of São Paulo, is that during the first decades of the 20th century, economic activities generated by the urban agglomeration in the region did not attract the interest of the leaders of the coffee export segment – the dominant owners of capital and economic resources. Reasons for this relative absence of interest have been attributed to various factors: the perception of lack of legitimacy, derived from the ownership of what was seen as 'minor' businesses; the uncertainties regarding the profitability of the new ventures; the involvement with a more profitable activity; or, simply, the lack of necessary skills and entrepreneurial initiative (Dean, 1971).

São Paulo's urban population growth, with the consequent development of an entirely new range of economic activities, created the proper environment for the blending of these two social roles – of immigrant and entrepreneur – and the emergence of this new social actor: the immigrant entrepreneur. The growth itself of the city was fueled by immigration, with the majority of the new arrivals coming there directly from their countries of origin. Other immigrants came from the coffee-growing regions in the state, as they were being replaced by the successive waves of newly arrived workers. At the same time, the city needed capital, investments, and resources applied to urban services and activities that were until then virtually unknown to the local society, which was focused on the large capital requirements of the coffee export business.

As a result, entire new sectors of economic activity, related not only to basic urban services associated with the extremely fast population growth of the city (e.g., restaurants and food markets), but also to some areas of manufacturing (e.g., textiles), had very few entry barriers to entrepreneurial immigrants. Using skills or knowledge developed in their country of origin, coupled with the resources gained by working in the state's coffee plantations, and supported in many cases by the social capital provided by their communities, a number of individuals of different ethnic backgrounds took advantage of these opportunities. The almost exponential growth of the city's population, as shown in Table 2, provided them with the necessary scale for the success of many of these initiatives.

A few immigrant entrepreneurs, some from the ethnicities presented earlier in this study, became the first captains of the embryonic industrial class that was developing in Brazil in the first decades of the 20th century. However, it was not until the first years after the Second World War that this group surpassed the coffee export business as the dominant economic power in the country. In spite of the rather secondary role of urban economic activities,

Table 2.   Population Growth of the City of São Paulo (1872–1934).

Year	Population
1872	23,243
1886	44,030
1890	64,934
1893	130,775
1900	239,820
1914	400,000 (approx.)
1920	579,033
1934	1,060,120

Source: Trento (1988).

these emerging businesses were fundamentally important for the creation of the infrastructure of South America's largest city. The immigrant entrepreneurs of that period were in a sense spreading the seeds of industrial development, which bore fruit after the Second World War, when the axis of Brazil's economy switched from primary agricultural activities to the industrial sector. These social actors had, as a result, a critical role in São Paulo's and Brazil's industrialization processes during most of the last century.

Among the most successful entrepreneurs of that time, the name of Italian immigrant and industrialist Francesco Matarazzo stands out, having already been the subject of a number of studies (e.g., Pereira, 1972; Martins, 1973, 1981; Araújo, 2000, 2003; Couto, 2004). Matarazzo was the founder of what became Brazil's largest business group ever, Industrias Reunidas F. Matarazzo, which at its heyday had 30,000 employees working in 365 associated companies, with total sales just slightly lower than the state of São Paulo's budget.[8] Matarazzo's business activities were also relevant for the relations between Brazil and Italy during the Italian Diaspora of the first half of the last century, in which Latin America had an important role. They served as an economic bridge between the two countries and represented a critical factor in Italy's balance of payments and public finances, since one of the most important companies in Matarazzo's group was a financial institution that was the main channel for the sizeable flows of money transfers from Italian immigrants in São Paulo to their families in Italy (Araújo, 2003).

The introduction of Francesco Matarazzo as the epitome of the successful immigrant entrepreneur in São Paulo is used as a symbol of the many anonymous cases that were mentioned in earlier sections of this paper. While less famous, they triggered an important new direction in Brazil's path of economic development. The initiatives of immigrant entrepreneurs were in many cases successful not only because they occupied market and functional niches that did not attract the interests of the local economic elite, but also because they were based on a set of resources (Light & Gold, 2000) – mainly social capital – that were at that time possessed almost exclusively by the immigrant communities. The networks of ethnic solidarity described in earlier sections were also common in the large Italian immigrant community in São Paulo, as evidenced by the fact that the majority of Matarazzo's employees were Italians or Italo-descendents, and that his relationship with the workers was essentially based on shared feelings of ethnic-based solidarity (Hall, 1989).

4. CONCLUSION

The joint examination of the dual phenomenon of immigration and entrepreneurship in the city of São Paulo, presented in this study, provides some elements for the understanding of the broader perspective of immigrant assimilation into that region. On the one hand, it offers one of many alternative explanations for the city's history of population growth and economic development. On the other, the dual perspective is an important element in explaining the reasons for the economic success of some of the ethnic groups in their entrepreneurial initiatives in specific sectors of activity.

A number of common elements to the Syrian/Lebanese, Armenian, and Korean immigrant communities in São Paulo emerge from the brief comments presented in earlier sections. First, the agglomeration itself of the groups in the urban space of the city had a direct connection with the preservation of community spirit; a symbolic reproduction of the links (not necessarily strong or even real), of cultural and identity-protection natures, the group had in the country or region of origin. All of these groups created their own urban *territories*: the *Bom Retiro* district as a reference to the Korean community (and before them the Jewish community), the *25 de Março* street to the Syrian/Lebanese, and *Tiradentes* avenue to the Armenians.

Second, the importance of religious associations and charities not only for the maintenance of community-identity links, but also as critical elements to support the business projects of immigrant entrepreneurs (e.g., the *kye* developed by the Korean group). These mechanisms had a direct impact on the creation of the proper level of social capital to assist the emerging entrepreneurial initiatives. Acting jointly with the natural sociability derived from the physical agglomeration, those institutions in turn strengthened the links and the communication channels available to the community. The associations and charities connected to the groups' churches also facilitated the creation of mechanisms that were critically important in the assistance to the new arrivals and to their integration. Religious communities have been said to be capable of promoting common interests of their members, functioning as a space for social interaction, discussion, and contact (Martes & Rodriguez, 2004). These exchange opportunities create awareness of community problems, mobilize members' collective initiatives, and have been found to increase trust and solidarity (Warner, 1993, 1997). As a result, religious groups can provide their members not only with such 'solidary resources,' but also with 'collective resources' that arise from unified political representation (Lane & Bachmann, 1997).

The third common element – although stronger in some groups than in others – was the practice of endogamy that facilitated not only the preservation of the culture's ancestral features, but also provided a cost-effective workforce to assist in the economic improvement of the family unit. The Koreans are once again a good example of this trend. In the case of other ethnicities, especially of the relatively less numerous Armenians, the endogamy served both as a mechanism of group aggregation and reproduction.

Finally, the division of labor within the communities, which legitimized the hierarchical structure of the group but that also provided a shelter for the assimilation of new arrivals into its functional specialization. Financing instruments such as the rotating credit associations, essentially based on the *enforceable trust* source of social capital, were critical elements assisting entrepreneurial initiatives in the usually difficult initial years.

The case of the Spanish immigration, as mentioned earlier, served in a sense as a counter-example to the trends identified in the other groups. The brief examination of the assimilation of this group into the host society indicated that the four common elements identified here were not present. While a more detailed historical and sociological analysis would be needed to identify the reasons for the dissimilar path followed by these immigrants, these elements can be seen as a preliminary explanation for the paradox: the fact that the third largest immigrant group in the history of Brazil did not imprint the host society with the same marks of other, smaller groups.

In conclusion, this paper examined the phenomenon of immigrant entrepreneurship in São Paulo, Brazil, and its role in that region's economic development. We hope to have contributed to broader analyses of the impacts of entrepreneurial initiatives to the development of regions with higher levels of risk derived from under-developed or emergent institutional infrastructures. However, an important issue not in the scope of the present work was the examination of the interactions between the effects of national culture of the four immigrant groups and the characteristics of the institutional environment of the host society. It is known that national cultural characteristics can impact entrepreneurial behavior, as shown by the differences in rates of entrepreneurship among immigrants from different cultures that were operating in the same environment (Waldinger et al., 1990). A long tradition of studies about the nature of institutions and their impact on society (e.g., North, 1990; Scott, 1995), as well as more recent empirical analyses (e.g., Tan, 2002), also indicate that there are differences in rates of entrepreneurship among groups of individuals from the same national culture operating in different national institutional environments. In any case, more efforts seem warranted to unravel the effects of these various sets of factors on immigrant entrepreneurship and regional economic development.

NOTES

1. It is important to mention that the social sciences literature treats mass movements such as immigration not as context-free choices of individual immigrants, but as collective events determined by economic and political factors. The work of sociologist Sayad (1999), for example, is a good example of this perspective.

2. Mainly from Spain and Portugal, but in the case of Brazil more from Portugal, the country's colonial power until 1822.

3. There is a significant body of research on the immigration movements to the state of São Paulo. This phenomenon has been investigated extensively in the social sciences, with significant contributions from the history, sociology, demography, and economic literatures. While it is not in the scope of this study to summarize the main works in each field, we would like to refer researchers interested in a more detailed examination of this topic to Fausto (1991).

4. Between 1887 and 1900, almost one million immigrants arrived in the state (Paiva, 2000).

5. In the 1920 census, approximately 6,000 Syrian/Lebanese were living in São Paulo. A significant number had settled in the capital, in an area north of the *Se* and south of the *Santa Ifigenia* districts, forming roughly a triangle with sides defined by the *25 de Marco* and *Cantareira* streets, and by the *Estado* avenue (Truzzi, 1991).

6. Both Syrian and Lebanese arrived in Brazil with Turkish passports, as their countries were under control of the Turkish–Ottoman Empire. The use of the common name 'Turkish' to describe the Syrian and the Lebanese has always been a source of annoyance to members of these communities.

7. According to Trento (1988), 56 percent of all immigration to Brazil arrived or settled in the state of São Paulo.

8. A recent study by Couto (2004b) indicates that Francesco Matarazzo's net worth at the time of his death in 1937 was, in current prices, approximately $20 billion.

320   JOSÉ RENATO DE CAMPOS ARAÚJO ET AL.

REFERENCES

Araújo, J. (2000). *Imigração e Futebol: O Caso Palestra Itália*. São Paulo, Brazil: Fapesp/ Editora Sumaré.
Araújo, J. (2003). *Migna Terra: Migrantes Italianos e Fascismo na cidade de São Paulo (1922/1935)*. Unpublished doctoral dissertation. Programa de Doutorado em Ciências Sociais, Instituto de Filosofia e Ciências Humanas, Universidade Estadual de Campinas (UNICAMP), Campinas, Brazil.
Baker, T., Gedajlovic, E., & Lubatkin, M. (2005). A framework for comparing entrepreneurship processes across nations. *Journal of International Business Studies, 36*(5), 492–504.
Baron, R., & Markman, G. (2003). Beyond social capital: The role of entrepreneurs' social competence in their financial success. *Journal of Business Venturing, 18*, 41–60.
Bolino, M., Turnley, W., & Bloodgood, J. (2002). Citizenship behavior and the creation of social capital. *Academy of Management Review, 27*(4), 505–522.
Bonacich, E., & Modell, J. (1980). *The economic basis of ethnic solidarity*. Los Angeles: University of California Press.
Bourdieu, P. (1985). The forms of capital. In: J. G. Richardson (Ed.), *Handbook of theory and research for the sociology of education* (pp. 241–258). New York: Greenwood.
Burt, R. (1992). *Structural holes: The social structure of competition*. Cambridge, MA: Harvard University Press.
Cano, W. (Ed.) (1983). *Raízes da Concentração Industrial em São Paulo*. São Paulo, Brazil: Editora T. A. Queiroz.
Coleman, J. (1988). Social capital and the common good. *American Journal of Sociology, 94*(Suppl.), S95–S120.
Coleman, J. (1990). *The foundations of social theory*. Cambridge, MA: Harvard University Press.
Couto, R. (Ed.) (2004). *Matarazzo. Colosso Brasileiro*. São Paulo, Brazil: Editora Planeta.
Dean, W. (1971). *A Industrialização de São Paulo*. São Paulo, Brazil: DIFEL.
Fausto, B. (1991). *Historiografia da Imigração para São Paulo*. São Paulo, Brazil: FAPESP/ Editora Sumaré.
Freitas, S. (2004). Brasil. Corea en el barrio de Bom Retiro. In: Banco Interamericano de Desarollo, *Cuando Oriente llegó a América. Contribuciones de Inmigrantes Chinos, Japoneses y Coreanos*. Washington, DC: BID.
Fukuyama, F. (1995). *Trust: The social virtues and the creation of prosperity*. New York: Free Press.
Fukuyama, F. (2001). Social capital, civil society and development. *Third World Quarterly, 22*(1), 7–20.
Greene, P. (1997). A resource-based approach to ethnic business sponsorship: A consideration of Ismaili-Pakistani immigrants. *Journal of Small Business Management, 35*(4), 58–71.
Grun, R. (1992). *Negócios & Famílias: Armênios em São Paulo*. Série Imigração (Vol. 3). São Paulo, Brazil: FAPESP/Editora Sumaré.
Hall, M. (1989). *Trabalhadores Immigrantes*. Série Trabalhadores. Campinas, Brazil: Secretaria de Cultura, Esporte e Turismo de Campinas.
Halter, M. (1995). Introduction – Boston's immigrants revisited: The economic culture of ethnic enterprise. In: M. Halter (Ed.), *New migrants in the marketplace: Boston's ethnic entrepreneurs* (pp. 1–22). Amherst, MA: University of Massachusetts Press.

Klein, H. (1994). *A Imigração Espanhola no Brasil*. Série Imigração (Vol. 5). São Paulo, Brazil: FAPESP/Editora Sumaré.

Lane, C., & Bachmann, R. (1997). Co-operation in inter-firm relations in Britain and Germany: The role of social institutions. *British Journal of Sociology*, *48*(2), 226–254.

Levy, M. (1974). O Papel da Migração Internacional na Evolução da População Brasileira (1872–1972). *Revista de Saúde Pública*, *8*(suplemento), 49–90.

Light, I. (1972). *Ethnic enterprise in America: Business and welfare among Chinese, Japanese, and Blacks*. Berkeley, CA: University of California Press.

Light, I. (1998). Immigrant entrepreneurs in America. In: D. Jacobson (Ed.), *The Immigration reader – America in a multidisciplinary perspective*. Malden, MA: Blackwell.

Light, I., & Bonacich, E. (1988). *Immigrant entrepreneurs*. Berkeley, CA: University of California Press.

Light, I., & Gold, S. (2000). *Ethnic economies*. San Diego, CA: Academic Press.

Martes, A. (2000). *Brasileiros nos Estados Unidos – Um Estudo sobre Imigrantes em Massachussets*. São Paulo, Brazil: Editôra Paz e Terra.

Martes, A., & Rodriguez, C. (2004). Afiliação Religiosa e Empreendedorismo Etnico: O Caso dos Brasileiros nos EUA. *RAC – Revista Brasileira de Administração Contemporanea*, *8*(3), 117–141.

Martins, J. (1973). *Conde Matarazzo. O Empresário e a Empresa*. São Paulo, Brazil: HUCITEC.

Martins, J. (1981). Empresários e Trabalhadores de Origem Italiana no Desenvolvimento Industrial Brasileiro, Entre 1880 e 1914: O Caso de São Paulo. *Dados*, *2*(24), 237–264.

Nahapiet, J., & Ghoshal, S. (1998). Social capital, intellectual capital, and the organizational advantage. *Academy of Management Review*, *23*(2), 242–266.

North, D. (1990). *Institutions, institutional change, and economic performance*. New York, NY: Norton.

Paiva, O. (2000). *Breve História da Hospedaria de Imigrantes e da Imigração para São Paulo*. São Paulo, Brazil: Memorial do Imigrante/ Museu da Imigração.

Pereira, L. (1972). *Empresários e Administradores no Brasil*. São Paulo, Brazil: Brasiliense.

Podolny, J., & Baron, J. (1997). Relationships and resources: Social networks and mobility in the workplace. *American Sociological Review*, *62*, 673–693.

Portes, A. (1987). The social origins of the Cuban enclave economy in Miami. *Sociological Perspectives*, *30*, 340–372.

Portes, A. (1998). Social capital: Its origins and applications in modern sociology. *Annual Review of Sociology*, *24*, 1–24.

Portes, A., & Landolt, P. (2000). Social capital: Promise and pitfalls of its role in development. *Journal of Latin American Studies*, *32*, 529–547.

Portes, A., & Rumbaut, R. (1990). *Immigrant America: A portrait*. Berkeley, CA: University of California Press.

Portes, A., & Sensenbrenner, J. (1993). Embeddedness and immigration: Notes on the social determinants of economic action. *American Journal of Sociology*, *98*(6), 1320–1350.

Putnam, R. (with Leonardi, R., & Nanetti, R.). (1993). *Making democracy work: Civic traditions in modern Italy*. Princeton, NJ: Princeton University Press.

Santos, C. (1998). *Nem tudo era italiano. São Paulo e pobreza (1890–1915)*. São Paulo, Brazil: Annablume/FAPESP.

Sayad, A. (1999). *A Imigração ou os Paradoxos da Alteridade*. São Paulo, Brazil: EDUSP.

Schumpeter, J. (1934). *The theory of economic development: An inquiry into profits, capital, interest, and the business cycle*. Harvard, MA: Harvard University Press.

Scott, W. (1995). *Institutions and organizations.* Thousand Oaks, CA: Sage.

Seibert, S., Kraimer, M., & Liden, R. (2001). A social capital theory of career success. *Academy of Management Journal, 44*(2), 219–237.

Shane, S., & Cable, D. (2000). Network ties, reputation, and the financing of new ventures. *Management Science, 48*(3), 364–381.

Shane, S., & Stuart, T. (2002). Organizational endowments and the performance of university start-ups. *Management Science, 48*(1), 154–170.

Shane, S., & Venkataraman, S. (2000). The promise of entrepreneurship as a field of research. *Academy of Management Review, 25*(1), 217–226.

Tan, J. (2002). Culture, nation, and entrepreneurial strategic orientations: Implications for an emerging economy. *Entrepreneurship Theory and Practice, 26*(4), 95–111.

Trento, A. (1988). *Do Outro Lado do Atlântico.* São Paulo, Brazil: Nobel/Instituto de Cultura de San Paolo/Instituto Cultural Ítalo-Brasileiro.

Truzzi, O. (1991). *De Mascates a Doutores: sírios e libaneses em São Paulo.* Série Imigração (Vol. 2). São Paulo, Brazil: FAPESP/Editora Sumaré; Brasília, DF: CNPq.

Tsai, W., & Ghoshal, S. (1998). Social capital and value creation: The role of intrafirm networks. *Academy of Management Journal, 41*(4), 464–476.

Waldinger, R., Aldrich, H., & Ward, R. (1990). *Ethnic entrepreneurs: Immigrant business in industrial societies.* Newbury Park, CA: Sage.

Walker, G., Kogut, B., & Shan, W. (1997). Social capital, structural holes and the formation of an industry network. *Organization Science, 8*(2), 109–125.

Warner, R. (1993). Work in progress toward a new paradigm for the sociological study of religion in the United States. *American Journal of Sociology, 98,* 1044–1093.

Warner, R. (1997). Religion, boundaries, and bridges. *Sociology of Religion, 58*(3), 217–238.

Williamson, O. (1975). *Markets and hierarchies.* New York: Free Press.

Wilson, K., & Portes, A. (1980). Immigrant enclaves: An analysis of the labor market experiences of Cubans in Miami. *American Journal of Sociology, 86,* 305–319.

Woolcock, M. (1998). Social capital and economic development: Toward a theoretical synthesis and policy framework. *Theory and Society, 27,* 151–208.

PART VII:
ENTREPRENEURSHIP AND
BUILDING HUMAN CAPITAL

ACQUIRING THE SKILLS AND LEGITIMACY TO BETTER MANAGE LOCAL ECONOMIC DEVELOPMENT: THE CASE OF JALISCO, MEXICO ✩

Nichola Lowe

1. INTRODUCTION

During the past decade, sub-national government agencies in the late industrialized nations have taken on greater responsibilities in the area of economic and industrial planning. This has been especially true in Mexico where fiscal and planning decentralization, shifting local politics, the recent entry into the North American Free Trade Agreement (1995), the peso crisis and resulting job-loss (1995–1997) and the latest wave of investment opportunities (in part an outgrowth of NAFTA) have, to varying degrees,

✩ Funding for this research was provided by the World Bank as part of a larger study on the decentralization of industrial promotion and the Inter-American Foundation. I am grateful to Michael Piore, Paul Osterman, and Guillermo Woo for their insightful comments and suggestions. I also wish to thank the participants of the 2nd annual Alfred P. Sloan globalization workshop for junior scholars and the MIT's BNB group for their input during an earlier iteration of this research.

Developmental Entrepreneurship: Adversity, Risk, and Isolation
International Research in the Business Disciplines, Volume 5, 325–354
ISSN: 1074-7877/doi:10.1016/S1074-7877(06)05017-3

facilitated greater intervention in the local economy by state-level planning and development authorities. Since the mid-1990s most state governments in Mexico have substantially increased the number of staff and working budgets of their economic development ministries.

However, expanded bureaucracies and budgets alone cannot prepare state governments for the arduous and complex task of managing industrial growth and development. In addition to making important choices about which tools to use in order to encourage new investment and upgrade existing industries, state planners in Mexico also grapple with the following concerns: how to effectively disperse information about available resources and support services to their local constituency; how to allocate and reallocate resources in ways that are most effective for both short-and long-term development; how to gain the trust of business owners and leaders that have long viewed local government as dormant, ineffective or worse, corrupt; how to convince constituent firms to willingly accept government support, advice and financial assistance; and finally, how to regulate and monitor subsidized firms.

2. ECONOMIC DEVELOPMENT AS SKILL BUILDING

The complex nature of the exercise, both in terms of the high number of tasks involved and the diverse paths available for identifying and completing such tasks, is often overlooked by scholars of contemporary economic development. Instead the current trend includes viewing economic development, especially at a sub-national level, as a simple choice between two distinct tasks and related strategies. Do local authorities take advantage of the latest flows of foreign-capital and seek to lure large-scale foreign-owned and managed operations to their state, what in Mexico is commonly referred to as the "*Maquila* model" (Bair & Gerreffi, 1998, 1999; Buitelaar & Padilla Pérez, 2000)? Or, do they focus their energies on building new industries from the ground-up and supporting pre-existing industries and firms through technical support services, marketing-assistance, employee training programs, technology transfer agreements and subsidized credit, the "entrepreneurial model" (Piore et al., 2001)?

According to this framework, state and local authorities pursuing the Maquila model, use most of their resources, financial and bureaucratic, to attract large, mobile foreign-owned, and export-oriented firms in mature industries, such as garments, especially denim products, textiles, chemicals, consumer electronics, autoparts, and computer and peripheral-assembly. It is often argued that economic developers employing this strategy are most concerned with immediate job-creation and export promotion (Eisinger, 1988; Buitellaar et al., 2000). In achieving this end, developers use a variety of fiscal incentives, including tax breaks and cash subsidies to compensate firms for their start-up training and infrastructure costs.

In contrast, state developers using an entrepreneurial approach are more interested in generating new capital through the creation of new businesses and efforts to upgrade micro and small-sized businesses. Here, "government's role is to help identify investment opportunities that the private sector may either have overlooked or be reluctant to pursue, including opportunities in new markets, new products and new industries" (Eisinger, 1988, p. 12). This is achieved through business development services and state-managed training programs that focus on supply chain management, increased local sourcing, production upgrading, skill retention and technology acquisition.

Although normatively speaking, the entrepreneurial strategy is favored by development analysts and evaluators, it is often believed that state governments (in both industrialized and less industrialized nations) when given a choice, will prioritize recruitment or luring over entrepreneurial activities. Drawing on conventional theories of political behavior and decision-making in which governors and their appointed staff seek to maximize future votes, it is argued that "given its apparent, immediate gratification and the possibilities for dramatic credit-claiming, capturing a footloose firm is far more satisfying politically than waiting for slower and riskier entrepreneurial programs to mature" (Eisinger, 1995, p. 155). Recruiting outside firms or what is commonly referred to as "supply side" economic development policy is therefore considered "a symbolic act for public consumption than for its economic effect ... Local politicians need to show that they are hustling business for their community" (Gilbert, 1995, p. 17; See also, Bartik, 1991; Schweke, Rist, & Dabson, 1994; Lynch, 1996; Buchholz, 1998).

While this analytical frame has considerable predictive power and helps fuel continued (and, at times, much needed) policy debate, its reliance on simplistic behavioral models and theories obscures the complex learning processes and real constraints faced by state governments as they tinker and experiment with and vary their "strategies of action" in the face of shifting national and international economic pressures (Barzelay, 1991; Sabel, 1994; Tendler, 1997; Lowe, 1999a, b; Perez-Aleman, 2000). More importantly, by separating out activities and tasks and placing normative values on them independent of their function within a broader sub-national policy regime, scholars of economic development tend to ignore dynamic (and often surprising) interactions between activities and models, as well as the important lessons and skills that state governments derive from them. Rather than ask why state governments continue to lure mobile capital when entrepreneurial-related tasks appear to have greater long-term development potential, we should be concerned with addressing the follow questions: *How do state governments acquire the skills and legitimacy needed to better manage the economic and industrial adjustment and growth of their region? What historical legacies and relationships can local authorities build on and further develop in order to help them hone these skills and design more "inclusive" development strategies? What events and actions trigger policy innovation and reform in the area of economic development?*

These questions emerge from and are informed by an extended case study of economic development planning in Jalisco, Mexico. The evidence presented in this paper draws on (a) 130 semi-structured interviews conducted by the author between June 1999 and July 2000 with business leaders, firm owners, government officials, and business consultants from the state of Jalisco and (b) a review of government documents, periodicals and other secondary sources. Interviews were also conducted with state developers and business leaders from the Western-central states of Michoacan and Guanajuato. The statistics used throughout this paper were compiled by the author using data provided by state-level business associations and Jalisco's Secretary of Economic Development and Promotion, SEPROE.

Since 1995, state-level economic developers in Jalisco have significantly altered their approach to development planning in ways that have enabled smaller firms in the state's traditional industries to have greater access to much-needed support services, training programs, and other public resources, both financial and bureaucratic. This assistance comes at a critical juncture as many of these industries face considerable competition resulting from tariff reductions on Asian-made imports. This new planning style represents a major departure from earlier administrations (spanning almost 50 years) in which state-level, public-sector authorities in Jalisco earmarked a substantial share of federal and state resources for those activities (e.g., cash giveaways, tax breaks, and subsidized training and infrastructure) that promoted large-scale investment in and recruitment of more capital-intensive industries, such as chemicals, textiles and, more recently, electronics.

While many local analysts, including high-level officials within the state government, see this shift as an expected outcome of the state's changing political leadership and the new administration's initial awareness of the benefits of entrepreneurial rather than recruitment-based activities, closer analysis reveals a much more complex, discursive and negotiated process of reform. After presenting more details on the scope and scale of this planning reform, I will examine the factors that helped to facilitate and inspire this shift in development praxis and that have enabled the state government in Jalisco to acquire the skills and legitimacy needed to both identify and follow out their desired and shifting goals.

3. TRADITIONAL SECTOR SUPPORT IN JALISCO: PROGRAM DEVELOPMENT AND DESIGN

Jalisco's industrial profile and growth trajectory is quite different to that found in other industrialized states in Mexico (see Table 1). Starting in the late 1920s, the State's industrial development, particularly in Guadalajara, the state's densely populated urban capital, was fueled primarily by the growth of firms in labor-intensive, traditional industries, such as footwear, garments, metal-mechanics, furniture, jewelry and artisan goods (Arias, 1983; Arias, 1992; Zamora, Diester, de Leon Arias, & Alejandre, 1988). In contrast to other states which have tended to specialize in one or two of these traditional, labor-intensive industries, total production and employment in these industries is more evenly balanced in Jalisco (see Tables 2 and 3). In most of these industries, Jalisco ranks second through fourth in the nation in total annual output (value in pesos) (see Tables 4 and 5). Most of the firms in these industries are 100 percent locally owned and operated. The state has few traditional sector maquila or export-processing assembly operations (e.g., garments).

A second distinction relates to the state's large share of micro and small-sized manufacturing establishments. In 1996, Mexico City, Mexico State,

Table 1. Total Industrial Output in Millions of Pesos.

State/Region	Gross Output in 1996 (1996 Pesos)
Mexico city	98
Mexico state	81
Nuevo Leon	43
Jalisco	35
Coahuila	27
Veracruz	23
Chihuahua	21

Source: INEGI. Producto Interno Bruto 1999.

Table 2. Traditional Industries in Jalisco (1998 Figures).

Industry	No. of Firms or Workshops	No. of Employees (Formal)
Artisan goods	3,315	NA
Graphic design	1,500	12,750
Shoes	1,063	20,000
Garments and textiles	1,436	27,000
Jewelry	800	9,300
Furniture	1,405	10,600
Total	9,519	79,650*

Source: Seijal.
*90,000 if we include estimates on total employment in the artisan goods industry.

Table 3. Jalisco's Industrial Sector Employment and Registered Owners by Industry, October 1998.

Sector	Employment	Registered Owners
Machinery & equipment	70,732	2,887
Food processing	68,227	2,854
Plastics & rubber	26,216	662
Shoes & leather	21,123	1,156
Apparel	20,398	1,283
Chemical	18,197	432
Furniture & wood	16,465	1,389
Minerals & metals	14,900	779
Textiles	9,840	265
Publishing & graphic design	7,815	796
Construction	6,689	168
Paper products	4,714	91
Petrochemical	1,011	17
Other industries	12,519	607
Total	298,846	13,386

Source: Seijal, IMSS.

and Nuevo Leon – the top three regions in the country in terms of total industrial output – had a greater share of large-sized, modern capital-intensive establishments and traditional sector firms when compared to Jalisco (ranked fourth in total industrial output) (Arias, 1983; Pozas, 1993; Spener & Pozos, 1996; Alba Vega, 1998). In Coahuila, Veracruz, and Chihuahua – fifth, sixth and seventh, respectively, in total manufacturing output – industrial jobs are mostly concentrated in medium and large-sized

Table 4. National Shoe Production, by State.

State	Value of Production (1993) %	No. of Firms (1997) %	Employment (1997) %	Specialty
Guanajuato	36.8	49.4	51.3	Men, Child
Jalisco	24.1	19.4	16.2	Women
DF	19.5	8.1	4.8	Men
Mexico state	7.7	5.4	5.6	Men
Nuevo Leon	3.1	2.4	3.6	Men, Child
Subtotal	91.2	84.7	81.5	
Others	8.9	15.3	18.5	

Source: Grupo Financiero Bancomer. Economic Report. June–July 1998. p. 53. Using data from INEGI. Column 4, UNAM study

Table 5. National Apparel Production, by State.

State	Share of Total Value (1995)[1]
Mexico city	48
Mexico state	12
Puebla	5
Jalisco	4
Guanajuato	3
Others	28

Source: Seijal, 1995.
[1]Total national apparel employment was 712,523 in 1998, Jalisco accounted for 4.2% of total employment and 7.02% of national production.

maquila plants. The exception is Veracruz, which depends heavily on petroleum-related industrial operations. The historical presence of small-sized establishments in Jalisco's capital city, Guadalajara, has earned it the nickname "the big city of small industry" (Arias, 1983). In the late 1980s, formal sector, small-sized businesses accounted for over 90 percent of all manufacturing operations in the city (Spener & Pozos, 1996).

The contemporary industrial policy regime of the state government reflects this industrial structure. SEPROE channels a considerable share of its financial (approximately 65 percent of the agency's annual budget) and bureaucratic resources to programs and policy innovations that target micro-, small- and medium-sized businesses in the state's core traditional industries, including footwear, garments, metal-mechanics, furniture, artisan goods, graphic arts, and jewelry. SEPROE's professional core and top-level management consider traditional sector firms to be a key industrial asset and resource for the state. They often justify program and policy interventions in terms of the state's long-term industrial competitiveness and capital (and skill) formation. Small firms in traditional sectors not only provide much needed jobs for the state (35–40% of all manufacturing jobs, depending on estimates), but are expected to (a) improve the quality of local jobs as they build on and further develop a rich and locally rooted skill base and (b) expose the state to (and localize) higher-value added processes and support services with the development of their own design capacity and the implementation of new technologies and manufacturing systems. State economic developers in Jalisco are also aware of the vulnerability of firms in these industries. Focused and well-designed interventions are seen as a means to stabilize these industries, as well as increase chances of firm survivability.

SEPROE's dedication to small-firm, traditional-sector upgrading is best represented through its direct involvement in four interconnected technical support and business training programs. These programs are designed, administered, and financed by SEPROE (using state and federal funds), the state's sectoral trade associations (see Table 6) and, in the case of the Agrupamiento Empresarial and FOJAL, the state's main Jesuit University, ITESO. The largest program in terms of allocated public resources, both financial and bureaucratic (e.g., number of staff and personnel assigned to this program) is the *Agrupamiento Empresarial* or AGREM program. AGREM is a "group consulting" program that facilitates joint problem solving among local manufacturers and suppliers through a mix of classroom training, factory visits and group critiques. Each AGREM consists of 15 to 25 micro-, small- and medium-sized firms, runs for approximately six months and is financed through state and federal grants and fees collected from participating firms. Government approved consultants run the programs with the administrative guidance and institutional support of the sectoral trade associations. Officials from SEPROE are responsible for determining program costs (see Table 7), negotiating the fees paid by participating firms, lobbying state and federal authorities for additional program funding, promoting the program to other industries and evaluating the program's progress. They also act as the key intermediary between the business consultants (trainers) and associations (participating firms).

Eight AGREMs have been initiated in four industries, footwear, garments, metal-mechanics and artisan goods, since 1997 (see Tables 7 and 8). SEPROE and local trade associations have also partnered to create CEJALDI, a multi-industry design center that opened last year in order

Table 6. Key Sectoral Business Associations in Jalisco.

Name	Industry	Year Established	Independent or Regional Office of National Organization
Camara de la industria Del Calzado de Jalisco	Footwear	1940s	Independent
Camara regional de la industria de Transformacion del Estado de Jalisco	Industries not represented by other chambers	1940s	Independent
Camara de la industria Alimenticia de Jalisco	Food processing	1940s	Independent
Camara textil de occidente	Textiles	1960s	Regional
Camara nacional de la industria del Vestido Delegacion Jalisco	Apparel	1960s	Regional
Camara regional de la industria de Joyeria y Plateria del Estado de Jalisco	Jewelry	1968	Independent
Consejo de Camaras industriales (before 1979, known as Junta de presidentes de las Camaras industriales)	Federation of all industrial business associations in Jalisco	1965/1979 (formal)	Independent
Asociacion de fabricantes de Muebles de Jalisco and Camara de Fabricantes de Muebles de Jalisco	Furniture	1979/1999	Independent
Camara nacional de las Artes Graficas delegacion Jalisco	Graphic arts and design	NA	Regional
Camara regional de La industria de Curtiduria	Leather goods/ tannery	NA	Independent
Camara nacional de Comercio, Tlaquepaque and Tonola delegacion (artisan division)	Artisan goods	NA	Regional
Camara nacional de la industria electronica y de telecomunicaciones e informatica delegacion Regional Occidente	Electronics	1991	Regional

Source: Camara de la Industria del Calzado del Estado de Jalisco, Camara Nacional de la Industria del Vestido Delegacion Jalisco and SEPROE.

to provide manufacturers and designers in Jalisco with the skills, resources and technology needed to develop a *linea propia*, or contemporary regional style or "look." CEJALDI's mission is to help smaller firms realize the full design potential embodied in their existing machinery and equipment.

Table 7.   Agrupamiento Empresarial Program Costs (6 Months, US Dollars).

	Shoe Industry[1]	Garment Industry[2]
SEPROE-state government	21,055	2,631.5
CIMO-federal government	15,790	2,631.5
Participants share	26,315	2,631.5
ITESO	0	2,631.5
Total program costs	63,160	10,526
Total program costs, per firm	2,526	877

Source: Camara de la Industria del Calzado del Estado de Jalisco and Camara Nacional de la Industria del Vestido Delegacion Jalisco.

[1]Costs for 25 participants. Includes cost of international trip to observe production processes overseas.

[2]Based on costs for the first garment Agrupamiento, with 12 participants. Costs are significantly lower for the garment industry agrupamientos as ITESO provides much of the services and overhead costs free of charge in addition to covering 25% of direct costs.

Table 8.   Overview of the Agrupamiento Program, Shoe and Garment Industry.

	Industry	Date Started	No. of Firms	Core Focus	Administrators
Group 1	Footwear	March-1998	22	Marketing	Chamber/ IPADEM/ ITESO
Group 2	Footwear	December-1998	16	supply chain management	Chamber/ IPADEM
Group 3	Footwear	June-1999	25	Labor force development	Chamber/ IPADEM
Group 4	Garment	October-1998	12	Marketing	Chamber/ITESO
Group 5	Garment	May-1999	18	Supply chain management	Chamber/ITESO
Group 6	Metalmechanics	December-1999	16	Marketing	Chamber/ITESO
Group 7	Garment	June-2000	15	Marketing collective	Chamber/ITESO
Group 8	Artisan goods	May-2000	14	Marketing/ quality control	Artisan institute/ ITESO

Source: Camara de la Industria del Calzado del Estado de Jalisco, Camara Nacional de la Industria del Vestido Delegacion Jalisco, IPADEM (private business consultant) and ITESO.

Design studies have been completed in the region's footwear, garments and artisan goods industries.

SEPROE's Division of Trade and Commerce (JALTRADE) has worked with officials from traditional sector business associations in order to facilitate the development of export alliances and marketing collectives. Two collectives, one in footwear and one in garments, have been created in order to expose medium-, small- and micro-sized firms to more demanding consumer markets and buyers in the United States and, eventually, in Europe. Finally, in recent years, SEPROE has contributed money and personnel to the garment industries *Camino de Vestido-*, a week long, promotional campaign that takes prospective investors, manufacturers, and suppliers to existing industrial complexes and small-firm clusters located outside of the metropolitan zone. By endorsing this project, public authorities hope to inspire other industries that currently face severe labor shortages (e.g., shoe and furniture manufacturers) to consider locating certain production processes in less urbanized regions of the state. In addition to these more formal efforts, SEPROE has offered assistance with local trade shows, international trade missions and industry-specific vocational training centers. The agency has also administered low-interest loans to small-sized, pre-existing firms using money allocated to them through federal temporary employment and job-creation programs, such as FOJAL and GEMICRO.

Early evaluations of the AGREM program show considerable, post-program improvements in the area of product design, international marketing, logistics and supply chain management (see Tables 9 and 10). Anecdotal evidence suggests that as a result of this program, participating firms are also learning how to identify, locate and apply new and appropriate technologies, improve work conditions in order to attract and retain semi-skilled and skilled employees, and collaborate with new and existing suppliers and partner firms on process and product improvements. A significant share of participating firms in the first three AGREMs have been able to draw on the

Table 9. Agrupamiento Empresarial Program Post-Group Evaluation, Summary Statistics, Group 1, Shoe Industry.

	Pre-Group	Post-Group	Total Change (%)
Installed capacity	83,750	89,790	7.2
Actual production	49,665	56,550	13.9
Total utilized capacity (%)	59	63	

Source: Instituto Para la Alta Direccion de Empresas. Resultados E Informacion Relevante del Pimer Programa de Agrupaminento Empresariel de la Industria del Calzado, September 1998.

Table 10. Agrupamiento Empresarial Program Post-Group Evaluation, Various Indicators, Group 1, Shoe Industry (Six Month Period).

Participant (Asterisk Indicates Firm that Exports[1])	Starting Employment (Asterisk Indicates a Post-Group Increase in Employment)	Starting Productivity (Pairs Per Person Per Day)	Ending Productivity (Pairs Per Person Per Day)	Percentage Change (Values in Bold Indicate Increase)	Order to Delivery Time, No. of Days, Pre-Group	Order to Delivery Time, No. of Days, Post-Group	Change in Order to Delivery Time, No. of Days
1	59	5.51	4.23	(0.23)	15	15	0
2	145*	4.83	6.4	**0.33**	30	17	−13
3	52*	6.73	8.00	**0.19**	5	4	−1
4	30*	6.67	6.11	(0.08)	22	8	−14
5	34	7.35	7.35	0.00	5	4	−1
6	180	8.33	8.33	0.00	NA	NA	NA
7*	198	6.06	6.06	0.00	NA	NA	NA
8*	66	5.76	7.30	**0.27**	22	10	−12
9	54	9.26	10.00	**0.08**	20	6	−14
10	40	3.75	7.35	**0.96**	28	21	−7
11	16*	6.25	6.67	**0.07**	30	15	−15
12	37*	9.81	10.00	**0.02**	7	5	−2
13	99	6.06	8.59	**0.42**	40	22	−18
14	27*	5.56	8.73	**0.57**	30	20	−10
15	18	4.44	6.67	**0.5**	22	7	−15
16*	55*	5.45	6.33	**0.16**	20	10	−10
17	23	6.96	7.83	**0.13**	60	30	−30
18	25	10.40	10.48	**0.01**	40	20	−20
19	44	5.45	6.14	**0.13**	60	12	−48
20*	41	36.59	38.05	**0.04**	22	15	−7
21	86*	4.65	4.44	(0.05)	22	9	−13
22	30	8.00	8.00	0.00	NA	NA	NA

Source: Instituto Para la Alta Direccion de Empresas. Resultados E Informacion Relevante del Pimer Programa de Agrupaminento Empresariel de la Industria del Calzado, September 1998.
[1] 4 firms export 5,635 pairs of shoes per week, or 10% of total group production. Firm 7 exports 92% of its total output. Remaining firms export approximately 3% of total production. 92% of the groups exports go to the U.S., 8% to Central and South America.

skills learned during the programs in order to secure a place in higher-end, more quality-conscious segments of the national footwear and clothing market.

JALTRADE's export alliance program has faced more difficulties. The first alliance, a collective of 25 manufacturers and suppliers selling women's shoes under the trademark Andiamo, performed well during its first two years in operation. In one season, Andiamo secured orders for over 35,000 pairs of shoes from top US retailers, including Nordstroms, Bloomingdales and Spiegels. However, due to unresolved disputes, the cooperative's governing board decided to liquidate the corporation in May 2000.

Interestingly, the major source of conflict was over the cooperatives targeted market, the United States. While a handful of participating firms in Andiamo, particularly medium-sized firms with more available working capital, continued to value the US market and see access to it as a key part of their own learning process, a significant share of Andiamo's firms felt vulnerable vis-à-vis large US buyers – e.g., orders and prices are often changed at the last minute; determinants of quality (and thus rejected shipments) were not always clearly specified. Furthermore, smaller sized firms have complained about payment schedules in the United States. Whereas domestic and regional buyers in Latin America guarantee payment in 10–20 business days, Andiamo's average was usually 95 days.

Andiamo's struggles have not gone unnoticed. Under the direction of JALTRADE (and thus, SEPROE), the second alliance known as Cactus West (15 garment firms) has proceeded more cautiously. The initial financial investment required from each firm has been much lower, thereby freeing up working capital for smaller-sized firms. Potential US clients are drawn from a list of buyers that participating firms have prior experience selling to and working with (i.e., Cactus West is in a better bargaining position vis-à-vis its US clients). Finally, project leaders have been more strict in their selection and evaluation criteria of both participating firms and US buyers. In contrast to Andiamo, firms wishing to join Cactus West were not required to have prior export experience – rather during group interviews firms were asked to clearly demonstrate their ability and willingness to work with, listen to and trust other firms. Project leaders, in making the final cut, also looked for shared experiences and characteristics across firms. It is not surprising therefore that many of the short-listed firms have also participated in garment industry AGREMs.

There are key differences between JALTRADE's export alliance program and the AGREM program that might also help explain why the former has faced greater obstacles. The primary concern of AGREM program designers is to first break traditional patterns of interaction between local firms and create a "culture" of trust and collective identity that will last beyond the confines of the AGREM. The formation of formal alliances and collectives, until recently, has been a lower priority item. This is reflected in initial program evaluations which examine individual, rather than collective metrics. In contrast, program administrators of the export alliance program are responsible for creating active, functioning marketing cooperatives or corporations by grouping together small businesses. While the foundations of collective action and cooperation are laid during the AGREM program, foundational cracks and weaknesses only become visible when a formal structure is in place. With time, this division of labor is becoming less pronounced.

Taken together these initiatives and on-going improvements to them reflect considerable forward thinking on the part of Jalisco's state government. This is true not only in terms of the types of industries targeted by SEPROE, but also the institutional arrangements the agency has developed (and strengthened) in order to better define and direct its core industrial policies and practices. Although many of the initiatives described above were first developed by the state's sectoral business associations, SEPROE played a key role in identifying and reinforcing, through public presentations, press releases and continued financial and administrative support, those initiatives that are most representative of a broader set of regional concerns. Through their actions, SEPROE has not only been able to scale-up local training programs by promoting them to other industry associations, but they have also been able to encourage elected officials and administrators of the associations to continuously upgrade and make improvements to their training programs and support services. They have also persuaded the board members of these associations to consider region-wide and multi-industry concerns and constraints, especially those affecting smaller-sized firms, when designing and developing new initiatives.

4. SHIFTING FRAMES AND PRIORITIES

Interestingly, even though Jalisco historically has had a large share of small firms in traditional sectors, the state government and development agency has not always concentrated its energies and resources here. While public-sector assistance at the state level was available to traditional-sector firms during earlier administrations, a greater share of the state's economic development budget, between 1940 and the mid-1990s, was reserved for subsidizing large-sized, export-oriented firms and new investments in more capital-intensive sectors (Arias, 1983; Rabellotti, 1995, 1999; Spener & Pozas, 1996). Resources that were channeled to the state's traditional sectors went disproportionately to larger-sized firms. This bias was often reinforced through SEPROE's day-to-day operations and routines; business owners of larger sized firms were able to secure meetings with higher-ranking bureaucrats and those most active in shaping state level industrial policy; the concerns of smaller firms were typically assigned to lower-ranking bureaucrats and assistants. Assistance that targeted smaller firms in the state's traditional industries – when available during earlier administrations – tended to be classified under the heading of rural industrialization and poverty alleviation or remained the responsibility of federal development authorities and agencies.

How do we explain this recent shift in planning praxis and resource allocation on the part of Jalisco's state government? Why are smaller sized firms in traditional industries now considered a key asset for the state and its future growth and development? Finally, what can development scholars and practitioners take from this case in light of on-going debates about the nature of the state and the institutional determinants of "good governance"?

As with other cases of public-sector reform, especially those deemed a success, it is easy to identify a rich, local narrative in Jalisco that is used to explain and understand these recent events. The shift in planning praxis on the part of SEPROE is typically attributed to the 1995 electoral victory of Alberto Cardenas, then gubernatorial candidate for *Partido Acción Nacional* (PAN). Reversing over 60 years of *Partido Revolucionario Institucional* (PRI) rule at the state level, the PAN and Cardenas claimed victory promising to dismantle PRI-style corporatist structures that disproportionately benefited a handful of large-sized producers in the state. The growing commitment to small firm, traditional sector development and upgrading is considered proof that the PAN is making good on its earlier campaign promises to support small business owners.

As will be discussed in more detail below, the PAN's victory in Jalisco has, without a doubt, helped to shape and redirect the state's contemporary industrial policy regime. However, the conventional narrative and its fixation with changing local politics, overlooks a critical irregularity in state-level politics and industrial policy making in Mexico. Specifically, local analysts, in attributing reform to the PAN and its broader mission to assist small businesses, fail to recognize considerable variation in development policy and practice across PAN-governed states even though each governor entered public life touting the same pro-small-business rhetoric.

In the northern state of Chihuahua, under the direction of the PAN (1992–1997) industrial policies continued to disproportionately target foreign-owned maquilas and a small number of traditional sector firms that have a direct stake in the rapid growth of these firms, including the state's construction-based industrial groups and families (Mizrahi, 1995). Interviews with development practitioners from the state of Guanajuato, where president Vicente Fox governed between 1989 and 2000, suggest that a large share of the state's economic development budget has been used to finance programs that support new investment in capital-intensive industries, particularly chemicals and autoparts. Resources available for the state's historically-rooted shoe industry, the largest traditional sector industry in the state, appear to have disproportionately benefited large- and medium-sized operations even though approximately 90% of all shoe manufacturers in the state are micro- or small-sized.

5. BUSINESS-OWNERS AS BUREAUCRATS

A more compelling argument relates to the PAN's explicit and conscious strategy of turning to and building on pre-existing industrial structures and systems within the state. In contrast to the PRI, the PAN, thus far, has not reserved its top cabinet posts for career politicians, top-ranking party members or those most active in managing the gubernatorial campaign. Instead, top-level bureaucrats and state cabinet secretaries of economic development are normally selected from the surrounding business community. Chosen candidates tend to be active and vocal members of well-established and highly reputable business associations or related organizations. Furthermore, under the direction of PAN-appointed personnel, reforms to the organizational structure of the secretary often reflect and reinforce the dominant industrial structures and representative business organizations in the state.

In Chihuahua, for example, the state's post-1992 Secretary of Economic Development was quick to adopt a structural form similar to that found in the states largest and most vocal business association. A large share of the secretary's professional core had direct links to this association, either as prior board members or high-ranking administrators (Mizrahi, 1995). Similar patterns exist in Guanajuato, where top-level bureaucrats in the state's Secretary of Economic Development are typically drawn from a handful of powerful industrial think tanks and manufacturing technology research centers in the state. In Jalisco, economic development officials from SEPROE have adopted an institutional structure somewhat similar to that used by CCIJ, the state's federation of industrial associations. Similar to CCIJ, in 2001 SEPROE has a single administrative body that determined the broad development policies and goals of the agencies and eight decentralized, thematic or sectoral divisions that were responsible for defining program procedure and protocol.

The strategy of consciously blurring the boundaries between the state and active business community, in part, reflects initial political constraints. The PAN, in an attempt to distinguish itself from the long-ruling PRI, adopted a much stricter membership process – extensive background checks and lengthy waiting periods of up to 5 years were initially the norm and were used to limit the type of inter and intra-party "corruption" often associated with the PRI. This has meant that as a political entity, the PAN had fewer card carrying members to draw from when selecting cabinet officials and top level bureaucrats during early state-level victories, such as those in Guanajuato and Jalisco. Some scholars of Mexican political reform have taken the argument further suggesting that this strategy, given its non-partisan nature, also enabled the PAN to gain much needed, earlier support from PRI-led federal agencies and PRI-affiliated state legislators. Ultimately, this translated into less resistance and struggle in the area of local policy innovation and budgetary discretion (Mizrahi, 1995). The nature of this strategy, insofar as the boundaries between business and the state bureaucracy have become more fluid, suggests the need for a richer and more nuanced understanding of Jalisco's existing business institutions and industrial structures.

The remaining sections of this paper look at the historical and institutional evolution of the state's key business associations, as well as how recent changes to these organizations have affected state–business relations in Jalisco. Close attention is paid to associations that have been most influential in shaping the direction of policies and the type of programs adopted by the state development agency after 1995. However, as will be illustrated below, the state government, while composed of individuals from these associations, is not just an expression or extension of the state's changing business community. Rather, as business owners-turned-government officials, especially those now responding to the needs of smaller-sized firms, SEPROE agents are often forced to grapple with, take on and understand greater bureaucratic challenges than those presented to them by vocal business associations and their constituencies. In turn, they are learning how to become more sophisticated agents of change. Informal links and networks to the local business community (and more recently, to a group of university extension agents and local business consultants) are not only used to shape the direction of policy but also provide government agents with important channels for monitoring, evaluating and influencing the progress and dispersion of the state's business support programs.

6. "SHOW ME THE MONEY": CRISIS, UNEMPLOYMENT AND, EVENTUALLY, LEGISLATIVE LEGITIMACY

Governor Alberto Cardenas entered office at the height of the national banking and fiscal crisis of 1995/1996. Not surprisingly, SEPROE and the state's local economy were in a severe state of shock when Sergio Garcia de Alba took charge of SEPROE in 1995. Official unemployment in Guadalajara, the state's capital city, and its surrounding urban counties was close to 7 percent. In 1994, unemployment in the Guadalajara Metropolitan Zone had been 3.1 percent, slightly higher than the 10-year average. Between December 1994 and 1995, the state lost 51,949 or 8 percent of all manufacturing jobs; the majority of job losses were due to plant closings in the state's traditional industries. Underemployment was an even greater concern. Approximately 3000 or 6 percent of all registered manufacturing establishments, the majority of which were traditional sector firms, closed shop or pulled out of the formal market during this same period.

While SEPROE's directors seemed to be genuinely interested in assisting the state's traditional sector firms, they were limited in what they could do given initial budget constraints, the extent of the crisis and their own lack of experience with development and crisis planning. In 1995, the agency had an annual working budget of less than US$80,000 to cover agency overhead, payroll and supplies. Given the states rising unemployment, SEPROE had little choice but to look to industries that would guarantee immediate and secure jobs. Traditional sector firms, at least those seeking public-sector support during this time, were often more interested in learning how to "reengineer" their plants so as to shed, rather than absorb, local labor. Micro and small-sized operations in the state's traditional industries often fluctuated between informal and formal markets and therefore were either not eligible for or avoided public-sector assistance altogether.

By the end of 1995, SEPROE began to embark on an ambitious campaign of recruiting second tier, original equipment electronics manufacturers and their suppliers from the United States and Asia. In this it had the help of a handful of electronics industry giants already present in the state, including IBM, Motorola and Hewlett Packard, all of which had assembly operations in Jalisco since the late 1970s. Key firms and regions had already been identified and targeted through extensive research done by a group of active business owners in the state, known as the Jalisco Investment Board (JIB). This organization was created, managed and financed by 10 wealthy business owners and investors from the state. Given financial troubles related to the banking crisis, the organization was eventually disbanded in the first months of 1996. SEPROE, however, was able to benefit from the group's prior knowledge and experience by absorbing key administrative personnel into its ranks. Investment missions to the United States and Asia, while attended by top-level officials from SEPROE, were typically financed by the regional electronics association and larger electronics assemblers. Financial incentives offered to new investors in the electronics industry came from state tax breaks, discounts from municipal utilities and the public-works and planning department and federal funds available for employee training. SEPROE's total financial bill was therefore minimal.

Local content rules and other conditions set under the NAFTA in the mid-1990s meant that Mexico, given its lower wages relative to the United States and Canada, was already considered a strategic location for Asian electronics firms and their second and third tier suppliers. Armed with financial incentives and detailed information on logistics and the local labor market, SEPROE helped ensure that Jalisco would benefit from this geographic shift West. In the mid-1990s, the bulk of fiscal incentives granted by SEPROE went to large-sized electronics firms employing upwards of 400 workers.

The figures speak for themselves: between 1994 and 1996, state employment in the electronics industry rose from 12,000 to 29,000, an increase of 134 percent. By 1999, 80,000 workers were employed in this industry, an increase of over 540 percent (see Table 11). Between 1995 and 1997, Jalisco received US$1.6 billion in new investment in this industry. Large original equipment manufacturers, including Flextronics, Jabil Circuit, Nat Steel, SCI Systems, Lucent, and Selectron, opened manufacturing facilities in the state during this period. Between 1994 and 1996, exports of electronic goods from Jalisco rose by 120 percent. During this same period, non-electronics exports rose by less than 10 percent. Unemployment in all manufacturing industries in Guadalajara dropped from a high of 7 percent in 1995 to 4.3 percent in 1996 and 3 percent in 1997. By 2001, the city's unemployment rate, 1.8 percent, was one of the lowest in the nation.

Not surprisingly, due to their aggressive and much publicized luring strategy and resulting job-creation, SEPROE gained much-needed legislative support and recognition. During his first days in office, Governor

Table 11. Electronics Industry, Total Employment, Jalisco.

Year	Employees	% Change	Share of Employment
1994	12,360		
1995	17,250	40	
1996	29,000	68	3.55
1997	50,000	72	5.29
1998	60,000	20	6.03
1999	80,000	33	7.89

Source: CANIETI, SEPROE.

Cardenas had promised the agency greater financial support and autonomy. However, in order to achieve this goal, he first needed to convince state-level congressional representatives of the relative importance of SEPROE, its responsibilities and capabilities. The rapid expansion of the electronics industry, the reduction in the state's unemployment rate and the over-whelming public support of these efforts was proof enough. In 1996, the state legislature substantially increased SEPROE's budget. Using this money, SEPROE was able to hire an additional 50 researchers and tech-nical service experts. The agency's growth has continued throughout the current administration. Between 1995 and 2000 (July), the agency more than doubled its permanent staff, raised employee salaries by over 75 percent, moved into its own 10-store modern glass building that towers high above other government and commercial offices in the area and increased its annual budget to over US$20 million, a 250-fold increase from 1995 (Ocho Columnas 9-15-2000, 1-E; Mural 9-15-2000, 3-A).

7. "SON, STEP RIGHT UP!": TEACHING SMALL BUSINESSES HOW TO ASK FOR AND ACCEPT GOVERNMENT SUPPORT

Although the majority of SEPROE's financial resources between 1995 and 1997 went to recruitment-type activities that disproportionately benefited firms in the electronics industry, the state development agency devoted a considerable amount of time and personnel to developing a long-term stra-tegic plan with the state's traditional industries in mind. The idea for the plan came from the governing board of the state's shoe association, CICEJ. The association got its inspiration from the bi-annual meeting of CONCA-MIN, a national federation of all industrial associations, during which business owners from all parts of Mexico discussed ways to better influence and shape post-Salinas, national industrial policy. Arturo Marcel, a shoe manufacturer in Jalisco, then president of the state's shoe association, the president of CCIJ (the state's federation of industrial associations) and a vice-president of CONCAMIN was present at this meeting.

In 1996, CCIJ formally adopted the idea and created twelve sectoral research commissions. With the institutional backing and support of SEP-ROE and using advisors from the Guadalajara campus of Tec de Mon-terrey, CCIJ completed a detailed six month study of the state's core industries. Each commission, made up of 10 business owners from the sector and directed by a strategic analyst, was responsible for locating, analyzing and compiling sectoral statistics (e.g., changes in number of firms and employees overtime, average industry wage, workforce profile and skills mix, geographic location, local content rates, export history and national and international market focus); identifying key weaknesses in the industry; and recommending possible directions and future markets given national and global industrial trends. The final report and 30 slide presentation, "Vision Jalisco" was made public by officials from SEPROE and CCIJ in the first months of 1997. The findings of this report had a significant influe nce on the types of initiatives adopted by SEPROE between 1997 and 2000.

7.1. The State's Contribution

The dialog between SEPROE and the state's traditional sector associations (and CCIJ, the federation which represents them) has not always been so fluid. Instead, trade associations in Jalisco, like those elsewhere in Mexico, tended to devote most of their time and resources to federal government lobbying. During Mexico's import-substitution-industrialization (ISI) period (1950–1985), associations lobbied the federal government for greater tariff protections. Decisions were often made on an industry-by-industry basis and were renegotiated annually (CITATION). Association presidents and governing board members spent, on average, three days per week in Mexico City. CCIJ, formalized in 1979, helped relieve some of this travel burden; CCIJ coordinators and representatives took turns traveling to Mexico City in order to voice concerns related to a wide array of local and traditional industries. Such patterns continued into the post-ISI period, as traditional sector industries lobbied federal authorities to investigate and respond to charges of unfair trade practices on the part of the Chinese. The shoe, garment and plastics industries were most successful in their efforts.

As secretary of SEPROE, Sergio Garcia de Alba, also a local business owner from the plastics industry, a former president of the local business association CAREINTRA (1990–1992) and former vice president of CCIJ (1993–1994), helped establish a stronger link to the local business associations and create the conditions that would lead to the "co-production" arrangements (i.e., business–state partnering) visible today. Interestingly, Governor Cardenas selected Garcia de Alba based on advice given to him by CCIJ's governing board. At the time, Sergio Garcia de Alba, also a vice president of CONCAMIN, was considered to be one of Jalisco's most vocal and visible critics of President Salinas and his industrial policy record. Once appointed secretary, Garcia de Alba quickly reached out to CCIJ, its member organizations and the wider business community; the presidents of all state trade associations were given the phone number to Garcia de Alba's private line. He maintained an open door policy and met with any business owner and business association representative who stopped by his office, even when unannounced.

Garcia de Alba and his core advisors set up weekly brainstorming meetings with officials from CCIJ and representatives from the state's association of commerce. Key individuals from the state's universities, financial institutions, business consulting firms and related federal agencies were often invited to join in the discussion. Initially, he drew from the ranks of existing business associations in order to staff the agency and select key advisors. Garcia de Alba, like many other business owners active in the state's business associations, had been extremely critical of SEPROE and the state government during earlier administrations. Now as secretary, he and his staff were learning that the credibility of the agency and its developmental record and reach, depended on the agency's local rootedness.

7.2. The Role of the Associations

The associations, and recent changes to their own internal structure, helped to strengthen the link with the state government and SEPROE. These changes also help explain SEPROE's shift in praxis, including recent efforts to target and support smaller sized firms. By 1995, leaders of the state's traditional sector trade associations, especially CAREINTRA and the footwear, metal mechanics, garments and jewelry industry associations had started (or in some cases, were just ending) a process of organizational reform. Between 1988 and 1995, most of the associations represented by CCIJ had lost almost 50 percent of their member firms. In the early 1990s, the state's shoe industry association, for example, had only 280 members or less than 40 percent of all registered footwear establishments – in the late 1980s, membership had fluctuated between 500 and 600 firms. Similar patterns appeared in other traditional sectors in the state.

The drop in association membership in the state can be traced back to the following events: First, a large number of medium-sized businesses in the state's traditional sector were, as a result of their growing debt burden, forced out of their respective industries between 1990 and 1996. Others shed a substantial share of their existing workforce and therefore were reclassified as small-sized. The influx of Chinese-made goods in the late 1980s and the shock of the banking crisis in 1995 only compounded the problem. Imports of cheaply priced Asian goods also motivated a large share of the state's micro-sized and very small firms, many of whom were formally registered in the 1980s, to seek refuge in the state's growing informal markets.

The shakeout of the traditional sector in Jalisco was far from uniform. While medium-sized firms, especially those that relied heavily on bank credit, and micro-sized establishments in Jalisco were most vulnerable and continued to suffer into the mid-1990s, small-sized firms employing between 30 and 80 workers actually grew substantially during the national banking crisis in 1995, in some cases doubling their total weekly production. Smaller firms, particularly those in the shoe, garment, metal mechanic and furniture industries, were able to fill market voids and niches in the regional and national market that resulted from the closure of medium-sized producers. They were also able to absorb skilled labor quickly and cheaply. Finally, smaller firms were in a better bargaining position vis-à-vis local raw materials, parts and equipment suppliers that now depended on them for their own survival. By 1996, most supplier firms in Jalisco gave their clients as long as 90 days to settle outstanding bills. This provided firms with much needed expansionary capital and low-interest credit. Tewari (1999) and Tendler and Amorim (1996) have found similar arrangements and patterns in India and Brazil.

Interestingly, the economic crisis and the need by business associations to increase membership rates, raise more revenue and fill vacant seats of governing boards presented smaller firms in the state's traditional industries with a unique opportunity to become more active in the political institutions and structures of their representative associations. Prior to the late 1980s, the core political elite of Jalisco's business associations was made up of owners of medium-sized establishments (101–300 employees). This stands in contrast to the norm elsewhere in Mexico, where business associations, including those representing firms in traditional industries, continue to be dominated by the interests of large firms. In Jalisco, however, there were few large-sized traditional sector firms. By the early 1980s, only one shoe manufacturer, Calzado Canada, employed more than 300 workers. The state's three large-sized garment producers, owned by Lebanese and Jewish families who emigrated to the state in the 1930s, went out of business in the mid-1980s.

By 1996, 50–75 percent of the governing boards of all traditional sector business associations were made up of small business owners. Three of four last presidents of the shoe industry association have all owned businesses employing less than 100 workers. Similar trends have emerged in CARE-INTRA and the state's jewelry, metal mechanics, garment and furniture associations. In some cases, the sons, daughters, nephews, nieces and grand-children of traditional sector manufacturers, many of whom worked for medium-sized, family-owned operations in the 1980s and received profes-sional degrees and training after they closed, reentered the industry, started their own small-sized establishments and became more active in associational life and politics.

Under the direction of smaller sized firms, traditional sector trade as-sociations have focused less on federal government lobbying and more on developing training and support services with the help of SEPROE and local business consultants. Part of this shift can be explained by changes in national and international institutions – as a member of GATT, the federal government is limited in its ability to protect domestic indus-tries. While negotiations with federal authorities continue, they tend to deal with issues like the smuggling of contraband goods and national transportation safety.

Interestingly, trade association staff and representatives often attribute this shift to events related to the growth of the state's electronics industry. The visible and much-publicized growth of this sector and SEPROE's role in it provided an important signal to local trade associations and their indus-trial constituency – namely, that state government was "open for business" and was available and willing to subsidize and support firms within its jurisdiction. Through their discussions with Sergio Garcia de Alba and others at SEPROE, trade association officials are learning how to ask for public-sector assistance, how to encourage member firms to participate in government-supported programs and finally, how to use these new pro-grams and initiatives in order to encourage greater firm participation and increase membership rates.

Similarly, through their initial exposure to and experience with this nar-row set of activities and tasks (i.e., luring new investors and firms in the electronics industry) and exposure to large-sized foreign-owned and export-oriented operations, SEPROE also developed a set of skills that they con-tinue to draw on for designing policies and programs that target existing, traditional sector industries and firms. In addition to teaching firms and associations to ask for and accept their support, SEPROE has learned how to identify shifting trends in global markets, sourcing and production sys-tems, how to identify, rank and address related weaknesses in local firms and industries, and how to detect and correct for major gaps in the state's physical and institutional infrastructure, gaps that can ultimately hinder the adjustment and development of locally rooted firms. They have also learned how to collect, analyze and present statistical data on the state's local industrial mix, workforce development and current and future consumer markets.

7.3. Discursive Planning

The dialog between SEPROE and the state's business associations is best characterized as a series of on-going "conversations" (Piore et al., 2001). Interestingly, as the conversation between the public-sector and mediating agencies continues to evolve in Jalisco, so too does the institutional connections between industries, organizations and activities. Three inter-related trends have emerged. First, people and ideas appear to flow freely between SEPROE, manufacturing extension agencies and the state's business associations. Second, the relationship between the formation of the state's policy agenda and the administration of individual programs is itself becoming more fluid and dynamic. Finally, as the state continues to take a more active role in the adjustment process of traditional sector firms, it is also in a better position to identify and respond to broader social and economic concerns. A pressing concern in recent years, for example, has been competition for semi-skilled labor between firms in the electronics industry and traditional sector. SEPROE has used this as leverage to pressure traditional sector associations and their constituent firms to focus on improving work conditions and employee benefits in order to attract and retain skilled and semi-skilled workers.

SEPROE's participation in the *Agrupamientos Empresariales* (AGREM) program is illustrative of these broad trends. In 1996, the footwear association worked with a private consultant and manufacturing extension staff from ITESO, Jalisco's main Jesuit university, to design the AGREM program. The program's methodology builds on an older federal program that ended in the late 1980s. In exchange for financial assistance, planners from SEPROE were invited to participate in and observe the first training session. Twenty five shoe manufacturers and suppliers participated in the six month course. In 1998, SEPROE, with the help of officials from ITESO extended the program to the garment and metal working industries. At the same time, SEPROE sought to institutionalize the program by hiring staff from ITESO University on both a permanent and temporary basis. In 2001, SEPROE's head regional planner, for example, retained formal links to ITESO's small business extension program. As a state planner, he coordinated weekly AGREM meetings between extension experts from ITESO and associations representing footwear, leather goods, garments, textiles and metal mechanic industries. Other examples of this sort exist. The general directors of CAD-ELEC, a supplier development initiative in the electronics and telecommunications industries and CEJALDI, a multi-sector design center, were also former researchers and planners at SEPROE; the latter directed SEPROE's AGREM program for one year.

This flow of people across organizations and activities has helped create an environment of continuous reflection and improvement both in the implementation of existing technical support programs and the formation of broad-based, strategic planning initiatives. As a result of their active participation in the AGREM program, SEPROE agents have grown increasingly aware of the larger constraints of and limitations to joint-consultation and collaboration across associations and other policy-shaping organizations. They have been able to draw on their knowledge of inter-firm collaboration gained through the exposure to the AGREM program in order to effectively identify and respond to rising tensions between and within some of the local trade associations. In the case of CEJALDI, the state's design center, tensions did eventually emerge between the center's board members and those of the trade associations they are expected to represent. While solutions were often task-specific and thus customized at the program level, SEPROE was able to build on processes and experiences that cut across tasks in order to identify, analyze and isolate problem areas and concerns.

Through this process, the state government in Jalisco has not only grown more effective in policy formation and planning practice but has started to craft a new approach to local economic development planning. This style of planning involves the simultaneous adoption of a wide range of subjects, tasks and objectives. Planners seek out and identify connections between sets of activities; coordination and learning across tasks and agencies is prioritized; and finally, the identification of problem areas and constraints emerges out of earlier planning struggles and shifts with additional examination and policy exploration (Schön, 1983; Piore et al., 2001). This style differs from traditional technical problem solving, in which planners approach tasks in a more routinized and scientific manner. Through this frame, planners optimize strategies with the resources available to them. Well-defined and pre-tested causal models help direct the course of action taken by these agencies. Program efficiency is given priority over long-range learning and skill development on the part of local decision makers (Piore et al., 2001).

8. CONCLUSION: RETHINKING THE CONDITIONS OF GOOD GOVERNANCE IN LIGHT OF THE JALISCO CASE

"The analysis moves further up the causal chain to consider the threats and vulner-
abilities that encourage state and business elites to invest in cooperation and in institutions that diminish incentives for 'opportunism with guile.' These threats differ across
actors; business usually responds to economic competition and state actors to political
threats to their survival."

(Schneider and Maxfield, 1997, p. 5.)

This quote captures the standard thinking on good governments in late industrialized nations. Meritocratic and Weberian bureaucracies (Amsden, 1989; Evans, 1995), hard budget constraints (Doner & Ramsay, 1997) and highly visible intra-government tensions and hostilities (Schneider & Maxfield, 1997) are considered to be the underlying causes (and prerequisites) of growth-enhancing interventions on the part of public-sector authorities. Each of these factors also ensures greater distance between the state and business community, thereby limiting opportunities for growth-diminishing clientelism and corruption.

Similar assumptions pattern the literature on the role of business associations in shaping industrial policy. It is often argued that business associations need to be "all-encompassing" or representative of a wide-spectrum of firms and industries (e.g., multi-sectoral) in order to behave "developmentally" in their lobbying and service-creating activities. In contrast, business associations that represent a narrow set of interests – i.e., single sectors or industries – will be more likely to engage in "directly unproductive" and "rent-seeking" activities with public officials (Bennett, 1998; Schneider & Maxfield, 1997; Moore & Hamalai, 1993). The same logic applies to "captive" government agencies. This approach to analyzing state–business interactions draws heavily on Mancur Olson's theory of collective action. It is also influenced by the wide-spread acceptance and application of rational choice theory in development studies in the 1980s.

The dynamic and evolving relationship between SEPROE, local business and their representative agencies in Jalisco, however, underscores the limits of this analytical approach to understanding and identifying cases of good governance. None of the standard explanatory variables outlined above seem to hold in this case. The state bureaucracy cannot be easily categorized as Weberian, in fact, the current administration often relies on loose social contacts and hiring practices when filling higher-level planning and research posts; there are no civil service exams or standard testing procedures; local budget constraints are easily softened through private contributions, changing fiscal policies and subtle changes in program design and protocol that generate additional federal resources and support; intra-government tensions, while evident, do not appear to be permanent and fixed; intra-governmental territoriality continue to change as the current administration takes on new tasks and responsibilities, and this has only been compounded by federal efforts to decentralize authority and decision-making; participating trade associations, while forming part of a broader multi-industry, multi-agency coalition, still identify with particular sectors and industries; finally, there are few visible boundaries between the state and wider business community.

Yet in simply refuting each of these proposed variables, we miss a more fundamental limitation to conventional explanations of good governance, the inability to account for and recognize complex learning processes and on-going institutional shifts, not only within government agencies, but also across public-sector agencies, quasi-public organizations (e.g., manufacturing extension services) and representative business groups. While fixed organizational and structural attributes may help to explain developmental interventions at a particular moment in time, they fail to adequately explain improved performance over time and the circumstances under and processes by which states and associations learn to work together in more growth-enhancing ways.

REFERENCES

Alba Vega, C. (1998). *Tres Regiones de Mexico Ante la Globalización: Los Casos de Chihuahua, Nuevo Leon y Guadalajara. Las Regiones Ante La Globalización, Competitividad territorial y recomposición sociopolítica.* Carlos Alba, Ilán Bizberg, Hélene Riviere d'Arc. México: El Colegio de México.

Amsden, A. (1989). *Asia's next giant.* Oxford: Oxford University Press.

Arias, P. (1983). *Fuentes para el Estudio de la industrialización en jalisco. Siglo XX.* Mexico. D.F.: Centro de Investigaciones y Estudios.

Arias, P. (1992). *El Calzado en la región Jalisciense: La industria y La Cámara.* Guadalajara: Cámara de la Industria del Calzado de Jalisco.

Bair, J., & Gerreffi, G. (1998). Interfirm networks and regional divisions of labor: Employment and upgrading in the apparel commodity chain. Paper presented at the international workshop on global production and local jobs: New perspectives on enterprise networks. Geneva: ILO.

Bair, J., & Gerreffi, G. (1999). The impact of NAFTA on the apparel commodity chain: Linking corporate strategies, inter-firm networks, and local development. Paper presented at the Alfred P. Sloan foundation globalization workshop for junior scholars.

Bartik, T. (1991). *Who benefits from state and local development policies.* Kalamazoo: WE Upjohn Institute.

Barzelay, M. (1991). Managing local development: Lessons from Spain. *Policy Sciences, 24,* 271–290.

Bennett, R. (1998). Business associations and their potential contribution to the competitiveness of SMEs. *Entrepreneurship and Regional Development, 10,* 243–260.

Buchholz, D. (1998). *Competition and corporate incentives: Dilemmas in economic development.* Unpublished doctoral dissertation. Duke University, Durham.

Buitelaar, R., & Padilla Pérez, R. (2000). Maquila, economic reform and corporate strategies. *World Development, 28*(9), 1627–1642.

Doner, R., & Ramsay, A. (1997). Competitive clientalism and economic governance: The case of Thailand. In: S. Maxfield & B. Schneider (Eds), *Business and the state in developing countries.* Ithaca: Cornell University Press.

Eisinger, P. (1988). *The rise of the entrepreneurial state.* Madison: University of Wisconsin Press.

Eisinger, P. (1995). State economic development in the 1990s: Politics and policy learning *Economic Development Quarterly, 9*(2), 146–158.

Evans, P. (1995). *Embedded autonomy: States and industrial transformation.* Princeton: Princeton University Press.

Gilbert, J. (1995). *Accountability mechanisms: Smart bombs in the bidding wars or false sense of security?* Masters Thesis, Massachusetts Institute of Planning.

Lowe, N. (1999a). From lobbying to local learning: The origins of successful public–private partnering in Jalisco's traditional sectors. Paper presented at the Alfred P. Sloan foundation globalization workshop for junior scholars.

Lowe, N. (1999b). The foundations of high road policy: Rethinking the origins of economic crisis and reform in 20th century Mississippi. Report for the Bank of the Northeast, Brazil.

Lynch, R. (1996). *Do state and local tax incentives work.* Washington, DC: Economic Policy Institute.

Mizrahi, Y. (1995). Entrepreneurs in the opposition: Modes of political participation in Chihuahua. In: V. Rodriquez & P. Ward (Eds), *Opposition government in Mexico.* Albuquerque: University of New Mexico Press.

Moore, M., & Hamalai, L. (1993). Economic liberalization, political pluralism and business associations in developing countries. *World Development, 21*(12).

Perez-Aleman, P. (2000). Learning, adjustment and economic development: Transforming firms, the state and associations in Chile. *World Development, 28*(1), 41–55.

Piore, M., Kuznetsov, Y., Clemente, R. D., & Charles, S. (2001). *Think globally, act locally: Decentralized incentive framework for Mexico's private sector development.* Research Report, World Bank, Washington, DC.

Pozas, M. (1993). *Industrial restructuring in Mexico: Corporate adaptation, technological innovation, and changing patterns of industrial relations in Monterrey.* San Diego: Center for U.S.-Mexican Studies.

Rabellotti, R. (1995). Is there an industrial district model? Footwear districts in Italy and Mexico compared. *World Development, 23*(1), 29–41.

Rabellotti, R. (1999). Recovery of a Mexican cluster: Devaluation bonanza or collective efficiency. *World Development, 27*(9), 1571–1585.

Sabel, C. (1994). A measure of federalism: Assessing manufacturing technology centers. Mimeo.

Schneider, B., & Maxfield, S. (1997). Business, the state and economic performance in developing countries. In: S. Maxfield & B. Schneider (Eds), *Business and the state in developing countries*. Ithaca: Cornell University Press.

Schön, D. (1983). *The reflective practitioner: How professionals think in action*. Basic Books.

Schweke, W., Rist, C., & Dabson, B. (1994). *Bidding for business: Are cities and states selling themselves short*. Washington, DC: Corporation for Enterprise Development.

Spener, D., & Pozos, F. (1996). U. S.-Mexico trade liberalization and its effects on small-scale enterprise in two distinct regions: West Central Mexico and the Texas border region compared. *International Journal of Sociology and Social Policy, 16*(7–8), 102–147.

Tendler, J. (1997). *Good government in the tropics*. Baltimore: Johns Hopkins University Press.

Tendler, J., & Amorim, M. (1996). Small firms and their helpers: Lessons on demand. *World Development, 24*(3), 407–426.

Tewari, M. (1999). Successful adjustment in indian industry: The case of Ludhiana's woolen knitwear cluster. *World Development, 27*(9), 1651–1671.

Zamora, R., Diester, C., de León Arias, A., & Alejandre, J. (1988). *Jalisco Desde la Revolución XIII: Crecimiento industrial y manufacturero 1940–1980*. Guadalajara: Universidad de Guadalajara, Gobierno del Estado de Jalisco.

BUILDING HUMAN CAPITAL IN DIFFICULT ENVIRONMENTS: AN EMPIRICAL STUDY OF ENTREPRENEURSHIP EDUCATION, SELF-ESTEEM, AND ACHIEVEMENT IN SOUTH AFRICA

Christian Friedrich and Kobus Visser

1. INTRODUCTION

The lack of traditional employment opportunities for many students and the oft-repeated cry for South Africa to invest in developing black entrepreneurs prompted the University of Western Cape's Department of Management to introduce an Enterprise Management stream at graduate level and Entrepreneurship as a subject at 2nd and 3rd year levels in recent years. All these initiatives are based on a strong capability in entrepreneurship and small business that has been developed in the department since the introduction of the Enterprise Development Unit in 1997.

The originators of the concept developed and implemented a year-long entrepreneurship major for 2nd year management students. This module was realised in the Department of Management during the 2001 academic

Developmental Entrepreneurship: Adversity, Risk, and Isolation
International Research in the Business Disciplines, Volume 5, 355–378
Copyright © 2006 by Elsevier Ltd.
All rights of reproduction in any form reserved
ISSN: 1074-7877/doi:10.1016/S1074-7877(06)05018-5

year when Entrepreneurship was introduced as a 2nd year subject to a small pilot group. Subsequently, in 2002 the module has been revised, adapted and adjusted and currently it is presented for the 4th consecutive year.

In terms of the three generally accepted obligations of tertiary institutions (i.e., teaching, research and technology transfer), entrepreneurship education and training ought to be regarded as a response to one of the numerous requirements by commerce and industry. In the context of developing countries that face increasingly complex environments, instilling self-esteem and achievement through entrepreneurship education, present a unique set of challenges.

In this chapter, we report on the design of this innovative module, its practical implementation and assessment of its efficacy by means of a longitudinal survey. Our chapter is divided into three sections: Section 1 presents an overview of literature relating to academic programmes aimed at promoting student enterprise with a view to ascertain similarities and dissimilarities of such approaches in an academic context. Section 2 describes how different South African and European expertise and experience were brought together to build and deliver an innovative module suited specifically to the South African environment and to UWC, a "historically black university." Section 3 presents the empirical findings from a longitudinal study describing the impact and outcome of the module on students' perceptions of entrepreneurship training as a viable work-related option.

The chapter concludes with a summary of what went right, and what changes would be suggested to improve this module or others similar to it. It is hoped that our experiences will help our colleagues in developing economies to design, plan, and implement similar modules, and will provide impetus for discussions through which we can improve future iterations of this entrepreneurship major module.

2. REVIEWING THE LITERATURE

It has been said that there are courses *about* entrepreneurship and courses *for* entrepreneurship. This chapter describes an innovative university module both about *and* for entrepreneurship.

Laukannen (2000) proposes each as: Education *about* entrepreneurship, which develops, constructs and studies the theories referred to the entrepreneurs, the creation of firms, the contribution to economic development, the entrepreneurial process and small- and medium-sized enterprises. It addresses both graduate and undergraduate students, masters, Ph.D.s, policy makers and researchers; in other words, everyone interested in entrepreneurship as a social phenomenon; whereas, education *for* entrepreneurship addresses current and potential entrepreneurs. The objective is to develop and stimulate the entrepreneurial process, providing all the necessary tools for the start-up of a new venture both inside and outside existing organizations. According to Mason's (2000) definition, "it is proposed to develop the core skills and attributes necessary to roll out a new venture and to identify pre-start-up needs."

There is a fundamental difference between the above definitions. The first definition is based on the construction and transfer of knowledge about the field, while the second one focuses on the learning experience and the development of competencies, skills, aptitudes and values; therefore, the teaching methods used in each of these areas are not the same.

Most of the empirical studies reviewed, indicate that entrepreneurship can be taught and that education can enhance entrepreneurial skills, competencies and attitudes (Ronstadt, 1987; Braukmann, 2000; Hisrich & Peters, 2002; Saffu, 2003; Laukkannen, 2000; Timmons & Spinelli, 2004; Siteman, 2004; Green, Katz, & Johannison, 2004; Edwards & Muir, 2004).

Based on the above notion that entrepreneurship can be learned and that tertiary institutions can (in all probability) act as the conduits for such learning in a South African context, Davies (2001) postulates that these tertiary institutions can assist in creating and contributing to an entrepreneurial society by means of five interventions, namely changing the mindsets of students from potential employees to employers; equipping students with practical business skills and facilitating experiential learning; developing a faculty of entrepreneurial role models; researching problems, needs and constraints of entrepreneurs; and, influencing governmental policy and actions. The latter discourse brings us to the question discussed in the next section.

3. WHAT IS KNOWN ABOUT UNIVERSITY ENTREPRENEURSHIP EDUCATION?

Internationally, entrepreneurship and small business development have been studied at university level from the early 1970s; for example, entrepreneurship education and training have been scholarly assessed and analysed in North America by several authors including, Timmons and Spinelli (2004), Finkle and Deeds (2001), Vesper and Gartner (1997); in Europe by Bolton and Thompson (2004), Perren and Grant (2001), Levi (1999), Hisrich and O'Cinneida (1992), Katz (1991); on the subcontinent by Patel (1986), Singh (1990); and, in Africa by Rwigema and Venter (2004), Nieman, Hough, and Nieuwenhuizen (2003), Kiggundu (2002), Davies (2001), Driver, Wood, Segal, and Herrington (2001), and Vosloo (1994).

In general, literature on entrepreneurship education reveals a relatively eclectic approach to the teaching areas of entrepreneurship education. In broad terms, literature suggests that entrepreneurship education ought to contain teaching and exposure to activities, which will assist the student (and therefore the potential entrepreneur) to perform at levels above that of being an employee (Klandt, 2004; Antonites, 2003; Hamilton, Asundi, & Romaguera, 2002; Falkäng & Alberti, 2000; Levi, 1999).

Anderson and Visser (2002) present teaching and exposure to activities as the ability of the potential entrepreneur to improve/increase formation of new ventures, likelihood of self-employment, growth rates of emerging firms, graduates' personal assets, likelihood of developing new products, and likelihood of graduates owning a high-technology business.

Most of the elements of entrepreneurship education indicated above are contained in a model for entrepreneurial performance training, as espoused by Ladzani and Van Vuuren (2002). Ladzani and Van Vuuren postulate that entrepreneurship education and training consist of three dimensions with each being influenced by a number of factors, as presented in Table 1. For example, the factors of need for achievement, ability to inspire and reaction to success/failure influence the dimension of motivation. In the same way,

Table 1. Content of Entrepreneurial Performance Training.

Motivation	Entrepreneurial Skills	Business Skills
Need for achievement	Creativity	Management/leadership
Ability to inspire	Innovation	Business plans
Expectations of the high achiever	Ability to take risks	Financial skills
Obstacles or blocks	Ability to identify opportunities	Marketing skills
Help	Ability to have a vision for growth	Operational skills
Reactions to success or failure	Interpret successful entrepreneurial role models	Human resource skills

Source: Ladzani and Van Vuuren (2002).

creativity, innovation, interpreting role models, etc., influence entrepreneurial skills, whereas the functional areas of finance, marketing operation and human resources, etc., influence the dimension of business skills.

4. A MODEL FOR ENTREPRENEURSHIP EDUCATION AT INSTITUTIONS OF HIGHER EDUCATION

The model for entrepreneurship education and training followed at 2nd year level in the Department of Management at UWC is based on Hytti's model as implemented at the Turku School of Economics and Business Administration, Finland (Hytti & Kuopusjärvi, 2004a, b; Hytti, 2002).

In brief, the Hytti model is designed to include three important components of entrepreneurship training and enterprise education in a teaching and research context. It is based on three interrelated and interdependent sets of aims that focus, first, on learning about entrepreneurship, second on a non-business focus with an emphasis on becoming entrepreneurial, and third, with a focus on business by learning to become an entrepreneur.

Hannan, Hazlett, and Leitch (2004) describe the interrelationship between the three aims of the Hytti model as "development along the entrepreneurship education continuum, from being aware of entrepreneurship, to developing entrepreneurial skills, to the intention to be an entrepreneur."

5. TAXONOMY OF START-UP RELEVANT COMPETENCIES (HYTTI'S MODEL)

Based on Hytti's model, an area of critical importance in the UWC project is the integration of entrepreneurial education into the university, which concurs with Hannan et al. (2004, p. 4) that what we experience here is a "... dynamic process of changing the cognitive mechanisms within students. These cognitive mechanisms, such as belief, values and attitudes, develop allowing students to understand their capabilities and skills more fully.

As such, as students become more aware and independent they are more likely to become entrepreneurs and act on their intentions established by their attitudes and beliefs in a business setting." As indicated previously, entrepreneurship education at tertiary level does not receive a high priority in an African context. In this regard, Kiggundu (2002, p. 54) suggests that

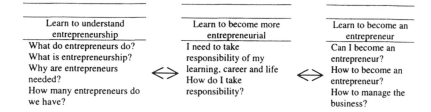

Learn to understand entrepreneurship	Learn to become more entrepreneurial	Learn to become an entrepreneur
What do entrepreneurs do? What is entrepreneurship? Why are entrepreneurs needed? How many entrepreneurs do we have?	I need to take responsibility of my learning, career and life How do I take responsibility?	Can I become an entrepreneur? How to become an entrepreneur? How to manage the business?

Source: Hytti, U. (Ed.). (2002). *State-of-art of enterprise education in Europe - Results from the Entredu project.* Turku, Finland: Small Business Institute, Business Research and Development Centre, Turku School of Economics and Business Administration and ENTREDU project partners.

Fig. 1.   Hytti Model of Entrepreneurship Education.

entrepreneurship education ought to become a "mainstream" activity in the education systems of African countries.

The interactive nature of the Hytti model is shown in Fig. 1 in which the different roles assigned to entrepreneurship education are summarised.

In essence, each of these three categories has the purpose of identifying and monitoring progress as the student moves from becoming familiar with the concept of entrepreneurism to developing a level of maturity that will enable the student to start an enterprise to a stage where the student/prospective entrepreneur now possess most of the elements required for business success.

6. MEASUREMENT

Over the past 40 years, a number of measuring instruments have been developed to study entrepreneurship (see Wickham, 2004). Based on a body of research on personality and entrepreneurship (Robinson, Huefner, & Hunt,1991a), four constructs were identified that have generally been used in research on the entrepreneur, namely, the need for achievement, locus of control, self-esteem and innovation.

In view of the four constructs identified above, Kiggundu (2002, pp. 243–245) indicates in an assessment of empirical studies linking education training to entrepreneurial success, that the factors of achievement, personal control, self-esteem (as psychological factors) and innovation (as a core competence) all indicate positive correlates to success.

For the purposes of measuring the impact of entrepreneurship training at university level, the instrument selected is based on the entrepreneurial attitude orientation (EAO) scale, as developed and validated by Robinson, Stimpson, Huefner, and Hunt (1991b).

Based on attitude theory, this measuring instrument has been specifically designed to predict entrepreneurship. In this regard, "attitude" is defined as "the predisposition to respond in a generally favorable or unfavorable manner with respect to the object of the attitude" (Robinson et al., 1991a, p. 17). In addition, the EAO was developed to predict entrepreneurship, based on the tripartite model of attitude, rather than on demographics or personality theory. In order to increase the content validity of each subscale, Robinson et al. (1991a) postulate that the attitude components are included in the EAO.

Furthermore, the EAO was created specifically to measure entrepreneurship and has successfully discriminated between entrepreneurs and non-entrepreneurs in several research contexts (Robinson et al., 1991a, b; Hunt, Huefner, Voegele, & Robinson, 1989).

These four EAO subscales (with support from the literature for each subscale) are briefly described below.

- *Achievement in Business* (ACH) referring to concrete results associated with the start-up and growth of a business venture, i.e. it refers to tangible outcomes which can be associated with business formation and growth (Spencer, McClelland, & Spencer, 1992; Robinson et al., 1991a; Roberts, 1991; McClelland, 1965, 1986; Hermans, 1970).
- *Innovation in Business* (INN) relating to perceiving and acting upon business activities in new and unique ways, i.e. this factor relates to the ability to recognize business activities in unique ways and to act upon these challenges (Robinson et al., 1991a; Kirton, 1976, 1978; Hornaday & Aboud, 1971).
- *Perceived Personal Control of Business Outcomes* (PC) as a factor refers to the perception of control by the individual and the influence over his/her business (Robinson et al., 1991a; Rotter, 1966, 1990; Levenson, 1981; Brockhaus, 1976; Rotter, 1966).
- *Perceived Self-Esteem in Business* (SE) pertaining to the self-confidence and perceived competency of an individual in conjunction with his or her business affairs (Robinson et al., 1991a; Crandall, 1973).

Huefner, Hunt, and Robinson (1996, p. 56) state that the "EAO was selected because it was specifically developed through rigorous scale development procedures to measure entrepreneurship based on attitude rather than personality theory."

In a South African context, these four subscales achievement, innovation, personal control and self-esteem were re-assessed for construct validity in a study by Van Wyk, Boshoff, and Owen (1999).

7. HYPOTHESES

In terms of the constructs to be measured in this research project (as identified above), the following hypotheses have been set:

H1. Achievement orientation improves after having attended the training module.

H2. Personal control improves after having attended the training module.

H3. Innovation improves after having attended the training module.

H4. Self-esteem improves after having attended the training module.

8. PROGRAMMES AND MODULES

Students at the 2nd year level attend Entrepreneurship classes for four terms of 7 contact weeks each for the academic calendar year, beginning in early February and ending early in December.

Student micro-enterprise businesses are located on the UWC campus, serving mostly UWC students and staff. By the end of Term 2, micro-enterprise teams are ready for initial funding and start-up, and the businesses are fully functional and operating at the start of Term 3 and for the duration of Term 4.

In the four sequential terms, classes begin with an introduction to *Entrepreneurship* and by acquainting the students with the concept of entrepreneurship as a career choice. In addition, the students are familiarised with the structure and cross-functional business concepts of the formal business plan, and choose small businesses to study and write on for individual business plans. Classes consist of lectures and frequent class discussions to reinforce course concepts through use of examples that the students are familiar with from their own experience. The module focuses on the practicalities of starting and operating a small firm in the local context. Students are required to interview, interact and present a report on a successful entrepreneur and to reflect on the lessons they have learned from this encounter. A major focus of the first-half of the module is for students to develop a business plan for the micro-enterprise, which they will establish during the Term 2 and continue to operate until Term 4.

In Term 2, students prepare for intensive group involvement in micro-enterprise teams. Each team produces a charter, a contract of expectations for team performance and a consensus-driven peer evaluation instrument to rate individual contributions towards achievement of the team's goals. In addition, students study survey techniques and the customer-orientation necessary for successful businesses. The micro-enterprise teams design questionnaires and survey several hundred prospective customers (i.e. the wider campus community) to ascertain their preferences for small businesses the students might develop. Micro-enterprise teams determine which business ideas they want to pursue, and they begin to plan and move toward implementation of their plans and realisation of their businesses. With loan funding (to a maximum of R1,000) provided by the Department of Management, as well as their own capital contributions and sponsorships, micro-enterprise teams can receive and raise venture capital of up to R3,000 (equivalent to approximately US$500).

The focus of Term 3 is on the practical establishment and operation of a new business by students working in small teams. Students are introduced to and defined the factors of success and begin to set goals for their enterprises. Students meet in tutorial sessions with the instructor to reflect on, and collectively address the problems that arise in establishing and initially operating their businesses. During the module students continue to operate the micro-enterprise that they established at the beginning of the term. The initial focus of the module is to help ensure that the start-ups survive and thrive so that the students are able to learn valuable practical lessons from continued operations. Additionally, they learn about success factors. Students use their own experience of operating a micro-enterprise as the basis for studying the challenges of acquiring, franchising and operating various kinds of more formal small businesses. The material is sequenced in a similar way to the events likely to be encountered when starting or buying a small business and provides the building block of the 3rd year programme.

During Term 4 the micro-enterprise teams continue with their enterprises on campus. Typically, this is a period when complacency sets in, individuals lose interest and the enterprises may suffer as a result of a lack of commitment. During this period a sustained effort is made by the faculty to maintain the impetus of the enterprises and to assist in resolving matters that threaten group dynamics, group performance and group cohesion. In order to address these potential threats, senior students act as business mentors to guide and assist the micro-enterprise teams in matters relating to group performance.

Table 2 presents a summary of the components constituting the full module, which consists of curriculum content, practical work and academic compliance requirements for the four terms.

The academic module sets aside 4 hours of lecturer contact time per week. Once the enterprises operate on campus, members of the respective micro-enterprise teams attend lectures on a rotational basis.

For Terms 3 and 4 one lecture-hour per week is forfeited to enable the enterprise teams to work in the businesses. Regular class attendance is made compulsory by means of unannounced class tests, attendance records and group tutorials all of which generate marks towards a final term mark. Full academic compliance is maintained during all terms by means of credit-bearing activities as identified in Table 2.

8.1. Evaluation Components

Typically, the final term mark in institutions of higher education in a South African context consists of a composite of work based on the model of continuous evaluation. This method of evaluation consists of components such as: case studies, assignments, weekly journals, entrepreneur interview and assessment of relevant articles, tutorials, peer evaluation, term test and an examination.

8.2. Teaching Method

During Term 1 of the module, the preferred method of knowledge transfer is by means of classroom-based lectures, controlled interaction with entrepreneurs and group work. From Term 2 until the completion of the module, a radical change in knowledge transfer takes place when action learning takes precedence as the dominant learning method; in this regard, students learn-by-doing and learn-by-taking responsibility for their decisions. Action training in entrepreneurship has proved to be a successful training method and training intervention (Frese, Beimel, & Schoenborn, 2003; Friedrich, Glaub, Gramberg, & Frese, 2006; Glaub, 2002).

In terms of the proposed enterprises on campus, students are required to form their own groups and establish working, financial and administrative relationships. Experience from previous groups showed that groups that do

Table 2. Curriculum, Practical Work and Academic Requirements.

	Curriculum Content	Practical Work	Academic Compliance
Term 1	MAN201: Starting a business (theory) 1. Entrepreneurship as a career choice 2. Environmental analysis 3. Learning about entrepreneurs: Traits and behaviours 4. New venture opportunities 5. Business planning: Marketing, industry, competition 6. Presentation skills 7. Interviewing an entrepreneur 8. Fit and feasibility of new venture ideas	Marketing survey on campus	1. Weekly journals 2. Idea generation 3. Interview an entrepreneur 4. Marketing research 5. Term test 6. Examination
Term 2	MAN202: Starting a business (Practice) 1. Group building exercise, group dynamics, idea generator 2. How to develop a business plan, market need, customers 3. Competitors, situation analysis 4. Positioning, promotion, location, distribution 5. Start-up plan/costs, operational plan 6. Financial management, cash flow, profitability, Finance required 7. Presentation of business plans	On-campus presentation by entrepreneurs Forming a stable work group Funding a successful enterprise	1. Weekly journals 2. Student peer evaluation 3. Business plan 4. Assignment
Term 3	MAN203: Operating the small business (practice) 1. Reviewing business plans of MAN 202, Start up of own business on the campus 2. Introduction into success factors of SMEs, goal setting for own business 3. Planning strategies 4. Innovation 5. Personal initiative 6. Presentation of results of own business	Work in enterprise Funding the enterprise	1. Weekly journals 2. Student peer evaluation 3. Group report/ enterprise progress report

Table 2. (*Continued*)

	Curriculum Content	Practical Work	Academic Compliance
Term 4	MAN204: Harvesting the enterprise (practice) 1. Micro-enterprise operation 2. Exit strategies and issues 3. Business valuation 4. Harvesting and liquidation issues 5. Shutting down the micro-enterprise 6. Entrepreneurial life strategies 7. Journaling and peer evaluation 8. Micro-enterprise and programme reflection and assessment	Work in enterprise	1. Bi-weekly journals 2. Student peer evaluation 3. Four case studies 4. Group final report 5. Term test 6. Examination

not formalise these relationships contractually, tend to fail at the first onset of conflict.

In order to assist the enterprise groups after formation, two student assistants (senior students) are appointed to act as a "sounding board" for the indifferences arising within a group context, as well as to act as intermediaries between the groups and the lecturers.

8.3. Entrepreneurship Module Growth

When this module was first introduced in 2001, only 19 students registered for the module with four enterprises started on campus. Subsequently, as the success and popularity of the module grew and the awareness had been created, the number of students quadrupled over a period of four years from 19 in 2001, to 32 students in 2002, to 51 students in 2003 to 85 students in 2004.

The increasing number of female students registering for this module is certainly of interest; for example, the female representation grew from 8 in 2001 to 14 in 2002 to 25 in 2003 to 45 in 2004. This growth in female participation is in line with international trends that entrepreneurship is increasingly considered as a career choice by women (Minniti, Arenius, & Langowitz, 2004; Timmons & Spinelli, 2004; Reynolds, Hay, Bygrave, Camp, & Autio, 2000).

8.4. Research Method

Table 3 shows the design of this study. The study represents a design which takes the format of a pre-test (i.e. T1) and a post-test (i.e. T2) together with a non-randomised control group (Cook, Campbell, & Peracchio, 1990). Students of the experimental group and control group were tested at the beginning of the academic year and at the end.

8.5. Sample Selection

The experimental group who participated in T1 and T2 consisted of $N = 69$ 2nd year students, while the control group had $N = 45$ students who did not participate in any entrepreneurial education and training for the period under review. The gender profile is presented in Table 4.

In terms of the ethnic categorisation of the sample (as depicted in Table 5), in both the experimental group as well as the control group,

Table 3. Study Design.

	T1	Intervention	T2
	Before Training		7 Months After
Training group	0	Entrepreneurial training	0
Control group	0	No training	0

Note: 0 = Evaluation measures collected.

Table 4. Student Profiles: Gender.

	Frequency	Percent
Experimental group		
Male	25	36.2
Female	36	52.2
Total	61	88.4
Missing system	8	11.6
Total	69	100
Control		
Male	15	33.3
Female	27	60
Not reported	3	6.7
Total	45	100

Table 5.   Student Population: Ethnic Group.

	Frequency	Percent
Experimental group		
Asian	4	5.8
Coloured	22	31.9
Sotho	5	7.2
Tswana	2	2.9
Xhosa	19	27.5
Zulu	3	4.3
Other	9	13
Total	64	92.8
Missing system	5	7.2
Total	69	100
Control group		
Asian	4	8.9
Coloured	22	48.9
Sotho	1	2.2
Tswana	5	11.1
Xhosa	4	8.9
Zulu	9	20
Other	0	0
Total	45	100

Coloured students were the highest percentage. Other students included
Sotho, Tswana, Xhoso, Zulu and Asians.

9. RESULTS

Table 6 shows the means, standard deviations for both the experimental and
the control group in a paired sample comparison. The univariate comparison
shows that the means of the experimental group for the variables achievement, innovation, self-esteem and control improved between T1 and T2.
Unexpectedly, the results of the control group between T1 and T2 show a
decline of means for all the four variables (Table 7).

Table 8 shows the comparison between training group and control group
at T2. Achievement, innovation and self-esteem of the training group were
found to be significantly higher than for the same variable in the control
group, while no significant difference for locus of control between training
group and control group could be found.

Table 6. Paired Samples – Statistical Comparison between T1 and T2.

		Mean	N	Standard Deviation	Standard Error Mean
Experimental group					
Pair 1	achav1	7.9108	60	0.66397	0.08572
	achav2	8.1990	60	0.81062	0.10465
Pair 2	inovav 1	6.4475	60	0.67938	0.09493
	inovav 2	6.7183	60	0.73531	0.08771
Pair 3	cntlav1	6.9846	65	1.08448	0.13451
	cntlav2	7.2462	65	1.12614	0.13968
Pair 4	slfav1	7.4638	63	0.94482	0.11904
	slfav2	7.6825	63	0.81451	0.10262
Control group					
Pair 1	achav1	8.2202	35	0.84552	0.14292
	achav2	7.9462	35	1.08375	0.18319
Pair 2	inovav 1	6.5912	34	1.00178	0.17180
	inovav 2	6.4338	34	0.91102	0.15624
Pair 3	cntlav1	7.2525	43	1.26968	0.19362
	cntlav2	7.1794	43	1.18752	0.18109
Pair 4	slfav1	7.8041	38	1.02600	0.16644
	slfav2	7.4561	38	1.13893	0.18476

Table 7. Paired Samples Test T1-T2.

	T	df	Significance (two-tailed)
Experimental group			
Pair 1 achav1 & achav2	−2.760	59	0.008**
Pair 2 inovav1 & inovav2	2.833	59	0.006**
Pair 3 cntlav1 & cntlav2	−1.718	64	0.091
Pair 4 slfav1 & slfav2	1.425	62	0.159
Control group			
Pair 1 achav1 & achav2	1.55	34	0.13
Pair 2 inovav1 & inovav2	−0.696	33	0.339
Pair 3 cntlav1 & cntlav2	0.387	42	0.701
Pair 4 slfav1 & slfav2	−2.080	37	0.044*

*$p<0.05$.
**$p<0.01$.

Table 8. Comparison between Training Group and Control Group After Training.

Source	df	Mean Square	F	Significance
Achievement	1	3.493	8.574	0.004
Control	1	1.449	1.449	0.170
Innovation	1	1.989	5.913	0.017
Self-esteem	1	3.805	5.735	0.019

Table 9. Comparison between Parents of Students who are Entrepreneurs/ Employed Parents, Chi-Square Tests.

	Value	df	Asymp. Significance (two-sided)
Achievement	42.884	32	0.95
Innovation	35.123	36	0.510
Locus of control	23.776	24	0.474
Self-esteem	25.360	23	0.332

Table 9 deals with the results of the question whether there are differences between students who have parents, who are self-employed and those who are employed concerning the variables achievement, innovation, locus of control and self-esteem. The chi-square test did not show any significant differences between the two groups concerning the tested variables.

10. DISCUSSION

The main aim of this study was to test whether certain variables of entrepreneurial orientation can be increased among historically disadvantaged students by a new nine-month long entrepreneurial training course at university. The results described in this survey show that it is possible to improve achievement orientation, innovation and self-esteem of South African students within a university entrepreneurship course. Participants not only acquired skills and knowledge how to start and run a business (learning *about* entrepreneurship), but also improved their entrepreneurial orientation in comparison to a control group (learning to be more entrepreneurial). The result for locus of control over time showed an increase of the mean between T1 and T2, but no significant change in comparison to the control group. Overall, the results confirm three of our four hypotheses. Each is briefly discussed:

As hypothesized in Hypothesis 1, the training had a significant positive effect on Achievement. The trained students showed a significantly higher score in the post training measure than the control group. This is in line with previous research with different groups of entrepreneurs (McClelland, 1986).

Hypothesis 2 could not be confirmed. It does not seem to be possible to change this mindset with an intervention we used, or internal/external locus of control, since this factor is an attitude which cannot be changed in a relatively short period of time.

We assumed that innovation can be increased through the university course. The results show that students increased their innovation score significantly between T1 and T2 as well as in comparison to a control group. This confirms earlier results (Friedrich et al., 2006) in which with a three-day training intervention innovation in entrepreneurs could be improved significantly.

In Hypothesis 4 we assumed that perceived self-esteem would increase by attending the entrepreneurial university training. The results confirm our hypothesis. At the end of the academic year the self-esteem of the training group was significantly higher than that of the control group. Students are gaining higher self-esteem in starting and running a business successfully. Since there is not much competition and they do not have to pay a significant amount for renting business premises on the campus, almost all the businesses of the students are successful.

10.1. Student Reflection and Assessment

On completion of a particular module standard practice requires that all modules be subjected to student assessment by means of a questionnaire. In broad terms, the questionnaire focuses on the following important sections, namely learning objectives; the efficacy of the presenters; and an assessment of the module itself. Students were required to present their assessment on 30 questions on a five-point Likert scale. A summary of the elements of assessment is presented in Table 10.

In terms of the feedback acquired from students by means of in-class feedback and the completion of anonymous course evaluation forms (see Table 10), students have found this year-long module overwhelmingly positive and they regard the module as excellent. Furthermore, since entrepreneurship education and training is not specific to enterprise only, students reported learning outcomes sometimes outside of entrepreneurship; in other words, what they learned in this module had a significant impact on other events and

Table 10. A Summary of the Elements of Assessment and Score Values
(N = 85).

Learning Objectives	Efficacy of Lecturers	Assessing the Module
Elements of assessment: • Skill-building approach • Developing and using my skills • Creating practical learning tools • Behaviour modelling • Exposure to the 'world of work' • Covering key topics • Reinforcing concepts through tutorials • Applying the concepts	Elements of assessment: • Present material effectively • Interested in subject matter • Care for students' learning • Stimulate my thinking • Good knowledge of subject matter • Willing to help students • Marked tests and assignments promptly • Encouraging a student/ presenter partnership • Felt free to ask questions • Fair and impartial • Well-prepared for lectures	Elements of assessment: • Improved my ability to analyse and evaluate • Increase my ability to solve problems • Improve my understanding of concepts & principles • Students team-exercises effective • Course objectives clearly stated • Course content met course objectives • Course material contributed to my comprehension

High[a]	Medium	Low[b]	High[a]	Medium	Low[b]	High[a]	Medium	Low[b]
74.10%	14.20%	11.70%	82.50%	10.30%	7.20%	86.00%	11.80%	2.20%
	9 Questions			13 Questions			8 Questions	

[a]Average of the two highest points of the 5-point Likert scale.
[b]Average of lowest two points of the 5-point Likert scale.

activities in their lives; the acquisition of cross-functional skills abound and there has been an enthusiastic appreciation of the innovative format of this module. Finally, students wanted more time to run their businesses, especially those enterprises where the success is based on strong group cohesion.

10.2. Reflections by Presenters

From the perspective of the presenters, the outcome of the module was regarded as very positive. From an empirical perspective, it – proved that entrepreneurial training at the level of higher education impacts positively on the target group. Students gained significant benefit in terms of building their self-confidence, knowledge acquisition and skills development for starting their own businesses. Furthermore, the module appears well-worth repeating and therefore continues at the university.

However, further refinement and support mechanisms need to be developed and put in place to aid students. For example, improved financial monitoring and reporting are required; more training in peer evaluation is needed; and students need more time to run the businesses.

11. STRENGTHS AND LIMITATIONS

The results from this research project should be considered as a starting point of the debate on the extent to which entrepreneurship can be taught at the tertiary level, especially in an African context.

It would have been useful to do follow-up research to determine whether students who have attended the training are more frequently starting businesses than those of the control group. Many of our students are coming from different provinces and in terms of the geographic dispersion it is very difficult to trace them, because they are mostly going back to their home provinces after they have finalised their studies.

Another limitation of the study is the relatively small sample size of experimental and control group. Thus an issue of further research would be to have a larger sample size, especially for the control group.

However, a significant strength of the study is the experimental design with a control group and that the questionnaire used, was validated in South Africa. It is within the same context that the researchers wish to open the debate with their peers on the African continent, and elsewhere, on developing evidence of an empirical nature on how entrepreneurship can be taught.

12. SUMMARY, CONCLUSION, RECOMMENDATIONS

This chapter presented an innovative method at the level of higher education of training and educating a group of undergraduate students in entrepreneurship, brought about by the challenges of establishing self-esteem and education in the context of developing economies by means of a programme in entrepreneurship education and training. This year-long module has been operational for four years and a longitudinal survey was done to ascertain if there is any implication in this form of training. In terms of the four elements tested in the survey, namely achievement, innovation, locus of control and self-esteem, the study found significant improvements in three of these variables. However, from our findings it does not seem possible to change the locus of control variable in the context of the intervention we used.

Based on our experience of entrepreneurship training and education at the level of higher education, we can now conclude that this module has been instrumental in

- changing the mindsets of students by offering self-employment (i.e. entrepreneurship) as a viable alternative to becoming a job-seeker;
- presenting students with the necessary business skills to start and run an enterprise;
- facilitating and further enhancing experiential learning by running and managing their own enterprises on campus;
- subjecting students to real-life examples of the typical problems, needs and constraints entrepreneurs face; and
- developing role models based on the successful examples of similar student enterprises from previous years.

In terms of recommendations, three important aspects can be highlighted, namely:

- Future training: Future entrepreneurship training must be based on practical, "hands-on" experiences. Three of the four elements tested in the survey (i.e. Achievement, Innovation and Self-esteem) support the practical interventions about entrepreneurship and that students can learn to be more entrepreneurial.
- Length of training courses: Short training courses in entrepreneurial training as found in business schools, do not have the same results as found in training courses of longer duration. This recommendation is based on our finding that the changing of attitudes do not easily occur over a short period of time; rather, a longer period of time is required to influence this process which is especially true in larger groups.
- Training over a longer time period impacts positively on the outcome. The results from this survey, prove that we have the right approach as reflected in the patterns of attitude towards being more entrepreneurial, especially in the context of South Africa with its high rate of unemployment, starting a business is crucial to the growth of the economy.
- Courses, such the one described in this chapter, should be initiated at other tertiary institutions, not only in South Africa, but also other parts of Africa.

REFERENCES

Anderson J., & Visser, K. (2002). Student micro-enterprise teams for South Africa: A university-based experience. 9th annual international EDINEB conference, June 20–24. Monterrey Technical University, Guadalajara, Mexico.

Antonites, A. (2003). *An action learning approach to entrepreneurial creativity, innovation and opportunity finding.* Unpublished doctoral dissertation. University of Pretoria, Pretoria, South Africa.

Braukmann, U. (2000). Fostering of entrepreneurships by Universities – Outlines of an entrepreneurship education within the scope of the 'Bizeps-Project'. *Proceedings of the 2000 USASBE annual national conference: The entrepreneurial millennium,* San Antonio, Texas. February 16–19.

Bolton, B., & Thompson, J. (2004). *Entrepreneurs: Talent, temperament, technique.* Oxford: Elsevier Butterworth-Heinemann.

Brookhaus, R. (1976). *Locus of control and risk taking propensity as entrepreneurial character isitics.* Unpublished doctoral dissertation. Washington University, St Louis.

Cook, T., Campbell, D., & Peracchio, L. (1990). Quasi experimentation. In: M. Dunette & L. Hough (Eds), *Handbook of industrial and organizational psychology.* Palo Alto: Consulting Psychologists Press.

Crandall, R. (1973). Measurement of self-esteem and related constructs. In: J. Robinson & P. Shaver (Eds), *Measurement of social psychological attitudes.* Ann Arbor: University of Michigan.

Davies, T. (2001). Entrepreneurship development in South Africa: Redefining the role of tertiary institutions in a reconfigured higher education system. *South African Journal of Higher Education, 15*(1), 34–39.

Driver, A., Wood, E., Segal, N., & Herrington, M. (2001). *Global Entrepreneurship Monitor: 2001 South African Executive Report.* Cape Town: Graduate School of Business, University of Cape Town.

Edwards, L., & Muir, E. (2004). "Tell me and I'll forget; show me and I may remember; involve me and I'll understand" – Developing enterprise education through theory and practice. *Proceedings of the 13th nordic conference on small business research,* Tromsø, Norway, June 10–12.

Falkäng, J., & Alberti, F. (2000). The Assessment of Entrepreneurship Education. *Industry and Higher Education, 14*(2), 101–108.

Finkle, T. A., & Deeds, D. (2001). Trends in the market of entrepreneurship faculty during the Period 1989–1998. *Journal of Business Venturing, 16*(6), 613–630.

Frese, M., Beimel, S., & Schoenborn, S. (2003). Action training for charismatic leadership. *Personnel Psychology, 56,* 671–697.

Friedrich, C., Glaub, M., Gramberg, K., & Frese, M. (2006). Does training improve the business performance of small-scale entrepreneurs? *Journal of Industry and Higher Education* (Accepted for Publication). London: IP Publishing.

Glaub, M. (2002). *Cognitive and behavioral factors in entrepreneurship training in South Africa and firm success.* Unpublished Diploma thesis. University of Giessen, Germany.

Green, P., Katz, J., & Johannison, B. (2004). Entrepreneurship education. *Academy of Management Learning and Education, 3*(3), 238–241.

Hamilton, L., Asundi, R., & Romaguera, J. (2002). Innovative practices for teaching entrepreneurship and business formation courses: An assessment of the six year program at

UPR-Mayagüez, College of Business. *Proceedings of the 47th world conference of the international council of small business*, San Juan, Puerto Rico. June 16–19.

Hannan, M., Hazlett, S., & Leitch, C. (2004). Entrepreneurship education: How do we measure success? *Conference proceedings RENT VII conference*, Copenhagen, Denmark. November 24–26.

Hermans, H. (1970). A questionnaire measure of achievement motivation. *Journal of Applied Psychology, 54*(4), 353–363.

Hisrich, R., & O'Cinneida, B. (1992). Research trends in entrepreneurship: The potential in expanding europe and transatlantic perspectives. *Proceedings of the 7th nordic conference on small business research.*

Hisrich, R., & Peters, M. (2002). *Entrepreneurship.* Boston: Irwin McGraw-Hill.

Hornaday, J., & Aboud, J. (1971). Characteristics of successful entrepreneurs. *Personnel Psychology, 24*(2), 141–153.

Huefner, J., Hunt, H., & Robinson, P. (1996). Comparison of four scales predicting entrepreneurship. *Academy of Entrepreneurship Journal, 1*(2), 56–80.

Hunt, H., Huefner, J., Voegele, C., & Robinson, P. (1989). The entrepreneurial consumer. In: G. Hills, R. LaForge & B. Parker (Eds), *Research at the marketing/entrepreneurship interface.* Chicago: University of Illinois at Chicago.

Hytti, U. (Ed.), (2002). *State-of-art of enterprise education in Europe – Results from the Entredu project.* Turku, Finland: Small Business Institute, Business Research and Development Centre, Turku School of Economics and Business Administration and ENTREDU project partners.

Hytti, U., & Kuopusjärvi, P. (2004a). *Evaluating and measuring entrepreneurship and enterprise education: Methods, tools and practices.* Small Business Institute, Business Research and Development Centre, Turku School of Economics and Business Administration. European Community Project # FIN/02/C/P/RF-82501. Entrava-project, Leonardo da Vinci-programme of the European Commission, Turku, Finland.

Hytti, U., & Kuopusjärvi, P. (2004b). Three perspectives to evaluating entrepreneurship education: Evaluators, programme promoters and policy makers. *Conference proceedings RENT VII conference*, Copenhagen, Denmark. 24–26 November.

Katz, J. (Ed.). (1991). Special issue editor's introduction: Infrastructure reporting in the field of entrepreneurship. *Entrepreneurship Theory and Practice, 15*(3), 5–10.

Kiggundu, M. (2002). Entrepreneurs and entrepreneurship in Africa: What is known and what needs to be done. *Journal of Developmental Entrepreneurship, 7*(3), 239–257.

Kirton, M. (1976). Adaptors and innovators: A description and measure. *Journal of Applied Psychology, 61*(5), 622–629.

Kirton, M. (1978). Have adaptors and innovators equal levels of creativity. *Psychological Reports, 42*, 695–698.

Klandt, H. (2004). Entrepreneurship education and research in German-speaking Europe. *Academy of Management Learning and Education, 3*(3), 293–301.

Ladzani, W., & Van Vuuren, J. (2002). Entrepreneurship training for emerging SMEs in South Africa. *Journal of Small Business Management, 40*(2), 154–161.

Laukkannen, M. (2000). Exploring alternative approaches in high-level entrepreneurship education: Creating micro mechanisms for endogenous regional growth. *Journal of Entrepreneurship and Regional Development, 12*(1), 25–48.

Levenson, H. (1981). Diffferentiating among internality, powerful others and chance. In: H. Lefcourt (Ed.), *Research with the locus of control construct: Assessment methods*, Vol. 1. New York: Academic Press.

Levi, J. (1999). *Entrepreneurship education in higher education in England: A survey.* London Business School and Department of Higher Education, London: Crown.

Mason, C. (2000). *Teaching entrepreneurship to undergraduate: Lessons from leading centers of entrepreneurship education.* Southampton: University of Southampton, Department of Geography.

McClelland, D. (1965). Need for achievement and entrepreneurship: A longitudinal study. *Journal of Personality and Social Psychology, 1*(4), 389–392.

McClelland, D. (1986). Characteristics of successful entrepreneurs. *Journal of Creative Behavior, 21*(3), 219–233.

Minniti, M., Arenius, P., & Langowitz, N. (2004). *Global entrepreneurship monitor: 2004 Report on women and entrepreneurship.* Center for Women's Leadership at Babson College, Boston: Babson College.

Nieman, G., Hough, J., & Nieuwenhuizen, C. (2003). *Entrepreneurship: A South African perspective.* Pretoria: Van Schaik.

Patel, V. (1986). Integrated entrepreneurship development programs: The Indian experience. Regional workshop on training for entrepreneurship and self-employment. Manila.

Perren, L., & Grant, P. (2001). *Management and leadership in UK SMEs: Witness testimonies from the world of entrepreneurs and SME managers.* London: Council for Excellence in Management and Leadership.

Reynolds, P., Hay, M., Bygrave, W., Camp, S., & Autio, E. (2000). *Global entrepreneurship monitor: Executive report.* Kansas City: Kauffman Center for Entrepreneurial Leadership.

Roberts, E. (1991). *Entrepreneurs in high technology.* London: Oxford University Press.

Robinson, P., Huefner, J., & Hunt, H. (1991a). Entrepreneurial research on student subjects does not generalize to real world entrepreneurs. *Journal of Small Business Management, 29,* 42–50.

Robinson, P., Stimpson, D., Huefner, J., & Hunt, H. (1991b). An attitude approach to the prediction of entrepreneurship. *Entrepreneurship Theory and Practice, 15*(4), 13–31.

Ronstadt, R. (1987). The educated entrepreneurs: A new era of entrepreneurial education is beginning. *American Journal of Small Business, 11*(4), 37–53.

Rotter, J. (1990). Internal versus external control of reinforcement. *American Psychologist, 45,* 489–493.

Rotter, J. (1966). Generalized expectations for internal versus external control of reinforcement. *Psychological Monographs: General and Applied, 80*(1), 1–27.

Rwigema, H., & Venter, R. (2004). *Advanced entrepreneurship.* Cape Town: Oxford.

Saffu, K. (2003). The role of 'acadepreneurs' in entrepreneurship education in Australian universities. *Proceedings of the 48th world conference of the international council of small business,* Northern Ireland. 15–18 June.

Singh, J. (1990). Entrepreneurship education as a catalyst of development in the third world. *Journal of Small Business and Entrepreneurship, 11,* 44–47.

Siteman, A. (2004). Can entrepreneurship be taught? Reflections on the MIT experience. (Online), http://www.esmas.com/emprendedores/startups/eresemprendedor/401446.html. February 20, 2005.

Spencer, L., McClelland, D., & Spencer, S. (1992). *Competency assessment methods.* Boston: Hay-McBer Research Press.

Timmons, J., & Spinelli, S. (2004). *New venture creation: Entrepreneurship for the 21st century.* Boston: Irwin McGraw-Hill.

Van Wyk, R., Boshoff, A. B., & Owen, J. H. (1999). Construct validity of psychometric in-
     struments developed in the United States, when applied to professional people in South
     Africa. *South African Journal of Economic and Management Sciences, SSI*(Special Issue),
     1–72.
Vesper, K., & Gartner, W. (1997). Measuring progress in entrepreneurship education. *Journal
     of Business Venturing, 12*(5), 403–421.
Vosloo, W. (Ed.) (1994). *Entrepreneurship and economic growth.* Pretoria: Human Sciences
     Research Council.
Wickham, P. (2004). *Strategic entrepreneurship.* Harlow, England: Pearson Education.

EDUCATIONAL CURRICULA AND SELF-EFFICACY: ENTREPRENEURIAL ORIENTATION AND NEW VENTURE INTENTIONS AMONG UNIVERSITY STUDENTS IN MEXICO

Ricardo D. Alvarez, Alex F. DeNoble and Don Jung

1. INTRODUCTION

By almost any index Mexico has historically struggled in the last century with economic and social growth. For example, Kearney's (2005) well-respected Globalization Index ranks Mexico 42nd in the world and the U.N. Human Development Reports (2003) rank Mexico 53rd in its Human Development Index. Recently, however, Mexico appears to have made a commitment to transform into a competitive nation by privatizing state-owned industries, reducing international commerce barriers and tariffs, attracting foreign investment, and establishing free-trade agreements (NAFTA) with

Developmental Entrepreneurship: Adversity, Risk, and Isolation
International Research in the Business Disciplines, Volume 5, 379–403
Copyright © 2006 by Elsevier Ltd.
ISSN: 1074-7877/doi:10.1016/S1074-7877(06)05019-7

neighbors such as the United States and Canada (Young & Welsch, 1993). However, to sustain the changes, a strong and capable group of domestic entrepreneurs are needed in Mexico.

According to Wachtel (1999), three types of obstacles are inhibiting entrepreneurial success in Mexico: (1) business environment, (2) individual culture, and (3) family centered society. First, accessing capital funding, or obtaining loans to get the necessary start-up assets, is very difficult for new business ventures, because of high-interest rates, increasing consumer prices, and volatile foreign currency exchange rates. Start-up equity financing, such as venture capital and business angels, is extremely scarce. Without access to this investment, it is difficult for start-up companies that need substantial capital, particularly those in the mid- to high technology sectors, to reach break-even or gain a reasonable return on investment without additional support. In addition, because Mexican federal taxes are at record levels, there is a lack of fiscal private investment stimulus. Although the Mexican government and associated economic institutions regularly reforms itself, they are still considered overly bureaucratic, regulated, and corrupt as evidenced by the low ranking on the various global business indices, such as IMD International's "business efficiency" index (47th) and Transparency International's "corruption" index (67th).

Second, small to medium size family centered organizations represent the largest number of businesses in the country, which usually reinvest their capital in new related family business ventures. They are extremely closed and myopic, and rarely allocate money in other diversified companies outside of the family. In addition, it has been suggested that Mexican family business is also generally adverse to risk, shows a lack of confidence, and has discriminatory practices against women – dimensions that often make it difficult for emerging entrepreneurs, particularly female (Lee & Peterson, 2000). Many have suggested that Mexico must take more aggressive measures to develop and maintain an adequate environment that promotes and nurtures new business start-ups, enterprise creation, and risk-taking entrepreneurs.

An "entrepreneurial environment" can be defined as the combination of factors that play an important role in the development of new business ventures. It refers both to the overall exogenous factors that influence people's willingness to undertake entrepreneurial activities and to the availability of assistance and support services that facilitate start-ups. According to Covin and Slevin (1991), the external environment can include economic, political/legal, and socio-cultural forces that provide a broader context for an organization's operation.

Entrepreneurship in developing economies can flourish if potential entrepreneurs find opportunities in the environment, and if environmental conditions motivate and enhance entrepreneurs' ability to start and manage a new business (Gnyawali & Fogel, 1994; Ussman & Postigo, 2000). While certain infrastructure elements, like the existence of research and development programs, and a well-educated and technically skilled labor force, can make a substantial impact on the entrepreneurial environment (Bruno & Tyebjee, 1982), previous research (Pennings, 1982; Vesper, 1990; Davidsson, 1991), also indicates that factors such as the presence of universities for training and research are found to be very important to increase the rate of new venture creation. Thus, countries that have low levels of technical and business skills could prevent motivated entrepreneurs from starting a new venture – and according to UNESCO, Mexico ranks at best somewhere in the mid-point of the world in secondary educational achievement (2000 statistics), and according to the Organization for Economic Cooperation and Development (OECD), last of the member countries in "technical literacy" (1999 statistics).

Vesper (1990) identified four elements in venture creation: a profitable business opportunity, technical know-how of the entrepreneur, business know-how of the entrepreneur, and entrepreneurial initiative, which comprises at the same time education and intentions. This suggests that education is a key environmental force that enables and provides a way for nascent entrepreneurs to gain the necessary business and technical skills to nurture their self-efficacy to the point of initiating actions toward starting a new venture (Lüthje & Franke, 2003).

Previous research (DeNoble, et al., 1999) has demonstrated a positive relationship between perceived self-efficacy and entrepreneurial intentions, and there is also empirical evidence showing a positive relation between formal education and new venture success. A study by Veciana (2002) found that the failure rate between entrepreneurs without higher education and entrepreneurs with education is almost four to one.

Accordingly, the purpose of this project was to investigate the impact of entrepreneurship education on students' perceived self-efficacy and orientation toward new venture intentions within a sample of Mexican universities. We examine some of the following key research questions:

1. With Mexican students, to what extent does entrepreneurial education exposure help nascent entrepreneurs and students develop entrepreneurial intentions and orientation?
2. Is Entrepreneurial Self-Efficacy (ESE) enhanced by Mexican entrepreneurial education?

3. Is there a positive relationship between Mexican universities' entrepreneurial curricula and students' entrepreneurial intentions?
4. How is self-efficacy related to entrepreneurial intentions and orientation?

If universities do not promote entrepreneurship education, we would expect that students would be less likely to pursue efforts toward starting a new business venture. Particularly, as Gnyawali and Fogel (1994) have suggested, it seems that training and education services are very important in emerging market economies because entrepreneurs lack basic business skills.

The need for economic development and prosperity is influencing universities to include entrepreneurship courses in their curricula to promote entrepreneurial capabilities among students (Laukkanen, 2000; Hindle & Rushworth, 2000). There is growing consensus that education plays an important role for the creation of new ventures, enhancing students' managerial skills which increases the probability of developing entrepreneurial activities (Van Praag & Cramer, 2001; Kantis, Postigo, Federico, & Tamborini, 2002).

In Mexico, a number of universities have recently instituted entrepreneurial courses in their curricula. However, the vast majority still have not, although there is a trend toward more entrepreneurial education. This developing situation presents an ideal setting to investigate the issues posed in this study.

2. LITERATURE REVIEW

2.1. Entrepreneurship Education: Historical Overview

Entrepreneurship education constitutes a novel academic field, particularly in countries and cultures where even the term "entrepreneurship" has somewhat different meanings. The discipline is still unknown by a large number of university professors, students, business owners, and community members within developing countries. The introduction and promotion of new entrepreneurship curricula at both graduate and undergraduate levels, embraces major challenges for universities' entrepreneurship program developers and business school faculty.

Within the United States, for example, more than half a century ago the first entrepreneurship courses were introduced at the Harvard Business School, but the subject evolved very little and was not generally popular in the decades that followed. By the 1960s less than 10 universities offered some type of entrepreneurship education. In 1970, the number of business schools and universities in the United States that offered entrepreneurship courses began to increase. From the 16 universities that were offering entrepreneurship courses at the time, 12 had started to include them in the preceding two years (Vesper & Gartner, 1997). The first entrepreneurship majors were offered in some American universities by the 1980s (Sexton, Upton, Wachlotz, & McDougall, 1997). In 1993, about 400 colleges and universities in the United States were offering one or more courses in entrepreneurship. By the late early 2000 every business program in the United States probably offered one or more courses in entrepreneurship, with many universities offering or developing actual concentrations in entrepreneurship (Vesper, 1993; Fiet, 2001; Solomon, Duffy, & Tarabishy, 2002; Katz, 2003).

In an emerging field such as entrepreneurship, there is likely to be less educator consensus than in other better-established fields (Finkle & Deeds, 2001). A major challenge faced by most entrepreneurship educators in universities is the existing organizational and institutional structures. Most university business schools are highly departmentalized by functions and often do not have an identifiable "home" for "entrepreneurship." Entrepreneurship education is inter-functional and does not properly fit within any business department. Entrepreneurship course-work is generally offered in management departments in Business Schools and less often within the marketing and finance areas (Hills, 1988).

Several universities offer more than one or two related courses. Early research by Vesper (1985) identified at least three models for an entrepreneurship program. First, there is the "conceptual baseline" that includes the business plan, the business life cycle, and business functions. Most introductory courses in entrepreneurship focus on an overview of the business plan. Another model, often used in MBA programs, is highly related to the "business life cycle" stages. Some universities offer a course in small-business management with a focus on established firms. The third model is the one that treats entrepreneurial education as a set of "additional courses" within the finance, accounting, legal, and/or marketing areas, fitting the functional organization of business colleges (Hills, 1988; Gorman, Hanlon, & King, 1997; Solomon et al., 2002). Some authors stated the need to experiment with an unstructured approach to teaching entrepreneurship, much like a doctoral seminar, which is a partial response to evidence that entrepreneurship students exhibit characteristics that demand more flexibility (Hills & Welsch, 1996; Relf, 1995; Vesper & Gartner, 1997). In this regard, Ronstadt (1985) implies that students must be oriented into a multiple venture career and toward adaptive flexibility to evolve successful configurations. Many students should not be required to develop full business plans, but instead create, less detailed feasibility studies. Such variations are based on evidence as to the different types of students who take entrepreneurship courses and the strength of their entrepreneurial intentions (Hills & Barnaby, 1977). While entrepreneurship education has clearly progressed over the years (Gorman et al., 1997; Solomon et al., 2002) the basic models of entrepreneurship education appears to have remained fairly constant, with the exception that more specific majors are now being offered. Similar models, with some variations unique to the European educational system, have been developed at many universities in Western and Central Europe.

The entrepreneurial phenomena has also impacted Latin American universities, as increasingly more schools are now committing to develop and nurture entrepreneurial capabilities among students (Ussman & Postigo, 2000; Varela & Jimenez, 2001; Postigo & Tamborini, 2002). According to a recent study regarding Latin America business development, half of most enterprising new start-ups were ventures created by university graduates (Kantis, Ishida, & Komori, 2002).

Entrepreneurship education in Mexico has evolved at a slower pace than in the United States, however the first entrepreneurial education efforts started in 1978, when the ITESM (Instituto Tecnologico y de Estudios Superiores de Monterrey) created their revolutionary "Business Enterprise Program" ("Programa Empresario"), which later became the "Entrepreneur Program" ("Programa Emprendedor").[1] The program was conceptualized as a series of integrated entrepreneurship courses to promote a proactive approach to business venturing among undergraduate students that were studying in their last few semesters. The program is still running and it is considered as the pioneer project of entrepreneurial education in Mexico.

By the early 1990s, a decade or so after the "Programa Emprendedor" was launched, several Mexican universities started including different entrepreneurship courses in their Business Administration programs. Some of these courses, such as "New Product Development" or "Strategic Planning," do not have formal academic support and are not related to any entrepreneurial curricula. Most schools tend to include new business or new product development courses in their curricula just because competitor universities are offering them. The Mexican educational environment that can nurture future entrepreneurs' skills, competencies, and capabilities appears to be at the moment, very limited.

2.2. Self-Efficacy

Bandura (1978) defines self-efficacy as "a judgment of one's ability to execute a particular behavior pattern" or the "personal assessment of the capability to accomplish a certain level of performance." Thus, an individual's behavior, environment, and cognitive factors are highly interrelated, and play a key role in that individual's motivation and achievement. Self-efficacy beliefs determine how much effort a person will spend on a task and how long he or she will persist with it. People with strong self-efficacy beliefs exert greater efforts to master a challenge while those with weak self-efficacy beliefs are likely to reduce their efforts or even quit. There are four major sources of information, in which some of them education plays an active role, are used by individuals when forming self-efficacy judgments:

- "Performance Accomplishments" refers to personal assessment information that is based on an individual's personal mastery accomplishments (i.e. past experiences).
- "Vicarious Experience" is gained by observing others success activities and performance (modeling).
- "Social Persuasion" refers to activities where people lead, through suggestion, into believing that they can cope successfully with specific tasks. Coaching and giving evaluative feedback on performance are common types of social persuasion.
- The final source of information is physiological and emotional states. The individual's physiological and emotional state influences self-efficacy judgments, both positive and negative of one's ability to complete a task (Bandura, 1977; Bandura & Cervone, 1986).

Perceived self-efficacy helps to account for a wide variety of individual behavior, including: changes in coping behavior produced by different modes of influence, levels of psychological stress reactions, self-regulation, achievement strivings, growth of intrinsic interest, and choice of career pursuits (Bandura, 1982).

2.3. Entrepreneurial Self-Efficacy

ESE has to do with the self-belief, willingness, and persistence to overcome the initial anxiety that a new start-up process delivers. Entrepreneurs with a high degree of confidence in their potentiality and capabilities to successfully accomplish the needed tasks and required actions to create a new venture or launch a new product to the market will have more positive results and outcomes than others. Self-efficacy beliefs may support direction, intensity, and the entrepreneur's persistence (DeNoble, Jung, & Ehlrich, 1999; Lüthje & Franke, 2003; Arenius & Minniti, 2005).

Self-efficacy has a number of practical and theoretical implications for entrepreneurial success because initiating a new venture requires unique skills and mind sets. Self-efficacy is linked to initiating and persisting a behavior under uncertainty, to setting higher goals, and reducing threat-rigidity and learned helplessness (Bandura & Cervone, 1986). This is important because opportunity recognition depends on situational perceptions of controllability (Dutton, 1993) and self-efficacy (Krueger & Dickson, 1994).

Entrepreneurs pursue opportunity regardless of the resources at hand. Individuals who perceived themselves as "entrepreneurial capable" are expected to be alert and sensitive to opportunities, and able to take advantage of such opportunities if they consider the endeavor worthwhile. Doubts upon self entrepreneurial skills and initial capital funding, were perceived by university students as two of the key obstacles associated with new venture creation (Postigo, Iacobucci, & Tamborini, 2003), while increased self-efficacy may facilitate opportunities perception (Krueger & Dickson, 1994). If entrepreneurial competence is understood as the combined capacity to identify and pursue opportunities, and to obtain and coordinate resources (Erikson, 2002), universities' entrepreneurial courses may be a fundamental element to provide the needed skills and the right knowledge to future entrepreneurs.

DeNoble et al. (1999) developed a scale to measure a person's "entrepreneurial self-efficacy" (ESE) or the personal belief of one's abilities to carry out the required tasks to create a new enterprise, based on several entrepreneurial skills that were uniquely different from general managerial skills. They identified six dimensions of entrepreneurial skill requirements and utilized them as a basis for developing the ESE scale. The measure can help researchers understand what makes entrepreneurs persist in their efforts to capitalize on new venture opportunities, and explain their cognitive characteristics.

One key implication that DeNoble et al. (1999) found, is the possibility of nurturing the necessary skills and to build the supportive confidence among university students, through entrepreneurial education, coursework, and training, reinforcing their self-belief as would-be entrepreneurs. Noel (2001) found that students who had taken entrepreneurship courses showed higher levels of self-efficacy and intentions to launch new business ventures than those who did not. Although these findings demonstrate a positive relationship between entrepreneurial intentions and perceived self-efficacy, in contrast, a subsequent study by Cox, Mueller, and Moss (2002) found that entrepreneurial education may in fact, decrease a student's ESE as a result of revealing the complex nature of entrepreneurial pursuits to these nascent individuals.

2.4. Entrepreneurial Intentions Models

Intentions are generally the single best predictor of any planned behavior, including entrepreneurship (Bagozzi, Baumgartner, & Yi, 1989). In his Theory of Planned Behavior (TPB), Azjen (1991) proposes a model that in its simplest form shows that intentions predict behavior, while in turn certain specific attitudes predict intentions. There are three attitudinal antecedents of intention. The first two, which are personal attitudes toward outcomes of the behavior (expectations and beliefs about personal impacts) and perceived social norms (expectations and beliefs about social groups impacts), reflect the perceived desirability of performing the behavior. The third, perceived behavioral control reflects perceptions that the behavior is personally controllable. Perceived behavioral control reflects the perceived feasibility of performing the behavior and is thus related to perception of situational competence (self-efficacy). Feasibility perceptions drive career-related choices, including self-employment as an entrepreneur.

Intentions toward behavior are absolutely critical for understanding other antecedents. These include situational role beliefs, subsequent moderators, including the perceived availability of critical resources, and the final consequences, including the initiation of a new venture. To understand the consequences of intentions -particularly actions- requires that we understand the antecedents of intention. Much of entrepreneurship is intentional, and therefore, the use of well thought-out and research-tested intention models should provide a good means of examining the precursors to business start-up (Krueger, Reilly, & Carsrud, 2000).

Shapero's (1982) "Entrepreneurial Event" model (EE), which is an implicitly intention construct, states that intentions to start a business derive from perceptions of desirability, feasibility, and a certain disposition to act upon opportunities. In such a case, behavior depends on the relative "credibility" of alternative behaviors plus some "propensity to act." "Credibility" requires a behavior to be seen as both desirable and feasible. "Perceived desirability" is the personal attractiveness of starting a business, including both intrapersonal and extra-personal impacts. "Perceived feasibility" is the degree to which one feels personally capable of starting a business (he proposes a testable eight-item inventory of questions aimed at different aspects of perceived desirability and feasibility). Shapero (1982) conceptualizes "propensity to act" as the personal disposition to act on one's decision, based on control perceptions and reflecting volitional aspects of intentions: that is, the desire to gain control by taking action.

A well-established conceptualization of this phenomenon is "learned optimism," which is a valid, reliable measure that consistently predicts commitment to goal-directed behavior in many settings (Seligman, 1990). A person who has a high propensity to start a business is more likely to start it if he or she sees an opportunity in the environment and feels confident in his or her ability to enterprise. The greater their entrepreneurial business skills, the greater their ability to enterprise (Vesper, 1990; Gnyawali & Fogel, 1994). This was demonstrated by a study about job creation in various states of the US, showing that for every 1% increase in a state's college-educated population, there was a 1.2% increase in jobs created by small firms (Phillips, 1993).

Attitudes influence behavior through effects on intentions. Intentions and attitudes depend on the situation and person. Accordingly, intentions models predict behavior better than either individual or situational variables, and provide superior predictive validity. Personal and situational variables typically have an indirect influence on entrepreneurship by influencing key attitudes and general motivation to act (Krueger et al., 2000). As much self-efficacy predicts opportunity recognition, self-perceptions are also pivotal to self-employment intentions (Scherer, Adams, Carley, & Wiebe, 1989).

Research findings suggest that individual self-addressed intentions to start a new business are increased by exposure to entrepreneurship education. Particularly, participatory courses have demonstrated to enhance students perceived desirability and feasibility (Delmar & Davidsson, 2000; Cowling & Taylor, 2001; Fayolle, 2002; Peterman & Kennedy, 2003).

2.5. Entrepreneurial Orientation

Entrepreneurship is a multi-dimensional process that starts with an opportunity, and opportunities are rooted in the external environment. Whether or not certain contexts nourish the development of enterprises, a strong Entrepreneurial Orientation (EO) within potential entrepreneurs or firms depends on a wide array of environmental conditions. The abundance of resources in the environment seems to have an impact on the firm's EO. Entrepreneurs can only know their environment via their perception, and their perceived environmental munificence may be a key determinant of their EO and self-belief of acquiring the necessary resources (Chandler & Hanks, 1994).

Brown and Kirchhoff (1997) found that small businesses owner's perception of resource availability affects her or his EO and subsequently, the firm's rate of growth. Self-reported competencies are predictive of entrepreneurial performance (Chandler & Jansen, 1992).

According to Lumpkin and Dess (1996), "Entrepreneurial Orientation" (EO) refers to the entrepreneurial process, namely how entrepreneurship is undertaken – the methods, practices, structures, and decision-making styles (behaviors) used to act entrepreneurially. Individual's EO can be determined by assessing five salient dimensions consisting of autonomy, innovativeness, risk taking, proactiveness, and competitive aggressiveness.

Autonomy refers to the independent spirit and necessary freedom to create a new venture. However, in order for the autonomy dimension of EO to be strong, entrepreneurs must operate within contexts that promote them to act independently, to maintain personal control, and to seek opportunities in the absence of social constraints. Whether or not entrepreneurs operate in environments that support new ideas, experimentation, novel solutions to problems, and creative processes of entrepreneurs will determine the strength of the innovativeness dimension of EO. Risk taking is the willingness of entrepreneurs to assume risk and accept the uncertainty associated with being self-employed. Risk-taking is an important component of a strong EO. Proactiveness has to do with the implementation stage of the entrepreneurial process. Proactive individuals do what is necessary to bring their concepts to fruition and gain an advantage by being the first to capitalize on new opportunities. Competitive aggressiveness refers to the tendency on assuming a combative posture toward rivals and to employ a high level of competitive intensity in attempts to surpass them. This is another key component of EO because new ventures are much likely to fail than established firms. Thus, an aggressive stance and intense competition are critical to the survival and success of new start-ups (Lumpkin & Dess, 1996).

2.6. Entrepreneurial Intensity

A given individual or organization is capable of producing a number of Entrepreneurial Events (EE) over time (Stevenson & Jarillo, 1990). Schumpeter (1934) defined entrepreneurship in terms of five types of events: introduction of new goods or new quality of goods, introduction of new methods of production, opening of a new market, utilization of new sources of supply, and carrying out new organizational forms (Gartner, 1985; Vesper, 1990). Whereas pursuing one of these events is entrepreneurship, there is some evidence to suggest that entrepreneurship is also associated with multiple events. Covin and Slevin (1991) argue that entrepreneurial organizations are those in which behavioral patterns are recurring. A continued effort to develop new products, services and/or markets, is indicative of a highly entrepreneurial operation and frequency (Morris & Sexton, 1996).

Accordingly within an educational context, comparative research regarding entrepreneurial education intensity between Colombian universities, showed that highest investment in entrepreneurial courses and training, resulted in higher-new venture creation rates among students (Varela & Jimenez, 2001).

Entrepreneurial intensity, as stated by Morris and Sexton (1996), can be defined as a variable that results from the combination of the "entrepreneurial frequency" or the number of events (new ventures, products, services, processes) in which a firm becomes involved, and the "entrepreneurial degree," which is the extent to which any one event is innovative, risky, and proactive. Accordingly, entrepreneurship is not an either/or determination, but a question of "how often" and "how much." The "entrepreneurial degree" and "entrepreneurial frequency" constructs derive from previous research.

Underlying entrepreneurial attitudes and behavior are three key dimensions: innovativeness, risk-taking, and proactiveness (Miller, 1983; Ginsberg, 1985; Morris & Paul, 1987; Covin & Slevin, 1989; Miles & Arnold, 1991). Innovativeness refers to the seeking of creative unusual or novel solutions to problems and needs. Risk-taking involves the willingness to commit significant resources to opportunities having a reasonable chance to costly failure. Proactiveness is concerned with implementation – with doing whatever is necessary to bring an entrepreneurial concept to fruition. It usually involves considerable perseverance, adaptability, and a willingness to assume some responsibility for failure. To the extent that an undertaking demonstrates some amount of innovativeness, risk taking and proactiveness, it can be considered an EE and the person behind it an entrepreneur (Morris & Sexton, 1996).

3. RESEARCH MODEL AND HYPOTHESIS

Based on the previous literature review, we developed a research model that explains the type of relationships that we are assessing and that exist

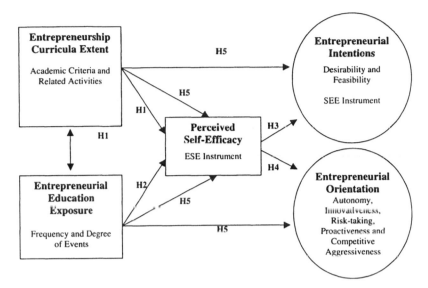

Fig. 1. Entrepreneurial Education Research Model.

between entrepreneurial education self-efficacy, and entrepreneurial intentions and orientation among university students in Mexico.

Fig. 1 graphically depicts how university students' EO and intentions, as would-be entrepreneurs, are positively influenced by their perceived ESE, and how this self-confidence in their capability of starting new business ventures is also directly related to the extent of entrepreneurship courses and seminars at their current universities, and their previous exposure to them.

3.1. Hypotheses

Hypothesis 1. Our first hypothesis suggests that "Entrepreneurial Education Intensity," which is the frequency and degree of exposure to EE as perceived by both Mexican faculty and students (courses, conferences, seminars, etc.), is positively and directly related to the "Entrepreneurship Curricula" extent, or the number of mandatory and optional entrepreneurship courses that a university includes in its academic programs, the new product development workshops, and/or business start-up simulations and seminars that schools offer to students. Academic courses, workshops, conferences, and seminars are infrastructure elements and environmental conditions that motivate and enhance students' entrepreneurial abilities (Bruno & Tyebjee, 1982; Gnyawali & Fogel, 1994).

A university extent of entrepreneurship educational curricula will have a positive impact in the level of students' perceived ESE. Our assumption is that a broader extent will result in higher perceived self-efficacy.

Hypothesis 2. Departing from Morris and Sexton's (1996) definition of "entrepreneurial intensity" and the Self-efficacy theory implication that an individual's behavior, environment, and cognitive factors are highly integrated, and are major influences in that individual's motivation and achievement (Bandura, 1978), our second hypothesis assumes that students perceived "Entrepreneurial Self-Efficacy" (self-believed entrepreneurial capabilities and competencies) is an outcome of "Entrepreneurial Education Intensity."

Thus, students' frequency and degree of exposure to entrepreneurship education will influence students' perceived ESE. We expect that a higher intensity (frequency and degree of exposure to entrepreneurial courses, seminars, workshops, etc.) will lead to higher perceived self-efficacy within our sample of Mexican universities.

Hypothesis 3. Our third hypothesis drives from the concept that intentions are the best predictors of any planned behavior, including entrepreneurship (Bagozzi et al., 1989).

Since certain specific attitudes predict intentions, such as situational role beliefs and perceived behavioral control (Azjen, 1991), the perceived feasibility of performing a behavior, (starting a new business) is based on perceived situational competence (Shapero, 1982). Students' propensity to act (intentions) is an outcome of students' perceived ESE (control and feasibility perceptions).

We suggest that higher perceived ESE will result in higher intentions for developing a new venture.

Hypothesis 4. Considering that entrepreneurs behavior results from their environmental perceptions and self-beliefs (Chandler & Hanks, 1994), and that by definition, "Entrepreneurial Orientation" refers to the entrepreneurial process (undertaken methods, practices, structures, and decision-making behaviors) to act entrepreneurially (Lumpkin & Dess, 1996), our fourth hypothesis suggests that perceived ESE has a positive impact on the students' EO.

Students' high perceived ESE will be directly related to a higher orientation toward developing a new venture, as measured by their autonomy, innovativeness, risk-taking, proactiveness, and competitive aggressiveness levels.

Hypothesis 5. Previous research has found evidence of the relation between the different types of students who take entrepreneurship courses and their behavioral entrepreneurship intentions strength levels (Hills & Barnaby, 1977). Based on this, we suggest that students' level of exposure to EE (i.e. courses, seminars, workshops, etc.), which we expect to be directly related to the educational curricula extent, will eventually have a direct impact in students' perceived entrepreneurial intentions and orientation. Students with higher entrepreneurial intensity (frequency and degree of exposure to EE) will have higher perceived entrepreneurial intentions and orientation.

4. DATA AND METHODOLOGY

We selected three local, major universities from the city of Tijuana, B. C., Mexico, to conduct our research. The three institutions are well known for their business schools and high academic standards: Centro de Enseñanza Técnica y Superior or CETYS Universidad, Universidad Autónoma de Baja California (UABC), and Universidad Iberoamericana (UIA). Owing to its close proximity with San Diego, California which has several university programs in entrepreneurship (San Diego State University, University of San Diego, etc.) it was felt that Tijuana schools would also have a fairly broad selection of entrepreneurial courses compared with other locations in Mexico.

CETYS Universidad is a private school with a regional presence in Baja California. It was founded 45 years ago and has three major campuses in Mexicali, Tijuana, and Ensenada, and is considered among the top ten private universities in the country, according to the Mexican Private Colleges and Higher Education Institutions Federation (FIMPES).[2] CETYS Universidad offers 12 different undergraduate and 14 graduate academic programs, ranging from Engineering to Law, and from Business Management and Accounting to Psychology.[3]

The UABC, or Autonomous University of Baja California, is a state-owned institution with the largest number of enrolled students in Baja California and in the city of Tijuana. UABC comprises 17 schools and 8 research institutes with a broad variety of undergraduate and graduate programs. It has the largest School of Business Administration and Accounting among local universities and is recognized by its high-academic standards as compared with other state-owned institutions nationally.[4]

While UABC and CETYS are both regional universities, Universidad Iberoamericana, or UIA, is a renowned national and international private university with more than 60 years of history. The Iberoamericana University is part of the UIA-ITESO system, Mexico's second largest privately owned educational conglomerate with campuses in Mexico City, Guadalajara, Tijuana and three other major mid-size Mexican cities. UIA offers 30 undergraduate and 31 graduate programs, and more than 190 Extended Studies courses.[5]

To test the stated hypothesis in this study, data were collected from administration faculty and students at each institution. We measured faculty perceptions of entrepreneurial education intensity within each school by conducting personal interviews with each university's School of Business principals and with the faculty in charge of the Entrepreneurship Program. A total of 6 professors were interviewed (two from each university). During the interviews we applied to the professors a 34 item questionnaire adapting the Morris and Sexton instrument (Morris & Sexton, 1996) to measure their perceived school's "entrepreneurship intensity" (frequency and degree of entrepreneurship education events).

We gathered academic curricula and counted and categorized the entrepreneurship courses, both optional and mandatory, that each school was offering at the graduate level. We then compared the entrepreneurship curricula of the three different universities to establish the entrepreneurship courses extent and differences between them.

As for the "would-be entrepreneur" data, we conducted a survey with approximately 300 students attending the three universities. Respondents were randomly selected and 195 usable questionnaires were obtained with a 65% rate of response (see Table 1).

The survey consisted of 104 items that was translated from English to Spanish and then translated back to English. Several measures were

Table 1. Research Sample Questionnaires – Rate of Response.

	School 1 UIA	School 2 UABC	School 3 CETYS	Total
Total sample questionnaires	100	100	100	300
Returned usable questionnaires	75	79	41	195
Response rate (%)	75	79	41	65
Business Administration students	22	59	22	103
International Business students	13	13	13	39
Accounting students	0	1	6	7
Other programs students[a]	40	6	0	46

[a]Other programs: Engineering, architecture, graphic design and law.

sub-divided into three sections. Some of the questions were reverse-coded to reduce bias. The first part of the questionnaire was designed to assess student's self-belief and confidence in developing new ventures adapting the "Entrepreneurial Self-Efficacy" instrument ESE developed by DeNoble, et al. (1999). The second section of the questionnaire focused on determining students' entrepreneurial intentions, orientation, and general self-efficacy, adapting and combining the 'Conviction and Attitude' item inventory developed by Davidsson (1991), with the "General Self-Efficacy" scale used by Markman, Balkin, and Baron (2002) and Lumpkin & Dess (1996) 'Entrepreneurial Orientation' instrument, to measure students' level of autonomy, innovativeness, risk taking, proactiveness, conviction, change-orientation, valuation of money, achievement motivation, social contribution, payoff, and competitive aggressiveness, utilizing five-point scales.

On the third section, we measured the students' entrepreneurial educational exposure (intensity) by quantifying the frequency of "entrepreneurship education events" of every student (number of taken courses, feasibility studies conducted, market research projects, etc.) and their regretful thinking level, by once again adapting the Morris and Sexton instrument (Morris & Sexton, 1996), and Markman et al.'s (2002) regretful thinking questions.

Finally, we compared and statistically analyzed the findings, identifying the types of correlations that exist between exposure to entrepreneurial education and reported levels of ESE, orientation, and intentions.

5. PRELIMINARY FINDINGS AND RESULTS

5.1. Entrepreneurship Curricula

After reviewing and comparing the academic curricula of the Business Administration, International Business Administration, International Trade Management, Marketing, and accounting graduate programs from the three universities, we found minor differences between their "entrepreneurial curricula extent" (see Table 2). Moreover, of the 10 different academic programs that were reviewed, only three of them had some kind of mandatory entrepreneurship courses included. Thirty-six business management and accounting-related courses were quantified, and from these, only five were related to new product or new business development. We did not find any specifically designed "entrepreneurial curricula" in any of the three universities. Actually, there were not any "entrepreneurship programs" in the strict sense. Most of the schools offered just a few optional and isolated

Table 2. Curricula Analysis of Schools of Business Undergraduate
Programs.

	School 1 UIA	School 2 UABC	School 3 CETYS
School of business curricula (all courses)	52	54	54
Business administration program	Yes	Yes	Yes
International/trade management program	Yes	Yes	Yes
Accounting program	—	Yes	Yes
marketing management program	—	—	Yes
Hotel administration program	—	Yes	—
New product/new business related courses			
Mandatory	20	19	28
Optional	5	3	0
Entrepreneurship specific courses			
Mandatory	2	5	0
Optional	0	2	2
Workshops	1	1	1
Percentage of entrepreneurial courses			
From new product/new business related courses (%)	12.0	36.4	10.7
From total curricula (%)	5.8	14.8	5.6

Note: Based on information provided by school officials and registered undergraduate programs. Programs offered by different schools: UIA; UABC; CETYS.

"new business," "new product" or "small business development" courses, but without any formal continuum or programmatic instruction. UABC, the largest public university in the state, was the only one that offered a more comprehensive number of entrepreneurship related courses, including "entrepreneurship workshops." Entrepreneurship courses in UABC represented almost 27% of the total business related courses within four different graduate programs, and 15% of the total academic curricula.

5.2. Entrepreneurial Exposure and Entrepreneurial Curricula Intensity

Table 3 presents a Pearsons two-tailed bivariate analysis of students' perceived "entrepreneurial exposure" (aggregated sample) and faculty' perceived "entrepreneurial extent," showing a significant positive correlation at the 0.05% level. This finding positively supports our assumption that a higher entrepreneurial curricula extent and intensity may be linked to a higher students' "entrepreneurial exposure." After disaggregating the students'

Table 3. Research Variables Correlations/General Sample.

	1	2	3	4	5	6	7
1. Courses extent[a]	1.000						
2. Courses intensity[b]	0.742**						
3. Students exposure[c]	0.151*	0.025					
4. Entrepreneurial self-efficacy	0.075	0.59	0.297**				
5. Entrepreneurial intentions	0.47	−0.002	0.284**	0.286**			
6. Entrepreneurial orientation	0.20	0.033	0.277**	0.765**	0.662**		
7. General self-efficacy	−0.016	0.061	−0.116	0.058	−0.098	0.015	1.000

Note: $N = 195$
*$p < 0.05\%$ level (2-tailed).
**$p < 0.01\%$ level (2-tailed).
[a]Courses extent refers to the number of entrepreneurial courses within the educational curricula as perceived by faculty.
[b]Courses intensity refers to the degree and frequency of entrepreneurial education events (courses, seminars, workshops and conferences) as perceived by faculty.
[c]Students exposure refers to the number and degree of entrepreneurial courses, workshops or seminars taken by students during their undergraduate studies.

sample into separate arrays by school, we also found a significant positive correlation at the 0.01% level in the between UABC students' entrepreneurial exposure and their reported levels of ESE, intentions and orientation. At a general level, faculty' perceived entrepreneurial curricula extent at each school to be a significant indicator of the schools' entrepreneurial intensity and orientation.

5.3. Entrepreneurial Self-Efficacy and General Self-Efficacy

The results, however, do not support any significant relationship between students' perceived ESE and their general self-efficacy. This implies that a person's self-belief and conviction, does not necessarily indicate that at a given moment, his or her self-trust and willingness for developing and pursuing a new business venture.

5.4. Entrepreneurial Exposure, Entrepreneurial Self-Efficacy, Intentions and Orientation

The research results also indicated that students' exposure to entrepreneurship education has a positive impact on ESE, intentions, and orientation as perceived by the respondents (see Table 4). After dividing the sample into

Table 4.   Entrepreneurial Education Exposure and Entrepreneurial Self-Efficacy, Intentions and Orientation Correlation Levels among Business and Non-Business Administration Students.

	Business Administration Students[a]	Other Business Administration Related Students[b]	Non-Business Administration Students[c]
Entrepreneurial education exposure correlated with:			
Entrepreneurial self-efficacy	0.305**	0.317**	0.097
Entrepreneurial intentions	0.256**	0.283**	0.125
Entrepreneurial orientation	0.308**	0.306**	0.106

Note: $N = 195$
**$p < 0.01\%$ level (2-tailed).
[a]Business administration students only.
[b]International business/trade management, accounting, marketing management and hotel administration students.
[c]Engineering, architecture, graphic design and law students.

specific graduate programs, we found that Business Administration and related program students (Marketing, Accounting, and International Business), had significantly higher correlations in terms of their entrepreneurship education exposure, and their self-efficacy, intentions and orientation, than those that were studying non-business-related programs, such as Engineering, Architecture, or Law. This suggests that eventually entrepreneurial education does have an impact on future entrepreneurial outcomes for students.

6. CONCLUSIONS AND IMPLICATIONS

This study addressed a gap in the entrepreneurship education research literature highlighted by Bechard and Gregoire's (2005). Their comprehensive content analysis of 103 peer reviewed entrepreneurship education articles indicated a paucity of research focusing on social-cognitive implications. Our preliminary results indicate that entrepreneurial education is probably a major contributor in the formation of nascent entrepreneurs. Other related factors, such as family business background, personal entrepreneurship experiences, and other environmental conditions are important elements to be considered, but eventually cognitive know-how and self-confidence are a constant element for nurturing entrepreneurial intentions and orientation toward new business venture developments.

We found significant correlations between professors' perceived entrepreneurial curricula extent and students' perceived exposure to entrepreneurial courses, and a high relation between such instruction experience and students' ESE, intentions, and orientation toward starting their own business ventures. Although we did not find major differences between universities' entrepreneurial curricula and course extent, or between general self-efficacy and ESE, we did find positive correlations between schools' entrepreneurial courses extent, schools' entrepreneurial intensity, and mandatory entrepreneurial courses that students undergo. Given the correlative nature of our analysis, these results must be thought of as "preliminary" and focusing only on general and broad areas of interest.

The research results, however, may be useful for university decision makers and education officials in Mexico interested in supporting and promoting the establishment of formal coursework in entrepreneurship in order to design adequate educational policies which can nurture a better entrepreneurial environment. Such support is necessary in order to facilitate new business creation in the country, which may lead to future gains in economic growth and development. Supporting and promoting entrepreneurship education in universities will facilitate business creation.

The research findings are related only to students' entrepreneurial intentions and orientation. Future longitudinal studies should be conducted in order to determine whether such intentions and orientation will eventually translate into new business ventures.

The fact that this research was conducted in a specific geographic location, Ciudad de Tijuana, implies that results may vary depending on regulatory environment, culture, and economic factors associated with different locations. Future research questions will have to do with finding significant differences between students and entrepreneurial curricula extent from national, regional, and local schools or between inland and border cities universities, or within international institutions. Cultural dimensions between different locations in Mexico may also play an important role as moderating factors of entrepreneurial intentions.

NOTES

1. Programa emprendedor history. http://www.mty.itesm.mx/daf/centros/ceprode/historia/historia.html
2. Federación de Instituciones Mexicanas Particulares de Educación Superior. http://web.fimpes.org.mx
3. CETYS Universidad. http://tij.cetys.mx

4. Universidad Autónoma de Baja California. http://www.uabc.mx
5. Universidad Iberoamericana. http://www.uia.mx

REFERENCES

Ajzen, I. (1991). Theory of planned behavior. *Organizational Behavior and Human Decision Processes, 50*, 179–211.

Arenius, P., & Minniti, M. (2005). Perceptual variables and nascent entrepreneurship. *Small Business Economics, 24*(3), 233–247.

Bagozzi, R., Baumgartner, H., & Yi, Y. (1989). An investigation into the role of intentions as mediators of the attitude-behavior relationship. *Journal of Economic Psychology, 10*, 35–62.

Bandura, A. (1977). Self-efficacy: Toward a unifying theory of behavioral change. *Psychological Review, 84*(2), 191–215.

Bandura, A. (1978). Reflections on self-efficacy. *Advances in Behavioral Research and Therapy, 1*(4), 237–269.

Bandura, A. (1982). Self-efficacy mechanisms in human agency. *American Psychologist, 37*(2), 122–147.

Bandura, A., & Cervone, D. (1986). Differential engagement of self-reactive mechanisms governing the motivational effects of goal systems. *Organizational Behavior and Human Decision Processes, 38*(1), 92–113.

Bechard, J., & Gregoire, D. (2005). Entrepreneurship education research revisited: The case for higher education. *Academy of Management Learning and Education, 4*(1), 22–43.

Brown, T., & Kirchhoff, B. (1997). *The effects of resource availability and entrepreneurial orientation on firm growth. Frontiers of entrepreneurship research.* Babson Park, MA: Babson College.

Bruno, A., & Tyebjee, T. (1982). The environment for entrepreneurship. In: C. Kent, D. Sexton & K. Vesper (Eds), *Encyclopedia of entrepreneurship.* Englewood Cliffs, NJ: Prentice-Hall.

Chandler, G., & Hanks, S. (1994). Market attractiveness, resource-based capabilities, venture strategies and venture performance. *Journal of Business Venturing, 9*(4), 331–349.

Chandler, G., & Jansen, E. (1992). The founder's self-assessed competence and venture performance. *Journal of Business Venturing, 7*, 223–236.

Covin, J., & Slevin, D. (1989). Strategic management of small firms in hostile and benign environments. *Strategic Management Journal, 10*(1), 75–87.

Covin, J., & Slevin, D. (1991). A conceptual model of entrepreneurship as firm behavior. *Entrepreneurship Theory and Practice, 16*, 7–25.

Cowling, M., & Taylor, M. (2001). *Entrepreneurial women and men: Two different species? Small Business Economics, 16*(3), 167–175.

Cox, L., Mueller, S., & Moss, S. (2002). The impact of entrepreneurship education on entrepreneurial self-efficacy. *International Journal of Entrepreneurship Education, 1*(1), 229–245.

Davidsson, P. (1991). Continued entrepreneurship: Ability, need, and opportunity as determinants of small firm growth. *Journal of Business Venturing, 6*, 405–429.

DeNoble, A., Jung, D., & Ehlrich, S. (1999). *Entrepreneurial self-efficacy: The development of a measure and its relationship to entrepreneurial action. Frontiers of Entrepreneurship Research.* Wellesley, MA: Babson College.

Delmar, F., & Davidsson, P. (2000). Where do they come from? Prevalence and characteristics of nascent entrepreneurs. *Entrepreneurship and Regional Development, 12*(1), 1–23.

Dutton, J. (1993). The making of organizational opportunities: Interpretive pathway to organizational change. In: B. Staw & L. Cummings (Eds), *Research in Organizational Behavior*. Greenwich: JAI.

Erikson, T. (2002). Entrepreneurial capital: The emerging venture's most important asset and competitive advantage. *Journal of Business Venturing, 17*, 275–290.

Fayolle, A. (2002). Les déterminants de l'acte entrepreneurial chez les étudiants et les jeunes diplômés de l'enseignement supérieur français. *Revue Gestion 2000, 4*, 61–77.

Fiet, J. (2001). Education for entrepreneurial competency: A theory-based activity approach. In: R. H. Brockhaus, G. E. Hills, H. Klandt & H. P. Welsch (Eds), *Entrepreneurship education: A global view* (pp. 78–93). Hants: Ashgate Publishing Limited.

Finkle, T., & Deeds, D. (2001). Trends in the market for entrepreneurship faculty, 1989–1998. *Journal of Business Venturing, 16*, 613–630.

Gartner, W. (1985). A conceptual framework for describing the phenomenon of new venture creation. *Academy of Management Review, 10*(4), 696–706.

Ginsberg, A. (1985). Measuring changes in entrepreneurial orientation following industry deregulation: The development of a diagnostic instrument. In: G. Roberts (Ed.), *Proceedings: Discovering Entrepreneurship*. Marietta, GA: U.S. Affiliate of the International Council for Small Business.

Gnyawali, D., & Fogel, D. (1994). Environments for entrepreneurship development: Key dimensions and research implications. *Entrepreneurship Theory and Practice, 19*, 43–62.

Gorman, G., Hanlon, D., & King, W. (1997). Some research on entrepreneurship education, enterprise education and education for small business management: A ten year literature review. *International Small Business Journal, 15*(3), 56–77.

Hills, G. E. (1988). Variations in university entrepreneurship education: An empirical study of an evolving field. *Journal of Business Venturing, 3*, 109–122.

Hills, G. E., & Barnaby, D. J. (1977). Future entrepreneurs from the business schools: Innovation is not dead. *Proceedings of the international council for small business* (pp. 27–30). Wichita, KS.

Hills, G. E., & Welsch, H. P. (1996). Entreprenurial behaviorial intentions and student independence characteristics and experiences. In: R. Ronsadt, J. A. Hornaday, R. Peterson & K. Vesper (Eds), *Frontiers of Entrepreneurship Research* (pp. 173–186). Wellesley, Mass: Babson Center for Entrepreneurial Studies.

Hindle, K., & Rushworth, S. (2000). *Global Entrepreneurship Monitor: Australia 2000*. Hawthorne, Victoria: Swinburne University of Technology.

Kantis, H., Ishida, M., & Komori, M. (2002). *Entrepreneurship in emerging economies: The creation and development of new firms in Latin America and East Asia*. Inter-American Development Bank, Department of Sustainable Development, Micro, Small and Medium Business Division.

Kantis, H., Postigo, S., Federico, J., & Tamborini, M. (2002). The emergence of university graduates entrepreneurs: What makes the difference? Empirical evidences from a research in Argentina. RENT XVI conference, Barcelona, Spain.

Katz, J. A. (2003). The chronology and intellectual trajectory of American entrepreneurship education. *Journal of Business Venturing, 18*(2), 283–300.

Kearny, A. T. (2005). Measuring globalization. *Foreign Policy*, (May/June), 52–60.

Krueger, N., Jr., & Dickson, P. (1994). How believing ourselves increases risk taking: Perceived self-efficacy and opportunity recognition. *Decision Science Journal, 25*(3), 385–400.

Krueger, N., Jr., Reilly, M., & Carsrud, A (2000). Competing models of entrepreneurial intensions. *Journal of Business Venturing, 15*(5), 411–432.

Laukannen, M. (2000). Exploring alternative approaches in high-level entrepreneurship education: Creating micro mechanisms for endogenous regional growth. *Journal of Entrepreneurship and Regional Development, 12*(1), 25–47.

Lee, S., & Peterson, S. (2000). Culture, entrepreneurial orientation, and global competitiveness. *Journal of World Business, 35*(4), 401–416.

Lumpkin, G., & Dess, G. (1996). Clarifying the entrepreneurial orientation construct and linking it to performance. *Academy of Management Review, 21*, 135–175.

Lüthjec, C., & Franke, N. (2003). The making of an entrepreneur: testing a model of entrepreneurial intent among engineering students at MIT. *R&D Management, 33*(2), 135–147.

Markman, G., Balkin, D., & Baron, R. (2002). Inventors and new venture formation: The effects of General self-efficacy and regretful thinking. *Entrepreneurship Theory and Practice, 27*(2), 149–165.

Miles, M., & Arnold, D. (1991). The relationship between marketing orientation and entrepreneurial orientation. *Entrepreneurship Theory and Practice, 15*(4), 49–65.

Miller, D. (1983). The correlates of entrepreneurship in the three types of firms. *Management Science, 29*, 770–791.

Morris, M., & Paul, G. (1987). The relationship between entrepreneurship and marketing in established firms. *Journal of Business Venturing, 2*, 247–259.

Morris, M., & Sexton, D. (1996). The concept of entrepreneurial intensity: Implications for company performance. *Journal of Business Research, 36*, 5–13.

Noel, T. W. (2001). *Effects of entrepreneurial education on intent to open a business. Frontiers of Entrepreneurship Research.* Babson Park, MA: Babson College.

Pennings, J. (1982). Organizational birth frequencies: An empirical investigation. *Administrative Science Quarterly, 27*, 120–144.

Peterman, N., & Kennedy, J. (2003). Enterprise education: Influencing students' perceptions of entrepreneurship. *Entrepreneurship, Theory and Practice, 28*, 129–144.

Phillips, B. D. (1993). The growth of small firm jobs by state 1984–1988. *Business Economics, 28*(2), 48–53.

Postigo, S., Iacobucci, D., & Tamborini, M. (2003). Undergraduate students as a source of potential entrepreneurs: Comparative study between Italy and Argentina. Paper presented at the 13th global IntEnt – internationalizing entrepreneurship education and training conference, September 8–10, 2003, Grenoble, France.

Postigo, S., & Tamborini, M. (2002). Entrepreneurship education in Argentina: The case of San Andrés University. Internationalizing entrepreneurship education and training conference, IntEnt02, Malaysia.

Relf, W. (1995). The entrepreneurship curriculum: Victim of a life cycle or progenitor of the future. In: T. Monroy, F. Reichert & F. Hoy (Eds), *The art and science of entrepreneurship education* (pp. 25–32). Cleveland: Baldwin-Wallace College.

Ronstadt, R. (1985). The educated entrepreneurs: A new era of entrepreneurial education is beginning. *American Journal of Small Business, 6*, 7–23.

Scherer, R., Adams, J., Carley, S., & Wiebe, F. (1989). Role model performance effects on development of entrepreneurial career preference. *Entrepreneurship Theory and Practice, 13*, 53–81.

Schumpeter, J. (1934). *The theory of economic development*. Cambridge, MA: Harvard University Press.

Seligman, M. (1990). *Learned Optimism*. New York: Knopf.

Sexton, D., Upton, N., Wachlotz, L., & McDougall, P. (1997). Learning needs of growth-oriented entrepreneurs. *Journal of Business Venturing, 12*, 1–8.

Shapero, A. (1982). Social dimensions of entrepreneurship. In: C. Kent, D. Sexton & K. Vesper (Eds), *The encyclopedia of entrepreneurship* (pp. 72–90). Englewood Cliffs, NJ: Prentice-Hall.

Solomon, G., Duffy, S., & Tarabishy, A. (2002). The state of entrepreneurship education in the United States: A nationwide survey and analysis. *International Journal of Entrepreneurship Education, 1*(1), 65–86.

Stevenson, H., & Jarillo, J. (1990). A paradigm of entrepreneurship: Entrepreneurial management. *Strategic Management Journal, 11*, 17–27.

United Nations (2003). *Human development index* Wikipedia: The Free Encyclopedia.

Ussman, A., & Postigo, S. (2000). *O Papel da universidade no fomento da função empresarial. Anais Universitarios. Ciencias Sociais e Humanas.* 1990–2000 Yearbook Special Issue, 219–233.

Van Praag, C., & Cramer, J. (2001). The roots of entrepreneurship and labour demand. Individual ability and low risk aversion. *Economica, 68*(269), 45–62.

Varela, R., & Jimenez, J. E. (2001). *The effect of entrepreneurship education in the universities of Cali. Frontiers of entrepreneurship research.* Babson Park, MA: Babson College.

Veciana, J. (2002). Comentarios sobre los resultados de la investigación comparada sobre la empresarialidad entre América Latina y el Este de Asia. In: H. Kantis, M. Ishida & M. Komori (Eds), *Entrepreneurship in emerging economies: The creation and development of new firms in Latin America and East Asia.* Inter-American Development Bank: Department of Sustainable Development, Micro, Small and Medium Business Division.

Vesper, K. (1985). *Entrepreneurship education 1985*. Wellesley, MA: Babson College.

Vesper, K. (1990). *New venture strategies*. Englewood Cliffs, NJ: Prentice Hall.

Vesper, K. (1993). *Entrepreneurship education 1993*. Los Angeles, CA: UCLA.

Vesper, K., & Gartner, W. (1997). Measuring progress in entrepreneurship education. *Journal of Business Venturing, 12*, 403–421.

Wachtel, P. (1999). Entrepreneurship in the transition economies of Central and Eastern Europe. *Journal of Business Venturing, 14*, 417–426.

Young, E., & Welsch, H. (1993). Major developments in entrepreneurial development in central Mexico. *Journal of Small Business Management, 31*, 80–85.

ENTREPRENEURSHIP EDUCATION: A CAUTIOUS RAY OF HOPE IN INSTRUCTIONAL REFORM FOR DISADVANTAGED YOUTH

Howard S. Rasheed and Michelle Howard-Vital

1. INTRODUCTION

In 2001, the Elementary and Secondary Act legislation was reauthorized in the U.S. as The Leave No Child Behind Act (NCLB) to place special emphasis on the importance of basing educational practice on empirical research. The reauthorization also required that America's public school systems become more accountable for the learning of students, for improving the educational achievement of all students, and for closing the achievement gap between advantaged and disadvantaged segments of the student population.

In addition to accountability for the education of each child, the ultimate goal of the landmark federal legislation is to insure that future generations will be educated to maintain America's competitive edge in trade, manufacturing, technology, entrepreneurship, and higher education. The NCLB accountability efforts, the national high school reform movement, global

Developmental Entrepreneurship: Adversity, Risk, and Isolation
International Research in the Business Disciplines, Volume 5, 405–423
Copyright © 2006 by Elsevier Ltd.
ISSN: 1074-7877/doi:10.1016/S1074-7877(06)05020-3

competitiveness, and the 21st century workforce needs highlight the urgency to develop a highly educated, skilled, and creative workforce. There are abundant national data that traditional comprehensive high schools produce too many students who are underachieving, dropping out, turning to violence, and becoming disengaged in the civic and economic future of America (Balfanz & Legters, 2004; Hall, 2005). Students of color are often over represented among dropouts, underachievers, and disengaged adolescents. Many of these students graduate without the tools they need to succeed in higher education or in the workforce of the 21st century (Achieve, Inc. 2004; Balfanz & Legters, 2004; Barton, 2005; Brand, 2004; Haycock & Huang, 2001a, b; Harvey & Houseman, 2004). Unfortunately, research on middle school reform efforts (that began in the 1970s to identify best practices to engage and motive middle school youth) still does not seem to identify particular instructional strategies that are linked to student achievement (SREB, 2002).

Moreover, as indicated by the latest data from the National Center for Education Statistics and other national reports, youth in America are falling behind other industrialized countries in the academic achievement (Balfanz & Legters, 2004; Barton, 2005; Sen, Partelow, & Miller, 2005). To compete, America is depending more and more on its immigrant population for talent in areas such as science and engineering. Of the recent doctorates awarded in engineering, approximately 51 percent of individuals earning them were not born in the United States (Cavanagh, 2005).

Americans cannot afford the enormous societal losses of unrealized human potential – intellectual, creative, and entrepreneurial. These losses are borne as costs to all Americans, as the social systems strain to respond to the growing economic competitiveness of other countries (Barton, 2005). Even though there are numerous best practices throughout the United States that reflect exemplary schools and teachers, there is still a need to identify and implement effective instructional strategies that engage more students in America to become lifelong learners (Learning Outside the Lines, 2002).

Tatum (1997) makes a convincing case that teaching and learning in America occurs within the social context of racial and cultural identities of the students and teacher. This context includes predispositions about the intellectual capabilities of persons of color, negative messages regarding the future potential of developing adolescents of color, and oppositional identities assumed by some students of color. The social context of education highlights the need for supportive teachers and other adults to intervene to help students internalize their potential for success within the complex

American society. Most parents of these adolescents, Tatum goes on to state, want their children to develop an "internalized sense of personal security" that will help them recognize the social context of public education, respond effectively to it, and proceed to lead responsible and productive lives. In *Learning While Black*, Hale (2001) affirms that underachievement of students of color in public education in America is related to what happens in the classroom and the lack of support to navigate the cultural context. She attests that educational reform must acknowledge and employ appropriately the cultural context of education to improve the academic performance of students of color.

Wentzel and Wigfield (1998) also attest that there is an intricate connection between instructional strategies, psychological attitudes, and characteristics that emerge in learners. Positive attitudes toward learning, exploration, and future prospects are valuable learning characteristics that influence student outcomes. Entrepreneurial programs appear to offer one solution to help students emerge more empowered within the social context of learning. Research on entrepreneurial programs relates positive effects on overall attitudes of students toward learning and future goal setting when engaging in such instruction (Brockhaus, 1980; Begley & Boyd, 1987; Montago, Kuratko, & Scarella, 1986; Boyd & Vozikis, 1994; Krueger & Brazeal, 1994; Littunen, 2000).

Findings from an entrepreneurship educational project in New Jersey reinforce that there are promising, student-centered, instructional strategies that can be used for structuring self-employment career paths, engaging students, helping students develop a sense of personal control, and for rethinking how instruction is delivered in America's schools (Rasheed & Rasheed, 2003). This theme-based instructional intervention furnishes empirical support for varying instructional strategies and classroom practices to affect students' academic achievement, motivation, self-esteem, and personal control. Because the New Jersey project demonstrated that the entrepreneurial intervention did affect students' attitudes toward achievement, the New Jersey project was analyzed further to determine if the intervention also improved the academic achievement of students.

The analysis reviewed in this article contributes to the larger conversations on educational reform and the more focused conversations on instructional strategies that correlate with improved academic outcomes for students. The discussions in this article should have implications for policy makers and educators searching for instructional strategies to engage more youth, to motivate them, and to improve their academic achievement.

2. LITERATURE REVIEW

Entrepreneurship education generally refers to programs that promote awareness of self-employment as a career choice and skill training for business creation and development. It is distinguishable from other forms of business or career education and its purpose is to create a new business entity, product, or service results in higher economic value (Hansemark, 1998). Entrepreneurial education can prepare youth for new venture initiation by nurturing entrepreneurial motivation and helping them develop the knowledge and relevant skills that improve self-efficacy and effectiveness (Hatten & Ruhland, 1995; Gorman, Hanlon, & King, 1997; Ede, Panigrahi, & Calcich, 1998).

Banaszak (1990) suggests that entrepreneurial programs in middle grades provide knowledge of the role and function of entrepreneurs in a market-driven economy and help students understand and practice entrepreneurial characteristics such as self-esteem, willingness to take risks, innovativeness, and acceptance of responsibility for personal actions and persistence. Effective youth entrepreneurship education is also linked to preparing young people to be responsible, enterprising individuals who become entrepreneurs or entrepreneurial thinkers and contribute to economic development and sustainable communities, mitigating some of the limitations of traditional middle and high school curriculums (Ashmore, 1990; Harvey & Houseman, 2004). Moreover, research suggests identifying and nurturing potential entrepreneurs throughout the education process could produce many long-term economic benefits (McClelland & Winter, 1969; Hatten & Ruhland, 1995; Hansemark, 1998).

An inherent assumption in entrepreneurial education is that entrepreneurship characteristics and skills can be learned. Research suggests that the propensity toward entrepreneurship has been associated with several personal characteristics that can be influenced by a formal program of education (Gorman et al., 1997; Bechard & Toulouse, 1998). As stated earlier, there is empirical support for the efficacy of entrepreneurial education in developing entrepreneurial characteristics such as achievement motivation, self-esteem, and personal control. These are arguably also desirable characteristics for student development and needed interventions for students of color who are likely to receive negative messages regarding achievement potential. What prior studies have not adequately addressed is the effect of entrepreneurial education on academic performance.

The increased achievement motivation results revealed in the New Jersey project suggest the need for further analysis concerning academic performance in related coursework tested for this article. Since the need for achievement is based on expectations of doing something better or faster than others or better than the person's earlier accomplishments (McClelland, 1961, 1965), and it also relates to planning and striving for excellence (Hansemark, 1998), it was hypothesized that entrepreneurship education as an intervention would make a significant difference in academic performance:

Hypothesis 1. Students receiving entrepreneurial training will attain significant improvement in scores for academic subjects from the previous academic year.

Hypothesis 2. Students receiving entrepreneurial training will attain higher academic performance scores in academic subjects than students in the control group.

3. METHODOLOGY

Five hundred and two upper elementary and middle schools in Newark, New Jersey were selected to participate in a 26-week entrepreneurial program. This population included nine schools and 28 classes ranging from grades 4 through 8. Students were divided into a treatment group and a control group. The treatment group engaged in an entrepreneurship training class for 3 hours a week for 26 weeks using KidsWay curriculum as an alternative intervention strategy for improving academic achievement. Students in the 13 treatment classes engaged in entrepreneurship education and training. Students in 15 classes were designated as the control group, and they were involved in other activities, specifically art and music during the same class period (Rasheed & Rasheed, 2003). The goal of the program was to determine whether inner-city students could be motivated to improve academic achievement with a theme-based entrepreneurial educational and enterprise intervention.

KidsWay is a youth entrepreneurship curriculum that employs student-centered, active learning strategies. Teachers in the treatment group participated in standard KidsWay professional development to minimize differences in teacher effectiveness. Students were encouraged to explore course concepts by completing tasks that demonstrate reflection and elaboration on course content (Hammer, 2000). The active learning strategy is distinguishable from traditional methods because it includes mini-lectures integrated with group activities and games that reinforce learning objectives. Semi-structured experiential techniques involved completing a group task or project that used real business situations as the context for learning (Hammer, 2000).

The learning strategies in the KidsWay curriculum also include active experimentation, concrete experience, and behavioral simulations. The skill-building component includes negotiation, leadership, creative thinking, exposure to technological innovation, and new product development. Students were also taught how to detect and exploit business opportunities and long-term business planning. As part of the class, students developed and implemented a class-based enterprise.

The study population of 506 students consisted primarily of ethnic minority students (56.4% Hispanic/Latin; 34.7% African American; 3.6% Caucasian; 1% Asian; and 4.4% no response). Frequency distribution by grades was: 4th grade – 29%; 5th grade – 30%; 6th grade – 23%; 7th grade – 15%; and 8th grade – 3%. Males represented 49.3% and females 50.7% of the sample. A random sample of 144 students was selected for grade analysis, with equal distribution between the treatment and control groups.

The measurement variables were letter grades recorded on office copies of student report cards converted to numerical scores, i.e., Superior = 5, Excellent = 4, Good = 3, Fair = 2, Poor = 1.

4. RESULTS

To test Hypothesis 1, a descriptive statistical analysis was performed to determine differences within group and between groups, regarding academic performance. The within group analysis for the treatment group before the intervention and after, yielded positive results for the following specific subject areas:

- Reading – the difference in average scores was 13.2% higher.
- Language – the difference in average scores was 6.1% higher.
- Social Studies – the difference in average scores 11.3% higher.

To test Hypothesis 2 using descriptive statistical analysis, entrepreneurship classes (treatment group) scored better than non-entrepreneurial classes (control group) in the following subject areas:

- Reading – the difference in average scores was 16.4% higher.
- Language – the difference in average scores was 15% higher.
- Spelling – the difference in average scores was 15.3% higher.

- Math – the difference in average scores was 18.7% higher.
- Social Studies – the difference in average scores was 19.5% higher.
- Science – the difference in average scores was 39% higher.

Using inferential statistics, a *t*-test analyzed within group differences between the academic performances of the treatment group in the academic year prior to participating in the entrepreneurial education program. The results indicated the following:

- Reading grades were higher for the entrepreneurial group ($p < 0.05$); mean difference was 1.912.
- Language Arts grades were higher for the entrepreneurial group ($p < 0.10$); mean difference was 1.781.
- Social studies grades were higher for the entrepreneurial group ($p < 0.001$); mean difference was 3.868.

Comparing the entrepreneurial class to the control group using a t-test, the academic performance differences were as follows:

- Reading grades increased significantly ($p < 0.10$); mean difference was 0.1517.
- Language arts grades increased significantly ($p < 0.10$); mean difference was 0.1344.
- Spelling grades decreased significantly ($p < 0.10$); mean difference was 0.1909.
- Social studies grades increased significantly ($p < 0.01$); mean difference was 0.2534.
- Science grades increased significantly ($p < 0.001$); mean difference was 0.68.

The results of this analysis indicates support for the general hypothesis derived from the conclusion that students that are achievement motivated will have improved and better academic performance. Specifically, grades improved for the entrepreneurial class between years for reading, language arts, and social studies. Additionally, students in entrepreneurship classes scored significantly better than non-entrepreneurial classes in reading, language, spelling, social studies and science. By analyzing within group and between groups scores, this study confirms the effectiveness of entrepreneurial studies on academic performance and suggests promising implications for developing effective intervention strategies for minority students in primary grades (Table 1).

Table 1.   Statistical Comparisons of Education and Venture Treatment Groups.

Variables		Reading	Language Arts	Spell	Math	Social Studies	Science
Hypothesis 1							
Within group							
Pre-test	Mean	2.11	2.16	2.85	2.17	2.24	2.23
	Stan. Dev.	0.96	0.99	1.08	1.06	0.97	0.90
Post-test	Mean	2.26	2.29	2.66	2.18	2.50	2.17
	Stan. Dev.	0.86	0.83	1.25	0.93	1.02	0.95
	t-test	−1.81+	−1.68+	1.72+	0.19	−2.92**	0.78
Hypothesis 2							
Between group							
Training	Mean	2.39	2.41	2.81	2.33	2.67	2.43
	Stan. Dev.	0.83	0.85	1.04	0.97	1.01	0.93
No training	Mean	2.05	2.10	2.44	1.96	2.23	1.75
	Stan. Dev.	0.88	0.77	1.49	0.81	0.97	0.81
	$F_{1,143}$	5.42*	5.07*	2.80*	5.47*	6.63**	20.33***

*$P < 0.05$.
**$P < 0.01$.
***$p < 0.001$.

5. CONCLUSION AND DISCUSSION

How innovative was this intervention for students participating in the New Jersey program? There are indications that the traditional classroom instructional design is not particularly supportive of entrepreneurship and may result in the suppression of entrepreneurial characteristics (Chamard, 1989). Kourilsky (1980) finds that 25 percent of kindergartners demonstrate entrepreneurial characteristics (i.e., need for achievement and risk taking) compared to 3 percent of high school students. Singh (1990) concludes that the traditional instruction and education environment should be reoriented to emphasize and value entrepreneurial attitudes at the pre-collegiate level and to encourage entrepreneurship as a career choice. Students' improvement in academic achievement scores also supports the link between achievement attitudes and academic gains in traditional coursework. Moreover, the social context of the traditional classroom reinforces the social stratification for many students of color and results in oppositional strategies regarding learning and future potential (Hale, 2001; Tatum, 1997).

In *Learning Outside the Lines* (2002), six vignettes of promising instructional practices in schools located in various settings around the United States are highlighted. These vignettes describe diverse instructional strategies that serve underprivileged youth and help them become confident learners. Further, the six vignettes are brief but vibrant examples of instructional strategies that result in engaged, future-oriented, and high-achieving students. Research reviewed for this article supports the authors' assertions in *Learning Outside the Lines* that we know that youth thrive in settings where there are caring relationships that help them persist past obstacles; where there is challenging curriculum content that interests them; where there are learning communities that encourage peer support and collaboration; and where they can develop significant relationships with adults. However, effective instructional strategies and teacher–student interactions are often viewed in isolation, without empirical analysis, and not examined beyond surface levels.

To examine the effectiveness of the New Jersey entrepreneurship education project as an overall intervention strategy that can lead toward improved academic achievement for students, it is useful to view the interrelated components of the intervention: (1) theme-based curricular content that interests students, (2) specific instructional strategies, and (3) enabling classroom environment with positive student–teacher interactions. An analysis of the literature shows that each of these interrelated components contribute to improved academic achievement for students and can be found in effective schools around the nation.

5.1. Theme-Based Instruction

The Bill and Melinda Gates Foundation has become a major catalyst in stimulating national discussions on how we structure education particularly at the high school level. Responding to the national dropout rates and the lack of engagement by a significant portion of the high school population, the Gates Foundation has funded numerous reinventing high school projects around the nation. These *New School Projects* focus on the three R's: rigor, relevance, and relationships. The need for more rigorous academic content not only answers America's need to compete internationally, but it responds to the perceptions of numerous high school students that school is not challenging. The projects are based on the assumption that high schools will be more effective if they are smaller, more personalized, student-focused units that are rigorous, relevant to students' lives and places of significant relationships for students. The high school reform projects are themed high schools that are also smaller schools (100 students per grade) that afford teachers and students the opportunity to form smaller learning communities that respond to students' interests. In addition to serving as innovative experiments designed to discover various pathways to rigorous and relevant learning, the high school reform projects seek to identify learning strategies and organizational structures that will enhance positive relationships between students and teachers.

The results from the New Jersey project and the research on career academics (Brand, 2004) suggest that theme-based instruction can be effective in engaging students and ultimately improving students' academic performance in related academic subjects. Brand further states that teachers often work together in teams in career academics; students are grouped with a core of teachers; and the family-like environment often promotes close teacher–student relationships.

In Cincinnati, Ohio, Entrepreneur High School, a theme-based entrepreneurship high school, applies theories and concepts in core courses to the business world. Additionally, courses are available in advertising, market research, banking, investing, and forecasting a product's supply and demand to teach students how to start and operate a business. Early data from the entrepreneur school reveals that students have improved in academic proficiency and retention. The early success of Entrepreneur High School seems linked to the common curriculum focus and the positive behavior support for students embodied in the theme of the high school – Life is choice, choices matter. The entrepreneurial theme is viewed as valuable for preparing students for life-long learning and life after high school (Matthews & Morris, 2005). Entrepreneur High School implements several of the interrelated components identified in this article as affecting improved student academic performance. It is a theme-based high school instruction in core academic subjects relevant to the real world of business. Student–teacher and student–mentor relationships are encouraged. Students are paired with mentors from local small businesses or placed in internships at local companies. Instructional strategies include business simulations and writing a business plan to start a business. Most importantly, the combinations of the aforementioned interrelated components results in improved academic achievement for students.

The Southern Regional Education Board (1999–2006) highlights Project Lead the Way in *High Schools that Work* as an example of a national, theme-based, activity-oriented curriculum designed to increase the number of engineers in our country (Project Lead the Way, 1999–2006). The curriculum, when combined with middle school and college preparatory courses, introduces students to the discipline of engineering in a hands-on, problem-solving environment. The middle school curriculum, Gateway to Technology, is constructed to introduce students to project-based learning in an exciting and fun format. In the Gateway program, students are expected to pursue integrated study in math, science, and technology to strengthen their knowledge content and to provide a foundation of knowledge and skills for success in pre-engineering. In the high school theme-based curriculum, students take introductory engineering courses such as principles of engineering, introduction to engineering design, digital electronics, and computer-integrated manufacturing. The introduction of students to engineering content, project-based problem solving, and an integrated subject matter is designed to attract students and to demonstrate the relevancy of concepts. The need for empirical analysis on programs like Project Lead the Way is crucial for an in-depth understanding about theme-based best practices and future decision making regarding teacher practices and student achievement.

5.2. Instructional Strategies and Teacher–Student Interactions

Sanders and Rivers (1998) affirm that there is a growing body of research that supports the link between good teaching and academic achievement for all students. Good teaching is the crucial link in attaining and sustaining academic achievement for students, regardless of race and other variables. The contribution of good teaching to student achievement is so large that it exceeds any student characteristic (i.e. social economic status). Further, the research of Sanders and Rivers (1998) demonstrates that there is a statistically significant higher achievement for students taught for several years by effective teachers. Wenglinsky (2000) reports, however, that evidence has been inconclusive regarding specific instructional strategies that effective teachers practice in the classroom that are different from those ineffective teachers practice (to affect the academic performance of students). Possibly the case study approach used by Kubitskey and Fishman (2004) can be a valuable research methodology to examine classroom practice and to identify specific instructional strategies used by effective teachers.

The KidWays curriculum included learner-centered instructional strategies such as simulations, gaming, cooperative group work, starting an enterprise, and role-playing that allowed students to formulate responses that are entrepreneurial and active (Kent, 1990). Experienced-based programs that encourage students to be active rather than passive learners and empower students to actually make decisions tend to be successful in helping students acquire knowledge and skills (Wenglinsky, 2000). Current research on the effect of peer support (in group activity) on student achievement supports the hypothesis that peer interactions are positively linked to improved student achievement. Additionally, effective teachers tend to use cooperative groups in which students learn from the teacher and share their knowledge with their peers.

McKinley (2003) studies instructional strategies in 29 urban classrooms and concludes that changes in student/teacher interactions can result in improved achievement for African-American students. McKinley finds that improved achievement of African American students correlated with instructional strategies that are used in the context of caring and respectful relationships between teachers and students and among students. Furthermore, African American students responded well to instructional strategies that employed cooperative learning, collaborative and democratic practices, verbal expression and movement, and real-life activities relevant to the curriculum. Teachers who were effective in improving the academic achievement of African American students believed their success were related to the positive relationships they developed with the students and their overall fairness in classroom interactions.

Munns (2003) views the teacher's ability to engage students as the "centralizing factor" for implementing effective instructional strategies that led to improved student achievement. He affirms that student engagement results in an educational identity that is significantly influenced by the messages that students believe the teacher is communicating to them. Munns (2003) purports that students internalize these messages and the messages shape how students see themselves as learners. Sometimes students perceive that they are receiving disengaging messages from teachers regarding their ability, knowledge, place, and power in the classroom. Both Tatum (1997) and Hale (2001) also discuss the significant influence that imbedded racial and social messages have for influencing the learning environment and responses to learning for people of color. Acknowledging these interrelated racial and social contexts will empower students and help teachers become more effective in engaging students of color.

In *Learning Outside the Lines: Six Innovative Programs that Reach Youth* (2002), the authors note that youth thrive in programs where there are opportunities for them to have a *voice and a choice*. Kahle, Meece, and Scantlebury (2000) demonstrate that there is a link between inquiry-oriented teaching, strategies that involve interactive and stimulating laboratory experiences in a noncompetitive environment, and African American students' attitudes and perceptions of science. Wentzel and Wigfield (1998) review research on social and academic constructs that relate to, and predict, students' academic performance, persistence, and choice of academic pathways. They affirm that recent studies support theories that students' social motivation and their personal relationships with teachers and peers strongly influence their academic performance and overall adjustment to the school environment.

Similar to Wentzel and Wigfield (1998), McKinley (2003) discusses the links between social context, learning, and student achievement. McKinley relates how effective teachers negotiate the power relationships in the classroom to establish a climate of mutual respect. Effective teachers also promote collaborative, democratic processes in the classroom. They share responsibilities and appropriate decision making with students. Denbo (2002) affirms that all learning and teaching is filtered through a cultural lens. Often there is discord between the classroom activities and the culture of African American students. Teachers, however, can "tune into" their students' culture, worldviews, verbal communication, social values, and develop instructional strategies that will engage and motivate students. Brand (2004) affirms that the record of success of career academics has much to offer high school reform. Career academics have demonstrated the importance of responding to the needs of students and the communities they represent. Additionally, career academics have experience in improving academic achievement with personalized learning communities.

5.3. The Future

Can the aforementioned interrelated components be used on a larger scale as interventions for students of color who are not performing well academically in schools around the United States? Rushing (1990) recommends entrepreneurship education programs for African-American youth because they are underrepresented among successful entrepreneurs. Rushing further affirms that entrepreneurial instruction could help to mitigate obstacles many African-Americans encounter in formal education. He identifies these obstacles as the lack of role models, low self-esteem, and the frustration of failure. Yet, there has been limited evidence that entrepreneurship education has been used extensively as an intervention strategy for overcoming such obstacles. Barton (2005) agrees that we need to know more about what happens in alternative schools and intervention programs like *Talent Development*, especially if these programs seem to be effective in mitigating drop out rates and engaging students.

Carey (2005) points out that the academic achievement gap too often coincides with low-income students, and/or minority students, and inexperienced teachers. Some students are assigned to ineffective teachers for as many as 3 years exasperating the academic achievement gap. Contacts with significant teachers and counselors are often minimal or negative. As an alternative to these situations that disproportionately affect students of color, MacDowell (1990) suggests that a well-designed entrepreneurial training program can provide the hidden curriculum skills that are important to educators and employers. Gray (2004) offers that career academies and theme-based education can motivate students considered *at risk* to overcome academic deficiencies and social limitations to pursue desired careers.

Barton (2005) argues that even though America promotes public education to all; the social contract contains fine print. There are limited options for students who experience dissonance in the current educational structures. Further, there are limited opportunities for getting youth back on track to complete high school and lead their most productive lives. Barton states further that by examining the successful instructional strategies we have employed in public education we can learn much.

The New Jersey project was originally designed to investigate the effects of entrepreneurship training and enterprise on the entrepreneurial characteristics of intermediate level students with hopes that the results would be a positive intervention for motivation and academic performance. Moreover, the study was designed to determine if the findings would support the supposition that entrepreneurial training and enterprise creation was an intervention strategy that would have positive benefits for the academic performance of ethnic minorities. The research did provide empirical evidence to support these hypotheses, finding that a composite of entrepreneurial characteristics was significantly greater for students engaged in entrepreneurial training and a classroom-based enterprise (Rasheed & Rasheed, 2003).

Because the New Jersey entrepreneurial project employed a control and treatment group of comparable students, the findings also lend support to the research that argues that changes in instructional strategies and positive student–teacher relationships can affect students' achievement, self-esteem, and achievement goal orientations (Wentzel & Wigfield, 1998; McKinley, 2003; Munns, 2003). The findings indicate that some aspects of the instructional and classroom component of the treatment group served as mediating factors to stimulate students' motivation, achievement orientations, and higher sense of personal control (Wentzel & Wigfield, 1998). Likewise, the instructional experiences and classroom interactions in the treatment group resulted in students performing better in related academic subjects.

It is difficult to determine the exact influence of student and teacher relationships to the achievement results, as discussed by McKinley (2003) and Munns (2003). The findings from the New Jersey project do not include empirical data for analysis of relationship interactions. More empirical data are needed to identify further what type of student/teacher relationships are positively correlated with the higher academic performance of students, and when should these interactions be varied.

The findings of the New Jersey project relate to the effects of entrepreneurship training and enterprise experience on entrepreneurial characteristics on predominately ethnic minorities in a low-income urban setting (Rasheed & Rasheed, 2003) and improved academic performance of students in related subjects. Other research, however, suggests that changes in instructional strategies and student–teacher interactions would be as relevant to the general student population at all school levels (Wentzel & Wigfield, 1998). The instructional strategies and instructional climate employed in the New Jersey project have been identified in various research articles as having positive affects on students' self-esteem, academic achievement, and engagement. (Barton, 2005; McKinley, 2003; Munns, 2003). Research supports that the New Jersey project included components that are linked to student motivation and academic achievement. These interrelated components are curriculum of interest or theme-based instruction, instructional strategies that include active learning and real-life problem solving, and positive student–teacher and peer relationships.

What does our future look like? Our challenge remains to employ the cultural context for learning to empower and enable all students (Hale, 2001; Tatum, 1997). Wenglinsky (2000) affirms the need to link student achievement with recruiting, retaining, and developing high-quality teachers who can function well within the cultural context of educational environments. A scan of educational publications leaves us with a cautious ray of hope.

In May 2005, 5 years after the initial study the Commissioner of Education in New Jersey announced a major new initiative to change the organization and structure of middle and high schools in New Jersey's low-income communities. One of the plan's goals is to develop smaller learning communities that employ theme-based instruction by reconstructing middle and high schools into smaller units. Another is to strengthen the alignment between middle and high schools by preparing middle school students for college preparatory work. Likewise, high school students would be prepared for college work or demanding careers. New Jersey's new initiative is expected to emphasize personalized instruction and improve quality of instruction for academic gains for students (Vespucci, 2005).

In an article, "Game-Based Learning: how to Delight and Instruct in the 21st Century," Foreman (2004) foretells the benefits of game-based learning for a generation of students who have grown-up immersed in an information technology world in which they have learned by using commercial games. By highlighting the perspectives of leading thinkers in the game development field on the organization and structure of education, Foreman relates that our educational institutions are still organized around limitations of the last century. The "industrial classroom approach" does not mesh well with the way other aspects of the 21st century are organized and operate. One of the advantages of using game-based technology is that learners can be immersed in the game world that simulates how learning will be applied to solve actual problems in actual situations. The game world allows learners to interact and learn with other students and participate in solving a complex set of decisions. The game-based learning community corresponds to how the Internet has allowed us to interact and solve problems. Learners can experiment with different solutions, support their learning with visual cues in a multimedia environment, and become active participants in constructing an understanding of the relevance of a concept, theory, or skill.

Even though the US military has used simulations to educate for decades, USAF Captain Iverson (2001) discusses the need for the military to adapt its instructional strategies more to the characteristics of the current generation. A generation accustomed to entertaining itself with television, video games, and videos requires increased video, simulation, interactive games, and technological methods to engage learners and to emphasize the relevance of specific concepts. Iverson proffers that the current generation of learners might simply process information differently because of the technological enhanced experience of growing up in America.

An article in Education Week (Jacobson, 2005) reports there are recent efforts to relate, and gain more knowledge about the link between teachers' knowledge of content, instructional strategies, and the academic achievement of students. For instance, *Teachers for a New Era*, funded by the Carnegie Corporation, is a nationwide initiative designed to noticeably alter and link teacher education programs to effective teachers' instructional strategies, internships for teachers, and improved student outcomes. Discussions around the Gates Foundation supported activities in North Carolina call for the need for reflective practices among educators that lead to an examination of what happens in the classroom and how it affects the achievement of all students. Education should affect change in our society and interrupt the patterns of poverty and social injustice (Tatum, 1997).

With the continuous need for Americans to strive to be the best and the brightest, it seems apparent that it is time to look closely at the influences, and intricate links, between student-teacher relationships, theme-based curriculum, social environment, and instructional strategies used in the classroom. There is sufficient research also to suggest that African American and Hispanic youth perform better in an environment in which a sense of personal control and respect is coupled with active participation in relevant activities in personalized learning communities. As declared in *Learning Outside the Lines*, we know the answers, so what do we do now?

REFERENCES

Achieve, Inc. (2004). Creating a high school diploma that counts. *The American Diploma Project*. www.achieve.org

Ashmore, M. (1990). Entrepreneurship in vocational education. In: C. A. Kent (Ed.), *Entrepreneurship education* (pp. 211–230). Westport, CT: Quorum Books.

Balfanz, R., & Legters, N. (2004). *Locating the dropout crisis: Center for social organization of schools*. Baltimore, Maryland: John Hopkins University

Banaszak, R. (1990). Economics and entrepreneurship education for young adolescents. In: C. A. Kent (Ed.), *Entrepreneurship education* (pp. 165–182). Westport, CT: Quorum Books.

Barton, P. (2005). *One-Third of a nation: Rising dropout rates and declining opportunities*. Princeton, NJ: Policy Evaluation and Research Center, Educational Testing Service.

Bechard, J. P., & Toulouse, J. M. (1998). Validation of a didactic model for the analysis of training objectives in entrepreneurship. *Journal of Business Venturing*, *13*(4), 317–332.

Begley, T., & Boyd, D. (1987). Psychological characteristics associated with performance in entrepreneurial smaller businesses. *Journal of Business Venturing*, *2*(1), 79–94.

Bill and Melinda Gates Foundation (http://www.gatesfoundation.org/Education).

Boyd, N. G., & Vozikis, G. S. (1994). The influence of self-efficacy on the development of entrepreneurial intentions and actions. *Entrepreneurship: Theory and Practice*, *18*(4), 63–78.

Brand, B. (2004). *Reforming high schools: The role for career academies*. Career Academy Support Network, National Academy Foundation, Berkley, CA: National Career Academy Coalition. http://casn.berkeley.edu/resources/reforming.html

Brockhaus, R. (1980). Risk taking propensity of entrepreneurs. *Academy of Managing Journal*, *23*(3), 509–520.

Cavanagh, S. (2005). Born to science. *Education Week*, *24*(38), 27–29.

Chamard, J. (1989). Public education: Its effect on entrepreneurial characteristics. *Journal of Small Business and Entrepreneurship*, *6*(2), 23–30.

Denbo, S. J. (2002). Institutional Practices that Support African American Student Achievement. Improving Schools for African American Students. In: S. J. Denbo & L. Beaulieu (Eds), *Improving schools for African American students: A reader for educational leaders*. Springfield, IL: Charles C. Thomas Publisher.

Ede, F., Panigrahi, B., & Calcich, S. (1998). African American students' attitudes toward entrepreneurship education. *Journal of Education for Business*, 73(5), 291–296.

Elementary and Secondary Act (The No Child Left Behind Legislation). *The Elementary and Secondary Education Act (The No Child Left Act of 2001)*, www.ed.gov/legislation/ESEA02/

Foreman, J. (2004). Game-based learning: How to delight and instruct in the 21st Century. *Education Review*, 39(5), 50–66.

Gorman, G., Hanlon, D., & King, W. (1997). Some research perspectives on entrepreneurship education, enterprise education and education for small business management: A ten-year literature review. *International Small Business Journal*, 15(3), 56–79.

Gray (2004). *Is high school career and technical education obsolete? Phi Delta Kappan*. http://www.pdkintl.org/kappan/k_v86/k0410gra.htm

Hale, J. (2001). *Learning while black: Creating educational excellence for African American children*. John Hopkins Press: Baltimore, Maryland.

Hall, D. (2005). *Getting honest about grad rates: How states play the numbers and students lose*. Washington, DC: The Education Trust.

Hammer, L. (2000). The additive effects of semi structured classroom activities on student learning: An application of classroom-based experiential learning techniques. *Journal of Marketing Education*, 22(1), 25–34.

Hansemark, O. (1998). The effects of an entrepreneurship programme on need for achievement and locus of control of reinforcement. *International Journal of Entrepreneurship Behavior and Research*, 4(1), 28–50.

Harvey, J., & Houseman, N. (2004). *Crisis or possibility? Conversations about the American high school*. Washington, DC: Institute for Educational Leadership, National High Alliance.

Hatten, T., & Ruhland, S. (1995). Student attitudes towards entrepreneurship as affected by participation in an SBI Program. *Journal of Education for Business*, 7(4), 224–227.

Haycock, K., & Huang, S. (2001a). Are today's high school graduates ready? *Thinking K-16*, 5(1). Washington, DC: The Education Trust.

Haycock, K., & Huang, S. (2001b). Youth at the crossroads: Facing high school and beyond. *Thinking K-16*, 5(1). Washington, DC: The Education Trust.

Iverson, A. (2001). Professional military education for company grade officers: Targeting for affect. *Aerospace Power Journal*, 15, 52–57.

Jacobson, L. (2005). Teacher education homing in on content. *Education Week*, 24(39), 1–18.

Kahle, J., Meece, J., & Scantlebury, K. (2000). Urban African-American middle school science students: Does standards-based teaching make a difference? *Journal of Research in Science Education*, 37(9), 1019–1041.

Kent, C. (Eds). (1990). *Entrepreneurship/economics/education in the urban environment: The E3 project in entrepreneurship education* (pp. 271–283). Westport, CT: Quorum Books.

Kourilsky, M. L. (1980). Predictors of entrepreneurship in a simulated economy. *The Journal of Creative Behavior*, 14(3), 175–199.

Krueger, N., & Brazeal, D. (1994). Entrepreneurial potential and potential entrepreneurs. *Entrepreneurship Theory and Practice*, 19(2), 91–104.

Kubitskey, B., & Fishman, B. (2004). Impact of professional development on a teacher and her students: A case study, presented at the annual meeting of the American Educational Research Association.

Learning Outside the Lines (2002). Learning outside the lines: Six innovative programs that reach youth. Mongraph. W. K. Kellogg Foundation. Battle Creek, Mi. http://servicelearning.org/lib_svcs/lib_cat/index.php?library_id=4828

Littunen, H. (2000). Entrepreneurship and the characteristics of the entrepreneurial personality. *International Journal of Entrepreneurial Behavior and Research, 6*(6), 295–309.

MacDowell, M. (1990). Approaches to education for the economically disadvantaged: Creating tomorrow's entrepreneurs and those that will work for them. In: C. A. Kent (Ed.), *Entrepreneurship Education* (pp. 261–270). Westport, CT: Quorum Books.

Matthews, C., & Morris, J. (2005). Entrepreneurship education in the 21st century: Linking high school and college entrepreneurship programs. Presented at the Eastern Academy of Management, Cape Town, South Africa.

McClelland, D. (1961). *The achieving society.* Princeton, NY: Van Norstand.

McClelland, D. (1965). Need achievement and entrepreneurship, a longitudinal study. *Journal of Personality and Social Psychology, 1,* 389–392.

McClelland, D., & Winter, D. (1969). *Motivating Economic Achievement.* New York: The Free Press.

McKinley, J. (2003). Leveling the playing field and raising African American students' achievement in twenty-nine urban classrooms, *New Horizons for Learning Online Journal,* http://www.newhorizons.org/strategies/differentiated/mckinley.htm.

Montago, R., Kuratko, D., & Scarella, J. (1986). Perception of entrepreneurial success characteristics. *American Journal of Small Business, 11,* 1–8.

Munns, G. (2003). *A sense of wonder: Student engagement in low SES school communities,* www.aare.edu.au/04pap/mun04498.pdf

Rasheed, H., & Rasheed B. (2003). Developing entrepreneurial characteristics in youth: The effects of education and enterprise experience. In: C. Stiles & C. Galbraith (Eds), *Ethnic entrepreneurship: Structure and process.* Amsterdam: Elsevier.

Rushing, F. (1990). Economics and entrepreneurship education in the elementary grades. In: C. Kent (Ed.), *Entrepreneurship education: Current developments, future directions* (pp. 153–164). Westport, CT: Quorum Books.

Sanders, W., & Rivers. J. (1998). Cumulative and residual effects of teachers on future student academic achievement. In: *Education trust, thinking K-16: Good teaching matters: How well qualified teachers can close the gap,* www.ets.org/research/pic/teamat.pdf

Sen, A., Partelow, L., & Miller, D. C. (2005). *Comparative Indicators of education in the United States and other G8 countries: 2004. National Center for Education Statistics, U.S. Department of Education.* Washington, DC: U.S. Government Printing Office.

Singh, J. (1990). Entrepreneurship education as a catalyst of development in the third world. *Journal of Small Business and Entrepreneurship, 7*(4), 56–63.

Southern Regional Education Board, Pre-Engineering Curriculum: Project Lead the Way (1999-2006). http://www.screb.org/programs/hstw/specialnetworks/pltw/pltw-index.asp

Southern Regional Education Board (2002). Academic achievement in the middle grades: What does the research tell US? *A Review of the Literature.* Atlanta, GA.

Tatum, B. (1997). *Why are all the black kids sitting together in the cafeteria?* New York, NY: Basic Books.

Vespucci, R. (2005). DOE announces Abbott secondary education initiative: Four districts to participate in pilot program to improve teaching and learning. New Jersey Department of Education News Release.

Wenglinsky, H. (2000). *How teaching matters: Bringing the classroom back into discussions of teacher quality.* A Policy Information Center Report. Educational Testing Service.

Wentzel, K., & Wigfield, A. (1998). Academic and social motivational influences on students' academic performance. *Educational Psychology Review, 10*(2), 155–175.

Printed in the United States
86564LV00001B/2/A

9 780762 313587